SHELLEY'S

MYTHMAKING

SHELLEY'S

MYTHMAKING

by Harold Bloom

Cornell Paperbacks

CORNELL UNIVERSITY PRESS

ITHACA, NEW YORK

First published 1959

First printing, Cornell Paperbacks, 1969

Library of Congress catalog card number: 59-6793

PRINTED IN THE UNITED STATES OF AMERICA
BY VAIL-BALLOU PRESS, INC.

For Frederick A. Pottle

Preface to the Cornell Paperbacks Edition

IT is evident to me only now, on rereading, that the subject of this book is Shelley's internalized quest to reach the limits of desire. He touched those limits, abandoned the Promethean phase of the Romantic quest, and died, but not in despair of the quest's mature phase, upon which he had begun. If he passed a Last Judgment upon himself, in "The Triumph of Life" and the final lyrics to Jane Williams, it was perhaps because he had failed his own vision, and not because the vision had failed him. This book is offered again, as an experimental study of the limits of desire, and as a tribute, however inadequate, to the poet I find least dispensable among those I read.

Most of the first draft of this book was written in 1955. The book was published, in shortened and revised form, in January, 1959. It is here reprinted, without change. Since 1959 I have written twice more on Shelley, in *The Visionary Company* (1961) and in the Introduction to a Signet Poets volume of selections from Shelley (1966). These two later essays somewhat modify my earlier reading, extend it to "Adonais" and some of the final lyrics, and avoid for the most part both the polemics and the various technical vocabularies of *Shelley's Mythmaking*. The new texts available of "The Triumph of Life" do not make my discussion of the poem obsolete. The progress of Shelley criticism in the last decade has not been rapid enough to meet the demands of our changing literary sensibility. It is one of Shelley's peculiar strengths that he necessarily anticipates his own defenders, and so goes on burying his undertakers.

I have learned from the reviews of this book that I was wrong to think its procedure to be finely obvious. One British critic, representative of a number of others, animadverted upon what he termed my attempt to see Shelley through "Buberian spectacles," while another deplored the decadence of American education, which had granted a higher degree to an ephebe insufficiently versed in Plato. The use of Buber in this study is of course heuristic; I hardly know what a reductive use of the *I-Thou, I-It* dialectic would be, since what Buber calls "relationship" has to vanish when analyzed, or discussed. As to the influence of Plato upon Shelley's poetry, whatever it may have been, we will not know how to talk about it, as critics, until we understand more about the process of poetic influence than we do today.

H. B.

Ithaca, New York
October 27, 1968

Contents

Poetry, and the principle of Self, of which money is the
visible incarnation, are the God and Mammon of the world.
A Defence of Poetry

Can the servant of Mammon say *Thou* to his money?
Buber, *I and Thou*

I

Introduction: The Mythopoeic Mode

THE contemporary Jewish theologian Martin Buber makes a distinction between two "primary words," *I-Thou* and *I-It*. These combined words intimate relationships instead of signifying things, and, being spoken, bring about the existence of relationships which could not exist independently of the uttered primary words.

Man's attitude to the world is twofold, depending upon which of the two primary words is spoken. "When *Thou* is spoken, the speaker has no thing for his object. For where there is a thing there is another thing. Every *It* is bounded by others; *It* exists only through being bounded by others. But when *Thou* is spoken, there is no thing. *Thou* has no bounds." [1]

There are then two I's: the I which exists when the whole being of a man confronts a Thou, and the I of the other primary word I-It, which can never be spoken with the whole being. One I exists in the world of experience; I experiences a "She," "He," or "It." The other I establishes the world of relation. Buber writes:

> I consider a tree.
>
> I can look on it as a picture: stiff column in a shock of light, or splash of green shot with the delicate blue and silver of the background.
>
> I can perceive it as movement: flowing veins on clinging, pressing pith, suck of the roots, breathing of the leaves, ceaseless commerce with earth and air—and the obscure growth itself.
>
> I can classify it in a species and study it as a type in its structure and mode of life.
>
> I can subdue its actual presence and form so sternly that I recognise it only as an expression of law—of the laws in accordance with which a constant opposition of forces is continually adjusted, or of those in accordance with which the component substances mingle and separate.

1. Martin Buber, *I and Thou*, tr. Ronald Gregor Smith (Edinburgh, Clark, and New York, Scribner's, 1937), pp. 4–5. In these paragraphs I attempt to summarize the opening pages of Buber's book. Following quotations from pp. 7–8, 11, 18, 75, 33, 34.

I can dissipate it and perpetuate it in number, in pure numerical relation.

In all this the tree remains my object, occupies space and time, and has its nature and constitution.

It can, however, also come about, if I have both will and grace, that in considering the tree I become bound up in relation to it. The tree is now no longer *It*. I have been seized by the power of exclusiveness.

To effect this it is not necessary for me to give up any of the ways in which I consider the tree. There is nothing from which I would have to turn my eyes away in order to see, and no knowledge that I would have to forget. Rather is everything, picture and movement, species and type, law and number, indivisibly united in this event.

Everything belonging to the tree is in this: its form and structure, its colours and chemical composition, its intercourse with the elements and with the stars, are all present in a single whole.

The tree is no impression, no play of my imagination, no value depending on my mood; but it is bodied over against me and has to do with me, as I with it—only in a different way.

Let no attempt be made to sap the strength from the meaning of the relation: relation is mutual.

The tree will have a consciousness, then, similar to our own? Of that I have no experience. But do you wish, through seeming to succeed in it with yourself, once again to disintegrate that which cannot be disintegrated? I encounter no soul or dryad of the tree, but the tree itself.

I have quoted all of this long and beautiful passage because it states better than any others I have encountered the nature of what I take to be mythopoeic perception. Buber remarks further: "The relation to the *Thou* is direct. No system of ideas, no foreknowledge, and no fancy intervene between *I* and *Thou*." We have here a mode of imaginative perception which leapfrogs over Coleridge's Primary Imagination directly into his Secondary; an analogue to Blake's "Fourfold Vision." It comes as no surprise that Buber should claim further that "In the beginning is relation," and proceed to discover the I-Thou primary word to be dominant over the I-It in the speech of "primitive" peoples. The world of our ancestors, or of contemporary primitives, is one of relation and not experience. From the insights of a modern theologian, I pass to the utilization (apparently unacknowledged) of those insights by some distinguished scholars of ancient civilizations.

Henri Frankfort and Mrs. H. A. Frankfort begin their attempt to expound the nature of myth in ancient Egypt and Mesopotamia by making precisely Buber's distinction between the I-Thou relation, and the I-It experience.[2] However, their distinction is purely technical in purpose, while his is of course primarily religious. For Buber, "every particular *Thou* is a glimpse through to the eternal *Thou*," God, for God can only be *addressed* in the second person, never *expressed* in the third, the sphere of It. Man's world as *related* to his I ultimately leads to the eternal Thou, God; while man's world as *experienced* by his other, and very different I, can lead ultimately only to the eternal It, away from God. Now Buber acknowledges that every "particular *Thou,* after the relational event has run its course, *is bound* to become an *It*," but he counters this by asserting that every "particular *It,* by entering the relational event, *may* become a *Thou.*" As befits a theologian, Buber's conclusion is moral: "without *It* man cannot live. But he who lives with *It* alone is not a man."

After that warning, the Frankforts' dispassionate analysis causes me some uneasiness: "The fundamental difference between the attitudes of modern and ancient man as regard the surrounding world is this: for modern, scientific man the phenomenal world is primarily an 'It'; for ancient—and also for primitive—man it is a 'Thou.'"[3]

The Frankforts' excellent scholarly purpose is to demonstrate the inadequacy of "animistic" or "personalistic" interpretations of the meaning of ancient or primitive myth. Since all phenomena relate to him as Thou's, "primitive man simply does not know an inanimate world," a world to be experienced. "For this very reason he does not 'personify' inanimate phenomena nor does he fill an empty world with the ghosts of the dead, as 'animism' would have us believe."

True myth then, according to the Frankforts, "perpetuates the revelation of a 'Thou.'" The imagery of myth is thus not allegorical but anagogical. Mythical imagery "represents the form in which the experience has become conscious." Therefore, the Frankforts summarize, "Myth is a form of poetry which transcends poetry in that it proclaims a truth; a form of reasoning which transcends reasoning in that it wants to bring about the truth it proclaims; a form of action, of ritual behaviour, which does not find its fulfilment in the act but must proclaim and elaborate a poetic form of truth."

This seems to me to be an admirable summary of the nature of myth, and also of mythmaking poetry, though the Frankforts might not acknowledge the latter. However, I am concerned with looting the work of the Frankforts for my own purposes, and I do not acknowledge that to proclaim a truth is to transcend poetry.

2. Henri Frankfort, Mrs. H. A. Frankfort, John A. Wilson, Thorkild Jacobsen, *Before Philosophy,* London, Penguins, 1949. Chapters 1, "Myth and Reality," and 8, "The Emancipation of Thought from Myth," both written by the Frankforts, are relevant to my subject here. *I-Thou* is contrasted to *I-It* on pp. 12–14, in particular.
3. Frankfort et al., p. 12. Following quotations from pp. 14, 15, 16, 22, 32.

The Frankforts are concerned with the distinction between mythopoeic thought and rational, scientific thought. They note the paradox of mythopoeic thought. "Though it does not know dead matter and confronts a world animated from end to end, it is unable to leave the scope of the concrete and renders its own concepts as realities existing per se." Put another way, it does exactly what a certain kind of "idealistic" poetry does; it renders a vision in terms of Blake's "minute particulars."

The mythopoeic conception of time and space, the Frankforts observe, is "qualitative and concrete, not quantitative and abstract." As much so, I hasten to observe, in the work of certain poets, as it is for ancient or primitive man. Indeed, this is as much so to some extent for all of us, even now, in our daily lives.

Now, as the Frankforts (and many others) point out, both the ancient Greeks and the Jews broke away from mythopoeic thought. The Greeks "progressed," in F. M. Cornford's phrase, "from religion to philosophy," while the Jews made a covenant with a God who absolutely transcended mythopoeic thought, as indeed He transcended everything else. Or put another way, the God of the Jews is an ultimate achievement of mythopoeic thought. All mythopoeic relation culminates in the eternal Thou, and the Jews went completely beyond all natural religion to the revelation of the myth (if you would have it so) that there existed a Will of this eternal Thou. The Jewish myth is the I-Thou relationship in which the I is either God or "a kingdom of priests and an holy nation" and the Thou, conversely, either this chosen people or God. The myth is covenant according to the Will of God, so that one cannot speak accurately of either a choosing or a being chosen, but only of the mutual relation entered into, which contract in turn produces law, moral and spiritual, and a tradition of belief.

Scientific, critical, rational *Greek* thought became, as we all know, completely emancipated from, and eventually hostile to, myth. Jewish thought became hostile to all myth but the one Myth, while Christian thought in turn excluded all myth but its own modification and transformation of the Jewish myth. Myth, thus excluded from philosophy and philosophy's child, science, and from what came to be the dominant religion of the West, nevertheless did not die, nor did it survive only among primitives. With Plato, it re-entered philosophy and has never since quite departed; it re-entered religion, not always as heresy, though usually regarded as such initially. Most important, of course, it became a certain kind, and tradition, of poetry.

As is commonly recognized, the distinction between mythological, mythographic, and mythopoeic poetry is not a very easy one to make, especially in poems which have their place at the beginnings of European literary tradition. Mythographic poetry for instance is a very rare thing, and while there are traces of it in many classical and medieval poets, it does not really seem to exist *in extenso* until the Renaissance. Its essential characteristic is that it is aware not only of the existence of different mythologies but also of the element of parallelism between mythologies. Mythological poetry, properly speaking, is unicultural, or at least unitraditional. Exactly where mythological poetry becomes mythopoeic it is impossible to say, but I find useful a division of mythopoeic poetry, or the mythopoeic aspects of poetry, into three parts, though all of them shade together. In the first a poet utilizes a given mythology but extends its range of significance without violating it in spirit, or even very much in letter. Properly speaking, this does not seem to me to fall into the range of mythopoeia at all, but can be considered more naturally as the most creative kind of mythological poetry. English poetry of this kind has received full treatment in two excellent books by Douglas Bush.[4] Good examples in Shelley are the "Hymn of Apollo" and the "Hymn of Pan."

A second kind of mythopoeic poetry can be called primitive, in that it embodies that direct perception of a Thou in natural objects or phenomena that the Frankforts have described for us, "a confrontation of life with life." [5]

This kind of poetry frequently owes nothing even to the example of past mythology, and Shelley is richer in it than any other English poet:

I

Swiftly walk o'er the western wave,
                    Spirit of Night!
Out of the misty eastern cave,
Where, all the long and lone daylight,
Thou wovest dreams of joy and fear,
Which make thee terrible and dear,—
                    Swift be thy flight!

II

Wrap thy form in a mantle gray,
                    Star-inwrought!
Blind with thine hair the eyes of Day;
Kiss her until she be wearied out,
Then wander o'er city, and sea, and land,
Touching all with thine opiate wand—
                    Come, long-sought!

4. *Mythology and the Renaissance Tradition in English Poetry*, Minneapolis, Univ. of Minnesota Press, 1932; and *Mythology and the Romantic Tradition in English Poetry*, Cambridge, Harvard Univ. Press, 1937, with a chapter on "Shelley."
5. Frankfort et al., p. 19.

III

When I arose and saw the dawn,
                    I sighed for thee;
When light rode high, and the dew was gone,
And noon lay heavy on flower and tree,
And the weary day turned to his rest,
Lingering like an unloved guest,
                    I sighed for thee.

IV

Thy brother Death came, and cried,
                    Wouldst thou me?
Thy sweet child Sleep, the filmy-eyed,
Murmured like a noontide bee,
Shall I nestle near thy side?
Wouldst thou me?—And I replied,
                    No, not thee!

V

Death will come when thou art dead,
                    Soon, too soon—
Sleep will come when thou art fled;
Of neither would I ask the boon
I ask of thee, belovèd Night—
Swift be thine approaching flight,
                    Come soon, soon!

The "Thou" here (Night), like the Thou of ancient or primitive man, or Buber's Thou of relationship open to us even now, "has the unprecedented, unparalleled, and unpredictable character of an individual, a presence known only in so far as it reveals itself." [6] Shelley is not personifying the phenomenon of night; that is, he is not animating what is *for him* not animate. He is indeed humanizing the night, in that his "I" is not a subject experiencing the night as object. There is no thing here except day; the Night is "Thou," and Thou and the poet stand over against each other in relationship. "He who takes his stand in relation shares in a reality, that is, in a being that neither merely belongs to him nor merely lies outside him. All reality is an activity in which I share without being able to appropriate for myself. Where there is no sharing there is no reality. Where there is self-appropriation there is no reality. The more direct the contact with the *Thou*, the fuller is the sharing." [7]

6. Ibid., p. 13.
7. Buber, p. 63.

Novalis, emblematically linked with Shelley in James Thomson's imaginative pseudonym, hymned the Night as part of his complex longing for death. In Shelley's subtler hymn "To Night" the paradoxical longing is for life, and the urgent prayer (the poem is primarily prayer) links Night and imaginative life, the life of the poet which cannot be lived in the common day. The Night in stanza I moves westward, as the day dies in the west and thus makes its final stand there. The figure of the "misty eastern cave" in line 3 is beautifully accurate. As the day progresses to its close, the first core of darkness is seen in the east, and in its relation to the whole dome of the sky's light, it is seen as the dark mouth of a cave. The prayer of the stanza, and of the whole poem, is for the Night to be swifter in its coming. So the daylight is an It, not a Thou. The poet cannot stand in relation to it, but rejects it as a thing. He has experienced it, under the burden of time as an object ("long" in line 4), and differentiated it from his being ("lone" in the same line). But even while he has suffered the day, he knows that the all-but-hidden Night has been at work in him, weaving those fantasies "of joy and fear" which make the Night (all but equated here of course with the primordial poetry in him—the unconscious if you will) a deity to be worshiped in both awe and love.

The Night here is male and creative, the day female and passive, as in the very beautiful second stanza.[8] Though the life even of a poet demands participation in each, if indeed his life is to continue (as Buber observes, "without *It* man cannot live"), the poet in this poem has reached the extreme limit of existence. When he arises and sees the dawn, he will not even attempt to address it as "Thou," but turns again to the Thou of Night, accepting the day only as something to be experienced, the burden of common life that must be suffered. The "dew" of line 18 is regarded by him as the last grace of Night, and when it is gone, and the light is high, he feels only burden, in the line:

And noon lay heavy on flower and tree.

In the fourth stanza he begins the final clarification, the pinpointing of his prayer. His prayer is not for Death or Sleep, as is the prayer of Novalis when he calls upon Night. In the final stanza the clarification is complete, and the Night of the relationship which is embodied in the prayer that is this poem is exactly defined. The Death-in-Life of common day will come, all too quickly, when this Night is dead; the Sleep which is everyday consciousness will come when this Night goes to its rest.

8. I take "the weary Day turned to *his* rest" of line 19 as being a different "Day" than the "Day" of stanza II. The "Day" of stanza II is a mythic Day, the contrary to the "Night" which the poem addresses. The "Day" of line 19 is the Sun, as I have been accustomed to read the poem. Pottle compares this "exuberance of invention," which admittedly can be confusing, to the many mythic representations of the earth in "Prometheus Unbound."

Therefore, the poet asks neither Death nor Sleep to come more swiftly. His prayer to the Night, his attempt to stand in I-Thou relationship to it, is a prayer for the advent of that fully wakeful consciousness which alone is life for him, and which comes only in the creative Night of his spirit, in the depth of himself which is the poetic faculty in him. He dies to our life of day, that he may live the fuller life of his night.

I have offered "To Night" as an example of primitive mythopoeic poetry, in which the poet enters into relationship with a natural Thou, the relationship itself constituting the myth. What I take as a third variety of mythopoeic poetry is more complex, though its roots are in just such relationships. From the concrete, primitive I-Thou relationship with God, the Jews formulated the abstract, complex myth of the Will of God. Similarly, from his concrete I-Thou relationships, the poet can dare to make his own abstractions, rather than adhere to formulated myth, traditionally developed from such meetings. This third kind of mythopoeia, as it is manifested in the major poems of Shelley, is my subject in the following chapters.

A close reading of a group of Shelley's poems will demonstrate my argument. I do not claim that *all* of Shelley's major and mature poems are mythopoeic, especially in the precise and narrow sense of mythopoeia that I insist upon here. I do claim that a certain group of Shelley's poems manifest precisely the mythopoeia that I have defined above. Their myth, quite simply, *is* myth: the process of its making, and the inevitability of its defeat.

I have already analyzed "To Night," a poem written in 1821, as an example of Shelley's mythmaking, a technique of writing poetry which is in itself the dominant theme of that poetry. With a few exceptions, the poems read in the following chapters are dealt with in the order of their composition.

I begin with the 1816 Hymns, the "Hymn to Intellectual Beauty" and "Mont Blanc," for these are the poems in which it seems to me that Shelley finds his myth, his great theme; in effect, finds himself. "Alastor," composed in the autumn of 1815, is conventionally taken to be Shelley's first mature and valuable poem of some length. I admire much in "Alastor," but the poem confusedly mixes allegory and mythmaking. Much of Shelley's later poetry has its prototype in "Alastor," but the specific aspect of that later poetry which is my concern does not.

The myth of the I-Thou relationship does not precede the 1816 Hymns; it comes into being as those poems work themselves out. Subsequently, the myth disappears for a time from Shelley's poetry. "The Revolt of Islam" (April–September 1817), an abortive allegorical epic which I do not admire, does not manifest much consciousness of the myth. The dualism of the "Revolt" is a spiritual retrogression from the myth; the dubious allegorizing of the poem is a technical decline from the mythmaking of the 1816 Hymns.

"Prometheus Unbound" is the first great embodiment of Shelley's myth, and in my third chapter I prepare for a reading of that poem. The fourth chapter, a reading of the "Ode to the West Wind," breaks away slightly from chronological order in an attempt to complete the process of introducing the lyrical drama. Chapter 5, in turn, is a full-scale reading of "Prometheus."

The myth of relationship culminates in "Prometheus"; the poem provides a complete statement of Shelley's vision. Other aspects of the myth are emphasized in "The Sensitive Plant" (Chapter 6) and "The Witch of Atlas" (Chapter 7).

In Chapter 8, which is a reading of the "Epipsychidion," I begin to trace the downward course of Shelley's myth, its awareness of its own defeat. "Adonais" (1821) would be considered next, but I have reluctantly excluded a reading of it from these chapters. Much of the poem frankly denies the myth rather than chronicles its defeat. The last seventeen stanzas of "Adonais" are as fine as anything in Shelley, but they neither illuminate nor are illuminated by the dialectic of Shelley's mythopoeia.

The ninth and final chapter is a reading of Shelley's posthumously published fragment, "The Triumph of Life." With the triumph of life over Shelley's myth of relationship, my argument is complete.

Such valuable long poems as "Julian and Maddalo," "The Cenci," and "Hellas" have been excluded because they have no bearing on my subject or my subject on them. Two longish poems which I particularly admire, the "Lines Written among the Euganean Hills" and the "Letter to Maria Gisborne," have been omitted for the same reason. Many of Shelley's lyrics and shorter poems would have served my purpose, but have been excluded for lack of space. I particularly regret saying nothing about "The Two Spirits. An Allegory," a remarkable mythopoeic lyric composed in 1820.

I have not been able to answer, even to my satisfaction, one crucial question. Blake, Shelley and Keats, besides being mythmakers, are in one degree or another opposed to Christianity. Blake calls himself a Christian, but persuasively redefines Christianity as being his own apocalyptic humanism. Shelley sets himself against institutional and historical Christianity in all his poetry, from "Queen Mab" through to "The Triumph of Life." Keats believes only in the holiness of the heart's affections, but is usually content not to polemicize against formal Christianity to the extent that Blake and Shelley do. Which has primacy: the mythmaking impulse and commitment to the mythopoeic mode, or the religious position counter to that of Christianity?

I cannot decide, for each commitment induces the other. In Shelley's 1816 Hymns, the overt denial of Christian myth and the formulation, vivid though tentative, of the poet's own myth exist side by side and neither has primacy. Though I cannot answer the question, I acknowledge its importance and validity. I for one would like to believe that primacy here belongs to the mythopoeic impulse itself.

Though I refer to Blake, Wordsworth, Coleridge, Byron, and Keats often in these chapters, this is a study not of romantic mythopoeia in general, but of Shelley only. Even the analogues I have made (especially in Chapter 3) between romanticism and Titanism break down if applied to one poet too many. Blake, Byron, and Shelley are Prometheans, Titans; Keats in "Hyperion" attempts to mediate between Olympians and Titans. The mature Coleridge and Wordsworth stand with the sky gods. No easy generalization will sum the matter; accuracy demands something more.

Yet, despite this reservation, Shelley is not unique as a romantic mythmaker. Coleridge and Wordsworth are potent influences, negative as well as positive, on the poet of the 1816 Hymns. Byron's Promethean-ism is active in Shelley's lyrical drama, and "Manfred" is certainly a mythopoeic work. Much in Keats might profitably be studied as myth-making.

But Blake stands with Shelley here as being primarily a mythopoeic poet. Yeats, the major mythmaker in modern poetry, derives equally from Blake and from Shelley, as much in the following chapters will evidence. Because Blake is a system maker, a mythographer who catalogues his own meanings, I have not hesitated to use him as contrast and iconographer to Shelley in these pages, especially in regard to the archetype of the lower paradise, Beulah-land.

Throughout these chapters I have used the Thomas Hutchinson edition of *The Complete Poetical Works of Shelley* (London, Oxford University Press, 1904), for all quotations from and references to Shelley's poetry. Where I have deviated from Hutchinson's text, principally in "The Triumph of Life," I have tried to account for the divergence and to indicate the source of my alternate text.

2

The 1816 Hymns

I

COLERIDGE'S "Hymn in the Manner of the Psalms," published first in the *Morning Post,* September 11, 1802, is entitled "Hymn before Sunrise in the Vale of Chamouni." Coleridge had never stood in that vale, as he himself admitted, and drew instead upon his experience in viewing Scawfell, but his visualization of the awful grandeur of Mont Blanc, Europe's highest peak, does not seem to have suffered from being compounded of both literary and somewhat remote experiential elements.

The Hymn is an expanded version of the "Ode to Chaumony" addressed by Friderika Brun to Klopstock, but it is considerably more than a translation. In his prefatory note in the *Morning Post* Coleridge states his poem's burden: "Who would be, who could be, an atheist in this valley of wonders?" Shelley gives the answer to this some fourteen years later, in his powerful hymn to Mont Blanc and, rather more blatantly, in his categorizing himself as ἄθεος in the visitors' album at the Chartreuse at Montanvert, some three leagues from Chamouni, on July 25, two days after the composition of "Mont Blanc." The album signing was prompted, we are told, by Shelley's observing "that his last predecessor had written some platitudes about 'Nature and Nature's God.' "[1] We have no reason to believe that Shelley had Coleridge's poem in mind, either then or when he composed his "Mont Blanc," for there are no verbal echoes of the earlier "Hymn" in the later work. However, there is evidence that Shelley had read Coleridge's poetry before 1816 of course, and the "Hymn before Sunrise" had been reprinted in *The Friend* (*11,* Oct. 26, 1809) before it made its appearance in *Sibylline Leaves* (1817). On July 17, 1816, less than a week before the composition of "Mont Blanc," Shelley wrote to Peacock, inquiring "of England—its literature, of which when I speak Coleridge is in my thoughts,"[2] and it is possible, at least, that Coleridge and his

---

1. Roger Ingpen, ed., *The Letters of Percy Bysshe Shelley* (2 vols. London, Bohn's, 1909), *2,* 514, n. 1. The source of the footnote is William Michael Rossetti, "Memoir of Shelley," *The Complete Poetical Works of Percy Bysshe Shelley* (London, 1878), *1,* 64.

2. Ingpen, p. 504.

"Hymn" were in Shelley's thoughts when he stood in the vale of Chamouni, and when he composed "Mont Blanc." Whatever the genetic history, the two poems are in violent contrast, with Shelley's meditation replying to Coleridge's orthodox transport. The excuse for beginning an analysis of Shelley's "Mont Blanc" with an analysis of Coleridge's hymn is that the reaction to Mont Blanc in the hymn, fully apprehended, will make us more aware of the unique elements in Shelley's confrontation of the mountain.

H. W. Garrod, commenting on the "Hymn before Sunrise," remarks that "it is worth recalling that Goethe's thoughts, when he first stood upon the Brocken, found expression in a verse of the Psalm: 'Lord, what is man that thou art mindful of him; or the son of man that thou takest account of him?' " [3] Coleridge is no less than accurate when he says that his hymn is "in the manner of the Psalms," for it does share their manner and much of their spirit. The God of the Psalms dwells upon His "holy hill," Mount Zion; from His mountain heights He speaks with awful authority, and in His remote fastnesses hoards the sources of His power. Closer still to Coleridge's hymn are the great questionings spoken by God from out the whirlwind to Job. "Who hath divided a watercourse for the overflowing of waters? . . . Out of whose womb came the ice? and the hoary frost of heaven, who hath gendered it?" Even so, Coleridge asks variants of these fiercely rhetorical questions as he addresses this "dread ambassador from Earth to Heaven" and urges it to transmit to God his, and the earth's, praises.

The "Hymn before Sunrise" is not one of Coleridge's finest poems, but it deserves more than the condescending scrutiny it receives in F. R. Leavis' *Revaluation*.[4] Its prime fault is probably its high-pitched quality; there are only two periods in this poem of eighty-five lines, all the other full stops (and there are several dozen) being either exclamation or rhetorical question marks. The effect is that of a man trying to work himself into a state of continuous rapture, so that Coleridge's dogged attempt at the Hebraic sublime works a considerable strain upon us. The extenuation is that 1802 is a rather late and difficult time for a poet to be uttering a psalm of praise to Jehovah.

Coleridge begins, as does Shelley in "Mont Blanc," with an evocation of near terror. Mont Blanc is aptly named, for its "bald awful head" stands in silent white contrast to the noisy blackness about it, where the Arve and Arveiron at its base rave ceaselessly and the surrounding air is dark, substantial, black. This violent sense perception, in which a natural scene is made to reveal its spiritual signature, is of course not so much traditional or biblical as it is Wordsworthian. D. G. James is prob-

3. H. W. Garrod, ed., *Coleridge, Poetry and Prose* (Oxford, Clarendon Press, 1933), p. 182.
4. London, Chatto & Windus, and New York, Stewart, 1947, pp. 233–5.

ably correct in insisting that a response to landscape in which doctrine is evoked, rather than preconceived, is unique to Wordsworth and to his imitators (as Coleridge and Shelley certainly are, though, as will be shown, to a precisely limited extent in their poems on Mont Blanc).[5] Unfortunately, the value and usefulness of James's observation are limited; it is correct as a judgment of rhetoric rather than of, so to speak, spirituality or psychology or epistemological belief, whichever one may prefer as an apt verbal discipline for this context. There can be no doubt, *insofar as this is a question of poetic procedure,* that Wordsworth is original in not bringing to bear upon a natural scene the burden of a preconceived doctrine, rather letting the type and character of his insight develop out of the scene itself. However, the perception itself, being Wordsworth's, constitutes, as all students of Wordsworth come to know, a unique kind of natural religion. Such religion is to be found, not altogether successfully blended with historical revelation of religion, in Coleridge's "Hymn before Sunrise"; and such religion is rejected, in effect, in Shelley's "Mont Blanc," in which reminiscences of this personal religious doctrine (an inadequate term, but still more apt than "belief") seem to perform the function of rhetorical and doctrinal contrast to Shelley's perception of the mountain and its attendant features.

If a Wordsworthian perception of a natural scene is then in itself equivalent to being doctrinal, what remains of James's observation is its aptness as a description of rhetorical technique. We may apply this to the Mont Blanc poems of Coleridge and Shelley as a simple but useful formula: these "nature odes" are Wordsworthian, and probably directly so, insofar as they continuously follow the rather effective technique of first, closely and vividly describing natural phenomena without obtrusively commenting upon them during the presentation and, next, closely relating the insight to be drawn from those phenomena to the phenomena themselves, generally by analogies based again upon a close descriptive account of the ways in which different parts of the phenomena relate to one another. Conversely, these odes are not Wordsworthian insofar as one of them attempts overtly to accommodate the insight drawn from the natural scene to a traditional body of belief or myth, and the other *begins* the process of compounding a new myth (partially out of older elements, in this case) by fitting the insight derived from landscape perception into a personally fabricated vision.

The first case is Coleridge's "Hymn before Sunrise"; the second, Shelley's "Mont Blanc." The first situation is not, I hasten to add, completely alien to Wordsworth's poetry. Basil Willey, who forcefully makes the point that for Wordsworth "there must be no abstractions, no symbols, no myths, to stand between the mind and its true object," also states that, while all mythologies were exploded for Wordsworth, "a

5. D. G. James, *The Romantic Comedy* (London, Oxford Univ. Press, 1948), p. 75.

belief in the visible universe as the body of which God was the soul alone remained." [6] Despite the rhetorical force of "alone," that is still a great deal to retain of the Christian cosmos, though it is less than we find in the "Hymn before Sunrise." Wordsworth facing the Alps is not prepared to refer their creation back to its mythic source in Genesis as Coleridge unhesitatingly does. The Alps testify in "The Prelude" not so much to the glory of Jehovah as to the existence of a continuity in nature which is, to Wordsworth, divine. Wordsworth's first sight of Mont Blanc is, as presented in his poetry, not immediately a consoling experience. In a passage which Raymond Havens thinks is partially a direct reminiscence of Coleridge's "Hymn before Sunrise," [7] Wordsworth begins in the spirit of Yarrow unvisited, lamenting the death of a living expectation when:

> That very day,
> From a bare ridge we also first beheld
> Unveiled the summit of Mont Blanc, and grieved
> To have a soulless image on the eye
> That had usurped upon a living thought
> That never more could be. . . .

"Soulless image" because of its frozen blankness, can one surmise, anticipating Shelley's "Mont Blanc" and remembering also Blake's insistence on white as the archetypal color of the heavenly tyrant, the frostbitten Urizen; white as the "colorless all-color of atheism"; white as the color of the feared unknown? This is at best a psychological guess as to Wordsworth's reaction, though it will be shown to be a part of Shelley's general symbolism, with at least a tentative employment in "Mont Blanc." Whatever the cause of Wordsworth's first reaction to Mont Blanc, he and his companion are immediately reconciled to realities in "The Prelude," for "the wondrous Vale of Chaumony . . . made rich amends" to them, of a kind more fully developed in one of Wordsworth's greatest passages, some hundred lines later. The wonders of the Alps, fearful to Wordsworth as they are to Coleridge and Shelley, are depicted here with a vividness surpassing both the latter poets:

> The immeasurable height
> Of woods decaying, never to be decayed,
> The stationary blasts of waterfalls,
> And in the narrow rent at every turn
> Winds thwarting winds, bewildered and forlorn,
> The torrents shooting from the clear blue sky,

6. Basil Willey, *The Seventeenth Century Background* (New York, Anchor Books, 1953), p. 295.
7. R. D. Havens, *The Mind of a Poet* (Baltimore, The Johns Hopkins Univ. Press, 1941), p. 425.

> The rocks that muttered close upon our ears,
> Black drizzling crags that spake by the way-side
> As if a voice were in them, the sick sight
> And giddy prospect of the raving stream . . .

At this point the powerful presentation of the natural scene develops into perhaps the finest expression of Wordsworth's natural religion to be found in "The Prelude," and here one can see precisely how Coleridge in his "Hymn before Sunrise" is going back to a relative orthodoxy of belief and expression, as compared to the nakedness of Wordsworth's shedding of the coverings of Christian myth in his religious utterance. Signatures in nature have been seen and expressed by the poets of Christian tradition, and auguries of innocence found in the physical world by Blake and by Shelley, but what exists in the following climactic lines is unique to Wordsworth, for its peculiar nature is that it is independent of myth, whether received or personally created. We are offered a truth whose warrant is only that it is the product of a single individuality's reciprocal dealings with nature:

> The unfettered clouds and region of the Heavens,
> Tumult and peace, the darkness and the light—
> Were all like workings of one mind, the features
> Of the same face, blossoms upon one tree;
> Characters of the great apocalypse,
> The types and symbols of Eternity,
> Of first, and last, and midst, and without end.

I have said nothing original about Wordsworth and his salient poetic qualities, but my purpose has been served if a contrast has been drawn precisely between Wordsworth and Coleridge in their visions of what we may term the interpenetration of the Alps and the Divine. Leavis, in his extraordinary essay on Shelley, has preceded me in this contrast of Wordsworth, Coleridge, and Shelley, and a reminder of his conclusions may be of some use before attempting detailed analyses of "Mont Blanc" and the "Hymn before Sunrise." Wordsworth, as opposed to Shelley, is judged by Leavis to display a sureness in grasping "the world of common perception." Coleridge's poem is babyish by clear implication, while the opening of "Mont Blanc" elicits a comment which I shall refer to again when I have examined the first section of that poem: "The metaphorical and the actual, the real and the imagined, the inner and the outer, could hardly be more unsortably and indistinguishably confused." [8] Bearing so distinguished a recent judgment in mind, I return to Coleridge's poem for a closer inspection.

The "Hymn before Sunrise" is what Blake would have termed "a

8. Leavis, pp. 212, 235.

Urizenic Hymn," and it is likely that he would have classified it with such works as *The Analogy of Religion, The Sacred Theory of the Earth* and *The Wisdom of God in the Creation* as being deistic, whatever their intention (certainly antideistic in the case of Butler). Blake's violent antipathy to natural religion was, we now realize, neither mystical nor orthodox in its design. It was based rather on a firm conviction that "where man is not, nature is barren," [9] from which followed the Blakean conclusion that any analogy for the Divine drawn from the physical world could result only in a visualization of an antihuman divinity, a white Mystery whose sacred blankness could be merely an expressed embodiment of man's fear and ignorance in the face of the unknown. Blake surveying Mont Blanc would have visualized instantly his Urizen dwelling there, even as Shelley, in a letter to Peacock, in a passage to which I must refer later, sees the mountain as the throne of Ahriman, the Evil Principle. One can contrast immediately the Hebraic theism of the "Hymn before Sunrise" with the reaction of the religious humanist, Blake, in "The First Book of Urizen," where Jehovah as mountain god is presented as the inhumane thunderer and limiter of human desire, Urizen:

> His cold horrors silent, dark Urizen
> Prepar'd; his ten thousands of thunders,
> Rang'd in gloom'd array, stretch out across
> The dread world; & the rolling of wheels,
> As of swelling seas, sound in his clouds,
> In his hills of stor'd snows, in his mountains
> Of hail & ice; voices of terror
> Are heard, like thunders of autumn
> When the cloud blazes over the harvests.
>   (Keynes, p. 244.)

Urizen is always hazy and abstract, associated as he is with clouds and hills of ice and snow, for these aspects of his appearance represent his unreality, his status as a cloudy projection of the vague fears of men. In the white vagueness of Mont Blanc, the theistic vision of Coleridge finds an embodiment of the Sublime, the "pure serene" being a background for the cloud-veiled mountain.

We can begin categorizing the "Hymn before Sunrise" then, as a Coleridgean analogy of religion which passes from an initial, rather deistic apprehension of the mountain into a Hebraic identification of the mountain with its Creator, the Jehovah who commanded and the silence came. The hymn stops short of pantheism, though its depicted mountain has anthropomorphic qualities, as in its "five wild torrents fiercely

---

9. Geoffrey Keynes, ed., *Poetry and Prose of William Blake* (London, Nonesuch Press, 1927), p. 195.

glad" which in context are suggestive perhaps of the human senses when we remember the traditional interpretation of "the rivers of the water of life" that ran through Eden as being the unfallen senses of the First Man. Still further suggestive of anthropomorphic identification are the wonderful lines (the finest, I think, in the hymn) in which the mountain is given almost the status of a Miltonic angel, contending against the dark forces of night:

> O struggling with the darkness all the night,
> And visited all night by troops of stars . . .

However, the orthodoxy of the poem comes no further than this toward proper pantheism. The sequence of the poem itself is very clear, in its close relation of mountain, Coleridge's thought, and God, entities which begin by being separate but which come perilously close to what precisely could be called an emotional rather than mystical fusion when Coleridge's

> dilating Soul, enrapt, transfused,
> Into the mighty vision passing—there
> As in her natural form, swelled vast to Heaven!

The "mighty vision" here is compounded of Mont Blanc's "blending" with the "Thought" of the poet, a blending which is the result of religious terror inspired by the awful silence and white mass of Mont Blanc, set against the blackness of a presunrise vale of Chamouni.

This is a universal reaction, and with it we cannot quarrel. What is more likely to offend many readers, Shelley as a hypothetical one among them, is the posture of servility with which Coleridge proceeds to worship the Creator of this white leviathan, this "kingly Spirit throned among the hills," this "great Hierarch." These phrases are in the tone of God speaking out of the whirlwind, boasting that his leviathan or his behemoth is "king over all the children of pride." Like the closing sequences of Job, the injunction of the "Hymn before Sunrise" is "Submit!" and only the cyclonic ferocity of the questions from out the whirlwind are likely to be rhetorically persuasive of such an injunction. Coleridge is plainly imitating the poet of Job, but much of the fine force gained by that imitation is dissipated by Coleridge's typical softening of the harsh, strident original. We are disconcerted at finding the mountain, otherwise so terrible, addressed as "Earth's rosy star," and being decorated "with living flowers / of loveliest blue," and being surrounded by pine groves with "soft and soul-like sounds." The unsympathetic eye of a nontheist or unorthodox theist might be grimly amused at the vision Coleridge presents in his conclusion of a poet fearfully placating Urizen, that is, his own fear of the unknown. For me, the conclusion is uncomfortably close to the ironic Urizenic symbolism of Blake, as the mountain demigod rises "like a vapoury cloud" before the pious poet. Only a sharer of Coleridge's faith can be expected to add his voice to the earthly choir of the final lines:

> Thou too again, stupendous Mountain! thou
> That as I raise my head, awhile bowed low
> In adoration, upward from thy base
> Slow travelling with dim eyes suffused with tears,
> Solemnly seemest, like a vapoury cloud,
> To rise before me— Rise, O ever rise,
> Rise like a cloud of incense from the Earth!
> Thou kingly Spirit throned among the hills,
> Thou dread ambassador from Earth to Heaven,
> Great Hierarch! tell thou the silent sky,
> And tell the stars, and tell yon rising sun
> Earth, with her thousand voices, praises GOD.

Nevertheless, my criticism is directed at an aspect of Coleridge's formulation and not at his poem as poem. Moreover, there is no validity in my carping for those who are able (by the strength of their common faith) to share Coleridge's emotion. To have challenged the poet of Job, as Coleridge comes very close to doing, on his own prime ground is not an inconsiderable achievement. Moreover, it is unfair to the "Hymn before Sunrise" to remove it from its context in Coleridge's life and poetry, and my only plea of extenuation is that I am employing the poem as a useful opening contrast to Shelley's difficult and frequently misread "Mont Blanc." The "Hymn before Sunrise" belongs to the period of Coleridge's life and work which is best exemplified by the great "Dejection" ode, its chief poetic ornament. This hymn out of darkness, projected by Coleridge into the vale of Chamouni by means of Friderika Brun's ode, is best apprehended as a counterpart to the greater ode of "Dejection." The poet knows that Mont Blanc is part of the "inanimate cold world" until he himself makes it something that lives in his own life. His gazing on Mont Blanc (in vision) is "a vain endeavour" as much as his gazing "on that green light that lingers in the west," which also is, for him, of God, unless something of the life of God is still within him, and all this he knows better than we can know it. An unsympathetic reader might say of the "Hymn before Sunrise" that it attempts just what the "Dejection" ode says the poet ought not anticipate doing:

> I may not hope from outward forms to win
> The passion and the life, whose fountains are within.

But the sympathetic and therefore better reader will apprehend the pathos of the "Hymn before Sunrise" coming out of the darkness of

Coleridge's night. The quality of desperation in the poem is perhaps damaging rhetorically, but it suits a hymn before sunrise in a vale of affliction.

In his theology, perhaps the major labor of his maturer years, Coleridge would seem to have made one of the most influential adjustments (of his period) of the old belief to an age when the mythologies were held "exploded." But in his poetry, as the partial failure of the "Hymn before Sunrise" helps to demonstrate, he must be judged to have been less successful at that difficult adjustment. As with Blake and Shelley, his poems which best resolve the problem are probably the handful of mythopoeic creations.

2

> Hast thou a charm to stay the morning-star
> In his steep course? So long he seems to pause
> On thy bald awful head, O sovran BLANC?

We pass to Shelley, who so frequently in the shifting system of his poetry identifies himself with the morning star, the light-bearer, and whose steep poetic course is here marked for us by its pause before the awful charm of Mont Blanc.

His poem is best introduced by his own fanciful prose speculations in his letters to Peacock. "One would think that Mont Blanc, like the god of the Stoics, was a vast animal, and that the frozen blood for ever circulated through his stony veins." [1] The white terrors of the Alps move the poet to visualize the most archaic deities: in addition to this Stoic archetype there is "the overhanging brow of a black precipice on an enormous rock, precisely resembling some colossal Egyptian statue of a female deity." He sees too the most archaic and unpleasant of gods, the Zoroastrian power of darkness, Ahriman, a playful object of belief for a cheerful and eclectic pagan like Peacock, but evoked here in another spirit:

> Do you, who assert the supremacy of Ahriman, imagine him throned among these desolating snows, among these palaces of death and frost, so sculptured in this their terrible magnificence by the adamantine hand of necessity, and that he casts around him, as the first essays of his final usurpation, avalanches, torrents, rocks, and thunders, and above all these deadly glaciers, at once the proof and symbols of his reign;—add to this, the degradation of the human species—who, in these regions, are half deformed or idiotic, and most of whom are deprived of anything that can excite interest or admiration. This is part of the subject more mournful and less sublime; but such as neither the poet nor the philosopher should disdain to regard.

1. Ingpen, ed., *Letters of Shelley, 2*, 515. Following quotations from pp. 507–8, 513.

"As the first essays of his final usurpation" is to be borne in mind as we turn to Shelley's ode. We are also to recall the relevant text in Wordsworth, so frequently cited as Shelley's inspiration here. The lines echoed in the opening section of "Mont Blanc" are these:

> And I have felt
> A presence that disturbs me with the joy
> Of elevated thoughts; a sense sublime
> Of something far more deeply interfused,
> Whose dwelling is the light of setting suns,
> And the round ocean and the living air,
> And the blue sky, and in the mind of man;
> A motion and a spirit, that impels
> All thinking things, all objects of all thought,
> And rolls through all things. . . .

This is another of the great set passages that serve as a key and as an ornament to Wordsworth's variety of natural religion. It is certainly being remembered by Shelley as he begins his ode, but its function in that great opening is contrast, as though Shelley (consciously or not; it scarcely matters) counterpoints his vision against Wordsworth's.

Let me, at the risk of stating the obvious, spell out the very basic contrast between Shelley and Wordsworth here. What Wordsworth hears in nature is "nor harsh nor grating," for "nature and the language of the sense" anchor his "purest thoughts" and constitute the "soul" of all his "moral being." What "rolls through all things" here is purely beneficent and clearly moral, is in fact the ground of all morality, of the higher human impulses. The physical world, especially, it would seem, on the banks of the Wye, is a large signature of natural piety. The music it evokes may, at worst, be still and sad, but harsh and grating it is not. There is no menace in this landscape (though Wordsworth has landscapes as desolate as any in Shelley) for its inherent Power, though vast, is only mildly and benevolently invoked.

George Woodberry, in his note on "Mont Blanc," long ago pointed out that in lines 96–7 of that poem,

> Power dwells apart in its tranquillity,
> Remote, serene, and inaccessible . . .

we are given "an anticipation of the conception imaginatively defined in Demogorgon." Woodberry's realization that "Mont Blanc" and the "Hymn to Intellectual Beauty" "are forerunners of the main lines of thought in the *Prometheus Unbound*" [2] is so accurate and essential an observation that one learns to distrust any full-scale consideration of

2. G. E. Woodberry, ed., *The Complete Poetical Works of Percy Bysshe Shelley* (Boston, Houghton Mifflin, 1901), p. 639.

Shelley that slights the importance of those poems as the first embodiment of the mature myth later to be developed in Shelley's major poems.

James, in his consideration of "Mont Blanc," also sees the poem as
being Wordsworthian, since its landscape fits his standards for Wordsworthian perception. But James goes on to say rather vaguely that "in
'Mont Blanc' the Eternal is seen in its creation and destruction of what
is temporal and passing." And "Mont Blanc," as an image of this,

> necessarily falls short; expressive as it is, it does not succeed in
> uniting the eternal and the temporal as the imagination desires, or
> in showing how they may come together . . . Certainly, the image
> conveys truth; it is a vision of the life of God, overflowing indeed
> into a created world, yet complete in itself and transcendent; it
> communicates to us a sense of the complete sufficiency of God to
> Himself and of the smallness of the human world which we see as
> issuing from inexhaustible power which can destroy what is created
> with no loss to itself. Yet something more is desired than this,
> whether with justice or not; that is, that we should somehow be-
> hold the eternal inhabiting the temporal, or the temporal informed
> by the stillness and perfection of the eternal.[3]

James is making what we must accept as a quasi-theological declaration, and he is making it in the form of criticism of a poem, but he com-
mits the error of misparaphrasing the poem by failing to relate his paraphrase to the text of the poem itself. Even were his reading accurate
(and I will have to show that it is not) his critical verdict would still
be irrelevant to Shelley's poem, for he cannot demand of a poem or a
poet what they have no desire to give in the way of a theological or metaphysical formulation. James expects of one of the earliest of Shelley's
mature poems what only the complete body of work may be able to give.
Here I encroach on the borders of my canonic argument, and must turn
at last to the text of "Mont Blanc" for one of the opening affirmations
of Shelley's beliefs *as* a poet, or poetic beliefs, as opposed to his beliefs *of*
a poet caught up in history and in an age.

Newman White thinks that "in the first section [of "Mont Blanc"]
Shelley elaborates the idea that experience is simply a mighty river of
events and impressions flowing through the mind . . . The rest of
the poem is primarily only a graphic illustration of this philosophic
idea." [4] Aside from White's mistaking of a metaphor for a "philosophical
idea," his paraphrase of the poem's opening lines is simply inaccurate.
"Experience" is his term and not Shelley's, and there is nothing in the
lines in question to indicate that the metaphoric river is the counter for
human "experience" or, as White says later, "reality." This is cited

3. James, p. 79.
4. N. I. White, ed., *The Best of Shelley* (New York, T. Nelson, 1932), pp. 474–5.

not to discredit an individual critic but rather to indicate the danger
of reading Shelley's poem too quickly. We have a text before us which
is more complicated than its author states it to be. "Mont Blanc" may
well have been "composed under the immediate impression of the deep
and powerful feelings excited by the objects which it attempts to describe," but it is not therefore necessarily to be regarded "as an undis-
ciplined overflowing of the soul," and it need not rest its prime claim to
critical approbation "on an attempt to imitate the untamable wildness
and inaccessible solemnity from which those feelings sprang." [5]

A. M. D. Hughes makes the fine remark that " 'Mont Blanc' takes
the affrighted sense of the great world itself as spiritual and ideal." [6]
I may (at the last) wish to quarrel with the final word in Hughes's sentence, but I find that I can best begin by pondering the eloquence of that
remark. The subject of "Mont Blanc" is truly just that : our "affrighted
sense of the great world," our awe before creation, and more particularly
our fear of some of its aspects. The apprehension of the physical creation in this sense is better illustrated by example than by paraphrase.
The analogues are in Job's beholding of behemoth and leviathan and in
Blake's fierce and joyful irony in the beholding of his tyger. Shelley's
ravine of Arve, if we take the image complete, with mountain background added to valley and rushing river, is just such a mythical figure
as behemoth or tyger. Robert Graves remarks that a myth is best considered as a "poetic pictograph," [7] and clearly in this sense Shelley's
ravine is a myth. Myths of this sort are likely to be comprehensive and
arbitrary at the same time, so that the justification for their presump-
tion had better lie in their vividness. Part of the critical test for "Mont
Blanc" must therefore be the extent to which it excels in phanopoeia, for
its argument and music can be strong and beautiful only if the development of its image is coherent.

Two years after the composition of "Mont Blanc," Shelley, in his
preface to "Prometheus Unbound," was to write : "The imagery which
I have employed will be found, in many instances, to have been drawn
from the operations of the human mind, or from those external actions
by which they are expressed." [8] This is an ambiguous statement, as the
varied interpretations placed upon it by Shelley scholars might seem
to demonstrate, and needs to be considered in a reader's meditation upon
"Prometheus." Invoked here in opposition to the first section of "Mont

5. Shelley's own comments on "Mont Blanc," made in his *History of a Six Weeks'
Tour, and Letters from Switzerland,* and quoted by Mary Shelley in her "Note on
Poems of 1816."
6. A. M. D. Hughes, *The Nascent Mind of Shelley* (London, Oxford Univ. Press,
1947), p. 250.
7. Robert Graves, *Hercules, My Shipmate* (New York, Creative Age, 1945), p. 449.
8. Thomas Hutchinson, ed., *The Complete Poetical Works of Shelley* (London, Oxford Univ. Press, 1904), p. 222.

Blanc," this statement may be elucidated in at least one of its aspects, and may help clarify the rugged opening of the poem, which Leavis has chided for "confusion."

> The everlasting universe of things
> Flows through the mind, and rolls its rapid waves,
> Now dark—now glittering—now reflecting gloom—
> Now lending splendour, where from secret springs
> The source of human thought its tribute brings
> Of waters,—with a sound but half its own,
> Such as a feeble brook will oft assume
> In the wild woods, among the mountains lone,
> Where waterfalls around it leap for ever,
> Where woods and winds contend, and a vast river
> Over its rocks ceaselessly bursts and raves.   [1–11]

"The metaphorical and the actual, the real and the imagined, the inner and the outer, could hardly be more unsortably and indistinguishably confused," to quote Leavis again. On the contrary, those dichotomies are here subtly mingled and are resolved (in the poem's text) into a clear relation whose outlines suggest one meaning of the statement I have quoted from the preface to "Prometheus."

I suggest that one of the prime causes of Leavis' difficulty is probably Shelley's initial suppression of the first term of his very impressive metaphor. "Mont Blanc's" subject is the poet's contemplation of a natural scene, but Shelley rushes *in medias res,* with no touch of natural description in his first section. We must assume the Arve river and the ravine it rushes through, in order to comprehend that we are dealing with metaphor, albeit inverted metaphor. What compounds the reversal, and angers Leavis, is that Shelley is not content to describe the second term of his metaphor in its own particulars, but rather alternates its presentation by extensively looting the components of the suppressed first term. The justification for this mingling is that it enables the poet to write simultaneously on two levels of apprehension which can be understood on one level of meaning. Shelley is beginning to talk about an I and a Thou, one related to the other, and their relationship to the abiding phenomena that constitute the physical world as we experience it. He, at the same time, is telling us that he is viewing a great river rolling through its ravine, though we must deduce this. He suppresses this latter statement, makes it indirect, from rhetorical motives. At worst, he is liable to the charge of purposeful obscurity, but his lines are not confused. If in "Prometheus" Shelley was to employ imagery "from the operations of the human mind, or from those external operations by which they are expressed," then we may say that he here anticipates himself to an extreme, for in the first section of "Mont Blanc" the imagery is clearly drawn from the external operations of nature, which the poet holds to express the operations of a more than human, a universal mind which works in all things. If "mingling" of tenor and vehicle is *on principle* objectionable, then and only then can Shelley's lines be condemned.

C. D. Locock, in his excellent notes on "Mont Blanc," seems not to share in any of Leavis' difficulties, as he clearly and simply makes the elementary necessary equivalences between the ravine and "universal mind," the Arve river itself and the "everlasting Universe of things"; that is, in paraphrase, the abiding phenomena that constitute the world as we mentally experience it and the "feeble brook" of line 7 and *"individual human* mind, which borrows its inspiration from the everlasting Universe." [9]

Locock's inadequacy here is only in making his counters too precise, that is, of being less suggestive and tentative than Shelley himself is. If I paraphrase the poem in what follows, it is with the reservation that I am not concerned directly with evaluation, and do not therefore offer my explication as exhaustive or exclusive. My concern here is with what I take to be the beginning of Shelley's mature mythopoeia : his first statement (allied, as we shall see, with its complement in the almost simultaneously composed "Hymn To Intellectual Beauty") of what can be termed, almost precisely, a primal vision; that is, a strictly poetic attempt to compete with religion and philosophy as a coherent presenter of ultimate realities. Behind my reading must lie my previous readings of Coleridge and Wordsworth on Mont Blanc, for the sake of an orthodox poetic contrast. In a schematic sense I am trying to ascertain and to state as clearly as I can only one kind of meaning in Shelley's "Mont Blanc," a meaning on a tropological or moral, here a mythic level. The question I must ask is : "What is unique in Shelley's view of Mont Blanc and the natural phenomena that surround it ?" In seeking an answer for this, the beginning of my inquiry, I may neglect with some justification many aspects of the poem, provided that I do not ever forget that it is a poem, and that it does not communicate doctrinally in the same way that other verbal disciplines do, even though it dares to encroach upon those disciplines. If I do not forget this, then even my limited paraphrase may justify an evaluation, on my part, of "Mont Blanc" as a poem.

"Mont Blanc" may be said to have a twofold "subject." First, what is the relation between the I, the individual mind of a man, and the phenomena that surround him in the physical universe? To what extent is the mind independent on phenomena of this kind—does it actively

9. C. D. Locock, ed., *The Poems of Percy Bysshe Shelley* (2 vols. London, Methuen, 1911), *2*, 489–90.

construct them, or does it simply passively record them? Put another way, does it confront them in relationship as Thou's, or does it merely experience them as It's? Within this outer subject, primal to Shelley's mature poetry as it is to Blake's, is the inner theme of the poem. What directs this world of physical things, and what moral purpose has this direction? Unifying the two parts of the subject is the poem's postulate of the possibility of a Thou as a kind of universal mind in nature. So much, in crude terms, until I can refine my formulation after analysis.

No one (except Leavis) has ever disputed the meaning or clarity of the first five and one-half lines of the poem. They embody the initial metaphor spoken of above. The Arve goes down through the great ravine lending splendor to the ravine, but also borrowing physical appearance from the ravine, by reflecting its colors. Analogically, impressions of physical phenomena reach the human mind through the senses, but at the same time the mind alters these impressions, and colors them individually. The traditional first difficulty occurs at line 6—what is the referent of "its"? The possibilities are "the everlasting universe of things" in line 1, or "the source of human thought" in 5, the immediately preceding line. Shelley's dashes do not help us much here. What is the function of the dash after "of waters" in line 6? If the function is to divide "with a sound" from what directly precedes it, so as to refer it back to the first line, then "the everlasting universe of things," possessing a sound "but half its own," is so far compared to "a feeble brook." However, we surely do better to ignore Shelley's dash entirely here, for such a reading destroys what is otherwise the first appearance in the poem of what will prove to be an aspect of its central theme, the relationship of an individual I to a universal Thou, concurrent with the relationship of both entities to the world of things. The counterreading would involve Shelley in a redundant first stanza, for if it were the "universe of things," that is, the river, which had a sound "but half its own," then we would only be "told" again that our impressions come through the physical senses but that at the same time our minds alter these impressions as they are received. Or, in the direct language of the stanza as so read, the sound of the river is increased by being reflected back from the sides of the ravine. Aside from the redundancy of this, we would find that lines 7–11 of the first stanza lost all rhetorical significance or effect by this reading. The "feeble brook" and its activities and surroundings would be merely a rather feeble metaphor to drive in the single point of the stanza for the third time. Read however as I (following Locock) read it, the final five lines of the stanza are effective and frightening, perhaps effective through fright. The feeble brook which gathers sound greater than its own, transposed into the mind of the individual I reaching out toward the ravine's Thou, and then borne along the ravine by the rushing river of things, evokes a response of fearful identification from us as we visualize our apprehensive faculties feebly coursing along:

> In the wild woods, among the mountains lone,
> Where waterfalls around it leap for ever,
> Where woods and winds contend, and a vast river
> Over its rocks ceaselessly bursts and raves.[1]

1. My reading of the first section of "Mont Blanc" differs so radically from the most recently published detailed reading (by Peter Butter in his *Shelley's Idols of the Cave*, Edinburgh, Univ. of Edinburgh Press, 1954, pp. 118–22) that it may be useful to juxtapose our two readings, of which only one can be accepted as correct. Butter begins by accepting I. J. Kapstein's general conclusions about the poem and would have to dispute almost every specific interpretation which, following Locock, I have made of the poem's first section. Butter reads the poem as embodying contradictions; I do not. Butter and I agree only on the interpretation of the first five and one-half lines, except that even here Butter is ready to admit Kapstein's suggestion that Shelley has in mind Locke's distinction between primary and secondary qualities, which I myself do not. From line 6 on Butter's reading and my own are irreconcilable. He takes the "its" of line 6 to refer to the "universe of things" in line 1, basing this reading on the dash after "waters," which I argue had better be ignored. In his view then, it is the "universe of things" whose sound is "but half its own" and which is compared to "a feeble brook." Here is Butter directly: "The river's sound is but half its own, in that it is increased by being reflected by the sides of the ravine. . . . I do not agree with Locock and others who identify the 'feeble brook' with the individual mind as opposed to the ravine (universal mind) and the river (things). Shelley is not yet concerned with the relationship of the individual mind to universal mind but solely with that of mind in general to things" (p. 119). My reasons for holding the opposite view are in my text.

My reading of the remaining sections of the poem, I ought to add, also differs greatly from that of Butter. Butter reads lines 41–8 as meaning "little more than that the poet having looked at the scene now proceeds to write poetry about it" (p. 120). Again, Butter refers the cave of line 44 to the *Republic,* and interprets the "ghosts" as "our sensory impressions" which are only "shadows" of Platonic reality. Butter concludes his analysis of the second section by finding the whole section "obscure —with an obscurity of an unjustifiable kind" but still "pretty well in accordance with Berkeleyan idealism." However Butter also concludes that herein "Shelley's ultimate power is still Necessity . . . rather than Berkeley's God." Of the poem's final lines Butter observes: "This last question is a dramatic reversal of the conclusion to which the whole poem has been tending" (pp. 123–4). If my own reading is correct, then the obscurity, contradictions, and dramatic reversal found by Butter are all of his own creation. If my reading is wrong, as it may well be, I should then be obliged to admit the contradictions.

Frederick Pottle has recently referred me to still another full-scale reading of "Mont Blanc," published since my completion of this chapter. Charles H. Vivian in his article, "The One 'Mont Blanc'" (*Keats-Shelley Journal, 4,* Winter, 1955, 55–65), takes issue with Kapstein, as I do, on the question of the poem's consistency. Vivian and I are very much in agreement in opposing the views of Kapstein (and of Butter, to whom Vivian does not refer), but we differ in our positive accounts of the poem, though our differences are not absolute. The Power enshrined in "Mont Blanc" which I term the Thou, on the basis of my mythopoeic thesis, is named the "Principle of Permanence" by Vivian. To him, "Mont Blanc symbolizes this Principle of Permanence of which Shelley has awareness and which he is trying to understand" (p. 56). Again, "The Principle of Permanence is not manifested to mortal man, in the midst of his ever-changing sensations, except by intuition. All he can actually contemplate is ex-

As the poem's second section opens, the landscape's correspondences are in the background, and Shelley invokes the terrible grandeur of the natural scene itself. Behind the ravine is Power, or an ultimate Thou lurking within nature. Beginning in the latter part of line 15, we are given first intimations of the potentially destructive (to us) capacity of that Power, intimations made explicit in lines 100–25, later to climax the poem's fourth section. Here in line 16 the Arve is the ravine and not the river, as the grouping of correspondences re-enter the poem:

> awful scene,
> Where Power in likeness of the Arve comes down
> From the ice-gulfs that gird his secret throne . . .   [15–17]

A primeval worship of this Power is depicted as being embedded in the natural scene, in contrast to Coleridge's Jobean vision of the same view:

> thou dost lie,
> Thy giant brood of pines around thee clinging,
> Children of elder time, in whose devotion
> The chainless winds still come and ever came
> To drink their odours, and their mighty swinging
> To hear—an old and solemn harmony . . .

Here the "giant brood of pines" (their size suggestive of Titanic, pre-sky-god ages) are, in a submerged image, great censers swinging in the element, with the winds visiting them to worship, to breathe their incense ("drink their odours"). With this faintly suggested image of worship we are prepared for the shrine that follows in "the aethereal waterfall, whose veil / Robes some unsculptured image"; and being prepared, we pass from the shrine of this invisible divinity into religious trance, evoked in

---

perience; if he is able to intuit anything about the Principle, the latter can appear to him only as 'Power in likeness of the Arve' " (p. 58). I prefer my reading to Vivian's here, because "Principle of Permanence" is Vivian's phrase and conception, not Shelley's. Shelley simply says "Thou," and my analysis follows him in doing so. But I support Vivian's reading, as he does mine, and I gain added confidence in my reading on that basis. In his reading of lines 142–4, which conclude the poem, Vivian lacks (from my standpoint) only an awareness of the vocabulary of Shelley's mythopoeia. Otherwise, we complement one another: "If the human mind did not, in silence and solitude, plunge into these realms of speculation, and pursue its way until finally it came upon these insights and intuitions—then, in effect, the Principle itself ('thou') would have no significance. Neither would any of our ordinary experience, with the common objects of knowledge ('earth, and stars, and sea')" (pp. 64–5). Here, if you omit Vivian's "the Principle itself" and leave only the "thou," you have very nearly my own reading. The I of the human mind needs to enter into relationship with the Thou of Mont Blanc, but the Thou needs the I as well. Confrontation is mutual, else the Thou itself is reduced to the status of an object of experience, like "earth, and stars, and sea." Earth and stars and sea, like Mont Blanc, attain significance only when met in relationship, not when they are simply experienced as objects.

> the strange sleep
> Which when the voices of the desert fail
> Wraps all in its own deep eternity . . .

In line 30, with appropriate rush of sound, we see the ravine again and the river coming down in its path, and we finish this astonishing second section with a difficult meditation beginning in line 34. We are brought back again to that major thematic aspect of the poem first suggested in the image of the "feeble brook," the I of the individual mind in its relation to the Thou of the mind lurking behind phenomena, and in its relation to the phenomena more directly, as it receives them. I am stumbling here into the problem of a poet's epistemology, as opposed to his poetic vision or epistemology in a less philosophical sense, and here I must pause again for argument.

I. J. Kapstein, in his essay on "Mont Blanc," [2] properly places the poem at that point in Shelley's *philosophic* career when materialism had been abandoned and the idealism of Berkeley avowed. Kapstein reads the poem as a document with philosophic, that is, technical epistemological meaning. As a critic he means to determine exactly the extent to which the poem is Berkeleyan and to which it is materialistic. Kapstein's conclusion is that the poem, like the poet at the time at which he composed it, is in a state of conflict and philosophic confusion. Shelley, this critic says, alternates in this poem between his early worship of the Power of Necessity, and a later, idealistic defiance of that power.

Let me observe first that Kapstein comes to the poem with far too many philosophical notions. He is so much on the lookout for these notions that he reads into the opening lines of the poem Locke's distinction between primary and secondary qualities. The external movement and mass of the onrushing river are primary qualities, and therefore external to the viewer, while the color of the water ("dark" or "glittering") is secondary, and is therefore provided by the viewer himself. I cannot see any necessity in this reading, nor is it clear what enrichment of meaning it would contribute.

I can return to line 34 of the poem now, bearing in mind Kapstein's findings. Shelley is directly viewing and again addressing the ravine:

> and when I gaze on thee
> I seem as in a trance sublime and strange
> To muse on my own separate fantasy,
> My own, my human mind, which passively
> Now renders and receives fast influencings,
> Holding an unremitting interchange
> With the clear universe of things around . . .   [34–40]

2. I. J. Kapstein, "The Meaning of Shelley's *Mont Blanc*," *PMLA*, 62 (1947), 1046–60.

The only difficulty here found by either Kapstein or myself is in the word "passively," though it ought to be remarked that "interchange" is a rich word as employed here. "Interchange" rather than "exchange" suits the process of mutual dependence in perception and existence that is involved. However, "passively" has its difficulties. "Passively . . . receives" is possible, "passively renders" appears to be a paradox. Kapstein remembers the wind harp, the aeolian lyre which makes recurrent appearances in Shelley's poetry, as it does in that of his contemporaries. The lyre "passively renders" because its rendering of sound is involuntary. By analogy, impressions cause the mind to respond, impinge on it whether or not it wishes to be affected. This is plausible, but needs to be read exactly, that is to say, in context. It will not do for Kapstein to seek philosophy here, for this takes place "as in a trance sublime and strange," and not under everyday conditions. In his religious experience resultant from his confrontation of the ravine, Shelley "passively" interchanges fast influencings with the "universe of things around."

> One legion of wild thoughts, whose wandering wings
> Now float above thy darkness, and now rest
> Where that or thou art no unbidden guest,
> In the still cave of the witch Poesy,
> Seeking among the shadows that pass by
> Ghosts of all things that are, some shade of thee,
> Some phantom, some faint image; till the breast
> From which they fled recalls them, thou art there!   [41-8]

The "legion" is the state of Shelley's mind, which is only half at rest in the composition of the poem. "That" in line 43 is the mind of Shelley; "thou," what is confronted by it in the ravine. The "still cave of the witch Poesy" will concern me again, when I study "Prometheus" and "The Witch of Atlas"; here, it only need be remarked that it is the process of dwelling together in the cave of poetry that establishes the prime link between the individual mind and the Thou, the Power behind nature. While in the cave, the mind of the poet, gazing outward into the world of things, seeks "some shade of thee" (the Thou) in the ghostly world of our fancies. Readers who insist on remembering the cave in Plato's *Republic* will tend to confuse their reading of the poem at this point. The allusion to Plato's cave, *if* it exists here (and one can doubt that it does), serves no function that I have been able to discover. The ravine of Arve is, physically, allied to the source of the river in that glaciers feed the river. The Thou, the ultimate mind, is visible in the phenomena of nature, even on the surface of those phenomena, though fleetingly. Shelley in lines 45-7 is in fact describing what he is doing in the composition of his poem: he is seeking out the presence of the hidden Power in natural phenomena. The "breast" of line 47 is that of Shelley; "they" of line 48 are the "shadows" of line 45 and the "ghosts" of line 46. The poet tries to fit imaginative symbol ("shade," "phantom") after imaginative symbol to the "Power," only to confess defeat (his "breast recalls" the "phantoms"). Then suddenly when he stops searching, the symbol is given him. (I have borrowed these last two sentences verbatim from a suggestion by Frederick Pottle, to whom I am heavily indebted here as elsewhere.) The "thou" of line 48 is of course, by this reading, the Power itself, the Thou sometimes fleetingly evident in that world of things, and sometimes able to be communed with by a poet in his poem. We have here the harsh sister poem to that other great hymn that Shelley composed in the summer of 1816—the address to Intellectual Beauty, a report of the heart as contrasted to this report of the head (the phrasing is Pottle's again).

This is not Kapstein's reading of the second part of "Mont Blanc" —for I have found neither the idealism of Berkeley nor the necessitarianism of Godwin present, let alone a confused mixture of the two. A close reading of the second section, without philosophical preconceptions, ought not to find secondhand philosophy, but rather a firsthand account of a personal religious experience, an experience centered in the composition of poetry. As an epistemology in a technical philosophical sense, the relationship between individual mind, things, and a universal mind which Shelley is presenting in "Mont Blanc" is perhaps crude in the extreme, and need concern no one. As a beginning of a mythmaking poet's account of reality, the relationship enters another sphere of value.

My reading so far is offered to refute the "confusions" Leavis finds in the first section of the poem and the "contradictions" Kapstein finds in the second. Before proceeding to the three remaining sections, I must emphasize again that the opening sections have not committed the poet in regard to the problem of ordinary perception. Something has been traced of the extraordinary relationship between natural scene, underlying Thou, and the poet "as in a trance sublime and strange," out of which poetry emerges. In the seeming afterthought of the final three lines of the poem, Shelley will at last, and in the form of a question, begin to speculate on more general perception.

Section 3 opens with a characteristic Shelleyan speculation on the relationship between death, sleep, and knowledge, followed by the first of many uses of a veil as symbol. Here both speculation and symbol are employed to establish again how far the poet's vision of Mont Blanc is from ordinary vision. The speculation is that in sleep "gleams of a remoter world," of a reality lying behind phenomenal things, are able to visit the soul. This is possible because slumber is like death, and the shapes of reality are more numerable to the vision of the dead, or the sleepers. So, to introduce his direct vision of power enshrined in the mountain, Shelley wonders if he is asleep, or if "the veil of life and death" (that is, the veil that separates life from death) has been up-furled. (Shelley wrote "unfurled" here, but that would make scant sense. James Thomson wisely suggested "upfurled" as what Shelley meant, whatever he wrote.) No matter whence this trance of extraordinary perception, the poet is able by means of it to discern Divine Power in Mont Blanc:

> Far, far above, piercing the infinite sky,
> Mont Blanc appears,—still, snowy, and serene—
> Its subject mountains their unearthly forms
> Pile around it, ice and rock; broad vales between
> Of frozen floods, unfathomable deeps,
> Blue as the overhanging heaven, that spread
> And wind among the accumulated steeps . . .   [60–6]

Again the remoteness of the white terror of this Mountain Divinity, alienated from our cares, "still, snowy, and serene"; again also we can discern the strength of this power, of a measure that can be set off against the sky god, "piercing the infinite sky" and presiding over the unearthly forms of subject deeps, quite as "blue as the overhanging heaven."

Richard Fogle has made many perceptive comments on Shelley's employment of heat and cold imagery,[3] but he has failed to link up the use of this imagery to Shelley's development of a religious myth, with the result that he oversimplifies and therefore distorts a significant area of Shelley's imagery. In my discussion of "Prometheus Unbound" I shall have to return to this aspect of Shelley's imagery (and to Fogle's useful treatment of it), but here I can only note its use in "Mont Blanc," which Fogle does not consider. Fogle's generalization does not fit "Mont Blanc": "In sum, Shelley describes cold as if he hates it like an enemy, the Principle of Evil in a kind of Manichaean dualism of existence . . ." In refutation I must cite "Mont Blanc," precisely at the point which I have reached in my reading of the poem. Having again given us a vision of the divine majesty of the mountain, Shelley hints at its more destructive aspects:

> how hideously
> Its shapes are heaped around! rude, bare, and high,
> Ghastly, and scarred, and riven.—Is this the scene
> Where the old Earthquake-daemon taught her young
> Ruin? Were these their toys? or did a sea
> Of fire envelop once this silent snow?   [69–74]

3. R. H. Fogle, *The Imagery of Keats and Shelley* (Chapel Hill, Univ. of North Carolina Press, 1949), pp. 71–9.

This, ostensibly, confirms Fogle, but lurking behind it is doctrine obviating any "kind of Manichaean dualism of existence." The Power behind the natural scene has not our specific good *or* ill in mind, and we can be reconciled with nature only if we realize and accept this. For

> The wilderness has a mysterious tongue
> Which teaches awful doubt, or faith so mild,
> So solemn, so serene, that man may be,
> But for such faith, with nature reconciled . . .

To Shelley the "mysterious tongue" teaches "awful doubt" of the orthodox view of nature, or more specifically of Mont Blanc, and here we can remember Coleridge's "Hymn before Sunrise" as an eloquent, exact illustration of the belief which the mysterious tongue teaches Shelley to doubt. But also, and here we (and surely Shelley as well) must think of Wordsworth, the mysterious tongue may teach a "faith so mild, / so solemn, so serene" as to prevent us from being able to reconcile ourselves to the seemingly malevolent aspects of nature. (The rejected reading of line 79 in the Boscombe Manuscript, "in such a faith," would of course damage my interpretation.) It is not the case that Shelley is anticipating the argument of Aldous Huxley, in the latter's sardonic vision of the poet of "Tintern Abbey" in the tropics. The argument is not that the Wordsworthian variety of natural religion does not fit all the natural facts but rather that it stops short in its apprehension of nature and the force behind nature, and that this timidity will keep those who believe in it from fully reconciling themselves with nature, that is, from realizing that none of the operations of nature work, of themselves, for our specific good. The voice of the mountain, properly understood, tells us that the power to make our state good or ill, is to some extent in our own hands, for the source of Power, while it is in nature, in Mont Blanc, and expends itself from thence without notion of our fate, can be met in relationship by us, even as the poet meets it in composing his poem. Thus, the concluding lines of the third section of the poem are not to be read as a Godwinian invocation of necessity (as they have almost always been read) but rather as a close-packed assertion of the Shelleyan variety of religion that I have been expounding throughout my reading:

> Thou hast a voice, great Mountain, to repeal
> Large codes of fraud and woe; not understood
> By all, but which the wise, and great, and good
> Interpret, or make felt, or deeply feel.   [80-3]

Godwin, I might venture, does not understand the voice, and mistakes it for that of necessity, but is still able to "interpret" it sufficiently as to see that "large codes of fraud and woe" need to be repealed. Wordsworth does not understand the voice but, even so, he can make it felt in his best work, and at one time, at least, felt it deeply. Shelley understands the voice, and if we follow him closely in our reading of the poem, without preconceptions, then we can understand it too.

Scholars who insist on reading these lines as Godwinian invariably will see the whole poem as contradictory, for here, they will (and do) say, the poet worships necessity, and in the final lines of the poem, he idealistically defies that power and asserts that man's imaginative vision is primary, and Mont Blanc dependent upon that vision. As I have shown, this difficulty will come into being only if you insist upon introducing into the poem doctrines which are otherwise not there to be found.

The close of section 3 is the thematic climax of "Mont Blanc"; the two remaining sections develop and recapitulate what has been presented previously. With doctrine already established behind them, the two final sections achieve a majesty of phrasing surpassing anything Shelley had done until "Mont Blanc," and not in turn to be matched until the composition of "Prometheus Unbound." The opening lines of section 4 build up gradually to the incantatory climax of lines 96–7. First, the manifestations of nature are invoked:

> The fields, the lakes, the forests, and the streams,
> Ocean, and all the living things that dwell
> Within the daedal earth; lightning, and rain,
> Earthquake, and fiery flood, and hurricane,
> The torpor of the year when feeble dreams
> Visit the hidden buds, or dreamless sleep
> Holds every future leaf and flower;—the bound
> With which from that detested trance they leap . . .
>
> [84–91]

The skillful progression, moving from natural bodies to the overt operations of nature in weather, and thence into the natural cycle of the year, comes inevitably to

> The works and ways of man, their death and birth,
> And that of him and all that his may be;
> All things that move and breathe with toil and sound
> Are born and die; revolve, subside, and swell.　　[92–5]

After the measured perfection of those two last lines there comes the sublimity of the central doctrine of the poem:

> Power dwells apart in its tranquillity,
> Remote, serene, and inaccessible . . .

The remoteness of Divinity; the eternal gap between aspiration after the desired object and the means of attainment, between good and the means of good, poetry and the medium of poetry; the ultimate conflict between romantic humanism and the human condition; the inevitable collapse of a Thou into an It again, after the relational event has run its course: all of this characteristic complex at the heart of Shelley's mature poetry is contained, in embryo, in these lines. That the Power is partially accessible "Mont Blanc" has already told us; the "Hymn to Intellectual Beauty" will tell us more, and the cycle of Shelley's long mythopoeic poems will confirm and deepen our knowledge. But rhetorically there is no contradiction felt here: the secret Strength of things which governs thought is in its inmost center inaccessible to us, however much we may draw from its outer regions.

The remainder of section 4 is only eloquent representation of the natural scene, under its aspect of white terror. Fogle's fault in his summation of Shelley's imagery of coldness is, we now see, in his assigning to such imagery the role of one counter in a simple dualism. Fogle is influenced in this by his scholarly belief in Shelley's philosophical dualism. "Mont Blanc" is a proof that Fogle may be too single-minded in this, for in the poem divinity is seen to lie beyond our antinomies, and again, in it divinity is imagistically expressed only in what Fogle takes to be always emblematic of evil in Shelley. Here in "Mont Blanc" Shelley's use of the imagery of cold and ice is ironic, for all that we are shown of nature, an impartial nature, is what constitutes death to us. The irony is best appreciated when we remember our juxtaposition of the Mont Blanc odes of Coleridge and of Shelley.

The fifth and last section is coda to the poem, and those scholars who have seen in its final three lines anything that contradicts the foregoing portions of the poem are quite simply in error. The concluding statement of the poem is properly twofold: first, we are to be told again that the central power in the cosmos has its emblem in the mountain; second, we are to be told again that the importance of this emblem to us is in the "human mind's *imaginings*" (my italics), for it is in our imaginings that we draw upon that power, insofar as we can draw upon it. The first part of the statement is in

> The secret Strength of things
> Which governs thought, and to the infinite dome
> Of Heaven is as a law, inhabits thee!   [139–41]

The second, and much disputed (and perhaps not altogether well phrased), part is in

> And what were thou, and earth, and stars, and sea,
> If to the human mind's imaginings
> Silence and solitude were vacancy?

To read this as some vaguely Berkeleyan epistemological musing is to show that one has not read the poem "Mont Blanc," for those who do so read these lines take them as a defiance of necessity, the doctrine which they enshrine in the mountain. But we need only realize that the "thou" of the first of these lines is the mountain only, and *not* the Power, to see how mistaken such a reading is. In the immediately preceding lines we are told that "the secret Strength of things . . . inhabits thee," and the "thee" and "thou" are the same: merely the physical mountain. "Thou" is linked to "earth, and stars, and sea," and what the poet is clearly saying is not that these phenomena would cease to exist if our imaginings could do nothing with silence and solitude, but only that they would cease to be emblematic of the Power behind them, if our imaginings could not accomplish the symbolic linking. If our imagination is impoverished, then we cannot grasp nature as being more than blind to us. But if the silence and solitude in which imaginings are germinated are not simply a vacancy to our minds, then we can see phenomena like "thou," Mont Blanc, and earth and stars and sea as being outer forms of an inward Power, and our very imaginings are thus a kind of grace, in which we have been able to draw upon that Power. This far "Mont Blanc" has taken us; its sister ode of 1816, the address to Intellectual Beauty, will show us the more active side of this grace, supplementing the vision of latent grace in"Mont Blanc." "Mont Blanc," like Blake's poetry, denies the possibility of *natural* religion. The "Hymn to Intellectual Beauty" begins to explore the contrary possibility of a revelation of the Thou. I hope to have shown something more of the unity of "Mont Blanc" than it is usually credited with possessing, and perhaps, in the process, I may have helped to justify my judgment regarding its greatneess as a poem and its importance in the developing canon of Shelley's mature mythmaking.

3

The composition of the "Hymn to Intellectual Beauty" preceded that of "Mont Blanc" by probably just one month. The "Hymn" is not dated, but Mary Shelley tells us that it was conceived during Shelley's voyage around the Lake of Geneva with Lord Byron, a voyage which we know took place June 23–30, 1816 ("Mont Blanc" is dated July 23).[4] In form the two poems are of course completely different, "Mont Blanc" resembling as it does "Tintern Abbey" rather more than any other poem, in spite of its irregular rhyme scheme. The Wordsworthian blank verse of "Alastor" is replaced in "Mont Blanc" by a style that has little of Wordsworth in it, but the genre to which the latter poem be-

4. "Note on Poems of 1816."

longs is clearly the descriptive-meditative in relation to landscape, a contribution to poetry matured by Coleridge and Wordsworth.

I have hinted that the "Hymn" and "Mont Blanc" are in a complementary relationship, and together are the proper prelude to "Prometheus Unbound," positing that poem as Shelley's first mature mythopoeic creation. The all but inaccessible Power, the secret Strength of things, available momentarily to the poet in his perceptive trance, is here in this sister ode shown to offer itself to man under a different aspect, the Thou of mythic relationship. Browning first spoke of Shelley as the poet of two principles: Love and Power. Power and Love in the absolute, Beauty and Good in the concrete; Shelley's achievement, according to Browning, was in having "thrown swifter, subtler, and more numerous films" between these absolutes and their concrete complements than any other modern poet had done.[5] The absolute power is celebrated in "Mont Blanc." Here in the "Hymn" a concrete manifestation of Beauty is confronted. The Power and the Beauty are not one, but neither are they opposed.

At the very outset of my reading Hughes would remind me that, for Shelley, Beauty is " 'Intellectual' in the sense so often carried by the word in the eighteenth century of 'spiritual' or 'behind the senses.' " [6] That is, we would do well to begin by recognizing the generality of the poem's title as being its distinguishing feature. There have been scholarly readers, remembering Shelley's use of the term "intellectual beauty," in his translation of the *Symposium,* who have taken the title of the poem itself as being overtly Platonic, which is to misread from the start.[7] Platonic coloring the "Hymn" may have. I, for one, do not find the parallels so readily found by J. A. Notopoulos, Carl Grabo, Beach, and Benjamin Kurtz; and I venture the objection to all of them that their Platonic and Plotinian citations are too specific and technical to resemble, in more than outline, the general phenomenon that Shelley is describing. In fact, as will be shown mostly as counterstatement to all this Platonizing, the "Hymn to Intellectual Beauty" is much more closely parallel in its "statement" to the Christian doctrine of grace in its broadest outlines. Not, to repeat again, that this last has any great significance beyond its evidencing that Shelley is an original religious mythmaker rather than a secondhand philosopher. The "Hymn to Intellectual Beauty" is *overtly,* as will be shown, an anti-Christian

5. "An Essay on Shelley," in Robert Browning's *Complete Poetical and Dramatic Works,* Boston, 1895. My source for the quotation is Hughes, p. 260.

6. Hughes, p. 42, n. 1.

7. Cf. C. H. Grabo, *The Magic Plant* (Chapel Hill, Univ. of North Carolina Press, 1936), p. 179; Benjamin Kurtz, *The Pursuit of Death* (New York and London, Oxford Univ. Press, 1933), p. 94; J. A. Notopoulos, *The Platonism of Shelley* (Durham, N.C., Duke Univ. Press, 1949), p. 196.

poem, but nevertheless its categories, after careful examination, are more Christian than they are Platonic.

The "Hymn" opens with a lucid statement, notable for its restraint of style, of the central phenomenon that constitutes the poem's theme: the spiritual beauty that cannot be apprehended by the senses, but which paradoxically seems to flicker, sometimes just perceptibly, in a whole series of natural signatures:

> The awful shadow of some unseen Power
>> Floats though unseen among us,—visiting
>> This various world with as inconstant wing
> As summer winds that creep from flower to flower,—
> Like moonbeams that behind some piny mountain shower,
>> It visits with inconstant glance
>> Each human heart and countenance;
> Like hues and harmonies of evening,—
>> Like clouds in starlight widely spread,—
>> Like memory of music fled,—
>> Like aught that for its grace may be
> Dear, and yet dearer for its mystery.   [1–12]

What is being communicated here is not an idea (not even an idea of an Idea) but a vision whose reality is, and can only be, embodied in a chain of metaphors. Even if I could not defend each metaphoric comparison as inevitable, I can defend the notion of the chain or series of comparisons as being inevitable *here*. It is popular these days to accuse Shelley of a profusion of metaphors, of an inability or refusal to employ continuous and "organic" metaphor in an extended fashion. In "Mont Blanc" we have seen Shelley making appropriate use of an extended, continuous metaphor; here in the "Hymn" he appropriately gives us tenuously connected profusion. "Appropriately" because the single metaphor could not fit the evanescent nature of the phenomenon that is the poem's theme. This first stanza is at extraordinary pains to emphasize the intangibility and mutability of its subject, and it succeeds well enough to constitute a poetic success. The Power is unseen at a double remove, for its awful shadow is itself unseen by us, though we can know, beyond the senses, when it has come and when it has gone. The shadow "floats" among us—there is in the verb the suggestion of an indifference, though not a final indifference, to us, on the part of the Power. "Visiting," "various," "inconstant" reinforce the central effect of the arbitrariness of the phenomenon. *All of the natural citation is wavering:* summer winds, moonbeams, colors of the evening sky, clouds, followed by the uncertainty of the memory of a tune. All of this is obvious enough, but it is not far short of masterful in its context.

We must not lean too heavily on the "grace" and "mystery" of lines
11 and 12, for this grace can at most be glossed as "ineffable influence," [8]
but the conjunction of grace and mystery is troublesome, just as is the
conjunction of a similar grace with "truth" in line 36.

In the first stanza we have had only the fact of the visitations, and
hints as to their nature. In the second the visitations are linked to the
cyclic rhythms which alternately vivify and depress our lives, natural
rhythms in uncorrected forms. The questionings of this stanza are too
ultimate to bear summary, for the necessary responses would be the
truths of religion, or something akin to them. But not for the obstinate
questionings of this "Hymn":

> No voice from some sublimer world hath ever
> 　　To sage or poet these responses given—
> 　　Therefore the names of Demon, Ghost, and Heaven,
> Remain the records of their vain endeavour,
> Frail spells—whose uttered charm might not avail to sever,
> 　　From all we hear and all we see,
> 　　Doubt, chance, and mutability.
> Thy light alone—like mist o'er mountains driven,
> 　　Or music by the night-wind sent
> 　　Through strings of some still instrument,
> 　　Or moonlight on a midnight stream,
> Gives grace and truth to life's unquiet dream.　　　　[25–36]

The opening lines of this stanza constitute a flat denial of Christian
revelation and a linking of its categories to those of superstition: "Demon,
Ghost, and Heaven." After the denial the affirmation of the poem's peculiar phenomenon can be made again. The nightmare of this existence
is relieved by "thy light alone," but again the name and nature of that
light is avoided, and we go to natural comparison of its characteristic
qualities: what is invoked is the movement of mist over mountains, the
workings of an aeolian harp, the shining of the midnight moon upon a
stream. "Abstract and intangible" is the implied comment of Cleanth
Brooks and Robert Penn Warren in their popular poetry textbook,
where they invite neophytes to the demonstration that the images of this
"Hymn" do not make its "abstract and intangible quality" concrete. I
deny the relative abstractness of the poem's subject to begin with, for it
is no more abstract than personal religious experience seems when
verbally presented. Next, I deny that it is the proper business of this
poem to make concrete, by its images, its supposedly abstract and certainly intangible subject phenomenon. Rather, the success of its images

8. F. S. Ellis, *A Lexical Concordance to the Poetical Works of Percy Bysshe Shelley*,
London, 1892. See the listings under "grace."

is in their consistent reinforcement of the impression upon us of the subtle nature of the Power behind this subtle influencing, the intangible grace, the spiritual beauty that constitutes the poem's subject. The mountains, the aeolian harp, the midnight stream are at one in that, like the poet in his trance in "Mont Blanc," each of them "passively / now renders and receives fast influencings, / holding an unremitting interchange / with the clear universe of things around." There is no precise, intentional direction in the movement of mist over the mountains, winds over the harp, moonlight over the surface of the stream, but an effect of beauty can be produced in each instance. One Power, remote as it is, is at work, and the imagery tells us this, as well as that the Power is seemingly aimless and indifferent to the effects it produces. Embodying so much so well, this imagery surely deserves to be characterized as uniquely successful, for imagery and theme are unusually unified here. Only our recent dogma which dictates the universal necessity of concrete imagery could provide a basis for condemning the imagistic pattern of the "Hymn."

If we are to learn nothing more of the nature of Divinity in the "Hymn," we do at least pass in the fourth stanza to a consideration of the effects upon man of the Beauty whose unseen presence the opening stanzas have been celebrating. The fourth stanza is the nicely balanced center of the poem, being the transition from the general phenomenon to the poet's relationship to the phenomenon. It considers the status of all men with regard to the Intellectual Beauty and is as well as the most overt doctrinal statement in the poem (which may be why it seems to me the weakest stanza in the poem):

> Love, Hope, and Self-esteem, like clouds depart
> And come, for some uncertain moments lent.
> Man were immortal, and omnipotent,
> Didst thou, unknown and awful as thou art,
> Keep with thy glorious train firm state within his heart.
> Thou messenger of sympathies,
> That wax and wane in lovers' eyes—
> Thou—that to human thought art nourishment,
>   Like darkness to a dying flame!
> Depart not as thy shadow came,
> Depart not—lest the grave should be,
> Like life and fear, a dark reality.   [37–48]

The "Love, Hope, and Self-esteem" triad is an obvious equivalent to the Christian triad of love, hope, and faith, the "Self-esteem" for "faith" substitution being the essential and inevitable one in Shelleyan religion. In this poem it links up to, and helps gloss, the final line of the poem where, as Elizabeth Nitchie so plausibly argues, "fear" probably

means "revere" or "esteem." [9] With divinity completely remote, faith
in God is replaced by reverence for the divine in oneself, by imaginative
self-esteem, worship of what Blake calls the "Poetic Genius" or "Human
Form Divine." Blakean and Shelleyan theology are widely different,
for Blake is never a theist and the Shelley of "Mont Blanc" and the
"Hymn," as we can already state, clearly is, though a violently unorthodox one. The central doctrine of Shelley's 1816 Hymns, the existence of
a Power within or rather behind nature, an ultimate Thou to which
we can stand in relationship, is altogether un-Blakean, and would have
been condemned by Blake as a form of deism (just as Blake similarly
condemned Wordsworth). However, though Shelley is a remote theist
and Blake a thoroughgoing religious humanist, the ethical force of the
two poetic myths is, at this stage of the development of Shelley's poetry,
very nearly one. For faith Shelley substitutes self-esteem: "to fear himself, and love all human kind," while for Blake, the worship of God—
that is, faith—is to reverence the imaginative qualities in oneself and
other men:

> The Eternal Body of Man is The Imagination, that is, God
> himself.
> The worship of God is: Honouring his gifts in other men, each
> according to his genius . . .[1]

The claim made for the Intellectual Beauty in stanza IV (to return
to our reading) is altogether absolute and categorical. Not only do the
visitations and departures of this grace (using grace in its most general, though quasi-theological sense) control the operations of the three
prime virtues in us but the permanent state of this grace would suffice
to make us "immortal" and "omnipotent," that is, would make us our
own gods. All this, to be sure, is carefully modified by the poem's con-
tinual, and herein continued, refusal to explicate its mystery: "unknown
and awful as thou art." As in "Mont Blanc," we are being prepared, as
it were, for the explicit mystery of Demogorgon, who embodies the
dialectic of mythmaking.

The remainder of stanza IV extends the human range of the visitation's
effect into the fluctuations of human love and thought. The only difficulty here is imagistic, in the seeming paradox,

> Thou—that to human thought art nourishment,
> Like darkness to a dying flame!

Pottle's suggestion (unpublished) seems to me to have the solution to
this difficulty. Shelley says that Intellectual Beauty nourishes human
thought in a fashion similar to that in which darkness serves a dying

---

9. Elizabeth Nitchie, "Shelley's 'Hymn to Intellectual Beauty,'" *PMLA, 63* (1948),
752–3.
1. Keynes, ed., Blake, pp. 765 and 202, respectively.

flame. He is not being ironical: Intellectual Beauty *does* nourish human thought, though by fitful visitations. What has happened in the figure is another Shelleyan telescoping of tenor and vehicle, as in the opening lines of "Mont Blanc." The lines repeat the notion of "wax and wane" in line 43. "Thou that nourishest human thought [and then withdrawest; thou that feedest] the flame and then leavest it to die in darkness." Shelley has used only half of his tenor and half of his vehicle in this figure.

By now it should be obvious to a reader of the "Hymn" that there is nothing Platonic about the Intellectual Beauty. Surely this is not Platonism:

> Depart not—lest the grave should be,
> Like life and fear, a dark reality.

These are the accents of Christianity or a religion like to it, but not the accents of any philosophy. Scholars who Platonize the "Hymn" ought to attempt the dramatic device of visualizing Socrates uttering these lines. Surely they would sense the inappropriateness of these sentiments to a Platonic hero?

The three final stanzas of the "Hymn" dramatically focus on the poet's relation to the Beauty invoked in the earlier stanzas. The boy seeking for ghosts in Gothic surroundings is father to the young man, who comes forth from his superstition-haunted beginnings into the light of the Intellectual Beauty. By the paradox of this Beauty's relationship to us, it is in fact only a shadow of greater radiance which falls upon us. Among the superstitions that it sweeps away is clearly all the Christianity, such as it may have been, to which this poet was exposed:

> I called on poisonous names with which our youth is fed;
> I was not heard—I saw them not . . .

Unsought, the actual Spirit comes upon him, in the rebirth of the year. The depiction of his reaction will seem excessively emotional to many of us, if we do not carefully gauge the experience involved. The shadow of the Spirit, of the Thou, sweeps over him even as the outward resurrection of nature is taking place. Religious conversion is at best a difficult theme for a poem to attempt, but when the religion is as personal and undefined as it is here, readers are likely to feel a certain impatience with the emotion evoked by the enthusiast, emotion which is hardly transferable and therefore felt by them to be illicit in a poem:

> Sudden, thy shadow fell on me;
> I shrieked, and clasped my hands in ecstasy!   [59–60]

Making the proper allowance, this is prophetic convention, though it probably does not constitute a poetic excellence.

The sixth stanza is so straightforward that it requires no commentary, and its explicitness has kept its critics from differing. Necessary alone is the observation that here, as in lines 80–1 of "Mont Blanc," the connection is made between the religious Power and the revolutionary political hopes of the "I" of both poems. In my reading of "Prometheus Unbound" this relationship, with its striking analogue of Blake's conception of the "Orc cycle" placed in juxtaposition, will concern me at length.

> The day becomes more solemn and serene
> When noon is past—there is a harmony
> In autumn, and a lustre in its sky,
> Which through the summer is not heard or seen,
> As if it could not be, as if it had not been!
> Thus let thy power, which like the truth
> Of nature on my passive youth
> Descended, to my onward life supply
> Its calm—to one who worships thee,
> And every form containing thee,
> Whom, SPIRIT fair, thy spells did bind
> To fear himself, and love all human kind.   [73–84]

If the fundamental ideas of Christian theology were in any way appropriate to this poem, we should have small difficulty in glossing this stanza by their direct aid. We could say then that the subject of the entire poem was actual grace, God's transient act to help the poet. The early stanzas illustrate preventing grace, working with the soul and preceding the free determination of the will. With the poet's vow we move to co-operating grace, working with the will, following its determination. The final stanza is then a prayer for the continuance of co-operating grace. Throughout the poem, we could conclude, the poet has been at pains to emphasize that his theme is actual, and not sanctifying grace. Again and again, he has made it clear, imagistically, that the grace of his subject is a transient act and not a permanent state.

Now this would be a misreading, or rather an overreading, a forced baptizing of Shelley's verse, but it is my contention that such a doctrinaire Christian reading of the "Hymn" does the poem less violence than the Platonized readings I have cited previously. I have remarked before on the possible Christian interpretation of the conclusion to "Mont Blanc," and I shall have to face the problem again in "Prometheus Unbound," where the Platonizers have preceded me and where the Christian misreading is again more plausible than the Platonic malforming of the poem.

Of the splendid last stanza of the "Hymn," little remains to be said here except that, again, one may read it as a guidepost toward "Prometheus." The poet, in the stanza, feels secure of his increasing power; he has lost nothing and gained everything with the departure of his "passive youth" (contrast that to the "Immortality" ode, with its record of gain *and* loss). The descent of the Spirit upon him was "like the truth / of nature" and he asks only the extension of that truth, that he may venerate himself and others as being in possession of it. Most movingly he prays for "calm," with a sure insight into his own great need.

In "Mont Blanc" we are told primarily that "the Power is there," and we are given some intimations of what the Power is not. In the "Hymn to Intellectual Beauty" we are told primarily that the shadow of the Power floats among us, visits us, and imparts a portion of itself to us, and we are given again intimations of what the Power is not, with a very few hints of what it is. In "Prometheus Unbound," the first major work of Shelley's poetic maturity, this tentative myth receives its first full development, and to that we must now pass.

4

In January 1822, a few months before his death, Shelley returned to the theme of his 1816 Hymns, only this time in a different spirit. Kurtz interprets the fragmentary "Zucca" of 1822 as a kind of palinode to the "Hymn to Intellectual Beauty," [2] just as many critics call the fragmentary "Triumph Of Life" of 1822 a palinode to "Prometheus Unbound" and the "Epipsychidion." Palinodes they are not, but certainly they do manifest a change in emphasis on the poet's part. "The Triumph of Life" will concern me at considerable length later; "The Zucca" may best be considered here, as epilogue to the 1816 Hymns.

"The Zucca" is an explicit and somber summation of a poetic career, and it has aspects which are best illuminated by and illuminate the "Epipsychidion." Again, its central theme, the passing away from the earth of the spirit of Beauty, has close affinities with "The Sensitive Plant" and "The Witch of Atlas," so that it can be juxtaposed profitably with those poems. However, it is its first five stanzas which are my concern here, for they complement the "Hymn To Intellectual Beauty." But where the "Hymn" emphasizes the *coming* of the Thou, as the spirit of Beauty, "The Zucca" is concerned with its departure (as is, of course, "The Sensitive Plant") and with the consequent questing and questioning that such a departure makes necessary. The question is not the Wordsworthian "Whither is fled the visionary gleam?" so much as it is a general, Spenserian complaint:

> Wherefore, this lower world who can deny
> But to be subject still to *Mutabilitie?*

As the illumination of the "Hymn" came in the spring, so the departure of Shelleyan grace (for want of a better term as yet) comes with

2. *The Pursuit of Death,* pp. 323–7.

the death of the natural year. The Christian year is counterpointed
against the natural, pagan year by the beautifully symbolic birth of the
Christ at the winter solstice, when nature is most desolate and the correction of grace most desperately required. But the Shelleyan year, from
the beginning to the end of his poetry, is the natural year, and it is at the
nadir of that year that "The Zucca" opens:

> Summer was dead and Autumn was expiring,
>   And infant Winter laughed upon the land
> All cloudlessly and cold;—when I, desiring
>   More in this world than any understand,
> Wept o'er the beauty, which, like sea retiring,
>   Had left the earth bare as the wave-worn sand
> Of my lorn heart, and o'er the grass and flowers
> Pale for the falsehood of the flattering Hours.   [1–8]

So far, this is only a lament for the cycle of Mutability, though it contains one of those eloquent tags that justify Yeats's characterization of
Shelley as the poet of the star of infinite desire, and makes explicit part
of the final formulation of the Shelleyan myth of the gap between human
desire and any of its objects. When we have gone further into the poem
we suddenly discover the accents and the theme of the "Hymn To Intellectual Beauty," but viewed on their darker side:

> I loved—oh, no, I mean not one of ye,
>   Or any earthly one, though ye are dear
> As human heart to human heart may be;—
>   I loved, I know not what—but this low sphere
> And all that it contains, contains not thee,
>   Thou, whom, seen nowhere, I feel everywhere.
> From Heaven and Earth, and all that in them are,
> Veiled art thou, like a   star.
>
> By Heaven and Earth, from all whose shapes thou flowest,
>   Neither to be contained, delayed, nor hidden;
> Making divine the loftiest and the lowest,
>   When for a moment thou art not forbidden
> To live within the life which thou bestowest;
>   And leaving noblest things vacant and chidden,
> Cold as a corpse after the spirit's flight,
> Blank as the sun after the birth of night.
>
> In winds, and trees, and streams, and all things common,
>   In music and the sweet unconscious tone

> Of animals, and voices which are human,
>   Meant to express some feelings of their own;
> In the soft motions and rare smile of woman,
>   In flowers and leaves, and in the grass fresh-shown
> Or dying in the autumn, I the most
> Adore thee present or lament thee lost.   [17–40]

If this were palinode to the "Hymn," we should expect something like renunciation of the earlier belief in the Spirit which bloweth where it listeth, some affirmation of a less remote theism, in which Divine Power would be more responsive to human invocation and need. Clearly what we are given is reaffirmation of the doctrine of the "Hymn" itself. No voice from some sublimer world has come to answer the questions of the second stanza of the "Hymn." The poet of 1816, in his poem, attempted no resolvement of the problem involved in the departure of the afflatus, for his honest statement, on its own tenets, did not permit of resolvement. The poet of the "Hymn" was content to celebrate the advent of the visitation, praying only that the Power which had enabled him to go beyond his passive youth would not abandon him in his maturity. But the "Hymn" itself establishes the essential mutability of that Power, so much so that a good part of the aesthetic effect that the poem makes is due to the foreboding of departure and desolation that hovers over the final stanza, ostensibly a serene prayer. Both the "Hymn" and "The Zucca" focus on the poet as the prophet of the Intellectual Beauty, the I seeking to meet an ultimate Thou in mutual relationship, the man caught up in the Spirit, in the Hebrew tradition of the *nabi,* the prophet of the Lord. Necessarily then, the poet is justified in his claim: "I the most / Adore thee present or lament thee lost," the former in the "Hymn," the latter in "The Zucca."

Between the poles of arrival and departure of the Spirit, the dialectic of the movement from It to Thou and then again to It, the mature poetry of Shelley enacts itself. In "Prometheus," now to be considered, an attempt is made to visualize the full consequences of a complete and imminent advent of the Spirit. For all its Hellenic dressing, we do "Prometheus Unbound" violence if we do not approach it as an embodiment of the Hebraic apocalyptic impulse, for this impetus is at its center, probably helping to account for its striking similarities to the epics of Blake. As epigraph for my reading of "Prometheus" I take the admonition of Hillel, spoken a generation before the advent of Christianity and taken by Christians, properly from their standpoint, as being another omen of Advent: "If not now, when?" The few, heavily weighted words are as appropriate to the background of Shelley's millennarian lyrical drama as they proved to be to that of the impending prophetic literature of their own time.

3

"Prometheus Unbound": Introduction

I

SINCE there have been so many commentaries on "Prometheus Unbound," it is singular that no sustained examination of the significance of its epigraph has been made. On the title page of the first edition of "Prometheus," published by Ollier in 1820, appears the verse:

Audisne Hæc, Amphiarae, Sub Terram Abdite?

Hughes notes: "The verse quoted is in Cicero, *Tusc. Disp.* ii.60, from the *Epigoni* of an unknown author. Amphiaraus, a renowned Seer, took part in the war of the Seven against Thebes, and was saved from his pursuers by Zeus, who caused the earth to swallow him. He became an oracular God." [1] This note is helpful insofar as it puts the necessary materials, or most of them, for understanding the meaning of the epigraph into our hands, but in itself it makes no attempt at defining that meaning. The meaning is complex and properly Titanic, for its prime characteristics are fierce pride and a fierce, prophetic irony. We can begin to get at it by consulting the Cicero texts (incidentally, Hughes's section reference would seem to be wrong; the relevant section is ii.25):

> But what, you will say, have we in time of peace, at home, in our easy chairs? You call me back to the philosophers who do not often step into the battle-line, and one of whom, Dionysius of Heracles, a person certainly of little resolution, after learning from Zeno to be brave was taught by pain to forget his lesson. For upon an attack of kidney trouble, even amid his shrieks, he kept on crying out that the opinions he had himself previously held about pain were false. And on being asked by Cleanthes, his fellow-pupil, what was the reason that had reduced him from his former opinion, he replied: "Because if, after I had given such devoted attention to philosophy, I yet proved unable to bear pain, that would be sufficient proof that pain was an evil. Now I have spent many years in study-

1. A. M. D. Hughes, ed., *Shelley, Poems Published in 1820* (New York and London, Oxford Univ. Press, 1910), p. 183.

ing philosophy and am unable to bear pain: pain is therefore an evil." Then Cleanthes stamped with his foot upon the ground and, according to the story, recited a line from the *Epigoni:*

Do you hear this, Amphiaraus, in your home beneath the earth? meaning Zeno and grieving that Dionysius was false to his teaching.[2]

Cicero's meaning is clear enough. In his previous section he states, quite simply, the moral this anecdote is to adumbrate:

To enable us to bear pain quietly and calmly it is a very great gain to reflect with all our heart and mind, as the saying is, how honorable it is to do so. . . . This is given further emphasis by the contrast drawn later in XXV between the renegade Dionysius and the stoic Posidonius, who from his sick-bed discoursed to Pompey on the proposition: that there is nothing good but what is honorable, and who, as often as a paroxysm of pain attacked him, would say: "It is no use, pain! for all the distress you cause I shall never admit that you are an evil."

According to J. E. King, the *Epigoni* referred to is the lost play by Aeschylus in its Latin translation (also lost) by Accius.

Amphiaraus the soothsayer, with prophetic foresight, opposed the expedition of the seven against Thebes partially because of his expectation of its defeat, more largely because he feared and revered Zeus and knew that the assault against the city was impious. Persuaded against his will and convinced of his impiety, Amphiaraus joined the expedition. When ruin came upon the seven, Amphiaraus was saved from his pursuing enemies by the intervention of Zeus (gratified at the sage's piety), who opened the ground in front of the fleeing oracle with his thunderbolts. Once closed up in the earth, Amphiaraus received his ultimate reward of immortality; he became a prophetic god, a mouthpiece of Zeus, to be consulted by believers in the thunder god of heaven.

With knowledge of both the passage in Cicero and the career of Amphiaraus, we can appreciate the force and direction of Shelley's epigraph to his lyrical drama. The epigraph is both pridefully stoic and deliberately impious, a defiance of the sky god, Zeus, Blake's Nobodaddy, or, as Shelley would have it, the popular version of Jehovah, God of the Jews and Christians. On the stoic side Prometheus is to be contrasted with those like the unhappy Dionysius, who cannot bear pain and yield to it, confessing its reality as an evil. Shelley's Titan is to endure to the end, and the prideful epigraph calls upon Zeno, as the hero of stoic endurance, to bear witness to this, even as Cleanthes in Cicero invokes

2. Cicero, *Tusculan Disputations,* trans. J. E. King (London, Loeb Library, 1927), pp. 213, 215.

Zeno under the name of Amphiaraus, to realize Dionysius' desertion of stoic principle. On its first level then, Shelley's epigraph underlines the glory of his Titan, his courage never to submit or yield.

The more profound level of meaning underlies this, and has nothing to do with the passage in Cicero but is based on a contrast between the Zeus-defying Prometheus and the Zeus-fearing Amphiaraus, each figure eternally emblematic of his attitude toward the sky god. "Do you hear this, Amphiaraus, hidden beneath the earth?" is the defiant cry, and "this" is the whole drama of "Prometheus Unbound." "Amphiaraus" can be read as a multiplicity of orthodox poets (how farfetched would it be to see Shelley as classing the Lake poets as well as Aeschylus within that multiplicity, as former, rather halfhearted rebels become time-serving oracular gods?) or perhaps best of all as simply the pious prophet of Zeus. Prometheus, if he were to yield, would become Amphiaraus, and the defiant epigraph is therefore heavily ironic: "Hear this, Amphiaraus, and contrast it with your history."

A third possible reading of the epigraph is subtler, and would be based on the analogue of Cicero's Cleanthes calling on Zeus under the name of Amphiaraus, Zeno being Cleanthes' own oracular god so to speak. The epigraph would then be an appeal to Demogorgon in his home within the earth, the oracular god of this drama, manifestation of the Power worshiped by Shelley and therefore his Amphiaraus as Zeno was Amphiaraus to Cleanthes. However, this begins to be remote, and is less likely than the two significations for the epigraph that I have already proposed.

2

> The only imaginary being resembling in any degree Prometheus, is Satan; and Prometheus is, in my judgement, a more poetical character than Satan, because in addition to courage, and majesty, and firm and patient opposition to omnipotent force, he is susceptible of being described as exempt from the taints of ambition, envy, revenge, and a desire for personal aggrandisement, which, in the Hero of *Paradise Lost,* interfere with the interest. The character of Satan engenders in the mind a pernicious casuistry which leads us to weigh his faults with his wrongs, and to excuse the former because the latter exceed all measure. In the minds of those who consider that magnificent fiction with a religious feeling it engenders something worse . . .[3]

Both Shelley and Blake maintained a running warfare against "Paradise Lost" throughout their poetic careers, a warfare unique (but for its parallel in these two poets who evidently never knew of one an-

3. Shelley's preface to "Prometheus Unbound," in Hutchinson, ed., *Shelley,* p. 222.

other's existence) so that it remains misunderstood even now by the bulk of commentators. Too many of our contemporaries follow the dangerous practice of condemning Shelley and Blake for *misreading* Milton while they themselves proceed to misread the supposed misreaders.

Blake writes:

> Those who restrain desire, do so because theirs is weak enough to be restrained; and the restrainer or reason usurps its place & governs the unwilling.
>
> And being restrain'd, it by degrees becomes passive, till it is only the shadow of desire.
>
> The history of this is written in Paradise Lost, & the Governor or Reason is call'd Messiah.
>
> And the original Archangel, or possessor of the command of the heavenly host, is call'd the Devil or Satan, and his children are call'd Sin & Death.
>
> But in the Book of Job, Milton's Messiah is call'd Satan.
>
> For this history has been adopted by both parties.
>
> It indeed appear'd to Reason as if Desire was cast out; but the Devil's account is, that the Messiah fell, & formed a heaven of what he stole from the Abyss.
>
> This is shewn in the Gospel, where he prays to the Father to send the comforter, or Desire, that Reason may have Ideas to build on; the Jehovah of the Bible being no other than he who dwells in flaming fire.
>
> Know that after Christ's death, he became Jehovah.
>
> But in Milton, the Father is Destiny, the Son a Ratio of the five senses, & the Holy Ghost Vacuum!
>
> Note: The reason Milton wrote in fetters when he wrote of Angels & God, and at liberty when of Devils & Hell, is because he was a true Poet and of the Devil's party without knowing it.[4]

An unwary critic is apparently able to read this as a simple inversion of the orthodox and Miltonic categories of the divine and the satanic. This is to reduce Blake's criticism of Milton to the popular misconception of that criticism.

The passage from Blake is not simple and is barbed with irony (though not of the kind now so fashionable with our most distinguished critics), and its best explication is in an epic of some length by Blake, his "Milton." Here is a lucid short commentary by Northrop Frye:

> Milton's God, Blake says, is the real Satan, the prince of the power of the air, the creator of a physical universe which is the subter-

4. "The Marriage of Heaven and Hell," in Keynes, ed., *Blake*, pp. 191–2.

ranean cave or hell of eternity. The real God dwells in the real
Eden, a city of flaming fire. Milton's Satan is Orc, the power of
human desire which gradually and inevitably declines into passive
acceptance of impersonal law and external reason. Thus Blake's
point is not that Satan is the hero of *Paradise Lost,* but that there
is no hero of *Paradise Lost.* The poem simply traces the Orc cycle
to the point at which all the characters, from God the Father to
Eve, are caught in the same quicksand of fatalistic morality.[5]

To this I add, in explication of Blake's troublesome "note," that it is
no use trying to interpret that note until one knows how Blake is defining "Angels & God," and "Devils & Hell," for in the ironic vocabulary
of the "Marriage," built on a system of "contraries," "Good is Heaven.
Evil is Hell," but "Good is the passive that obeys Reason. Evil is the
active springing from Energy." And even these categories are "what
the religious call Good & Evil." Those who accept these categories of
moral virtue Blake calls angels; those who realize that "Without Contraries is no progression" Blake calls devils. An orthodox pillar of society is therefore an angel, and visionary poet a devil. If "Angels & God"
mean the guardians of organized society (including poets who write to
uphold society) and the supreme abstraction which restrains desire,
respectively, and if "Devils & Hell" mean visionary rebels and the state
of the "active springing from Energy," then even contemporary critics
might acknowledge that "The reason Milton wrote in fetters when he
wrote of Angels & God, and at liberty when of Devils & Hell, is because
he was a true Poet and of the Devil's party without knowing it."

Shelley is our other unwary reader of Milton and is of course my prime
concern here, the Blakean digression being justified only because the
similar protests of Blake and Shelley will serve to illuminate each other.
I began this section by quoting Shelley on Milton's Satan in the preface
to "Prometheus." Three years later, in *A Defence of Poetry,* the poet
of "Prometheus" speculated again on the same problem :

> Milton's poem contains within itself a philosophical refutation of
> that system, of which, by a strange and natural antithesis, it has
> been a chief popular support. Nothing can exceed the energy and
> magnificence of the character of Satan as expressed in *Paradise
> Lost.* It is a mistake to suppose that he could ever have been in-
> tended for the popular personification of evil. Implacable hate,
> patient cunning, and a sleepless refinement of device to inflict the
> extremest anguish on an enemy, these things are evil; and, although
> venial in a slave, are not to be forgiven in a tyrant; although re-
> deemed by much that ennobles his defeat in one subdued, are marked

5. Northrop Frye, *Fearful Symmetry, A Study of William Blake* (Princeton Univ.
Press, 1947), p. 219.

by all that dishonors his conquest in the victor. Milton's Devil as a moral being is as far superior to his God, as one who perseveres in some purpose which he has conceived to be excellent in spite of adversity and torture, is to one who in the cold security of undoubted triumph inflicts the most horrible revenge upon his enemy, not from any mistaken notion of inducing him to repent of a perseverance in enmity, but with the alleged design of exasperating him to deserve new torments. Milton has so far violated the popular creed (if this shall be judged to be a violation) as to have alleged no superiority of moral virtue to his God over his Devil. And this bold neglect of a direct moral purpose is the most decisive proof of the supremacy of Milton's genius.[6]

This lacks the subtle dialectic and careful vocabulary of Blake, and is therefore even more available for misreading. Nevertheless, my contention is that this passage and the passage quoted by us from "The Marriage of Heaven and Hell" tell the same story, or the same side of the story. Blake would have granted cheerfully and generously that these sentences of Shelley deserved to be headed "The Voice of the Devil," just as much as any section of his own work did.

The angels have misrepresented Shelley as much as they have Blake. C. S. Lewis, an eminent angel, has even maintained that the view of Blake and Shelley toward Satan must end in the conviction that "any real being like Satan if there were one, or a real human being in so far as he resembles Milton's Satan, is or ought to be an object of admiration and sympathy, conscious or unconscious, on the part of the poet or his readers or both." Again, following the late Charles Williams in believing Satan to be suffering chiefly from a Sense of Injured Merit, Lewis writes of Satan: "He thought himself impaired because Messiah had been pronounced Head of the Angels. These are the 'wrongs' which Shelley described as 'beyond measure.'" [7]

Now ultimately Lewis and (alas! let it be admitted) Milton cannot agree with Blake and Shelley on the major issue in hand, for, as Blake superbly observed, "this history has been adopted by both parties," and they do not agree on its interpretation. Still, Lewis ought not to misrepresent Blake and Shelley, whose respectable belief is that the poet Milton wrought better than the man Milton (or the theologian Milton) knew. (Lewis insists, as the man Milton would have insisted, that the poet Milton wrought *exactly* what the theologian Milton knew.)

A fair interpretation of the remarks on Satan in the preface to "Prometheus Unbound" should begin with an understanding of the

6. John Shawcross, ed., *Shelley's Literary and Philosophical Criticism* (London, Oxford Univ. Press, 1932), pp. 145–6.
7. C. S. Lewis, *A Preface to "Paradise Lost"* (London, Oxford Univ. Press, 1942), pp. 92, 94.

more comprehensive comments on the same subject in the *Defence*. This understanding in turn depends on an imaginative sympathy with theological views which are not orthodox, whether one shares them or not, and ultimately on one's own reaction to the complicated aesthetic *cum* moral problem involved in Milton's depiction of God in "Paradise Lost." If one is not at all disturbed, morally or aesthetically (probably no distinction can be made here between the two), by this vision of God, then Shelley and Blake are likely to seem very much beside the point. Lewis finds aesthetic as well as theological splendor in this God who is an uncomfortably (for some of us) close parallel to an earthly avenging tyrant, sitting in state surrounded by retainers singing his praises. Lewis is certainly worthy of attention here; he may well correct my misapprehensions, if they are such, but it is not likely that he would have succeeded in changing the reading of Shelley and of Blake.

What is clearly inaccurate about Shelley's remarks, if we take them literally, is that they certainly seem to misstate Milton's intentions. There are no obvious signs of irony in Shelley here, for his own intention is decidedly straightforward; he has a firm conviction that the Satan *in the poem* is a far superior moral being to the God *in the poem*. He does not say that Satan is morally admirable, whatever Lewis may think. Instead, like Blake, he makes a comparison between energy or desire, on the one side, and the restrainer of energy or desire, on the other. Like Blake's, his real point is that "Paradise Lost" has not and cannot have any hero. Its only possible hero, the embodiment of *human* energy and desire at their highest pitch of imaginative intensity, its Orc or Prometheus, is Satan. He is made to accept the same categories of morality as God by being portrayed as a being who lives, or tries to live, by a frank and simple inversion of the conventional theological and moral categories. Like Blake, Shelley is implying that the poet in Milton made an attempt to break through the categories of the theologian: "He [Milton] mingled as it were the elements of human nature as colours upon a single pallet, and arranged them in the composition of his great picture according to the laws of epic truth; that is, according to the laws of that principle by which a series of actions of the external universe and of intelligent and ethical beings is calculated to excite the sympathy of succeeding generations of mankind." [8] Epic, poetic truth conflicts in "Paradise Lost" with Christian "truth" according to Blake and Shelley. The two truths, they hold, are incompatible, the "true" poet being necessarily not of God's party but of man's, the party of Orc or Prometheus, of which Milton's Satan is a necessarily imperfect representative since both the poet and the Christian in Milton struggle to portray him and both in part succeed. Something like this is what Shelley means in the preface to "Prometheus" when he writes, as already quoted, that Prometheus is "a more poetical character than Satan," just as Blake claimed Orc to

8. Shawcross, p. 146.

be a more poetical character, that is, truer than Milton's titanic Rebel to what the archetype of a Divine Man in revolt against an abstract and "reasonable" God ought to be. Shelley's preface is not a naïve document any more than "The Marriage of Heaven and Hell" is. Prometheus, like Satan, is to display "courage, and majesty, and firm and patient opposition to omnipotent force," but, unlike Satan, he is to be "exempt from the taints of ambition, envy, revenge, and a desire for personal aggrandisement" which the theologian Milton prevailed upon the poet Milton to attach to Satan. Satan is therefore a jumble of good and bad, of poetry and bad poetry (i.e. Christian theology), which jumble "engenders in the mind a pernicious casuistry which leads us to weigh his faults with his wrongs, and to excuse the former because the latter exceed all measure." Surely Lewis ought to have brooded on the words "pernicious casuistry" before deciding that Shelley meant that we ought to excuse all Satan's faults because of his wrongs, and surely also Lewis ought to have realized that the "wrongs" involved are more than the "Sense of Injured Merit" arising from being ranked below Messiah in the heavenly hierarchy. The wrongs are those suffered by the spirit of divinity in man when it challenges the arbitrary rule of the sky god and is borne down by that arbitrary power. When applied to "Paradise Lost," in which this element exists side-by-side (according to Blake and Shelley) quite irreconcilably with the Christian version of that same conflict, our recognition of both faults and wrongs must result in "pernicious casuistry" one way or the other, depending on which story we prefer, the orthodox Christian or the heretic romantic-humanist, the vision of Lewis and Milton the man or of Blake and Shelley.

In sum, if we take the reading of Milton by Blake and Shelley on its own terms then we cannot dispute it, and if we take it *on Milton's terms* then we are obliged to see partial truth in it, unless we are prepared, with Lewis, to accept Milton's portrayal of Satan and God as being morally, theologically, and imaginatively just. In any case, we shall not understand Blake and Shelley on Milton unless, like them, we are willing to dispute orthodox categories, at least long enough to comprehend those who do so dispute. Lewis will not make this effort, and therefore will not understand the Blakean and Shelleyan criticism of Milton.

What justifies this long digression is that it helps us to understand the preface to "Prometheus" and, subsequently, a good deal about "Prometheus" itself, for "Prometheus," like Blake's epics, is a poem written in a spirit of what we might term "corrective competition" with "Paradise Lost" (and to such other orthodox theistic works as "Prometheus Bound," of course). In my first chapter I contrasted the mythmaking and doctrinal poets, and reached the tentative conclusion that it was scarcely possible to assign primacy either to the commitment to the mythopoeic mode or to the unorthodox theology, of the poets of the former grouping. Certainly in Blake it would be extraordinarily diffi-

cult to decide whether personal religion produces mythographic poetry
or an overwhelming mythopoeic impulse results necessarily in original
religious vision. Even the very young Blake, in the "Poetical Sketches,"
gives indications of both elements being already present. Shelley is perhaps even more baffling here, in that these factors seem to alternate in
taking primacy and then inducing the other in his poems.

In "Paradise Lost" the mythopoeic mode and the orthodox religious
categories tend toward conflict. The Promethean Satan of Books 1 and
2, read by Blake and Shelley as a momentary triumph for the mythmaking impulse over Milton's orthodox censor, becomes in Blake's earlier
prophecies the chief literary model for Orc, the rebel against Urizen, and
in Shelley's lyrical drama the primary model (with the Titan of Aeschylus) for Prometheus, especially in the opening scene of the Titan's defiance and torment.

The point of the remarks about Satan in the preface and the deliberate echoings of Satan at the opening of the drama is therefore twofold : Prometheus and Satan are paralleled, but are also contrasted. Milton's Satan is accepted as prototype and morally approved, precisely
insofar as he is a Promethean figure. Insofar as Satan cannot be ab-
sorbed into Prometheus *he is rejected,* and he is rejected on moral grounds
and for being bad poetry compared to Shelley's more ideal and, so to
speak, more Promethean Prometheus. A. C. Bradley was perhaps mistaken when he bracketed Shelley's comparison of Prometheus and Satan
with Shelley's rather curious theory "of the representation of heroic
and tragic imperfection," if my reading of the preface is correct: "We
find in the Preface to *Prometheus Unbound* the strange notion that
Prometheus is a more poetic character than Milton's Satan because he is
free from Satan's imperfections, which are said to interfere with the
interest. And in the *Defence* a similar error appears. Achilles, Hector,
Ulysses, though they exhibit ideal virtues, are, he admits, imperfect . . .
It [this idea] is an example of Shelley's tendency to abstract idealism
or spurious Platonism . . ." [9]

My suggestion, counter to this, is that we may err in assimilating the
first notion (Prometheus more poetical than Satan) to the second (the
hero of a poem ought to be all virtue). My previous remarks on
Shelley's attitude toward Milton's Satan ought to explain what I might
mean in thus disputing Bradley.

3

Prometheus has participated in the universal leveling, reaching his
nadir in Gide's work, *Prometheus Ill-Bound.* There the Titan, safely

9. A. C. Bradley, "Shelley's View of Poetry," *Oxford Lectures on Poetry* (London,
Oxford Univ. Press, 1926), p. 166.

off his crag, will not part from *his* eagle, but keeps it feeding on his vitals because he will not see it less handsome than it has grown to be on its grisly diet, and because, after all, it is now his own eagle, raised on his own heart's blood. Sadder still is the Prometheus of Kafka, who simply tires of it all, as do the gods, the eagle, and finally the wound of Prometheus, which wearily closes of its own accord, the whole issue forgotten: "Die Götter wurden müde, die Adler wurden müde, die Wunde schloss sich müde." All that remains of the once passionate myth at the close of this dry parable is the crag, quite inexplicable, as befits a myth which arose from the inexplicable.[1]

I need not labor the significance of this contemporary dead end of a story which lived for so long in poet after poet. Better for my purposes to go back to the beginnings of the myth, hoping to see afresh the liberating potentiality that it had for Shelley, the poet of the 1816 Hymns, so that perhaps I can surmise why the free-floating divinity of those hymns could come, and came to be expressed in the more rigid forms of the conflict between Olympians and Titans.

What is central to the myth of Prometheus, even in its earlier appearances, is its unique relationship to the human race, its association with the massive issues of the origin, survival, and destiny of mankind rather than of the gods. The line of Iapetos stands out among the Titans and Olympians because we are indebted to it and share its glory and its guilt.

The Orphic tradition held that the Titans were our direct and sinful ancestors. Hesiod has it that Ouranos gave the Titans their name, a punning name, a term of abuse, derived from *titainein,* "to overreach oneself," and *tisis,* "punishment." These punished overreachers, afflicted by *atasthalia,* "foolhardiness," exemplify by their very name the condition and chief characteristic of their human descendants. Their greatest venture, the long war against the Olympians, typifies them most completely by its result: utter defeat. Karl Kerényi shrewdly observes that "The Titans were gods of a sort that have no function except in mythology. Their function is that of the defeated: even when they win seeming victories—before the stories come to their inexorable conclusion. These defeated ones bear the characteristic of an older male generation: the characteristics of ancestors whose dangerous qualities reappear in their posterity." [2]

Our audacious forefathers, the Titans, were thrown down into Tartaros after their defeat, falling nine nights and days from the earth down into that iron-walled hell of darkness, where Satan was to follow them. Hesiod tells us that lightning won the battles for Zeus, lightning and a deluge of stones. The sons of Iapetos had a mixed but not less atrocious fate than that of their father and uncles. Menoitios, demonstrating at length the audacious qualities of his race, was struck by Zeus's lightning and fell down into Erebos. Atlas, possessed of dangerous wisdom gathered in the recesses of the ocean, was put to endless labor propping up the skies at the western edge of earth, near the Garden of the Hesperides. At the eastern edge of earth, on the highest crag of the Caucasus, the most cunning of the younger Titans eventually endured his torment.

Of this Prometheus (the "foresighted," "prophetic," or "provident") we know first that he supported Zeus against the Titans, in the foreknowledge that the developing Zeus represented an advance in divinity. The subsequent falling out between Titan and God cannot be summarized except from either an orthodox or an antinomian point of view; for once again this history has been adopted by both parties, say Hesiod on the one side, the romantics on the other (Blake, Byron, Goethe, Shelley, Spittleler, et al.). Aeschylus avoids telling one story and one story only, and envisions the tragedy of a *partially* justified Titan (see next section).

I had best adopt the orthodox view first, before passing to the modifications of Aeschylus and the antinomian vision of Shelley's Prometheus. As Blake and Shelley see a great deal of Prometheus in Satan, even so the orthodox properly can trace satanic qualities in the original mythical figure of Prometheus.

Prometheus, like Satan, has the lust for all knowledge, lawful or otherwise. This drive toward knowing is a major element in the Titan's *hubris,* and is most fully symbolized by the theft of fire, an archetypal image emblematic of the upward thrust of the spirit of man, aspiring toward divinity, toward an ultimate fullness of knowledge. To this foolhardiness and impiety Prometheus adds a trait which Zeus does not possess, cunning, a useful gift but also a failing, not to be found in the highest of gods. Prometheus is "of crooked thoughts," *ankulometes,* a quality which Kerényi wisely notes as covering a range from deceitfulness to inventiveness.[3] This combination of foreknowledge and cunning, both attributes lacking in Zeus, makes Prometheus so useful and yet so dangerous an ally for the sky god.

Is this primal mythic Prometheus more a god or a man? There are two tales of creation involved here: one in which gods and men are coeternal, both being children of Earth brought forth at the same time; the other in which Prometheus is the creator of men and we are his creatures. The common mythic feature of either story is well summarized by Kerényi: "In our mythology the double task of separating mankind from the immortals and of giving completion to mortals fell

3. Quoted by R. J. Zwi Werblowsky, *Lucifer and Prometheus* (London, Routledge, 1952), p. 57.

to Prometheus." [4] Whether we were made *with* the gods or *after* them by Prometheus, we were in any case clearly separated off from the gods *by* Prometheus, who atoned for his guilt in this separation by giving us completion, the gift of fire and the gift of woman, so that we could survive even after Zeus had become angered at us over the affair of the division of the slaughtered bull at Mekone, when for the last time gods and men met in common council.

Kerényi answers the question with which we began our last paragraph by telling us that Prometheus is a god despite his human advocacy. But even the Prometheus of Hesiod must endure suffering and calumny in a manner which is clearly human. R. J. Zwi Werblowsky, agreeing with Kerényi, insists on distinguishing between Prometheus (Hesiodic) as a god and the romantic Prometheus (of Goethe or Shelley) as a "man claiming the rank and dignity of God." Perhaps the best summation of the paradox is given by Werblowsky, directly following Kerényi, when he writes of the primal mythic Prometheus: "His suffering is that of mankind, but his protest is that of outraged divinity, or rather of the divine quality of his humanity. The only parallel to Prometheus would therefore be a gnostic *Urmensch, anthropos* or *Adam Kadmon.* In the mythological sphere Prometheus is thus the divine representative of the non-olympic, the human pole of the world." [5]

This analogue of the Urmensch or Adam Kadmon, which Kerényi cites for Prometheus, was seized on by Blake for his Titans, the Giant Forms who populate his epics. I shall attempt to show how Blake, like Shelley, took up the myth of the Titans as being germane to his symbolism, for the parallel here between Blake and Shelley is so exact that a knowledge of one poet may help in the reading of the other. What is immediately useful about my quotation from Werblowsky is that it may help us to appreciate the complexity of even Hesiod's Prometheus, before we confront the still more complex Titan of Aeschylus.

The hubris of the first mythic Prometheus is quite satanic. Prometheus in his cunning and audacity accepts no bounds, no divine restraint, as he drives toward ultimate increases in knowledge, in consciousness, in the *separateness* of humans from gods. Following Jung and parodying Goethe's devil, we might term Prometheus "the Spirit who differentiates." Werblowsky, following Jung, finds the fire stolen by Prometheus to be symbolic of consciousness, thought, and knowledge (Empedocles found the same, as Werblowsky again notes). Increase in knowledge past certain bounds may bring sin, if the knowledge itself is unlawful, by Greek, Hebrew, and Christian belief, the modern equivalent being the Kierkegaardian dictum that every increase in consciousness means an increase in despair. Prometheus violates the perfect, the bounded

4. Kerényi, p. 214.
5. Werblowsky, pp. 54, 55.

and regulated order of Zeus. For this Hesiod holds his punishment to be just; it is Aeschylus who develops the problem to the point at which Shelley takes it over.

4

"But, in truth, I was averse from a catastrophe so feeble as that of reconciling the Champion with the Oppressor of mankind. The moral interest of the fable, which is so powerfully sustained by the sufferings and endurance of Prometheus, would be annihilated if we could conceive of him as unsaying his high language and quailing before his successful and perfidious adversary." [6] So Shelley justifies his having "presumed" to employ a considerable licence in his treatment of the unbinding of Prometheus, rather than having attempted to restore the lost drama of Aeschylus. George Thomson, in his brilliant introduction to his edition of Aeschylus' *Prometheus Bound,* has a relevant comment:

> I still remember my dismay, when, after reading the *Prometheus Bound* for the first time at school, I turned to the introduction and found that, in the view of the editors, despite any appearances to the contrary, Prometheus was in the wrong and Zeus was in the right, and the comfort I derived from Shelley's reassuring words in the introduction to his *Prometheus Unbound:* "But in truth I was averse from a catastrophe so feeble as that of reconciling the Champion with the Oppressor of mankind." Not being a scholar, Shelley had not the means of reconstructing the Aeschylean sequel; but he was a poet, and, so far as the first play of the trilogy is concerned, his instinctive judgment was sound. There, Zeus *is* the "Oppressor of Mankind" and their champion's "perfidious adversary." Such must be the impression of every candid reader, and a little examination will show that such was the poet's intention.[7]

Zeus is a tyrant: harsh, irresponsible, unconstitutional, suspicious of his friends, implacable, and impervious to persuasion. Prometheus is consumed by pride and is utterly lacking in restraint. The first play in the trilogy thus ends in deadlock, as Zeus and Prometheus are, each in his own way, diseased. Zeus's power is new; it needs to be refined and developed. Aeschylus "is displaying to us the world, not as it is now, but as it was in the beginning." [8] In the course of ages, taught by experience, the adversaries will be reconciled. The play teaches that σωφροσύνη is the highest of the virtues, and both Prometheus and Zeus must travel the path of suffering before they can attain it.

6. Preface to "Prometheus Unbound," Hutchinson, ed., *Shelley,* pp. 221–2.
7. George Thomson, ed., *Aeschylus, The Prometheus Bound* (Cambridge Univ. Press, 1932), p. 6.
8. Ibid., p. 11.

At the close of *Prometheus Bound* neither Zeus nor Prometheus can be said to have realized this, and Zeus casts Prometheus down into Tartaros. At the opening of the fragmentary *Prometheus Unbound* Zeus seems to have gone some way toward the cure of his "diseased" state. He has restored Prometheus, still bound, to the light of day. Prometheus, however, is still unregenerate, though that he now longs for death is significant. His disease is in its final stage before the beginning of cure, that is, reconciliation with Zeus.

Zeus has now given over his desire to destroy mankind, so that the continued obduracy of Prometheus is no longer due to his fears for the future of the human race but rather to his continued resentment for past wrongs committed by Zeus.

Earth, the mother of Prometheus, and the Titans, his brothers now also released from Tartaros, beg Prometheus to reveal his secret to Zeus, on the grounds that Zeus is now ruling well and justly. Zeus is actually at this time in pursuit of Thetis, so that if Prometheus will hold out only a little longer, the now just ruler of gods will be overthrown.

Prometheus finally yields, overcoming his pride, and permits Earth (who in the first place revealed the secret to her son) to warn Zeus in time. Heracles, whose birth symbolized Zeus's good will toward mankind, comes to slay the eagle and, doing so, liberates Prometheus, on the Titan's assurance that Earth is in the act of revealing the secret to Zeus. Heracles provides Prometheus with a substitute in Cheiron, the accidentally wounded centaur who wishes to die.

In the third play (as he orders it) *Prometheus the Firebearer,* Thomson surmises that the Titan seeks readmission to Olympus, which is granted to him under the patronage of Athena.[9] The complete cycle of the development of Zeus has been fulfilled, as both God and men, through their representative, have learned wisdom and restraint through suffering. Shelley, had he known all this, would not have referred to it as a "feeble" conclusion, but would still have rejected it for something better, something nearer to his heart's desire, that is, for apocalypse.

5

Aeschylus then is to be regarded as holding a mediator's position between Olympians and Titans, in contrast both to the older Olympian orthodoxy of Hesiod and to the romantic Titanism of Shelley and Blake. The Zeus of Shelley is Blake's Old Nobodaddy, setter of limits and circumcizer of desire, separating Zoa and Emanation, Titan or Divine Man and his bride, Albion and Jerusalem, Prometheus and Asia. What remains to be explored, even after we have glanced at the first Prometheus and at the creation of Aeschylus, is the primal myth of the Titans once

9. Ibid., pp. 34-8.

again, for even Aeschylus is orthodox enough to have told the history
adopted by the party termed angelic by Blake. Lurking in the mythic
material are antinomian possibilities available even to men of Aeschylus'
time, let alone early nineteenth-century visionaries. My own eyes are too
romantic, even if they had the necessary keenness, to be trusted in spying
out such possibilities. The dispassionate vision of the distinguished Jane
Harrison is more to be trusted here, and will serve to show what there
was waiting to be taken up by such as Blake and Shelley:

> In Homer and Hesiod they [the Titans], unlike the Giants, are
> always gods, τιτῆνες φεοί. They are constantly being driven down
> below the earth to nethermost Tartarus and always re-emerging.
> The very violence and persistence with which they are sent down
> below shows that they belong up above. They rebound like divine
> india-rubber balls. . . . The Gigantes are children of Earth, the
> Titanes are children of Earth and Heaven, with a leaning towards
> Heaven. . . . The fight of the Gods against the Giants had right
> as well as might on its side. . . . the same can scarcely be said of
> the fight against the Titans. These powers of the upper air, these
> gods of storm and lightning, these μετάρσια may be, because not
> understood, lawless, but they are nowise impure and their worship
> can scarcely degrade. . . .[1]

Spenser, the father of mythopoeia in English poetry, still preserved the
orthodox outlook on the Titans, making Mutabilitie a Titaness in renewed rebellion against Jove. Blake is the first major English poet to
range himself with the Titans, anticipating Byron and Shelley by a generation. I have already contrasted Keats's treatment of the Titan-
Olympian conflict with that of the more extreme Blake, Byron, and
Shelley in my introductory chapter. This more extreme Titanism of the
romantics is what must engage us here.

Blake turned to the Titans, those "children of Earth and Heaven,
with a leaning towards Heaven," because they provided him with another contrapuntal strand for his complex archetypal myth of the Fall of
a Divine Man, the Albion of the prophecies. Blake's unfallen world,
dominated by imaginative perception, is peopled by humans with gigantic
powers, and in the various Titanic myths Blake found intimations of that
unfallen world. The Prose Edda, the Hebrew Cabbala, and the classic
myths of Greece told, according to Blake, one story and one story only.
An Adam Kadmon, a wholly human and therefore wholly Divine Man,
at first existed as comprising all things of heaven and earth in his own
limbs. When this god-man fell gigantic energies, sprung from his body,
fought for control of it. The wars between Zeus and the Titans, Odin and

1. Jane Ellen Harrison, *Themis* (Cambridge Univ. Press, 1912), pp. 454, 458, 460.

the Jötuns, Jehovah and the rebel angels are all traditional, scriptural accounts of the battle for control of the fallen Albion by his components. These accounts are all orthodox, that is, told from the viewpoint of the victors, the sky gods Zeus, Odin, and Jehovah, all setters of limits, orderers of the cosmos, restrainers of man's violent energies, like Blake's Urizen, the god with the compasses who is meant to embody them in Blake's attempt at one central myth. Man in Blake falls from Titan to Giant and finally to his present weak form, as the sky god presses his limits in. The chained Prometheus, the chained Loki, the Satan bound in hell are all embodied in Blake's Orc, the "imprisoned Titanic power in man, which spasmodically causes revolutions." [2] Blake calls him Orc, from *orcus* or "hell," because that is where orthodox morality holds these bound energies to originate.

Like Shelley, as we shall see, Blake sees Jesus as a Prometheus crucified by Zeus, or an Orc nailed to a tree, or the still developing Odin who hangs upon the gallows tree as a sacrifice to himself. This last Blake takes as an embodiment of the grim phenomenon of the Orc cycle, in which Orc always ends by *becoming* Urizen, Jesus by becoming identified with Jehovah, Prometheus one with Zeus; or on the historical level, all revolutions becoming reactions, that is, in Blake's time the French revolution becoming first the Terror and then Napoleonic despotism.

The analogues to the Orc cycle in Shelley's "Prometheus" are striking and exact, and will be considered when they arise. Orc, like Shelley's Prometheus, has an Adonis aspect attached to him, embodied in his emanation Vala (Shelley's Asia), whose withdrawal from him keeps the earth from its fecundity, delays the coming of spring. Unawakened nature itself in Blake is to be understood as the scattered and suffering manifold that once helped comprise a connected unity in the form of the body of a Titan. Once again we will be reminded of Blake in the depiction of a scattered and suffering nature at the opening of Shelley's "Prometheus."

Long before Blake and Shelley saw Prometheus as a type of the crucified Jesus, who then is confounded (deliberately) by the orthodox with Zeus or Jehovah, the same identification had been made, with less gnostic intent, in Christian writers. Aeschylus' *Prometheus Bound,* lines 702–74, were easily pliable for the workings of Christian commentary, for they are, as Werblowsky and many others point out, the definite expectation of a savior. The vicarious atonement of Prometheus for mankind and of Cheiron for Prometheus are very obvious types for the atonement of Jesus. Tertullian refers to the Promethean suffering as the *crucibus Caucasorum,* while other Fathers juggled a god-man anagram in *Protheus* and made close comparisons of the Passions of the Titan and

2. Frye, *Fearful Symmetry,* p. 129.

the Christ: Zeus's eagle being the Roman lance, the Oceanides the disciples, Cheiron's descent to Hades that of Christ to hell, even the virgin conception of Io that of Mary.[3]

The complexity and richness of the Prometheus myth can embrace a symbolic identification for its protagonist which ranges all the way from Satan to Christ, as we have seen. The "Satanic School" of Byron and Shelley (Southey would certainly have added Blake to his grouping, had he ever seen the "Marriage of Heaven and Hell") naturally appropriated Prometheus, as a higher type of Milton's Satan and as a fully appropriate type of Christ, with the advantage of not arousing the formidable association for the orthodox and the conventional, which still attached to the latter. Blake, in his epics, overtly creates a romantic Christ, antinomian and aggressively humanistic in his opposition to the harshness of heaven. Byron and Shelley hint at the same creation, but never amplify these suggestions, if only because both of them, but more especially Byron, are of more than one conviction about the figure of Christ, unlike Blake who displays his customarily massive and perhaps costly consistency on this as on all matters.

Byron's "Prometheus" is an ode of only three short strophes, but the Promethean "Manfred" serves as his really Titanic poem. The hubris of the drive toward unlimited knowledge is united in Manfred with the conviction of the truth of the Titanic myth, that men were equal to the gods and to everything else in the creation in a former age. So Manfred defies the spirits who have come to claim him:

> I do not combat against death, but thee
> And thy surrounding angels; my past power,
> Was purchased by no compact with thy crew,
> But by superior science—penance, daring,
> And length of watching, strength of mind, and skill
> In knowledge of our fathers—*when the earth*
> *Saw men and spirits walking side by side,*
> *And gave ye no supremacy* . . .   [112–19]

The italics are mine, the myth involved the same exploited by Blake and by Shelley. Byron's "Prometheus" proper, composed July 1816, in the company and perhaps under the overt influence of Shelley, can be read as a prelude to Shelley's drama, embodying as it does a simplification of what I seem to find to be the emergent theology of the drama:

> Thy Godlike crime was to be kind,
>   To render with thy precepts less
>   The sum of human wretchedness,
> And strengthen Man with his own mind;

3. Werblowsky, pp. 62–3.

But baffled as thou wert from high,
Still in thy patient energy,
In the endurance, and repulse
    Of thine impenetrable Spirit,
Which Earth and Heaven could not convulse,
    A mighty lesson we inherit:
Thou art a symbol and a sign
    To mortals of their fate and force;
Like thee, Man is in part divine,
    A troubled stream from a pure source;
And Man in portions can foresee
His own funereal destiny;
His wretchedness, and his resistance,
And his sad unallied existence:
To which his Spirit may oppose
Itself—and equal to all woes,
    And a firm will, and a deep sense,
Which even in torture can descry
    Its own concenter'd recompense,
Triumphant where it dares defy,
And making Death a Victory.   [35–59]

This is perhaps only rhetoric, but rhetoric of the highest order, as the
last speech of Demogorgon in "Prometheus Unbound" most certainly is.
However it may be ranked as poetry, this strophe of Byron's has its
affinities with the peroration which closes Shelley's drama. Byron has a
grasp of Blake's Orc cycle (which I shall explore by its analogies in
Shelley's drama) as manifested in what may be his worst poem, the
extraordinary "Ode to Napoleon Bonaparte." Napoleon is the Orc or
Prometheus turned into Urizen or Zeus, the revolutionary become the
oppressor. As Shelley's Prometheus is to be tormented by the Orc cycle,
the visions of Christ crucified into a heavenly tyrant, and the French
revolution metamorphized into the Terror, the rule of Napoleon, and
the return to legitimacy, so Byron reacts to the same phenomenon,
though hardly in the same spirit. A wolfish glee animates Byron as he
taunts the fallen Napoleon, once Titanic, then Olympian, and now without status, and compares him to the romantic Prometheus:

Or, like the thief of fire from heaven,
    Wilt thou withstand the shock?
And share with him, the unforgiven,
    His vulture and his rock!
Foredoom'd by God—by man accurst,
And that last act, though not thy worst,
    The very Fiend's arch mock;

He in his fall preserved his pride,
And, if a mortal, had as proudly died!

What is central here for my purposes is the association of Napoleon
with Prometheus. The liberation of Promethean energies in the French
people had made Napoleon possible, had permitted his personal Orc cycle from antinomian Titan to yet another representative of heaven's
tyranny on earth. The heavy irony of Byron's stanza is dependent on
the fallen Napoleon's being placed again in the position of the Titan
at the start of the cycle. For Napoleon the wheel has come full circle;
what disfigures Byron's presentation of this is the coarse and inhumane
satisfaction which he takes in the wheel's turn.

Having traced something of the fortunes of Prometheus in Shelley's
"satanic" contemporaries, I come at last to a reading of Shelley himself,
hoping to be prepared to comprehend this "most difficult" of the poet's
"beautiful idealisms of moral excellence."

4

"Ode to the West Wind"

THE "Ode to the West Wind," judged by Oliver Elton to be the "greatest of all those lyrics of Shelley, which do not, in brief compass, convey a single and a simple emotion," [1] is a "Prometheus Unbound" in miniature, an expressive and economical summary of much that is central in the lyrical drama, the apocalyptic third act in particular (the "Ode" being composed simultaneously with the third act). This "Ode" is the most "prophetic" of Shelley's shorter poems, in matter and manner, even as the "Prometheus" is the most "prophetic" of the major works.

The *King James* "prophet" translates the Hebrew word *nabi:* The nabi is never an oracle, but rather a visionary, literally a seer, who sees more clearly and comprehensibly into the ethical consequences of a situation than most men manage to do. Blake, with his magnificent grasp of the Bible, put this very eloquently in one of his marginalia to Bishop Watson's so-called *Apology for the Bible,* an answer to Thomas Paine's *Age of Reason,* in itself not a very Blakean book, of course. (Blake's commentary on the bishop's book opens with the bitterly ironic remark: "To defend the Bible in this year 1788 would cost a man his life.") On page 14 of his book, Bishop Watson attempted a sarcasm *contra* Paine: "You esteem all prophets to be such lying rascals, that I dare not venture to predict the fate of your book." Blake's laconic comment is prompted by the bishop's vulgar misunderstanding of what a prophet is: "Prophets, in the modern sense of the word, have never existed. Jonah was no prophet in the modern sense, for his prophecy of Nineveh failed. Every honest man is a Prophet; he utters his opinion both of private & public matters. Thus: If you go on So, the result is So. He never says, such a thing shall happen let you do what you will. A Prophet is a Seer, not an Arbitrary Dictator." [2]

"Every honest man is a Prophet": one is reminded of Numbers 2:24-9, a text that Hoxie Neale Fairchild might have consulted before reproving the romantic poets for not leaving religion in the accredited

---

1. Oliver Elton, *A Survey of English Literature 1780–1830* (2 vols. London, Arnold, 1912), *2,* 213.
2. Keynes, ed., *Blake,* pp. 949, 961.

hands of the churches.[3] "And there ran a young man, and told Moses, and said: 'Eldad and Medad are prophesying in the camp.' And Joshua the son of Nun, the minister of Moses from his youth up, answered and said: 'My lord Moses, shut them in.' And Moses said unto him: 'Art thou jealous for my sake? would that all the Lord's people were prophets, that the Lord would put His spirit upon them!' " One remembers also that Blake, in some humility, chose that exclamation of Moses as the epigraph to the prophetic poem, "Milton," placing it directly after the quatrains, "And did those feet in ancient time . . ."

Blake's correct notion of the nabi is confirmed in Buber's comparison of Greek and Hebrew prophecy, oracle contrasted to nabi: "The oracle gives answers to a situation which is brought before it as a question by emissaries who ask for information; the *nabi,* sent by God, speaks unasked into the biographical or historical situation. The answer of the oracle is prediction of an unalterable future; the warning of the *nabi* implies the indeterminism and determining power of the hour." [4] That last phrase embodies a concept of "the hour" very close to a concept prevalent in "Prometheus Unbound."

Now Blake and Shelley are poets, at their best, of the rank and kind of Ezekiel, and they are prophets as he was a prophet. They "speak unasked" into their historical situation as he spoke unasked into his, and we ought to be very wary before we condemn their prophetic aspirations. The God of the Hebrew-Christian Bible makes an ominous reply when Moses begs His name: *Ehyeh asher ehyeh,* which the King James version renders "I am that I am" but which literally is closer to "I shall be (present) when and where I shall be (present)."

I am following a recent article by Pottle in this approach to Shelley as a prophetic poet.[5] Shelley himself, as Pottle points out, identified poetry with prophecy in the *Defence:*

> But poets . . . are . . . the teachers, who draw into a certain propinquity with the beautiful and the true, that partial apprehension of the agencies of the invisible world which is called religion. Hence all original religions are allegorical, or susceptible

3. "The primary business of the poet is not to make a world, but to fashion works of art out of positive or negative responses to the qualities of a world which already exists. The romantic faith in imaginative power, however, can be satisfied only by the creation of a universe. The poems themselves are but confessedly inadequate blueprints of the cosmic mansion. For those who insist with Browning that a man's reach should exceed his grasp the hugeness of the romantics' ambition establishes the greatness of their poetry, but others will object that all this straining to make poetry do the work of metaphysics and theology is damaging not only to religion but to art." Hoxie Neale Fairchild, *Religious Trends in English Poetry,* Vol. 3: *1780–1830, Romantic Faith* (New York, Columbia Univ. Press, 1949), p. 507.

4. Martin Buber, *Mamre: Essays in Religion,* trans. Greta Hart (Melbourne Univ. Press, 1946), p. 127.

5. F. A. Pottle, "The Case of Shelley," *PMLA,* 67 (1952), 589–608.

of allegory, and, like Janus, have a double face of false and true. Poets, according to the circumstances of the age and nation in which they appeared, were called, in the earlier epochs of the world, legislators, or prophets: a poet essentially comprises and unites both these characters. For he not only beholds intensely the present as it is, and discovers those laws according to which present things ought to be ordered, but he beholds the future in the present, and his thoughts are the germs of the flower and the fruit of latest time. Not that I assert poets to be prophets in the gross sense of the word, or that they can foretell the form as surely as they fore-know the spirit of events: such is the pretence of superstition, which would make poetry an attribute of prophecy, rather than prophecy an attribute of poetry.[6]

Blake, in his engraved tract *All Religions Are One* (etched about 1788), wrote: "The Religions of all Nations are derived from each Nation's different reception of the Poetic Genius, which is everywhere call'd the Spirit of Prophecy." In "The Marriage of Heaven and Hell" he wrote of "the ancient Poets" who with "their enlarged & numerous senses could perceive" so much more than the poets of an age of deism, and who had written poems from which an incipient "Priesthood" had been able to form a "system" with which they "enslav'd the vulgar," the whole process being described as "Choosing forms of worship from poetic tales." The prophet Ezekiel, in his appearance in the "Marriage," tells Blake that "we of Israel" taught that the Spirit of Prophecy or Poetic Genius was the first principle of human perception, from which teaching the dominant religion came to develop.[7] Blake here and the Shelley of the *Defence* are as one in their views of the formation of religion from prophetic poetry, the nature of true prophecy, and the ultimate identity of poetry with this kind of prophecy.

A major purpose of this book, as I have said, is to demonstrate that Shelley is, as Clutton-Brock and Pottle say, "a passionately religious poet," [8] who formulates his religion by the actual writing of his poems, the making of his myths, and further, to demonstrate the nature of those myths, by a close reading of the actual figures in which they are embodied in the poems. The "Ode to the West Wind" is actually a poem about this process of making myths, a poem whose subject is the nature and function of the nabi and his relation to his own prophecies. Specifically, we can take it as being a poem about Shelley's relationship to "Prometheus Unbound," just as in the opening of the last stanza of "Adonais,"

6. Shawcross, ed., *Shelley's Criticism*, p. 124.
7. Keynes, ed., *Blake*, pp. 149, 195, 196.
8. Pottle, "The Case of Shelley," p. 594.

> The breath whose might I have invoked in song
> Descends on me . . .

we are justified in thinking that "breath" to be the west wind "invoked
in song" in the first line of the "Ode." And if we are dealing with a
poem of this particular kind, a poem about the incarnation of a nabi, in
short a more mature version of the "Hymn to Intellectual Beauty,"
then we ought to be prepared to recognize certain conventions which
are intrinsic to this kind throughout prophetic literature, and most
particularly in the Hebrew tradition upon which Blake and Shelley draw.
Already Pottle has pointed out that

> Over against the ecstatic apocalypse . . . there stands the despond-
> ent psalm . . . "Thou art the God of my *strength*," says the Psalm-
> ist, "why hast thou put me from thee? and why go I so *heavily*
> while the enemy oppresseth me?" And again, "Why art thou so
> *heavy*, O my soul?" Shelley's psalm employs the same vocabulary
> to express the same situation: "The impulse of thy *strength* . . .
> O uncontrollable! A *heavy* weight of hours has chained and
> bowed . . ." [9]

One thinks of Blake, focusing on himself as poet-prophet at the close
of "Milton," just as Shelley focuses on himself at the end of the "Ode."
Those who sneer at Shelley's falling upon the thorns of life ought also
to sneer at this:

> Terror struck in the Vale I stood at that immortal sound.
> My bones trembled, I fell outstretch'd upon the path
> A moment, & my Soul return'd into its mortal state
> To Resurrection & Judgment in the Vegetable Body,
> And my sweet Shadow of Delight stood trembling by my side.
>
> [Keynes, p. 548]

If it be objected that Blake is here describing the prophetic experience without self-pity, while Shelley dramatizes himself in the "Ode"
as the unheeded prophet, the neglected poet, a reader of Blake can recall the moving lines in which the poet laments public deafness to the
trumpet of his prophecy in Enion's Song, Night the Second of "The
Four Zoas." Lacking Shelley's private income, Blake is in the pathetic
position of an exploited craftsman, but the pathos of these lines is not
economic:

> Wisdom is sold in the desolate market where none come to buy,
> And in the withered field where the farmer plows for bread in vain.
>
> [p. 318]

9. Ibid., p. 596.

The "Ode" follows English poetic conventions, and I agree with M. H. Abrams that it is "still recognizably in the tradition of prosopopoeia and allegory represented by Collins' 'Ode to Evening' " but, as Abrams himself amends, it goes beyond prosopopoeia and allegory into explicit mythopoeia and "weaves around the central image of the destroying and preserving wind, the full cycle of the myths of death and regeneration, vegetational, human, and divine." [1] My own reading of the "Ode" which follows, though intended primarily as another entry into reading "Prometheus," seeks to contribute a closer inspection than any I have found of some aspects of Shelley's finest lyric, that is, its prophetic and mythopoeic aspects.

H. C. Pancoast contributed a valuable article on the natural setting of the "Ode," basing his remarks on Shelley's own note: "This poem was conceived and chiefly written in a wood that skirts the Arno, near Florence, and on a day when that tempestuous wind, whose temperature is at once mild and animating, was collecting the vapours which pour down the autumnal rains. They began, as I foresaw, at sunset with a violent tempest of hail and rain, attended by that magnificent thunder and lightning peculiar to the Cisalpine regions." [2] Pancoast pointed out that westerly winds rule in the Cisalpine most of the year. Shelley is observing the action of the wind which marks the end of summer and the beginning of the rainy season. Another westerly wind will bring in the spring to the western coast of Italy, and it is to this wind, Favonius, favorable to life, the "azure sister" of Shelley's wind, that Lucretius, Virgil, Catullus, and Horace (followed by Chaucer and Milton) addressed their praises. None of these poets ever invoked the stern, masculine brother of Favonius, the Spirit addressed by Shelley. From the beginning then, Shelley is offering us a kind of paradox in invoking a destroyer, not a creator as poets did before him. [3]

What poems does the "Ode To The West Wind" most resemble? The Psalms of David, Pottle hints, [4] and he is right in many ways. But the "Ode" is even a more formal and ordered construct than are any of the Psalms and the quality of elemental ferocity which the "Ode" has, the sense of being in the midst of the event described, of embodying a voice directly out of significant action, is not really akin to the Psalms so much as it is to certain even more formal compositions: the tremendous battle odes of triumph like the "Song of Deborah" and "Song of Moses," or parts of the poem of Job, or certain poems by the prophets themselves. The most nearly "secular" of these poems is the "Song of Deborah," and for that reason I choose it as my analogue to

1. M. H. Abrams, *The Mirror and the Lamp: Romantic Theory and the Critical Tradition* (New York, Oxford Univ. Press, 1953), p. 296.
2. Hutchinson, ed., *Shelley*, pp. 640–1.
3. H. C. Pancoast, "Shelley's 'Ode to the West Wind,' " *MLN, 35,* 97–100.
4. Pottle, "The Case of Shelley," p. 596.

Shelley's poem. Neither poem will be shamed in the comparison, as against Shelley's best lyric I set one of the supreme Hebrew poems.

What can the two poems have in common? The "Song of Deborah" is a dramatic ode, which tells the story of a desperate situation redeemed by battle and a victory aided by God. It is a poem that celebrates courage and faith as the prime virtues of a people, and castigates those among a particular people who have failed to demonstrate such qualities. The King James version, though inaccurate, captures from the outset what is central in the original: "Praise ye the Lord for the avenging of Israel, when the people willingly offered themselves" (Judges 5:2). The emphasis throughout is on the contrast between those who willingly offer themselves to the service of God, which is here the defence of their neighbors and fellow believers, and those who do not.

The best literary criticism I know of that deals with the "Song of Deborah" is by Buber,[5] who speaks of the singing *nephesh,* the breath-soul of the poem's speaking protagonist, which rises and falls in the beautifully modulated breath-rhythm of this ode and which, in a moment of exultation in the twenty-first verse, suddenly breaks out in an injunction to itself, encouraging itself to march on and gather the strength to finish its creative recounting of the battle. For the *nephesh* has begun to falter:

19   The kings came, they fought;
      Then fought the kings of Canaan,
      In Taanach by the waters of Megiddo;
      They took no gain of money.
20   They fought from heaven,
      The stars in their courses fought against Sisera.
21   The brook Kishon swept them away,
      That ancient brook, the brook Kishon.
      O my soul, tread them down with strength.[6]

(I have quoted the American Jewish version here because King James, at this point, has the magnificent but inaccurate rendering: "O my Soul, thou hast trodden down strength!" which dissipates the central meaning of the line, referring to the strength of the enemy rather than the strength of the singer.)

Buber renders the line: "Tread forth, my soul, with strength" [7] but the line is not strictly translatable. The breath-soul of the singer, the spirit breathed into his nostrils by God, has faltered, and the singer's cry to his soul is a mixture of sorrow, exultation, and self-admonition, something very like such lines as these:

5. Martin Buber, *The Prophetic Faith* (New York, Macmillan, 1949), pp. 8–12.
6. *The Holy Scriptures* (Philadelphia, Jewish Publication Society, 1917), p. 299.
7. Buber, p. 10.

Woe is me!
The wingèd words on which my soul would pierce
Into the height of Love's rare Universe,
Are chains of lead around its flight of fire—
I pant, I sink, I tremble, I expire!   [587–91]

and these:

The solemn harmony

Paused, and the Spirit of that mighty singing
To its abyss was suddenly withdrawn;
Then, as a wild swan, when sublimely winging
Its path athwart the thunder-smoke of dawn,
Sinks headlong through the aëreal golden light
On the heavy-sounding plain,
When the bolt has pierced its brain;
As summer clouds dissolve, unburthened of their rain;
As a far taper fades with fading night,
As a brief insect dies with dying day,—
My song, its pinions, disarrayed of might,
Drooped; o'er it closed the echoes far away
Of the great voice which did its flight sustain,
As waves which lately paved his watery way
Hiss round a drowner's head in their tempestuous play.
                    [270–85]

The first of these passages closes the "Epipsychidion" (except for its brief epilogue) while the second comprises the final lines of the "Ode to Liberty." We shall see lines very much like these as the "Ode to the West Wind" moves from its fierce beginnings to its deliberately "broken" closing strophes. The difference between the singer of the "Song of Deborah" and Shelley in this situation is that the poet of "Deborah" is hymning a victory. When the spirit falters he therefore calls upon it to rally, for he is singing a victory of Yahweh and Yahweh does not flicker on and off as Shelley's deity does: he is always present when he chooses to be present, and chooses not to be present to his worshipers and prophets only with cause. Shelley's Spirit, not so attuned to the deserts of his prophets, comes and goes with a measure of abandon, so that Shelley nowhere in his poems cries out the equivalent of "O my soul, tread them down with strength." Nevertheless, that is the sum of the difference between Shelley and the Biblical poet in this matter. If the falling of the poet out of the Spirit and onto the thorns of life in the "Ode to the West Wind" is regarded by the reader as manifesting self-pity, the self-pity of our everyday life, then the reader is not yet reading the poem closely enough.

But the analogue of the "Song of Deborah" to the "Ode," including its useful contrast, is still not exhausted. When I began to sum the "Song" above, I was aware that nothing I said of it—its exaltation of courage and faith, its contrast between those who fight for God and those who will not—was altogether remote from the content of the "Ode." But form and the spirit that moulds the form are the closest parallels between the "Song" and the "Ode." Here is Buber, commenting on the structure of the former:

> The "Song of Deborah," though early, is nevertheless a song of masterful formation. The strongest of its forms is the refrain. And this form obviously is not first created because of aesthetic motives and later appointed to serve religious purposes as well but, so far as we can judge, it was born of religion. It is known that many early lyric forms spring from a magical aim to set up against the hard, unbound, demonic element, one that was bound and binding: the secret of the likeness appears as something that silences and subdues. The class of Biblical forms especially noteworthy, the repetitive forms—alliteration, assonance, paranomasia, key words, key sentences, refrain, etc.—has the particular purpose of emphasizing the most important aspect of the religious message, to point again and again at the fundamental idea or ideas of the belief round which the rest are grouped, and which the recipient of the message is requested to perceive as such with concentrated attention.[8]

Buber's prime concern here is to indicate something of the function of the very formal structure of the "Song," remarkably elaborate in that it is one of the most ancient poems in the Bible. The means of repetition in the "Song" serve an altogether religious purpose, and seem to have been engendered by the need to serve a precisely and formally religious end, rather than to have been a secular transposition. Read Buber's paragraph again with Shelley's "Ode" in mind, and you may come to realize how remarkably primitive (in this present sense) a mythmaking poem it is. The "Ode" also has a "magical aim," and its "bound and binding" structure is set up against "the hard, unbound, demonic element," the velocity and fierceness of the driving west wind ushering in autumn. And the frequently noted iconicity of the "Ode," its success in giving what W. K. Wimsatt has termed "an impression beyond statement of the very wildness, the breath and power which is the vehicle of the poem's radical metaphor," [9] is to be understood, to my

8. Ibid., p. 9.
9. W. K. Wimsatt, Jr., *The Verbal Icon* (Lexington, Univ. of Kentucky Press, 1954), pp. 115–6.

mind, in the light of Buber's "the secret of the likeness appears as something that silences and subdues." The greatness of Shelley's form in the "Ode" is akin to the greatness of the structure of the "Song of Deborah": each masters the turbulence of the events in relation to which the singer takes his stand.

With this taking of a stand in *relation* to the wind and what the wind conveys in the poem, as opposed to *experiencing* the wind and what it symbolizes, I begin my own reading of the "Ode to the West Wind." In the first chapter, following the "philosophical anthropology" of Buber and the comparative anthropology of the Frankforts, I took the basis of mythmaking to lie in the *sui generis* relation between I and Thou as contrasted to the subject-experiencing-object involved in the contact between I and It. On this basis one might show how prosopopoeia in Spenser, at his best, passed into mythopoeia, and how this mythopoeia revived in Spenser's romantic disciples. My brief analysis of Shelley's "To Night" in that chapter was a first attempt to illustrate how a specifically literary criticism might employ a knowledge of mythopoeic modes of apprehension in order to understand better a poem in which prosopopoeia no longer plays even a preliminary creative role. Where there is *no* consciousness of an inanimate world, personification can have no place, for there is no It to be worked upon, no phenomena to be experienced. A reader who seeks to investigate "To Night" or the "Ode to the West Wind" as creations embodying personifications is himself bringing to those poems *his* consciousness of the "inanimate cold world," for the poems themselves possess no such awareness of separation.

Meditating on their recognition that "primitive man simply does not know an inanimate world," the Frankforts lucidly explored some of the consequences of that recognition when they wrote:

> The world appears to primitive man neither inanimate nor empty but redundant with life; and life has individuality, in man and beast and plant, and in every phenomenon which confronts man—the thunderclap, the sudden shadow, the eerie and unknown clearing in the wood, the stone which suddenly hurts him when he stumbles while on a hunting trip. Any phenomenon may at any time face him, not as "It," but as "Thou." In this confrontation, "Thou" reveals its individuality, its qualities, its will.[1]

As Pottle has insisted, Shelley also, in much of his poetry, simply does not know an inanimate world.[2] The I of the "Ode" is the I of the primary word I-Thou, and is therefore a different I from that of the primary word I-It. Since many critics insist on this second I when they evaluate

---

1. Frankfort, *Before Philosophy*, p. 14.
2. Pottle, "The Case of Shelley," pp. 594-5: "He believed literally that there is a spirit in Nature, and that Nature therefore is never a mere 'outward world.'"

this poem, as well as other poems by Shelley, they are simply misreading when they think they are condemning. Allen Tate's famous and violent judgment on some lines of the "Adonais" is without value for just this reason; he does not realize the distinction between the different I's, the one which stands in relation to the world as a Thou and the one which can only experience the world as an It. Shelley celebrates the first I of relationship, and laments the second I of experience. When the poet falls upon the thorns of life he has fallen out of Thou into It (Blake would say out of the threefold Beulah of innocence or relationship into the twofold Generation of experience). The "white radiance of Eternity" is an expression of the timeless relationship of I and the Eternal Thou; the "dome of many-coloured glass" is another representation of the I experiencing the manifold of time-bound It's, ultimately many where the Thou is ultimately one. Tate *ex cathedra* condemns a poet's attempt to pass from experience of the world to relationship with the world, from I-It to I-Thou, as being "not poetry" but rather an expression of "the frustrated individual will trying to compete with science." [3] Tate is in fact condemning poets, and all the rest of us, to the perpetual death-in-life so accurately portrayed by Coleridge in his "Dejection, an Ode"; condemning us to behold in our life (and our poems) no more

> Than that inanimate cold world allow'd
> To the poor loveless ever-anxious crowd.

If, in poetry, it is improper or impossible to affirm that in our best moments we can, and ought to, pass from I-It to I-Thou, from the world of phenomenal objects of the scientists to the world in which Nature wears a human face, the world of Blake and Shelley, then Tate is justified in his pronouncement. But more than Spenser and the romantics, more indeed than some very good poetry will be swept away if we honor Tate's assertion. When Thou has altogether become It, irredeemably, and the poet, like the scientist, dwells in the world of experience alone, we shall suffer more of the lovelessness and overanxiousness of Coleridge's crowd than we do even at present.

I do not affirm this as my moralizing, but as part of the meaning and justification of the "Ode to the West Wind." With the "thou" of the first line of the "Ode," I come finally to the text of the poem:

I

> O wild West Wind, thou breath of Autumn's being,
> Thou, from whose unseen presence the leaves dead
> Are driven, like ghosts from an enchanter fleeing,

3. Allen Tate, *Reactionary Essays on Poetry and Ideas* (New York, Scribner's, 1936), pp. 81–5.

Yellow, and black, and pale, and hectic red,
Pestilence-stricken multitudes: O thou,
Who chariotest to their dark wintry bed

The wingèd seeds, where they lie cold and low,
Each like a corpse within its grave, until
Thine azure sister of the Spring shall blow

Her clarion o'er the dreaming earth, and fill
(Driving sweet buds like flocks to feed in air)
With living hues and odours plain and hill:

Wild Spirit, which art moving everywhere;
Destroyer and preserver; hear, oh, hear!   [1–14]

Pottle, commenting by indirection on the opening line of this stanza, wrote of Shelley: "When he invoked the breath of Autumn's being, he was not indulging in an empty figure. The breath ('spiritus') that he invoked was to him as real and as awful as the Holy Ghost was to Milton." [4] This, it seems to me, is true, and moreover helpful to the reader; its unfortunate aspect is that it can be misunderstood, since it appears to base itself on the reality and awfulness *to him,* with the reader accepting the reality on a kind of faith in Shelley's subjective consciousness. But the reality *is* in the poem, is achieved there, and no faith need be asked of the most sceptical reader, if he will but read and not preconceive.

To invoke the Spirit that is in the wind is not to invoke the wind or the autumn only. Again the helpful analogue is in the Biblical poetry; the God of Job is not the God of the whirlwind or *in* the whirlwind, but He is God of the whirlwind *also.* This also is *Thou,* but this is not Thou. The Spirit that moves in the west wind need not be a Spirit that moves in the west wind only. One aspect is revealed, but others are hinted, and the treatment, precise but extraordinarily suggestive, can accommodate the beliefs of any of us.

The first visible image in which the "unseen presence" (consistent, as always, with the "Hymn to Intellectual Beauty," whose lines, 73ff, as Hughes notes,[5] are echoed in lines 58–61 of this "Ode") is manifested is that of "an enchanter," a necromancer who also exorcises. Before him the dead leaves flee to their own destruction, while the live seeds (winged as everything with a full potentiality for more abundant life is winged in Shelley, winged *here* to escape the groundling mutable death of everything that is of the earth only) are "charioted" to the bed where they

4. "The Case of Shelley," p. 595.
5. Hughes, ed., *Shelley,* p. 218.

will sleep out the mutable winter insofar as they are natural seeds, or the great Winter of the world insofar as they are more than natural—human. "Charioted" is not a loosely chosen word, though an understanding of its use here needs a background of more of Shelley's poetry than this "Ode" and of more poetry than Shelley's alone. The chariot, the vehicular form of divinity when it is conveyed as man in many traditions, including Hinduism and Judaism-Christianity, finds serious use again in "Prometheus" and (with a severe twist) in "The Triumph of Life," as I hope to show. It is utilized here as it appears in Spenser, Milton, and Blake (in a specific tradition probably derived directly from Ezekiel) [6] to suggest the awesomeness and wrath, the divine impulsiveness of the force that drives the seeds, that moves the cycle of life, that destroys and preserves, inexorably.

The spring wind, sister of the west wind, is "azure" not simply because it will bring azure skies but also because throughout Shelley's poetry azure or blue is the color of redemption, of happiness, of a peace achieved in the spirit.

Little else in the first stanza needs specific commentary. What is destroyed by the wind is presented by varied but apt images, because the point about what is destroyed is that it *is* varied, mutable, good *and* bad. So it can be conveyed through varied but related abstractions, on either side of its concrete form: the ghosts fleeing from their exorciser are one movement to the abstract conceptual plane of the "yellow, and black, and pale, and hectic red" leaves of autumn; the "pestilence-stricken multitudes" who flee from the total cure which is their death are another. The shifting abstract images can be condemned only if *on principle* one disapproves of images which shift or are abstract; in the structure of the stanza (and the poem) the images are brilliantly exact; the poem's meaning demands them. What is destroyed is impermanent, and the abstract images are those of sickness and of unreal survival, death-in-life and life-in-death, both best left to the unambiguous death-giving of the autumn wind of destruction.

With the "wingèd seeds" and "azure" spring wind we are in the second half of the stanza (the structure is perfectly balanced in its symmetry, the first movement dedicated to destruction, the second to preservation, the two aspects being blended in the concluding couplet). The seeds lie "like a corpse," but they are only "like"; they are alive. Fogle rightly suggests that a submerged image of human, of quasi-Christian resurrection is to be found here.[7] The spring wind (feminine complement to masculine west wind, suggestive therefore of grace and inter-

6. See the discussion of the chariot of Life in my chapter on "The Triumph of Life."
7. Fogle, *Imagery*, p. 225. The clarion is the clarion of judgment, but one might also point out its appropriateness to a shepherdess, for that is what the "azure sister of the Spring" is visualized as here.

cession) "shall blow / Her clarion o'er the dreaming earth" ("dreaming," not dead but asleep), ending the temporal, annual winter, but also, as Fogle notes, suggesting an end to the eternal Winter, which shall dissolve at the clarion blowing for the last judgment. The image following, as Fogle again notes, is religious-pastoral, suggesting the ingathering of the flocks:

> and fill
> (Driving sweet buds like flocks to feed in air)
> With living hues and odours plain and hill . . .

The parentheses, suggesting an undersong, an aside, are themselves here a successful poetic device. The "hues and odours" are to be fully "living" when "plain and hill" cease to be unpastured. The sweet buds driven over the landscape prophesy a finally redeemed nature which will accompany the last change of season. The sea pastoral of the beautiful second scene of Act III of "Prometheus," when "the unpastured sea hungering for calm" shall be fed, is to be read in conjunction with this sudden moment of pastoral vision.

The final couplet binds the close form of the first stanza together, in that the two aspects of the wind are coupled here. The emphasis is on immediacy, for the spirit is "moving everywhere"; the implied admonition is the prophetic call to the individual to turn *now*. Especially to be noticed at this stage in the reading is the pattern that has now been established in which the second and third stanzas follow the first exactly, the scheme of repetition bearing out the remarks quoted from Buber on the function of repetition as a binding and pointing device in prophetic poetry. Each of the first three stanzas ends by calling upon the frequently reiterated Thou of the wind to hear the prayer of the I of the poet. The action of the wind is described, with great literal exactitude, in all its three spheres of operation: earth, sky, and water. But the description in each case—with all that is symbolized in the description (and it is impossible in a commentary to exhaust all that is symbolized) —is secondary to the direct address to the wind which comes before and after it. The structure of each of the first three stanzas serves thus to emphasize what is central in the poem: the poet's prayer to enter into I-Thou relationship with the Spirit that is in the wind also. Three times in each of these three stanzas—at beginning, middle, and end—there is a repetition, a return to Thou (or its surrogate, "thy congregated might," and "thy voice"). When we come to the fourth stanza and the beginning of the psalm, the poet's prayer, we have been told what *kind* of prayer it is. Whatever its specific content, and what that content is I in no way mean to deprecate by this qualification, we know already a final significance of that prayer. What is entreated is to be a Thou to the Spirit's I, not an It to its other and dehumanizing I.

II

Thou on whose stream, mid the steep sky's commotion,
Loose clouds like earth's decaying leaves are shed,
Shook from the tangled boughs of Heaven and Ocean,

Angels of rain and lightning: there are spread
On the blue surface of thine aëry surge,
Like the bright hair uplifted from the head

Of some fierce Maenad, even from the dim verge
Of the horizon to the zenith's height,
The locks of the approaching storm. Thou dirge

Of the dying year, to which this closing night
Will be the dome of a vast sepulchre,
Vaulted with all thy congregated might

Of vapours, from whose solid atmosphere
Black rain, and fire, and hail will burst: oh, hear!   [15–28]

Leavis has commented on the opening lines of this stanza and his commentary has been influential:

> The sweeping movement of the verse, with the accompanying
> plangency, is so potent that, as many can testify, it is possible to have
> been for years familiar with the Ode—to know it by heart—without
> asking the obvious questions. In what respects are the "loose
> clouds" like "decaying leaves"? The correspondence is certainly
> not in shape, colour or way of moving. It is only the vague general
> sense of windy tumult that associates the clouds and the leaves; and,
> accordingly, the appropriateness of the metaphor "stream" in the
> first line is not that it suggests a surface on which, like leaves, the
> clouds might be "shed," but that it contributes to the general
> "streaming" effect in which the inappropriateness of "shed" passes
> unnoticed.[8]

Fogle replies:

> To Mr. Leavis's objections to the comparison of "loose clouds" with
> "decaying leaves" one can only assert that there are quite adequate
> resemblances between them. The clouds and leaves are carried in
> precisely the same fashion by the power of the wind. Furthermore,
> the resemblance holds for shape and color as well as movement.
> Swift-flying clouds may present the same angularities as leaves, and

8. Leavis, *Revaluation*, pp. 204–5 passim.

leaves flying horizontally through a gray sky will take the hue of their surroundings. . . . Mr. Leavis appears to be isolating some archetypal clouds and leaf from their relationships with the wind and with the composition of the scene.[9]

With Fogle's last sentence I agree, but the earlier sentences are unnecessary. Leavis' close reading is in fact a simple misreading, which Fogle ought to have pointed out (though in effect he has indicated it in that *he* reads correctly here). Shelley does *not* necessarily compare clouds and leaves, but he *does* compare the process of shedding. Just as down below (in the first stanza) the wind shakes some leaves loose from the boughs of the trees and then carries the loose leaves along, so up above (second stanza) the wind carries along the lower clouds, as opposed to the larger clouds which seem to be stationary and therefore are not to be regarded as loose (see Pottle's remarks, as quoted below). Leavis stands convicted of being so very anxious to find fault (the sole function he allows himself in all of his essay on Shelley) that he will not examine the possibility that the line in question may be read "Loose clouds are shed like [i.e. as] earth's decaying leaves are shed" rather than "Loose clouds, which are like earth's decaying leaves, are shed," even though the word order and punctuation of "Loose clouds like earth's decaying leaves are shed" may admit of either reading. It is true that the first reading, with expressed verb, produces a construction now considered slovenly, but such construction can be found in all periods of the language. Nevertheless, Leavis is too angry (I must assume) to notice this, but instead goes on to evidence his astonishing inability to read a simple figure: "What again, are those 'tangled boughs of Heaven and Ocean'? They stand for nothing that Shelley could have pointed to in the scene before him; the 'boughs,' it is plain, have grown out of the 'leaves' in the previous line, and we are not to ask what the tree is." [1] So sure of himself does Leavis sound here that René Wellek (probably ironically) offered to pacify him by suggesting that an allusion "to the old mystical conception of the two trees of Heaven and Earth intertwining" might be involved in Shelley's figure.[2] Leavis professed himself not contented with this gift of the esoteric Sephirotic Tree [3] (which does of course occur in Blake's poetry, but not, I think, here or elsewhere in Shelley's), and undoubtedly still considers Shelley's figure indefensible.[4] Both Fogle and Pottle have tried to set Leavis right, however, and I have nothing

9. Fogle, p. 265.
1. Leavis, pp. 204-5 passim.
2. René Wellek, "Literary Criticism and Philosophy," *Scrutiny*, 5 (March 1937), 375-83, esp. 380.
3. F. R. Leavis, "Literary Criticism and Philosophy: A Reply," *Scrutiny*, 6 (June 1937), 68.
4. Leavis has reprinted his reply to Wellek, with his repeated stricture on Shelley's figure, in *The Common Pursuit*, London, 1952.

to add to their accurate and just explanations of Shelley's figure. Fogle is rather less detailed and precise than Pottle, but still very much to the point when he writes: "It is quite true—in fact self-evident—that there are no 'boughs' in the sky, no boughs in the sea. But the clouds derive from these 'tangled boughs'—tangled because Heaven and Ocean intermingle, boughs because the clouds derive from the sky and sea in just such an organic process as causes the leaves to grow on the tree." [5] Pottle's analysis of Shelley's figure is valuable also for its general remarks on the scene in which the first two stanzas of the poem are set:

> The first stanza of the poem presents the action of the wind on the surface of the earth. The poet is watching a forest in autumn. Most of the leaves are still on the boughs, but the wind is shaking some loose and driving them away. The dead leaves are streaming along beneath a canopy of tangled boughs still covered, or partly covered, with leaves. The second stanza presents the action of the wind in the sky. The poet's eye goes up, and he sees there something very like the scene in the forest. High up is a canopy of solid, relatively stationary clouds; below are smaller, "loose" clouds driven swiftly along by the wind. Shelley calls the upper stationary cloud-formations the boughs of Heaven and Ocean because it consists of condensed water-vapor drawn up from the ocean by the heat of the sun.[6]

Leavis also challenges what he calls the "stream" metaphor ("that 'blue surface' must be the concave of the sky, an oddly smooth surface for a 'surge'—if we consider a moment") [7] but this challenge enters the category of the fantastic, and no reply to it is possible, except that I would claim that no poetic figure will stand pressing past a certain point. Clearly in this last instance Leavis is persecuting, not criticizing; he is finding objectionable what no other reader would find troublesome, unless such a reader, like Leavis, had started with a good morning's hate of Shelley.

To finish with Leavis on the "Ode," here he is objecting to yet another figure:

> Then again, in what ways does the approach of a storm ("loose clouds like earth's decaying leaves," "like ghosts from an enchanter fleeing") suggest streaming hair? The appropriateness of the Maenad, clearly, lies in the pervasive suggestions of frenzied onset, and we are not to ask whether her bright hair is to be seen as streaming out in front of her (as, there is no need to assure ourselves, it might be doing if she were running before a still swifter gale: in

5. Fogle, *Imagery*, p. 266.
6. "The Case of Shelley," p. 606.
7. Leavis, *Revaluation*, p. 207.

the kind of reading that got so far as proposing to itself this particular reassurance no general satisfaction could be exacted from
Shelley's imagery).[8]

"The approach of a storm" does not "suggest streaming hair," but who
except Leavis puts it in just that way? Shelley's figure is "the locks of
the approaching storm" and I myself (who has not?) on a few occasions
when I have found myself in such a physical position as to have been
able to see "even from the dim verge / of the horizon to the zenith's
height" have observed cloud formations which could suggest Shelley's
figure and which have in fact recalled it to me. As for the "appropriateness" of the Maenad, sarcastically questioned by Leavis: a Maenad's
onset is not just "frenzied," but may well have an object, as Orpheus
discovered and as other myths of men victimized by Bassarids may recall. The emphasis in this stanza is on the wind as destroyer, not preserver, and the "divinely" engendered and dangerous intoxication of a
Maenad is a powerfully appropriate figure to embody the "divinely" ordained destructiveness of the storm that this west wind prophesies, a
storm which tears down kingdoms and human lives as well as trees
and leaves. Leavis' pleasantry about hair streaming out in front of or
behind the Maenad—insofar as it deserves rejoinder—is answered by
Shelley's verb "uplifted."

Most of the figures in the "Ode's" second stanza have already been
discussed, or adequate accounts of them quoted. Of the others, I might
note that "Angels of rain and lightning" in line 18 is apt in that "Angels"
is to be read as having its root meaning of "messengers." This also sustains Pottle's reading of "the tangled boughs of Heaven and Ocean" in
line 17 as being the main cloudfront, messenger of the coming storm, an
angel which precedes the divine arrival in the form of the storm. The
last figures of the stanza ("dirge" and "dome") are successful evoca-
tions of an awe bordering on terror. The sound of the wind as it affects
the forest is dirgelike, commemorating the death of the year. The year
and all that lived with it are sepulchered by the blackening dome of the
storm-stricken sky, the associations being manifold but here, I think,
especially political:

> Vaulted with all thy congregated might
> Of vapours, from whose solid atmosphere
> Black rain, and fire, and hail will burst . . .

Something of the pent-up fierceness that is precipitated out in popular
rebellions is to be felt in that.

The next stanza completes the triad of identical structures which lead
up to the "Ode's" climax (fourth stanza) and resolution (last). But

8. Ibid., p. 208.

the emphasis is now changed, for here in stanza III all that is disturbed
and destroyed is at peace and is beautiful. This stanza is in effect a cry
that Nature makes against Grace. The equivalent is in Spenser's great
lament for all the natural beauty that is prey to mutabilitie. Spenser believes that Grace must correct Nature, but he is reluctant to see so
much abolished that he knows must be abolished. Even though his Dame
Nature can offer assurance that all things

> being rightly wayd
> They are not changed from their first estate;
> But by their change their being doe dilate:
> And turning to themselues at length againe,
> Doe worke their owne perfection so by fate:
> Then ouer them Change doth not rule and raigne;
> But they raigne ouer change, and doe their states maintaine.[9]

nevertheless Spenser cries out for the Nature that is being perpetually
wounded by this harsh and indirect order of Grace. And in the earlier
speech of the Titaness Mutability, we can hear Spenser's lament for the
things of earth:

> For, all that from her springs, and is ybredde,
> How-euer fayre it flourish for a time,
> Yet see we soone decay . . .[1]

and for those of water, air and even of fire, and most of all, for man, insofar as he is of the order of Nature.

Even so, in this third stanza of the "Ode" what we are given is the
plangency of regret. The calm of the Mediterranean idealizes the best
of the past, as Fogle puts it, but that calm must be shattered:

III

> Thou who didst waken from his summer dreams
> The blue Mediterranean, where he lay,
> Lulled by the coil of his crystàlline streams,
>
> Beside a pumice isle in Baiae's bay,
> And saw in sleep old palaces and towers
> Quivering within the wave's intenser day,
>
> All overgrown with azure moss and flowers
> So sweet, the sense faints picturing them! Thou
> For whose path the Atlantic's level powers

9. J. C. Smith, ed., *Faerie Queene* (2 vols. Oxford, 1909), *2*, Bk. 7, Canto VII, stanza
LVIII, ll. 3–9.
1. Ibid., stanza XVIII, ll. 1–3ff.

> Cleave themselves into chasms, while far below
> The sea-blooms and the oozy woods which wear
> The sapless foliage of the ocean, know
>
> Thy voice, and suddenly grow gray with fear
> And tremble and despoil themselves: oh, hear! [29–42]

Edward Dowden, White, Hughes, and Fogle [2] have all commented on the biographical experience which underlies the first eight lines of this stanza. Pancoast has commented on the shift to the North Atlantic west wind in the final six lines of the stanza. [3] Shelley himself in his note to the poem explained the natural phenomenon involved in those closing lines. [4] I have nothing to add to this biographical and descriptive information, which seems to me to be complete. Criticism of this stanza can be brief, and must be largely devoted to praise. I have noted already that the color blue was Shelley's favorite, and that to him it represented an Elysian state, so much so that he came to employ it to mean clear, or delicate, or light, with no reference to color; to use it of sound to mean clear or unbroken; even to mean simply pleasant or joyous. The "azure moss and flowers" in line 35, like "thine azure sister of the spring" in line 9 and like the use of "azure" in certain lines of "Prometheus," do not mean literally blue in color, but something much closer to a clearness of texture, delicacy of form, lightness of substance, all associated with a state of joyousness. [5] I instance all this because it may help to explain what the "blue Mediterranean" means to Shelley. The outward form that the sea presents to the poet, as he recalls it in vision, betokens to him a graciousness and peace that is Elysian and that can be found even in this life at its best moments. All this is surrendered up to the wind and the storm it prophesies. The fierce Spirit must destroy much that is valuable, in society as in nature, as it moves where it lists. The Grace that ideally ought only to correct has a tendency to abolish, and Shelley does not celebrate in this stanza, in consequence. But so skilfully is beauty evoked in this stanza, so subdued and mellowed have the emblems which were once despotical ("old palaces and towers") become that regret for what has passed and is passing is what is primarily expressed, though by a triumph of obliqueness. The idealizing that can come with time ("the wave's intenser day"), the odors sweet beyond sense, the Byzantine unreality of the ocean growth ("sapless foliage") are all valued highly in this stanza, yet all swept away, disturbed, made

2. Edward Dowden, *The Life of Percy Bysshe Shelley* (2 vols. London, 1886), *2*, 215; N. I. White, *Shelley* (2 vols. New York, Knopf, 1947), *2*, 586, n. 44; Hughes, ed., *Shelley*, p. 218; Fogle, *Imagery*, p. 223.
3. "Shelley's 'Ode to the West Wind,'" *MLN, 35*, 100.
4. Hutchinson, ed., *Shelley*, p. 641.
5. See "azure," in Ellis, *A Lexical Concordance to Shelley*, p. 33.

to "tremble and despoil themselves." No forcing of these figures is involved in seeing, however obliquely, an expression in them of that state of paradoxical truth, unreal and yet eternal beauty, that is more directly presented in the "Byzantium" poems of Yeats, in certain odes of Keats (especially, of course, the "Urn" and the "Nightingale"), and in Blake's state of Beulah. The best world that poems can make goes down before this wind of destruction also.

With leaf, cloud, and wave established in the poem, in themselves and in relation to the wind, the unifying and climactic fourth stanza becomes possible. We move from the natural to the human order, and the wind must confront a Thou for the first time. The deep tragedy, and it can be demonstrated to be that, of this fourth stanza is to be found in the despairing prayer of a Thou to be treated as an It. Unless we understand the total contrast between this hopeless prayer and the resolving prayer of the last stanza, then we will fail completely to understand the whole of the "Ode." Too many readers fail to comprehend that the fourth and fifth stanzas are deliberate contrasts, with the result that they either isolate the fourth stanza from the poem or, still worse, carry it over to the fifth, and fail to see how either the fourth *or* fifth stanza is related to the first three.

The situation of the poet as the poem's protagonist (and the protagonist of this poem *must* be a poet) at the close of the first three stanzas is that he confronts a choice. He can either surrender himself to the wind as an object for it to experience, as the leaf, cloud, and wave are objects for it, or else he can attempt to call upon the wind to take up a stand in relation to him, to enter into him, and he into the wind. This last has nothing to do with any kind of mystical union, nor is there any vagueness about it as an aspiration. The poet here is confronted by the categories of religious choice: the way of despair, which is a submission to the natural process, a dwindling out of the myth down to object status, a denial of poetry; or another way (which on the natural level is also, of course, a way of despair, but which at least aspires toward hope), a renewal of myth, an affirmation of images and image-making power, a refusal to live with It alone, in relation to the wind and whatever is behind the wind. In the fourth stanza, most simply, the poet counts the human cost, the pervasive feeling that he is only an It to the I of the wind. That throughout he still addresses the wind directly, still acknowledges Thou, is what makes this stanza so Jobean in quality. This is not *self-pity*; perhaps indeed no pity is involved but only recognition of an aspect of the human situation:

IV

> If I were a dead leaf thou mightest bear;
> If I were a swift cloud to fly with thee;
> A wave to pant beneath thy power, and share

> The impulse of thy strength, only less free
> Than thou, O uncontrollable! If even
> I were as in my boyhood, and could be
>
> The comrade of thy wanderings over Heaven,
> As then, when to outstrip thy skiey speed
> Scarce seemed a vision; I would ne'er have striven
>
> As thus with thee in prayer in my sore need.
> Oh, lift me as a wave, a leaf, a cloud!
> I fall upon the thorns of life! I bleed!
>
> A heavy weight of hours has chained and bowed
> One too like thee: tameless, and swift, and proud.   [43–56]

The conditional mood of the opening lines (down to 51) bears a complex meaning. If I were purely an object of nature borne along by you in the mutable cycle of decay, death, rebirth; but never cognizant that your impulse waned in me as well as waxed; only less free than you yourself, because fully subject to your uncontrollable impulse, whether vital or death bringing; in short, were I less than human, then I would not have to wrestle with you now in this prayerful song. Or even if I still possessed the imaginative powers of my boyhood, if I were more than human—as I seemed to be then, when I stood in relation to you, with as much freedom and strength of impulse as you had—then also I would not be uttering this prayer now.

Yet this first prayer, "Oh, lift me as a wave, a leaf, a cloud!" neglects the second "if" for the despairing first. Lift me, even though it be to my own destruction; for my song falters, I am no longer caught up in your Spirit, "I fall upon the thorns of life! I bleed!" (By now it ought to be evident that the thorns of life have nothing to do with Lord Chancellors, quarterly reviewers, despotic fathers, etc.) The concluding couplet, with its ironic "too like thee," embodies the depth of the protagonist's alienation from the Spirit in the wind.

The Wordsworthian analogue is useful here (though not perhaps so much as in the "Hymn to Intellectual Beauty" or, as will be examined later, in "The Triumph of Life"). The loss of vision, of the child's imaginative powers is offset in the "Immortality" ode by the gain in human sympathy, so that what the song loses in vividness, in its relational closeness to the Thou of Nature, is compensated for in the accession of "sober colouring." Even so, in this "Ode," the song that breaks in the fourth stanza has lost in tamelessness, swiftness, pride, when it rises again in the final stanza, but it has gained "a deep, autumnal tone, / Sweet though in sadness."

More directly analogous to the fourth stanza are the laments of Job, who prays for his own natural destruction, asking either to be swept away by the same "great wind from across the wilderness" which slew his children, or else to be again as he was "in the days of my youth . . . when the Almighty was yet with me." Here also is the equivalent of those "thorns of life":

> He hath cast me into the mire,
> And I am become like dust and ashes.
> I cry unto Thee, and Thou dost not answer me;
> I stand up, and Thou lookest at me . . .
> Thou liftest me up to the wind,
>   Thou causest me to ride upon it;
> And Thou dissolvest my substance.[6]

Yet the voice at length speaks out of the wind to Job, and reconciles him in awe. No such voice speaks out in the "Ode's" last stanza, which ends, suitably, in question. What rises in the final stanza is the prayer of a different kind of faith, one which neither *trusts in,* as Job does, nor *believes that,* as Christians do, but which holds to the humanizing possibility of mythmaking and affirms again the value of the relationship which can create poems:

> V
>
> Make me thy lyre, even as the forest is:
> What if my leaves are falling like its own!
> The tumult of thy mighty harmonies
>
> Will take from both a deep, autumnal tone,
> Sweet though in sadness. Be thou, Spirit fierce,
> My spirit! Be thou me, impetuous one!
>
> Drive my dead thoughts over the universe
> Like withered leaves to quicken a new birth!
> And, by the incantation of this verse,
>
> Scatter, as from an unextinguished hearth
> Ashes and sparks, my words among mankind!
> Be through my lips to unawakened earth
>
> The trumpet of a prophecy! O, Wind,
> If Winter comes, can Spring be far behind?   [57–70]

"One too like thee," at the close of the previous stanza, meant also one like thee in being a portent of the coming storm. From that link, the

6. *The Holy Scriptures,* p. 951; 30:19–21, 22–3.

prayer of the I-Thou is able to replace that of the I-It. Buber writes that "Only one *Thou* never ceases by its nature to be *Thou* for us. He who knows God knows also very well remoteness from God, and the anguish of barrenness in the tormented heart; but he does not know the absence of God: it is we only who are not always there." [7] The Thou of the wind does not cease to be Thou for Shelley in the fourth stanza, but the Thou of Shelley is not there. The return of the poet's Thou, to confront the wind's I, is the subject of this final stanza, carried in the figure of the making of poetry itself.

In the opening lines, the exultant self-surrender of "What if my leaves are falling like its own!" carries us back to the image with which the "Ode" opens, and connects to the "dead thoughts" to be driven "like withered leaves" to quicken rebirth. The difference of the prayer is in "my dead thoughts . . . Like . . . leaves" as opposed to the former prayers "lift me as . . . a leaf." The thoughts are dead only in that they have also become It, they are poems already written.[8] But the I of the poet is not dead, nor is it to be submerged in the wind, as Fogle believes.[9] Let your Spirit be my spirit is the prayer; that is, stand in relation Thou to I, and I to Thou, so that your impetuosity, your energy and life may also be mine, and that your message may be my message. The need here is *mutual;* poet needs Spirit but Spirit as desperately needs poet, as the prophet needs God but God also the prophet. No "mystical" merging into a larger Identity but mutual confrontation of two realities is what is involved here.

The aeolian harp of the forest must combine with the "mighty harmonies" of the wind-Spirit for the "deep autumnal tone" to be produced.

7. Buber, *I and Thou*, p. 99.
8. I take the liberty here of inserting a footnote by Pottle, which supplements my own reading of "dead thoughts":

There is a nice point here which I have seen brought out only by Arthur Wormhoudt, *The Explicator, 6* (Oct. 1947), 2. By the way there is also at this reference a note on "Be thou me" by R. H. Fogle. Both Wormhoudt and Fogle are answering a query by Douglass S. Mead in *Explicator, 5* (May 1947), Q 20. Readers generally equate Shelley's dead thoughts with *both* the leaves and the seeds of stanza I. (Cf. the new—1950 and later—Cleanth Brooks and Robert Penn Warren, *Understanding Poetry* (New York, Holt, 1953), p. 100: "In section five, the poet refers to 'my dead thoughts.' Are they really dead, or does he mean that they are only apparently dead like the 'ashes and sparks' of line 67?") Wormhoudt says, "For now his dead thoughts are not merely to be blown about by the wind, but, like last year's dead leaves, are to be mulch for next Spring's snowdrops." (There is a certain amount of humility in the comparison!) I should have preferred "compost" to "mulch," but I have no doubt that is precisely what Shelley means by "to quicken a new birth." His thoughts (some of them, at least) are really and truly dead, but they may help other people's live ideas to grow. "Thoughts" correspond to leaves, "words" to seeds. Or, if this is too precise, he realizes that only part of his mental labors have the germ of life in them. Still, even the dead ones may be useful in a way.

9. Fogle, *Imagery*, p. 226.

Even so with the poet and the *nephesh*, the breath-soul which is in the wind; each component needs the other in order that "the trumpet of a prophecy" may be sounded, to precede that "clarion" which the spring wind shall blow. Recall "Mont Blanc," II, and its myth of how poetry is created:

> Dizzy Ravine! and when I gaze on thee
> I seem as in a trance sublime and strange
> To muse on my own separate fantasy,
> My own, my human mind, which passively
> Now renders and receives fast influencings,
> Holding an unremitting interchange
> With the clear universe of things around;
> One legion of wild thoughts, whose wandering wings
> Now float above thy darkness, and now rest
> Where that or thou art no unbidden guest,
> In the still cave of the witch Poesy,
> Seeking among the shadows that pass by
> Ghosts of all things that are, some shade of thee,
> Some phantom, some faint image; till the breast
> From which they fled recalls them, thou art there!   [34–48]

I have ventured already on a reading of these difficult lines and will not recapitulate here, except to point out again why I began this study of Shelley with the 1816 Hymns and how the "Ode" to the West Wind reiterates the mythopoeic theme first developed by Shelley in these hymns.

The Thou of "Mont Blanc" is the ravine of Arve (until in the final section Thou expands to Mont Blanc itself); the Thou of the "Hymn to Intellectual Beauty" is the Spirit of Beauty; the Thou here in this "Ode" is the west wind. These are three different Thou's, and it would be a mistake not to discriminate among them; nevertheless, they are all glimpses through to the Eternal Thou which comprehends them. What ties together the three Thou's (and the three poems which directly address them) is that they manifest, in their themes and structures (the strength of all three poems is due to the near identity of their themes and structures), the common element of the dichotomy of the two primary words, I-It and I-Thou, the I of experience and the I of relationship. The passing from the first primary word to the second is what I have designated as the primal act of mythopoeia, and it is no accident (I believe) that the three poems under discussion, which are mythopoeic in technique and plot, should have mythopoeia, the writing of poetry, as their subject. In lines 34–48 of "Mont Blanc," quoted above, poetry is engendered by the relationship between the I of the poet and the Thou of the ravine, between an individual and a universal Mind. In the "Hymn," poetry is seen to depend on the ability of the poet to sustain an I-Thou relationship with the evanescent Spirit of Beauty, which continually moves from object to object, creating Thou's out of It's and then abandoning them to become It's again; which visits the poet, and then abandons him again. When he is visited by the Spirit, the poet is no longer an object of the Spirit's experience, but the Spirit and he confront one another in mutual relation. When the Spirit departs the poem departs also, and the poet is left desolate. Now, in this "Ode to the West Wind" the same mythopoeic pattern establishes itself. When the poet is made the wind's lyre, then he and the wind both "render and receive fast influencings," and out of that mutual relationship the poem, which is a prophecy, can be created. In the end, Shelley has written his own best commentary in the *Defence:* "Man is an instrument over which a series of external and internal impressions are driven, like the alternations of an ever-changing wind over an Aeolian lyre, which move it by their motion to ever-changing melody. But there is a principle within the human being, and perhaps within all sentient beings, which acts otherwise than in the lyre, and produces not melody alone, but harmony, by an internal adjustment of the sounds or motions thus excited to the impressions which excite them." [1]

That "principle within the human being, and perhaps within all sentient beings," is what I have taken in these chapters to be the mythopoeic principle. In turn I judge that to be the will of a human or any sentient being to stand in relation to all that is sentient and to what is the ground of all that is sentient, as an I confronting a Thou rather than an I experiencing an It. And conversely, since relation is mutual, that being will himself be confronted as a Thou and not as an It.

The "unextinguished hearth" of line 66 of the "Ode," to finish my reading, is again best glossed by Shelley in the *Defence,* when he writes, in similar vein, that "the mind in creation is as a fading coal, which some invisible influence, like an inconstant wind, awakens to transitory brightness; this power arises from within, like the colour of a flower which fades and changes as it is developed . . ." "The Ode to the West Wind" is such a fading coal, perhaps, but never altogether faded, and the hearth is never quite extinguished. When a poem is written a Thou passes over to an It, and all we get, possibly, is what Shelley terms "a feeble shadow of the original conceptions of the poet." [2] In a relevant passage Buber writes: "But the revelation does not pour itself into the world through him who receives it as through a funnel; it comes to him and seizes his whole elemental being in all its particular nature, and fuses

1. Shawcross, ed., *Shelley's Criticism,* p. 121.
2. Ibid., p. 153.

with it. The man, too, who is the 'mouth' of the revelation, is indeed this, not a speaking-tube or any kind of instrument, but an organ, which sounds according to its own laws; and to sound means to *modify*." [3]

So far, this may be taken as commentary on Shelley's "Be through *my lips* to unawakened earth / The trumpet of a prophecy" and as a partial correction to Fogle's emphasis on Shelley's being "the trumpet of a prophecy *not his own*." [4] Paralleling Shelley's other statement, quoted from the *Defence,* is this by Buber:

> But the destiny of the relational event is here set forth in the most powerful way. The stronger the response the more strongly does it bind up the *Thou* and banish it to be an object. Only silence before the *Thou*—silence of all tongues, silent patience in the undivided word that precedes the formed and vocal response—leaves the *Thou* free, and permits man to take his stand with it in the reserve where the spirit is not manifest, but is. Every response binds up the *Thou* in the world of *It*.[5]

"Every response binds up the *Thou* in the world of *It*"—this comes closer, I think, to catching the meaning of Shelley's passage on "the mind in creation is as a fading coal . . . ," than any of the explicit commentaries on that passage. Even Abrams, the latest and one of the best commentators on this, seems to me to obscure what Shelley is saying when he classifies Shelley's "theory" here into a three-part hypothesis: inspiration as the divine afflatus; imagination as "the blissful contemplation of the sempiternal Forms"; inspiration naturalistic, as "an empirical phenomenon of the mind itself." [6] Judged in the context of mythopoeia (its principles and the necessary defeat of those principles), what seems to be a welter of conflicting philosophical and psychological notions may be seen to emerge into a clearer and more consistent outline. And if this holds for Shelley's critical theory, then we may find it still more useful in a reading of the poems themselves.

3. Buber, *I and Thou,* p. 117.
4. Fogle, p. 226. Notice the link between the "trumpet" here in line 69 and the "clarion" of line 10, a link which helps establish the formal unity of the poem.
5. Buber, *I and Thou,* p. 39.
6. Abrams, *The Mirror and the Lamp,* p. 192.

5

"Prometheus Unbound"

I

THE single scene which constitutes the first act of "Prometheus Unbound" is set in "A Ravine of Icy Rocks in the Indian Caucasus." Shelley is following Aeschylus, in the opening words of κράτος: Σκύθην ἐς οιμον, the tract of Scythia. Prometheus is bound on a mountain in Scythia, and this mountain is in the Caucasus range, thought by the contemporaries of Aeschylus to be the most extensive in the world (Aeschylus follows accepted tradition in thus setting the scene for the Titan's ordeal). But the "Ravine of Icy Rocks" is Shelley's visualization, and should recall to us the 1816 vision of the ravine of Arve in "Mont Blanc." The confrontation of an enigmatical, indifferent, ultimate Thou in the ravine of Arve was (to borrow Pottle's phrasing) the mythopoeic report of the head (complemented by a mythopoeic report of the heart as confronting an even more enigmatical, but less indifferent, though transitory, ultimate *Thou* in the grace of Intellectual Beauty in the 1816 "Hymn") concerning the possibility of natural, Wordsworthian religion. The report (as I tried to demonstrate in my reading of "Mont Blanc") was decisive and negative: there is no natural religion. Nature, not confronted in mythopoeic relation, is an *It,* indifferent to us, something we experience. When we experience it at its worst, Shelley is likely to embody this event in images of cold and ice. In my discussion of "Mont Blanc" I have presented Fogle's analysis of Shelley's use of these images, and cite it again here as commentary on Shelley's scene setting. As Fogle points out, "the background of the fatal drama of *Alastor* is the 'icy caves' of the Caucasus (line 143), and the 'icy summits' of its 'ethereal cliffs' (lines 351–2)." Here, at the opening of "Prometheus," the icy caves and summits of the Caucasus are evoked again as background, not for a poet's death but for an archetypal man's agony *unto* death. But, once again, I am forced to amend Fogle's dualistic view as he states that "in a sense the action of *Prometheus Unbound* is a symbolic struggle between Cold, representing Evil, Reaction, and Death; and Warmth, the emblem of Good, Life, and Liberation." [1] This dualism is more extremely stated by Fogle than it is by Shelley. Warmth does not over-

1. Fogle, *Imagery,* pp. 74, 76.

come Cold in "Prometheus" so much as imagination overcomes selfhood, relationship overcomes experience, forgiveness and self-forgiveness overcome hatred and remorse. The icy Caucasus with its rocky ravine is not just Jupiter's torture chamber for recalcitrant Titans. Rather is it, like the icy ravine of Arve in "Mont Blanc," an emblem of the supreme indifference of the natural world to man; a Power he cannot direct or tap or even learn from, unless he meets it in relationship, perceives it as a Thou; human, not natural. The individual mind of the bound Prometheus, alienated from the indifferent "universal mind" (probably a misleading phrase here, though a space saver) of the icy ravine, experiences torment in a world dominated by experience, by Itness, in this opening scene.

The scene setting, at least, is masterly. The Titan is bound to the precipice; the Oceanides, Panthea and Ione, are seated at his feet. The time is night, but "during the Scene, morning slowly breaks." The real unbinding of Prometheus, being a matter for himself to settle, is accomplished by the close of the first act and by then morning has broken. There are three remaining acts, just as there are five books and a fragment besides after *The First Booke of the Faerie Queene* has reached conclusion. Book I of *The Faerie Queene,* like Act I of "Prometheus," culminates in apocalypse, in a revelation which liberates completely. Book I is a complete visionary epic in miniature, just as Act I of "Prometheus" is a complete visionary drama in miniature. They can be read as organic wholes, as poems which begin, work themselves out, and end so finally as to be anagoges of human finality, of religious apocalypse. The Knight of the Red Crosse recovers Una's kingdom, Eden, once a paradisal garden and now the fallen earth, after slaying the Dragon who expelled Una's parents from their kingdom. This is completion—the lower paradise is recovered and Cleopolis, the lower heavenly city, capital of the Faerie Queene, is glimpsed in the distance by Red Crosse. The remaining books of *The Faerie Queene* are magnificent, and no one (until quite recently, anyway) would wish to lose them, but Book I stands without them. Their business is not to advance the action of Book I, which cannot by its nature be taken further, but rather to explore aspects of Faerie Land with which Book I is not concerned. The outline of salvation has been sketched; the complexity of the fallen state of Faerie, its possibilities for redemption, the consequences that fall and potential redemption have had and will have among the inhabitants of Faerie: these are the matter of the remaining books of *The Faerie Queene.* "Prometheus Unbound" is exactly analogous (and not, I think, by accident). Prometheus wills himself back into relationship in Act I; everything else, in the three remaining acts, ensues from this. Because of this Asia journeys down to Demogorgon, and Demogorgon comes up to unseat Jupiter and drag him down. Critics who complain that everything in the drama is over at the conclusion of the first act are in the right, but not to complain. Action (what action there is in a drama more internal in the minds of its protagonists than either Aeschylus' *Prometheus* or Milton's "Samson Agonistes") is over, or at least determined as Act I closes. But this is not defect, any more than it is in *The Faerie Queene*. The structure itself is visionary here, as is inevitable in religious epic or drama which passes beyond a didactic level. First the poles of fall and redemption must be spoken. The rest (not just Act IV) is in effect a Song of Triumph.

As Prometheus sees the morning slowly break, so does Asia, who has been waiting alone in a "Vale in the Indian Caucasus" throughout the long night. As the "Ode to the West Wind" concerns itself with the beginning of autumn, so "Prometheus" deals with the very moment at which spring begins. The whole of the "Prometheus" is a giant ode to the spring, but just as the west wind of autumn prepared the way for his azure sister of the spring, so there are warnings, even at the close of "Prometheus," that another Fall will always be possible. The dialectic of "Prometheus" is very close to that of Blake's Orc cycle, a cycle from which Blake, in his most mature work, deliberately broke away and from which we shall see Shelley turning in *his* final work. Blake went on to a more refined dialectic, perfected in "Milton" and "Jerusalem," in which progression through contraries gives way to a vision of finality in which the unceasing creation of the artist is seen to be a type of individual revelation, of an apocalyptic salvation open to all. Shelley turned away from all mythmaking in a final despair, and "The Triumph of Life," as I read it, has for its theme the defeat of mythmaking, the collapse of all relationship into experience. That stage of the Orc cycle, the defeat of the myth, does not invalidate the apotheosis of the myth in "Prometheus Unbound." Indeed, as I shall try to show, "Prometheus" as a poem is complex enough, and quite *ironic* enough, in its individual way, to anticipate the defeat of its own myth. Prophetic irony, constantly aware of the "contrast between expectation and fulfilment," [2] is a basic element in all of Shelley's mythopoeic poems, and is reflected in the permanent Shelleyan influence upon Yeats, particularly in "The Second Coming" and the "Byzantium" poems, as Donald Weeks and G. Wilson Knight have noted.[3] This is prophetic irony:

> Things fall apart; the centre cannot hold;
> Mere anarchy is loosed upon the world,
> The blood-dimmed tide is loosed, and everywhere

2. I quote from the definition of "irony" offered by Brooks and Warren in *Understanding Poetry*, p. 690.
3. Donald Weeks, "Image and Idea in Yeats' 'The Second Coming,'" *PMLA, 53* (1948), 281ff. G. Wilson Knight, *The Starlit Dome* (London, Oxford Univ. Press, 1941), pp. 219, 225.

> The ceremony of innocence is drowned;
> The best lack all conviction, while the worst
> Are full of passionate intensity.[4]   [3-8]

And so is this, in the fiercely paradoxical lines of the last Fury in "Prometheus," which Yeats echoes:

> In each human heart terror survives
> The ravin it has gorged: the loftiest fear
> All that they would disdain to think were true:
> Hypocrisy and custom make their minds
> The fanes of many a worship, now outworn.
> They dare not devise good for man's estate,
> And yet they know not that they do not dare.
> *The good want power, but to weep barren tears.*
> *The powerful goodness want: worse need for them.*
> *The wise want love; and those who love want wisdom;*
> *And all best things are thus confused to ill.*
>   [618-28. Italics mine.]

These lines seem to have fused in Yeats's mind with lines from a great stanza in "The Witch of Atlas," when he wrote "The Second Coming":

> The solid oaks forget their strength, and strew
> Their latest leaf upon the mountains wide;
> The boundless ocean like a drop of dew
> Will be consumed—*the stubborn centre must*
> *Be scattered, like a cloud of summer dust.*
>   [228-32. Italics mine.]

I am not concerned here with tracing the influence of Shelley upon Yeats (though it is an enormous one, and is not sufficiently taken into account by recent critics of Yeats, possibly out of their generalized distaste for Shelley) but rather with the profound resemblance between the currently recognized irony of Yeats, and the too-little regarded and quite formidable irony of Shelley. Not "romantic irony" but the irony of Isaiah and Blake is present throughout "Prometheus Unbound" and "The Witch of Atlas." The irony the prophet confronts, and presents, is the fearful one stated so clearly by Buber in the vocabulary of mythmaking:

> The particular *Thou,* after the relational event has run its course, is *bound* to become an *It.*
>
> The particular *It,* by entering the relational event, *may* become a *Thou.*

---

4. William Butler Yeats, "The Second Coming," *Collected Poems* (London, Macmillan, 1955), p. 210.

... without *It* man cannot live. But he who lives with *It*
alone is not a man.[5]

And the irony is worse yet than these. For to speak the sound *Thou*
with the vocal organs is by no means the same as saying the primary
word I-Thou, the word of mythopoeic creation. Will and grace are
needed, and grace in Shelley is as capricious as his Witch of Atlas. Without it poems, like all other relationships, collapse under deep enough
probing. "Prometheus Unbound" might be shown to collapse ultimately
also, but not because it cannot sustain an ironical contemplation. If, in
my reading of "Prometheus" which follows, I place an emphasis on
Shelley's awareness of the precariousness of mythmaking, on his poem's
self-realization that apocalypse can roll over into the fallen state again,
that is because the contemporary danger this poem faces is that of readers
crediting a very subtle poet with too little awareness of what he was
doing. Like all of Shelley's important poetry, "Prometheus" is misread
because it is not read closely enough. The uncritical millennarianism
that critics have found in "Prometheus" is what they have brought to
the poem themselves. Whatever Shelley the man may have believed about
evil, early or late, even if it were what Mrs. Shelley believed him to have
believed ("that mankind had only to will that there should be no evil,
and there would be none"),[6] is of slight importance to my study compared to what Shelley's poem believes and communicates.

The first speech of the poem (lines 1–73) is its climax, in terms of
merely *dramatic* resolution. By line 58 (in which Prometheus determines
to recall his curse "once breathed on" Jupiter) drama is over and vision
proper begins. The conventions of drama and the legitimate expectations
which they arouse are at an end. The conventions of the marvelous story,
the waking "dream," of mythopoeic relationship replace them. Spenser,
not Aeschylus, becomes the prototype, and Faery Land, the complete
visionary projection with its ambiguous interleaving of the varying states
of existence (earthly paradise, our life, earthly hell), becomes the local
habitation out of which the poem's lyrical discourse arises.

Counterpointed in this opening speech of Shelley's Titan are the
speeches and situations of his two great archetypes (discussed in the last
chapter), the Prometheus of Aeschylus and the Satan of "Paradise Lost."
Deliberate echoes of each are scattered through these lines:

> *Prometheus.* Monarch of Gods and Dæmons, and all Spirits
> But One, who throng those bright and rolling worlds
> Which Thou and I alone of living things
> Behold with sleepless eyes! regard this Earth
> Made multitudinous with thy slaves, whom thou

5. Buber, *I and Thou*, pp. 33–4.
6. Hutchinson, ed., *Works of Shelley*, p. 291.

Requitest for knee-worship, prayer, and praise,
And toil, and hecatombs of broken hearts,
With fear and self-contempt and barren hope.
Whilst me, who am thy foe, eyeless in hate,
Hast thou made reign and triumph, to thy scorn,
O'er mine own misery and thy vain revenge.
Three thousand years of sleep-unsheltered hours,
And moments aye divided by keen pangs
Till they seemed years, torture and solitude,
Scorn and despair,—these are mine empire :—
More glorious far than that which thou surveyest
From thine unenvied throne, O Mighty God !   [1–17]

Hughes, in his notes on these lines, compared them to "Paradise Lost,"
Book 1, lines 84ff and 242ff,[7] two of Satan's great speeches of Promethean defiance, replete with that "diabolic" energy that Blake read as
an exaltation of the strength and persistency of human desire. With the
Aeschylean echoes, here and later, fully noted by Hughes, these Satanic
reminiscences unite to recreate the Titanic archetype in that "more poetic"
form claimed by Shelley for *his* hero in the preface I have already examined.

These are the overt, incontrovertible analogues for the situation at
the opening of the poem. Other analogues, parallels rather than influences, may be helpful toward a fuller understanding of this opening
visualization. Job, the Samson of Judges and of Milton's drama, and
the bound Orc of Blake's "The First Book of Urizen" and "Night the
Fifth" of "The Four Zoas," provide reflectors and contrasts for the
reading of Shelley, just as the Aeschylean Prometheus and the Miltonic
Satan do. The common vision is of an emblematic Man in torment, his
energies bound in, repressed by what is or claims to be more than man.
Obviously, much is not in common ; Job and Samson are believing Jews
and trust that the God who is perhaps passive in face of their degradation
is still a transcendent Thou, whom they need to address. But even here,
the common elements with Shelley's Titan do exist. Like Job, Prometheus has been given over to the Accuser, and again like Job in his
deeper comprehension, he has been given over by himself, by his selfhood, a term and concept Shelley and Blake share. Like the bound Orc,
Prometheus is nailed down not by an evil principle but by human faculties gone to the bad by their isolation from one another. In "The First
Book of Urizen" the rational intelligence gone wrong in Urizen binds
down the energies of the young Orc ; in the more definitive vision of
"The Four Zoas" the imaginative principle operative in Los chains Orc
and his desires. The contraries, the dialectic of paradox, apply also to

7. Hughes, ed., *Shelley,* p. 183.

the poet's vision. Los can go as dangerously insular as any of the Zoas; vision generates its own contrary. The Los in Shelley's Prometheus, as well as the Urizen, is responsible for his condition at the opening of the drama. We bind our own energies, stifle our own desires, abandon our relationships willfully, experience It, and are experienced as an It because will and not simply grace has failed. That last sentence is prose reduction, abstract moralizing of *Prometheus,* but at least it is accurate reduction and may be useful as such.

Fogle, in his suggestive recent article on "Prometheus," has formulated the same matter rather differently, holding as he does to a more dualistic reading of the poem than I do:

> Jupiter serves also to embody the complexity of the hero Prometheus; he is associated with Prometheus in dignity, in isolation, expressed in repeated images of height and bareness in Act I, and in unalterable determination. One can think of him, in fact, as the masculine principle in Prometheus of courage and unlimited aspiration, but perverted and made evil from want of balance and control, which in Prometheus is supplied by Asia, the feminine principle of Love. The force of Jupiter is partly determined by the vigor of Shelley's conception of the Good in Prometheus, which calls forth an equal power to oppose it. It has been noticed that there is an odd kind of Manichaeanism in Shelley, Ormuzd and Ahriman, light and darkness,—and this is one way of explaining it.
>
> Until the climax of *Prometheus Unbound* this opposition appears dramatically in the conception of a fatal bond between good and evil, in which every effort at advance becomes a retrogression, the aspiration of goodness is perverted into the fact of evil and misfortune.[8]

Most of this I am in agreement with, and am helped by. But that "odd kind of Manichaeanism in Shelley," while dominant in "The Revolt of Islam," does not seem to me to be present in any of the poems that I discuss in these chapters. In the 1816 Hymns, Shelley began to write mythmaking poetry in what I take to be its strict sense. "The Revolt of Islam" lapsed back into the mixture of allegory and mythopoeia that "Alastor" had been; with "Prometheus" what had begun in "Mont Blanc" and the "Hymn to Intellectual Beauty" emerged in clearer form.

Fogle's assumption of dualism is not compatible with his own realization of the relationship between Jupiter and Prometheus. Fogle has some interesting comparisons between "Prometheus Unbound" and Blake's epics, of the kind that I myself find useful in reading either Shelley or Blake. Jupiter stands to Prometheus as Urizen (or any other of the

8. R. H. Fogle, "Image and Imagelessness: A Limited Reading of 'Prometheus Unbound,'" *Keats-Shelley Journal, I* (Jan. 1952), 25–36.

Zoas) does to Albion, Blake's Divine Man. When Albion reconstitutes himself, he gathers the Zoas, the fragmented natural world, and his emanation Jerusalem unto himself again, thus re-establishing an archetypal unity, an unfallen state higher than that of Beulah, the visionary paradisal garden. Jupiter vanishes as Urizen vanishes; he has no existence once Prometheus has reintegrated himself. This is a vision of a unitary man, not of a dualism. Fogle's only fault is that he puts too little trust in his own very accurate reading of the poem and too much in the received judgments of past Shelley scholarship. The dualism is *outside the poem;* it is imported from the tradition of Shelley criticism, and that tradition, while it has value, is a monument to what Wimsatt has termed "the intentional fallacy." Wimsatt himself, in his influential essay on "The Structure of Romantic Nature Imagery," manifests the influence of the worst aspects of that tradition when, on its authority, he talks about "the conflict between French atheism and Platonic idealism which even in *Prometheus Unbound* Shelley was not able to resolve." [9] I cannot find either French atheism or *Platonic* idealism in the poem. I do find an apocalyptic humanism which cannot be categorized as theistic or atheistic, materialistic or idealistic, but which challenges those dichotomies, "cloven fictions" as Blake called them, with a myth which is its own synthesis and which resists philosophy and theology by being its own discipline, explicable only in its own mythopoeic, concretely human terms.

I do not think that the point here can be stressed too much, because until it is acknowledged (and my limited reading of the poem is meant as demonstration of it) criticism of Shelley will always be crippled by its tradition of intentionalism. Thus, the reading of "Prometheus" which seems to me to be most free of the intentional fallacy, Fogle's (I take Knight's reading, for all its suggestiveness, as a splendid embodiment of Wimsatt's twin "fallacy," the "affective" variety), is still afflicted by the received identifications of Demogorgon as "Necessity," Asia as "Love," and the vision of the whole poem as being that of "Platonic idealism." Fogle does not demonstrate any necessity in these readings; he takes them for granted. So, unfortunately, do Baker and the other able recent critics of the poem. C. S. Lewis and Yeats have given us more elastic readings, but in terms that enter the realm of appreciation. Yeats on Demogorgon is rhetorically impressive but not very helpful:

> Why then does Demo-gorgon, whose task is beneficent . . . bear so terrible a shape, and not to the eyes of Jupiter, external necessity, above, but to those of Asia . . . Why is Shelley terrified of the Last Day like a Victorian child?
> Demo-gorgon made his plot incoherent, its interpretation im-

9. Wimsatt, *The Verbal Icon,* pp. 3–18, 103.

possible, it was thrust there by that something which again and again forced him to balance the object of desire conceived as miraculous and superhuman, with nightmare.[1]

John Todhunter had Demogorgon down as "Divine Justice," William Michael Rossetti as "Eternity," Vida Scudder as the "Ancient Principle of Reason."[2] More recently Joseph Warren Beach has interpreted him as "destiny or fate," Wilson Knight as "the human imagination or Holy Spirit," and Carlos Baker as "Necessity," with which last identification Fogle seems to agree.[3] When Jupiter (iii.i) is confronted by Demogorgon, he too inquires with the critics: "Awful shape, what art thou? Speak!" The reply is:

> Eternity. Demand no direr name.
> Descend, and follow me down the abyss.

Any source-hunting after Demogorgon, any intentionalistic fixation drawn from Shelley's life, prose, or other verse, any allegorizing will simply take us down that abyss. "Prometheus" is too long a work for me to examine line by line in a reading, but my commentary which follows attempts to work in closely to the text at all points which seem to me to be either crucial or especially difficult. With Demogorgon I shall come to grips several times, but always the Demogorgon in the poem will be taken as the interpretative problem. Beach's suggestion of destiny or fate, being most fluid, seems to me the least mistaken of past interpretations of Demogorgon. But even if, as seems likely, Beach has the analogue of Karma in mind rather than a Western concept of fate, the parallel is ultimately specious. Demogorgon emancipates; he is the agent of apocalypse. Prometheus subdues his experiential Self, and thus turns to Asia; Asia goes down to Demogorgon. But Asia goes for information, and to know the *when* of liberation. Prometheus has known of the agency of Demogorgon, this being the secret that Jupiter desires. Prometheus, by willing reintegration, by sending Asia has decided *when. When is now.* The admonition of Hillel is fully apt: "If I am not for me, then who will be for me, and if I am for myself only, then what am I, and if not *now, when?*"[4] But Demogorgon himself is the cause, not Prometheus. Prometheus is thesis and antithesis in the dialectic, with Jupiter

---

1. William Butler Yeats, " 'Prometheus Unbound,' " *Essays, 1931–1936* (Dublin, Cuala Press, 1937), pp. 56–7.
2. John Todhunter, *A Study of Shelley* (London, 1880), p. 137. W. M. Rossetti, Shelley's "Prometheus Unbound": *A Study of Its Meanings and Personages,* London, 1886. Vida Scudder, ed., *Prometheus Unbound* (Boston, 1892), p. xxxv.
3. Joseph Warren Beach, *A Romantic View of Poetry* (Minneapolis, Univ. of Minnesota Press, 1944), p. 120. Knight, *The Starlit Dome,* p. 204. Carlos Baker, *Shelley's Major Poetry* (Princeton Univ. Press, 1948), p. 104. Fogle, "Image and Imagelessness," p. 25.
4. Trans. from *Pirke Aboth,* ch. i, sec. 14.

as the Accuser, or contrary, the Self-within, playing as thesis here, and
the Titan on the rock as antithesis. The agent of synthesis is Demogorgon; he is the emblem of the whole myth, the dialectic itself. "*Karma*
is never the cause of emancipation," Shankara says. Karma is only the
causal sequence *in* time; when one dies to self one is delivered from it,
and from time and cause. Karma never dispels ignorance; it cannot, for
it is not in the category of knowledge. Demogorgon has nothing to do
with "necessity" or "justice" or even, finally, with "fate." Demogorgon
is in the question "if not now, when?" which provides its own answer.
The dialectic of personal apocalypse is always there; the individual determines the now or else the never. Demogorgon calls himself "Eternity,"
and not a "direr name." The "Eternity" is the sudden now, in which the
decision of the integrating will is put into time. The "direr name" is
whatever you prefer to term the dialectic of release (and of collapse,
necessarily, into time, experience, Itness again). Demogorgon is mythopoeic process, in which It's become confronted as Thou's, or relational
confrontations crumble away into experiences. Blake, in his 1810 commentary on the lost fresco, *A Vision of the Last Judgment,* put the essential aspects of this view of apocalypse very clearly:

> the Last Judgment begins, & its Vision is seen by the Imaginative
> Eye of Every one according to the situation he holds.

> Error is Created. Truth is Eternal. Error, or Creation, will be
> Burned up, & then, & not till then, Truth or Eternity will appear.
> I assert for myself that I do not behold the outward Creation & that
> to me it is Hindrance & not Action; it is as the dirt upon my feet,
> No part of me. [Keynes, pp. 828, 844.]

There is a great deal to be comprehended in these passages; all that
is relevant *here* is the notion of an apocalypse as being a judgment which
a man passes on himself, which his Imaginative Eye sees "according
to the situation he holds," which he *asserts for himself, now,* as Blake
does here. It is hindrance; Thou is action. One asserts for oneself. The
assertion brings mythopoeia into action, and in "Prometheus Unbound"
Demogorgon objectifies mythopoeia. He is *not* an *allegory* of mythopoeia.
Rather is he simply himself, myth, for dialectic cannot be allegorized;
dialectic is myth.

I return now to the speech of Prometheus which opens the drama. One
major meaning of the speech seems to have been overlooked by the commentators; it is that Prometheus describes mankind's (and his own)
situation as being a fallen one. You do not need apocalypse if you do not
have a fallen world and a fallen man, and if you have a fallen man, then

you do not have a situation which can be remedied by political action. Nature is fallen and fragmented, man is fallen from himself, experience rules, relationship is nowhere to be seen. The people of the earth, says Prometheus, are requited by the god they worship "with fear and self-contempt and barren hope" (line 8). "Love, Hope, and Self-esteem" were posited by the "Hymn to Intellectual Beauty" as the three prime mythopoeic virtues, "Self-esteem" taking the place of the Christian "faith" in God. Here are the three prime Shelleyan virtues completely fallen; love has been replaced by fear, hope by barren hope, self-esteem by self-contempt. Will a removal of *external* oppression replace fear with love, barren hope with hope, self-contempt with self-esteem?

Previously, I have suggested the injunction of Hillel—"If not now, when?"—as epigraph to "Prometheus." The complete saying of the sage would be better epigraph still, and provides the best gloss I know for what Shelley means by self-esteem, in opposition to remorse and self-contempt. The ethical admonition of Hillel parallels Shelley by linking a special kind of self-esteem to the apocalyptic impulse: "If I am not for me, then who will be for me? And if I am for myself only, then what am I? And if not now, when?" [5]

There, linked together as Shelley the poet links them, are the poet Shelley's three prime virtues; in order: self-esteem, love, and hope. Without self-esteem, no love for another; without love, no hope; and the hope is apocalyptic: *now*. I am not trying to make Shelley into a visionary Jew of the first century. The man Shelley, to his dying day, had a childish hatred for Moses and the Books of the Law, just as the man Shelley, to the end, preserved intact his immature contempt for doctrinal and institutional Christianity. I cannot agree with Bennett Weaver or Ellsworth Barnard that Shelley's attitude toward either Testament ever approached the condition of mature, responsible understanding. [6] Shelley learned to read and venerate Job and the Sermon on the Mount after his own fashion. The Pentateuch and the Epistles of Paul, the Old Law and the New, he never learned rationally to apprehend. When I call Shelley a prophetic or religious poet, I do not mean that I consider his works to be imbued with the spirit of the Bible, as Weaver and Barnard do. Manifestly, as it seems to me, those works are not so imbued; one distrusts a man's ability to read and emulate Isaiah or Ezekiel, if he is blindly incapable of sharing the beliefs of those prophets, if indeed he is incapable of anything but a wretched display of prejudice when confronted by that kind of belief. As ought by now to be clear, I have no respect whatsoever for the attitude which Shelley the man took to Juda-

5. Ibid.
6. Ellsworth Barnard, *Shelley's Religion* (Minneapolis, Univ. of Minnesota Press, 1936), passim; Bennett Weaver, *Toward the Understanding of Shelley* (Ann Arbor, Univ. of Michigan Press, 1932), passim.

ism and Christianity. No amount of scholarly special pleading will re-
habilitate that or many another aspect of the historical Shelley. My
thesis is that as mythmaking poetry, Shelley's works (or rather, a certain definite grouping of them) have helpful parallels to other prophetic
poems, precisely because they *are* religion-making works in parallel opposition to the mythmakings of formalized religions. The man was
afflicted by the limiting prejudices of the revolutionary intelligentsia of
his own age; the mythmaker in him was not. The poet of "Prometheus"
has learned to maintain the precarious balance so nicely adjusted in
Hillel's aphorism; the biographical evidence would seem to indicate
that, to the end, the man who happened to be that poet could not maintain such a balance. As I dogmatically affirmed in my first chapter, Shelley is perhaps the extreme case in the history of English literature of
the absolute cleavage between man and poet. Shelley the man was wise
enough to realize how drastic the split was; Shelleyan scholars and critics
have rarely emulated him in this realization, and the deplorable nature
of the critical result provides vociferous testimony to the consequences
of their biographical approach to his poems.

It is to the separated components of the shattered universe that Prometheus appeals for his curse to be given back to him, that he may cast it
forth. His impulse is a ritual one; to externalize the curse again is necessary, else the separate parts of a world will not be able to re-enter relationship with one another. The ritual analogue is fittingly a "primitive"
one; you cast out devils by forcing them to let themselves be visualized.

But mountains, springs, air, and whirlwinds, all Thou's that the Titan
attempts to confront, shrink away under the triple burden of fear, self-
contempt, and barren hope. They refuse to externalize the curse; the
Earth herself, the Titan's mother, "dare not speak like life," lest Jupiter
link her "to some wheel of pain / More torturing than the one" whereon
she rolls. The gods, being ever living, do not understand the language
of the dead, but Prometheus being "more than God" by virtue of being
a Man also, "being wise and kind," will understand, she thinks, if she
repeats the curse in the tongue "known / Only to those who die." But
he does not comprehend; even in his still separated, fallen state, with the
liberating process only begun, the language of Mutability cannot reach
him; too much divinity resides in him.

To meet this difficulty of communication, to provide a fit utterer for
the to-be-recanted curse, the poem creates one of the most astonishing
of its myths. To Prometheus' request: "But mine own words, I pray, deny
me not," the Earth replies:

> They shall be told. Ere Babylon was dust,
> The Magus Zoroaster, my dead child,
> Met his own image walking in the garden.

> That apparition, sole of men, he saw.
> For know there are two worlds of life and death:
> One that which thou beholdest; but the other
> Is underneath the grave, where do inhabit
> The shadows of all forms that think and live
> Till death unite them and they part no more;
> Dreams and the light imaginings of men,
> And all that faith creates or love desires,
> Terrible, strange, sublime and beauteous shapes.
> There thou art, and dost hang, a writhing shade,
> 'Mid whirlwind-peopled mountains; all the gods
> Are there, and all the powers of nameless worlds,
> Vast, sceptred phantoms; heroes, men, and beasts;
> And Demogorgon, a tremendous gloom;
> And he, the supreme Tyrant, on his throne
> Of burning gold. . . .   [191–209]

This passage, difficult and famous, has been an influential one in our own age. The late Charles Williams, in his supernatural thriller, *Descent into Hell,* quotes Shelley's lines to elucidate a central point in his story when his female protagonist encounters her own image. Eliot in *The Cocktail Party,* perhaps in a reminiscence of Williams, has his hierophant-psychiatrist quote these same lines when he seeks to expound the meaning of his vision of the martyr-heroine's double appearing behind her.[7] This image of the *Doppelgänger* is frequent in imaginative literature; one thinks of Poe's *William Wilson* and Dostoevski's *The Double* among others. Hughes cites the double of Heracles seen by Odysseus in Hades (Homer, *Od.* xi.601–14) as parallel.[8] The curious doctrine of lines 195–9 has an exact analogue in the *Elegien* of Rilke, with their belief that we reunite with our other Self in death, a belief that infuriated Yeats into the passionate protest of his own epitaph, with its injunction to cast a cold eye on life *and* death. Shelley, according to Thomas Medwin, "met his own image" at least once, at Casa Magni, and was asked by it: "How long do you mean to be content?"[9] A close examination of the passage ought at least to clarify its function in the drama, however impenetrable its final meaning may be.

"The Magus Zoroaster" is splendidly but imprecisely suggestive. No source hunter has encountered an instance of Zoroaster running into himself in a garden or elsewhere, and a fairly desultory glance at Zoro-

---

7. Whether Eliot's (or Williams') use of Shelley's passage at all illuminates their own points is at least disputable. Certainly, they cast scant light back on the passage itself.

8. Hughes, ed., *Shelley,* p. 185.

9. Thomas Medwin, *The Life of P. B. Shelley,* ed. H. B. Forman (London, Oxford Univ. Press, 1913), p. 405.

astrian research literature discloses no doctrine resembling that expounded in the Earth's speech.

Once past the puzzling Persian Magus, the lines would seem to read: "there are two worlds of life and death"; not, as might more commonly be said, a world of life and a world of death, but two worlds, each of which encompasses life *and* death. One is what we behold; the other is "underneath" the grave, not *in* it (as in the poems of Shelley's disciple Beddoes or near contemporary Novalis). *We* live here; our "shadows" live "underneath" the "grave," grave here being a way of looking at our own world. When we die, our shadows also will die, and then death will unite us and our shadows. There is no suggestion here that this is to be regarded as being in any way a good thing (as it clearly is in Rilke), but neither is the converse suggested. This is then to be taken only as a vision of the way things are; moral meaning is extraneous to it.

Now, these "shadows" are not only those of men but indeed "of all forms that think and live." Therefore, underneath the grave are to be found shadows also of our dreams and "light imaginings"; of the substance of what we hope for and the evidence of what we cannot see ("all that faith creates or love desires"). Shadows of mythmaking relationships and of poetic visions are in this curious Hades side-by-side with shadows of living men. Thus, Prometheus is there, hanging in his agony, and Jupiter on his throne, "and Demogorgon, a tremendous gloom." One misreading of this passage is to think of this world beneath the grave as being uniquely the home or realm of Demogorgon; clearly it is not. The *shadow* of Demogorgon, like the shadow of Prometheus and the shadow of Jupiter, is there but, as with Prometheus and Jupiter, there is a Demogorgon in the world we behold as well.

Out of the world of shadows arises the phantasm of Jupiter, summoned by Prometheus. The imaginative rightness of invoking this shadow to repeat the curse, so that Prometheus may then formally revoke it, has been commented on by previous critics. The dramatic irony of Jupiter's shadowy half externalizing the curse is evident and effective, but nothing in this device bears on the poem's thematic center, the re-establishment of relationship, the undoing of Prometheus' fall from his own divine humanity. The device is a causal connection and an ingenious one, but will not sustain extensive analysis; unlike what is best and most central in this lyrical drama, it is by no means inexhaustible to meditation.

Ione and Panthea do not take well to probing either, at this point (in Act IV this will not be true). As I have said before, I do not intend to add another group of allegorizings of the cast of "Prometheus" to those already extant, all of which seem to me to be equally valueless. Not the answer but the right question is what we require here. Grabo, seeking to comprehend Panthea, asks: "What abstraction does she personify?"

"Sympathetic love," is what he works out as an answer.[1] If one grants him the question, then one has no right to quarrel with the answer, or with the answers of other allegorizers either, e.g. Vida Scudder's "Faith" or Kenneth Cameron's "Hope."[2] But I do not grant the question as being a valid one in the reading of this poem. Panthea and Ione are Oceanides and subordinate sisters to Asia; Asia stands in relationship to Prometheus much as Blake's Jerusalem stands to his Albion, most simply as archetypal woman to archetypal man. Allegorizing is not in it; anagogy is. But what it is that we are given an anagoge of is something that must wait upon an apprehension of the whole of the lyrical drama, of the entire poem simultaneously perceived. Enough for now if, with every previous commentator, I note that Ione is subordinate to Panthea just as Panthea is to Asia. Ione covers her eyes rather than see the phantasm of Jupiter make his appearance; Panthea coolly observes and describes the shadowy figure. Being closer to the archetype, Panthea is further away from us than Ione is; in fallen human terms she will therefore be less sympathetic to us, though still more easily apprehended than Asia. The *why* of this trinity of gradation is possibly not a rational matter; one can assign genetic and superficially structural explanations, but they will not satisfy an analytic enquirer. Douglas Bush has some sly remarks: "Shelley is not content with a nameless chorus of Oceanides, he gives Prometheus a wife and two sisters-in-law, a typical Shelleyan household. The significance of Panthea and Ione is too speculative for discussion here; in some vague way they represent aspects of love. At any rate whenever the seraglio of feminine abstractions appear, they dissolve what elements of hardness belong to the fable and to Prometheus himself."[3]

Even if one does not read these ladies as being "feminine abstractions" ("seraglio" is a nice touch, but rather unfair, as Prometheus' relationship to his sisters-in-law is Platonic, though, one hastens to add, only in the popular meaning of the term), he can agree with Bush that Panthea and Ione, at least in the first three acts, tend to clutter things up. They sometimes gush a bit, and they are overfond of internal rhyme. Their presumed function is to humanize matters, to exhibit emotions and affections that are somewhat less than Titanic, and it may be that they fulfill their function too well. The real problem here is probably Pottle's "shift in sensibility": a generation less fashionably tight-lipped than ours once responded to Panthea and Ione more easily than we can respond; a later generation may do so again. In any case, I do not care to defend Panthea and Ione on mythmaking grounds; the tone of their

1. Carl Grabo, *"Prometheus Unbound," An Interpretation* (Chapel Hill, Univ. of North Carolina Press), p. 54.

2. Scudder, ed., *Prometheus Unbound*, p. xxxvii. K. N. Cameron, "The Political Symbolism of Prometheus Unbound," *PMLA, 58* (Sept. 1943).

3. Bush, *Mythology and the Romantic Tradition*, p. 146.

speeches seems to me sometimes to go over the line that separates Beulah-land from Namby-Pamby land, a region I do not regard as being vision-ary. Other readers (I hope) will disagree with me, but all of us hold that there is a public line somewhere separating the childlike from the childish; exactly where is rationally disputable.

The visualization of the Oceanides *may* be flawed; the remainder of Act I is masterly. We have now to consider, in order, the speaking and recantation of the curse; the furies and their torture scene; the extraor-dinary group of songs sung by the comforting spirits; and the daybreak that ends the act and begins the apocalyptic day. Each of these units is organically related, subtly, complexly, and meaningfully to what comes before and after it. The business of criticism, I take it, is to demonstrate this relation. My more particular concern here is with the original mythic aspect of these visionary events, but for my partial purpose to be served, the more general criticism must be accomplished also. Even if I am being unjust to previous critics of "Prometheus," the poem is so multi-form a creation that it can sustain a great many commentaries. No one approach will exhaust it; no approach responsible to the primacy of the poem's text will disfigure it.

A curse is a hard thing to transmute into a coherent and valuable poem: the poem of lines 262–301 would hardly stand by itself, wrenched from context. The first stanza is couched in the rhetoric of simple de-fiance; the second has more crucial lines:

> Thou art omnipotent.
> O'er all things but thyself I gave thee power,
> And my own will. . . .   [272–4]

The allegorical meaning usually read here begins with Prometheus = Mind of Man. Man makes Nobodaddy in his own worst image, giving him power over everything but himself and man's still free will. Better to stay close to the fable here, difficult as Shelley makes it for us. The lines are not single in meaning; running against the topmost current of statement is the ironic statement beneath: what power you have I give (not just gave), and what I give (and gave) is not omnipotence at all. In a cosmos of two, you have power over neither yourself nor what has primacy in me. Not power at all but a contrary-status is what I gave and give you. We are caught up together in experience, because we are divided. And in experience, dominance is mutable. The *mind* of man does not make Jupiter; rather it contains him as component, as it does Prometheus and a number of other energies. The shaper-in-fire Pro-metheus, not the stealer-of-fire, had something to do with giving Jupiter his mutable power. The stealer-of-fire, the one of crooked thoughts, knows something of how that power will be dissipated.

The actual curse, in the third stanza, winds itself like a shirt of Nessus around Jupiter, and wishes him a crown of pain in emblem of his "omnipotence," the crown to be of "burning gold," its fire at length to consume his brain. It will be remembered that in the world beneath the grave the phantasm of Jupiter sits upon a throne of "burning gold" (line 209). The Mammon aspect of Jupiter is a central one; he foreshadows the Mammon of the *Defence,* which stands incarnated in money as the principle of Self, opposed to poetry in the struggle for man's spirit.

The curse's last stanza is its best and most important:

> Heap on thy soul, by virtue of this Curse,
>   Ill deeds, then be thou damned, beholding good;
> Both infinite as is the universe,
>   And thou, and thy self-torturing solitude.
> An awful image of calm power
> Though now thou sittest, let the hour
> Come, when thou must appear to be
> That which thou art internally;
> And after many a false and fruitless crime
> Scorn track thy lagging fall through boundless space and time.
>
> [292–301]

"Be thou damned, beholding good": as Locock first noted,[4] there is an allusion to Milton here; the parallel is an ironic one, in Blake-like criticism of Milton's God. The relevant passage is Book 1, lines 209–20:

> So stretcht out huge in length the Arch-fiend lay
> Chain'd on the burning Lake, nor ever thence
> Had ris'n or heav'd his head, but that the will
> And high permission of all-ruling Heaven
> Left him at large to his own dark designs,
> That with reiterated crimes he might
> Heap on himself damnation, while he sought
> Evil to others, and enrag'd might see
> How all his malice serv'd but to bring forth
> Infinite goodness, grace and mercy shewn
> On Man by him seduc't, but on himself
> Treble confusion, wrath and vengeance pour'd.

Prometheus, in his curse, behaved as badly toward Jupiter as Milton's God here behaves toward Satan. The antinomian reversal is adroit; the irony is grim and altogether effective. The scheming God of Milton is coolly willing to give Satan his head, that he "might / Heap on himself damnation"; that is decidedly echoed by the scheming Prometheus of the curse who, like God, has foreknowledge; Jupiter, like Satan, "enrag'd might see / How all his malice serv'd but to bring forth / Infinite

4. Locock, ed., *Shelley, 1,* 601.

goodness"; eternally damned, beholding good. If Shelley had left it there, then he would deserve the popular misinterpretation of having simply inverted Milton's categories. But, like Blake, Shelley is not the naïve antinomian and childish rebel, overpowered by his own primary impulses, that New Critics want to read him as being; if you want the play acting of romantic Satanism you must go to Byron, not to Blake or Shelley. To invert the orthodox categories you must first accept them, as Byron in his depths did, being fundamentally a Christian and a Calvinist at that. But Shelley, like Blake, wars against the orthodox dichotomies, rejecting the "cloven fiction" of the orthodox great divorce between heaven and hell. Instead, he offers his visionary dialectic; the contraries progress. Prometheus and Jupiter, as Prometheus has learned to comprehend (instinctively learned, Shelley's drama would have it, for Prometheus does not consciously understand the mechanism of his own liberation, as a Zoa in Blake would), will never progress out of their impasse if Prometheus regards Jupiter as being simply his negation, as God regards Satan. The mechanism of release begins to operate when Prometheus recants his Miltonic curse:

> It doth repent me: words are quick and vain;
> Grief for awhile is blind, and so was mine.
> I wish no living thing to suffer pain.   [303–5]

At these lines, a whole series of pious commentators have clapped hands and cried out: "What a Christian the Titan has become!" They mistake not less than everything in doing so. The deliberate contrast is with Milton's God, who cannot be envisioned uttering these lines, so as to recall as "quick and vain" his malignant curse upon Satan. The soul is immortal, even in Satan; and Satan's soul, in hell, is therefore a living thing suffering pain, and Milton's God is evidently content that it should be so. Unless one wants to claim the silly paradox that Shelley's Prometheus is a better Christian than Milton's God, one had better refrain from baptizing the Titan. Myself, I agree with C. S. Lewis that Milton's God is being a very orthodox Christian indeed here. What it comes down to is that Prometheus does not believe that hell, in the orthodox sense, ought to exist; a traditional Christian (I speak under correction) would not agree with him. I cannot agree then with Baker when he writes of Shelley and "Prometheus Unbound" that "He has begun with Aeschylus and ended by the representation of an ethic which is close to that of the New Testament." [5] The New Testament knows of a savior who calls certain spirits "accursed" and sends them away from him into an "everlasting fire." Baker is perhaps endorsing Prometheus in this regard over the Christ of the New Testament, but if he *is* doing so then he owes it to his readers to show some awareness of

5. Baker, *Shelley's Major Poetry*, p. 101.

what he is doing. If I were a Christian, I should not want Shelley's Prometheus (or Shelley for that matter) assigned me as a coreligionist.

Jupiter, appropriately enough, is more of a mind with Milton's God than he is with Prometheus: he proceeds to intensify the Titan's tortures with technically admirable refinement. He is a victim of the prophetic irony of the dialectic of contraries; the liberating force has been released, but he can still see Prometheus as being only a negation of his own supreme will, just as Milton's God interprets Satan as a negation, not a contrary. Prometheus sees struggle; Jupiter, rebellion. And rebellion, by the law of negations, is to be put down. Hell is the best Jupiter, like Milton's God, can do when it comes to dealing with rebellion. Mercury, who reluctantly leads Jupiter's Furies in, delivers an address replete with ironic echoes of Milton:

> aye from thy sight
> Returning, for a season, Heaven seems Hell,
> So thy worn form pursues me night and day,
> Smiling reproach. Wise art thou, firm and good,
> But vainly wouldst stand forth alone in strife
> Against the Omnipotent. . . .   [357–62]

> Even now thy Torturer arms
> With the strange might of unimagined pains
> The powers who scheme slow agonies in Hell,
> And my commission is to lead them here,
> Or what more subtle, foul or savage fiends
> People the abyss. . . .   [365–70]

> bend thy soul in prayer,
> And like a suppliant in some gorgeous fane,
> Let the will kneel within thy haughty heart:
> For benefits and meek submission tame
> The fiercest and the mightiest.   [376–80]

Mercury is a time server, not a faithful Abdiel, but the practical advice given by two such different spirits is much the same:

> Cease then this impious rage,
> And tempt not these; but hast'n to appease
> Th' incensed Father, and th' incensed Son,
> While pardon may be found in time besought.
> [Bk. 5, lines 842–5]

The point I am attempting again is that "Prometheus Unbound" is a searching criticism of "Paradise Lost" (you could argue the converse, of course). Shelley, like Blake, clearly apprehends that something is wrong with the God presented in Milton's poem. It does not follow that something is therefore right about the poem's Satan; rather the necessary conclusion is that something is very wrong about him as well. I have heard it wisely argued that a moving self-chastisement is involved on Milton's part, in assigning so much human energy and initiative, so much imaginative force to Satan. Blake and Shelley did not believe this kind of self-chastisement, in which the human abnegates himself before a divinity which is supposedly more than merely human, to be anything but an evil act; in itself, and in its everyday consequences. Eternally, there will be disagreement among readers about this matter; whatever your own beliefs, you ought at least not to disqualify yourself as a reader of Shelley's "Prometheus" or of Blake's major poems by assuming, as so many now do, that Shelley's or Blake's attitude is less complex, subtle, meaningful, coherent, maturely founded on the facts of experience than your own. "Prometheus" may not be what C. S. Lewis so ably and persuasively argues it to be: the best long poem in English written in the nineteenth century.[6] But for extent of ambition and general excellence of execution, it has few rivals in its century; a modern critic who finds it "unreadable" (and many claim to do so) is only passing a severe judgment upon himself. My own generation, with only a handful of exceptions, finds the poem "unreadable" without ever having bothered to have read it, but then our peculiar literary vice is to have forgotten how to read a long poem, though we are all of us adept at reading and judging essays and even books devoted to the examination of long poems we ourselves have in fact not read, or are not able to read. As Sir Herbert Read remarks, if Shelley's poetry dies in our age it will not be because we have read it and found it wanting but because we have allowed ourselves to be persuaded into not reading it at all.[7] Critics as eminent as Eliot, Leavis, Tate, Brooks, and Ransom, among others, have assured us that the bulk of it is not good poetry, without evidencing that they know it well enough to judge dispassionately. On their authority (though, it must be granted, not at their advice) a generation has chosen to condemn a poet while remaining largely ignorant of his works.

My interrupted commentary on "Prometheus" has reached the point at which the Titan disdainfully breaks off his dialogue with Mercury: "how vain is talk! / Call up the fiends." I hasten to obey and pass on to a consideration of the Furies.

As the Furies come on, Mercury runs off, heavy with remorse and self-contempt. The manner of his movement is an ironic remembrance of Uriel's descent (and reascent) on a sunbeam to warn Gabriel that an evil spirit (Satan) "had escap'd the Deep, and past at Noon by his

6. C. S. Lewis, *Rehabilitations* (London, Oxford Univ. Press, 1939), p. 29.
7. Sir Herbert Read, "In Defence of Shelley," *The True Voice of Feeling* (London, Faber, 1953), pp. 212–13.

Sphere in the shape of a good Angel down to Paradise." [8] In contrast
to Uriel, Mercury waves the evil spirits on, knowing that they are evil;
as a servant of God, like Uriel, Mercury travels in an official way:

> *Panthea.* See where the child of Heaven, with wingèd feet,
> Runs down the slanted sunlight of the dawn.

These lines are ironic in another sense as well, for dawn is breaking,
and though we witness the advent of the Furies, Jupiter's power is wan-
ing. But the Furies, being subtle spirits, remain fearful enough, even
against a lightening background:

> So from our victim's destined agony
> The shade which is our form invests us round,
> Else we are shapeless as our mother Night.   [470–2]

The "destined agony" for Prometheus here is parallel to the later part
of Blake's Orc cycle; Orc at length becomes Urizen; the crucified Jesus
becomes Jehovah; the French Revolution becomes the Terror; similarly,
Prometheus will become Jupiter. The last Fury drives in the point, and
explicates the moral:

> *Fury.* Behold an emblem: those who do endure
> Deep wrongs for man, and scorn, and chains, but heap
> Thousandfold torment on themselves and him.   [594–6]

This horrible paradox is at the heart of Shelley's central myth, the
burden of which is the defeat of, the unmaking of myth. The means and
the end are irreconcilable; the relational event posited by mythmaking
runs its course, and a Thou is only an It again. Good and the means
of good are irreconcilable; and this holds whether the relational event,
the means of good, is a poem or a lovers' confrontation. Until "The Triumph of Life" finally commemorates this conflict, the most tragic statement of the failure of myth in Shelley is at this point in "Prometheus."
You may not agree with Prometheus in his lament (lines 597–615) for
what institutional Christianity has made out of Jesus; the expression in
these lines is perhaps overwrought. Blake put exactly this conviction
with rather more economy in the angry but effective "The Modern
Church Crucifies Christ with the Head Downwards." [9]

But whatever your sympathies here, the Fury's summary of the moral
results in the individual human heart that the Orc cycle brings about is,
beyond dispute, great poetry. Lingering in Yeats's consciousness, the
rhythms of this passage were to re-emerge in "The Second Coming."
Here in Shelley's drama, the passage presents the Titan's supreme agony,
the subtlest torture that Jupiter could devise:

8. "The Argument," Bk. 4, "Paradise Lost."
9. Keynes, ed., *Blake*, p. 724.

Fury.   In each human heart terror survives
The ravin it has gorged : the loftiest fear
All that they would disdain to think were true :
Hypocrisy and custom make their minds.
The fanes of many a worship, now outworn.
They dare not devise good for man's estate,
And yet they know not that they do not dare.
The good want power, but to weep barren tears.
The powerful goodness want : worse need for them.
The wise want love ; and those who love want wisdom ;
And all best things are thus confused to ill.
Many are strong and rich, and would be just,
But live among their suffering fellow-men
As if none felt : they know not what they do.   [618–31]

This is a speech to the consideration of which I shall return later in these chapters, for a study of Shelley's myth will lead us back to these lines, again and again. The Fury states a series of paradoxes, of hellish ironies which sum up something recalcitrant, something hardened in the human spirit. Something there is in us predisposed toward the condition of Itness, something that makes us prone to welcome experience at the price of relationship. C. S. Lewis, in a spirited appreciation of Shelley, insisted that no other "pagan" author so drives home the truth of original sin.[1] I find Lewis to be a better interpreter of Shelley's poetry in this regard than most critics, but original sin is a doctrine that Shelley's poetry repudiates, though like Blake's poetry it envisions a parallel "doctrine." Blake sees the Specter in our natures; Shelley, an unwilling dross that resists imaginative redemption. The Specter is the Selfhood, the subhuman self-absorption which both Blake and the mature poet Shelley identify with the state of nature, and to which they oppose mythmaking poetry. The Selfhood is the I which confronts no Thou's, but only experiences It's. With the original sin of doctrinal and institutional Christianity Blake and Shelley had no sympathy; neither was very far from an heretical tradition in Christianity which had affirmed, most vehemently in Eckhart and the *Theologica Germanica* and in English in William Law, that "only the Self burns in Hell." The most telling (and, I think, most central) statement in the *Defence* expresses the same truth : "Poetry, and the principle of Self, of which money is the visible incarnation, are the God and Mammon of the World."[2]

Blake, commenting on Lavater, stated the contraries of Poetry and Self even more clearly : "Man is a twofold being, one part capable of evil & the other capable of good; that which is capable of good is not also

1. *Rehabilitations,* p. 18.
2. Shawcross, ed., *Shelley's Criticism,* p. 152.

capable of evil, but that which is capable of evil is also capable of good." [3]

This is anything but a simple dualism, and if read too quickly will be misread. Comprehended, this statement summarizes the visionary ethic of Shelley's "Prometheus Unbound." If you brood on it, you may not agree with Douglas Bush that Shelley is the chief exponent in English poetry of "sentimental optimism." [4] Where is the sentimentality or the optimism to be found in "Prometheus"? The home truths that agonize the Titan do so because *they are truths,* "types of things which are." Terror gorges its "ravin," its prey in our hearts, and when full-fed on this carrion *still survives* its only proper food. The best among us fear all that we disdain to think is even true; we fear what we will not acknowledge. We retain, many of us, *in our minds,* the worship of creeds we know are outworn. We hide from ourselves the knowledge that we lack the courage to dare to improve or attempt to improve our neighbor's lot. When I paraphrase like this, these are only flat moralizings; things that we all of us know. But are they the moralizings of a sentimental optimist? The best lack all conviction, while the worst are full of passionate intensity. We take this now as being an acute insight into our present travail. Is it more acute than its model? Goodness, Power, Love, and Wisdom: these are the four cardinal virtues of Blake's unfallen Man and of Shelley's. They are also the virtues attributed to the God of the Jews and the Christians, and the virtues seen in human form in Jesus by the Christians. Does a sentimental optimist write like this about the state of those virtues in the human condition? Sentimentality and optimism:

> The good want power, but to weep barren tears.
> The wise want love; and those who love want wisdom;
> And all best things are thus confused to ill.

Mere anarchy is loosed upon the world, and the ceremony of innocence is drowned. Bush is a Christian humanist, and believes presumably that only a *Christian* humanism can avoid sentimentality or optimism in an examination of the human condition. Shelley the man was blinded all his life when it came to seeing that doctrinal Christianity, whatever you may do about accepting or rejecting it, is quite simply not to be dismissed by you as anything less than a mature analysis of your condition. But Bush is similarly blinded when it comes to seeing that a system of belief in competition to doctrinal Christianity—the apocalyptic humanism that Blake and Shelley create in their mythmakings—is also not to be caricatured with impunity. You can refuse to accept such belief if you are or want to be committed elsewhere, if you think that

3. Keynes, ed., *Blake,* p. 724.
4. Bush, p. 155.

you know the truth. But it will not do to misinterpret grossly such belief, on either side of the argument between the Christian with his received faith, or the religion-making poet with his insistence on creating
the reality in which he will believe. Blake would have summed it up in
the ironic vocabulary of "The Marriage of Heaven and Hell" : Shelley is
a devil and Bush an angel; they are contraries but not negations. They
cannot agree, but there is no reason why they should fail to understand
one another.

The final words of the Fury are the most frighteningly ironic. The
words echo Jesus, asking God to forgive his tormentors, on the grounds
that "they know not what they do." The tormentors are thus equated
with the "many" who could help their fellow men, the many who have
all the right intentions but who in fact do nothing :

> Many are strong and rich, and would be just,
> But live among their suffering fellow-men
> As if none felt: they know not what they do.

If you read this as a mixture of sentimentality and blasphemy, then
no one could rationally demonstrate that you are *misreading*. What
could be rationally questioned is your disinterestedness, and by that I
do not mean the nature of your own religious commitment but the degree to which it permits you to read poetry countered against your commitment, rather than be merely indifferent to it. The New Critics, for
all Richard P. Blackmur's vehemence of protest,[5] have become for their
followers the fathers of a new church, and daily one meets readers convinced of original sin who know nothing of and care not at all for Christianity or else who are Christian believers but think nothing of ripping
the doctrine of original sin out of its *theological* context and applying it
as a *literary* standard of evaluation. Shelley and Blake, with their own
vision of the radical evil *within* a man, are not likely to be comprehended
by either grouping of these instructed souls.

To cheer the state of the tortured Prometheus, his mother Earth summons "subtle and fair spirits," who sing to him of comfort. First, four
spirits celebrate in their songs the human creators of apocalypse: the
rebel, the self-sacrificer, the sage, and the poet. The fourth spirit is properly most in voice:

> On a poet's lips I slept
> Dreaming like a love-adept
> In the sound his breathing kept ;
> Nor seeks nor finds he mortal blisses,
> But feeds on the aëreal kisses
> Of shapes that haunt thought's wildernesses.

5. R. P. Blackmur, *The Lion and the Honeycomb* (New York, Harcourt, Brace,
1955), p. 207.

He will watch from dawn to gloom
The lake-reflected sun illume
The yellow bees in the ivy-bloom,
Nor heed nor see, what things they be;
But from these create he can
Forms more real than living man,
Nurslings of immortality!
One of these awakened me,
And I sped to succour thee.   [737–51]

This song is the *locus classicus,* or ought to be, of the passionate defence of visionary poetry in English; in itself it is one of the rewards
of reading Shelley. What Spenser began in English poetry culminates
here in the apotheosis of vision, in a confident assertion of the power of
poetry to create a golden world surpassing nature. Fuseli's "Nature puts
me out" becomes in Blake and Shelley: "I put nature out." Nature for
Blake is Hindrance, not Action; like the dirt upon his feet, it is no part
of him. Shelley in "Mont Blanc" broke with Wordsworth's nature, and
affirmed, with Blake, that there is no natural religion. If we confront
a Thou anywhere in nature, the credit is not nature's but ours. *We*
speak the primary word I-Thou; *we* initiate the dialogue. The relationship we make is *not* to be found in nature, and is of an order of reality
higher than the order of nature. So sings the fourth spirit, presenting
a poet who on principle will not keep his eye on the object, who denies
objects of experience, who despises commonplace, ordinary, *natural*
perception. It is no good crying out that Shelley has "a weak grasp on
the actual"—*whose* "actual"? The actual of hindrance, not action? The
actual of lazy, unimaginative perception? Shelley and his modern critic
may sit together from dawn to gloom, watching yellow bees in the ivy
by the light of the lake-reflected sun. At day's end the critic, if he has
the talents of a naturalist, might be able to turn out a more accurate description of the bees than Shelley could, but Shelley, never heeding or
seeing the bees, may have created *from them* forms "more real"—that is,
perceived with greater imaginative intensity—than a living man himself. And these forms will be "nurslings of immortality," auguries of innocence, visions of relationship. Examples of these forms are examined
in each chapter of this study, for these forms are precisely Shelley's
mythmaking poems. Accurate observation of nature may in itself be
a virtue; that it is a *poetic* virtue is nowadays taken rather too much for
granted. Wordsworth and Keats were interested in sensuous appearances and sensuous reality; Blake and Shelley, on principle, were not.
The "minute particulars" of Blake's poetry have nothing to do with
natural objects; rather they are attempts to visualize natural objects
as "men seen afar," to put a humanized Thou in place of a natural It.

The closing spirit-songs, fifth and sixth, have as theme the dialectic, the grim warning implicit in the whole of the drama. Love's shadow is ruin, the ruin that dogs all ideal endeavors, the cold common hell of isolation that replaces relationship. The songs echo against the aspiration of Prometheus to be reunited with Asia as the act comes to its close. We are moving out of ruin into love in the drama's overt progress; equally audible is the warning that we can move back, all too easily.

2

As in my analysis of Act 1, I shall take it for granted that I need not expend my space in summary of the events of the poem but am free to move to the mythic centers, elucidating only what I believe to be difficulties, defending only what has been attacked. Line-by-line analysis here, such as I gave in considering the "Ode to the West Wind," would produce an invidiously endless commentary. My readers, I assume, will have read "Prometheus" more than once, before they spare time to read commentary.

From Prometheus, bound to the precipice, the poem descends to Asia, standing in a vale at sunrise, a dawning that marks the advent of spring. The masculine landscape of the opening scene is replaced by the feminine receptiveness of Asia's surroundings. The dawn is timeless; it does not immediately progress onward to noon, but is suspended in its aspiration. And the morning star lingers on in it, until Panthea arrives to continue the progression toward liberation; then, reluctantly, the star fades in the light of the sun:

> *Asia.*   This is the season, this the day, the hour;
> At sunrise thou shouldst come, sweet sister mine,
> Too long desired, too long delaying, come!
> How like death-worms the wingless moments crawl!
> The point of one white star is quivering still
> Deep in the orange light of widening morn
> Beyond the purple mountains : through a chasm
> Of wind-divided mist the darker lake
> Reflects it : now it wanes : it gleams again
> As the waves fade, and as the burning threads
> Of woven cloud unravel in pale air :
> 'Tis lost! and through yon peaks of cloud-like snow
> The roseate sunlight quivers: hear I not
> The Æolian music of her sea-green plumes
> Winnowing the crimson dawn?   [II.i.13–27]

Fogle has what appears to me to be a definitive discussion of synaesthetic imagery in Shelley, in which he analyzes the final lines of this passage.[6] He can be read as a corrective here to Edward Hungerford, who makes too much out of those "sea-green plumes" in an attempt at geographical allegorizing.[7] My own concern with this passage is invested in the function of the morning-star figure, a recurrent one central to Shelley's mythopoeia. Like the Thou, the morning star has got to fade in the light of the experiential sun; here in "Prometheus" Shelley is attempting the task of apocalypse, which involves the conversion of the state of experience into a higher state of imaginative perception, not the lower state it occupies in relation to the world of innocence. The morning star belongs to the lower paradise, the state of innocence; better that than our common sun and the fallen world of experience to which it belongs. But, even as in Blake, we have got to pass out of the better into the worse state if we are ever to attain to a final, upper paradise in which the Thou will not fade into an It. Here, at the opening of Act II of "Prometheus," Shelley sacrifices the morning star in an attempt to attain to a sun beyond the sun. In "The Triumph of Life," when the cycle has rolled around again, when Orc has become Urizen, and Prometheus Jupiter, the prophetic Shelley will press home the lesson at which "Prometheus Unbound" hints so indecisively: the natural world and the natural man can never be redeemed. When the sun has been allowed to dim the morning star, then not a sun beyond the sun will illuminate us, but the chariot of life will advance upon us, with a cold glare, intenser than the noon but icy cold, shining forth from it, obscuring the sun as he the stars. The hope here in "Prometheus" is dialectical, but is still hope; Shelley believes in his myth. In "The Triumph of Life" faith in the myth is abandoned. This does not mean that Shelley rejects the myth, thinks it false. The myth itself is aware of its necessary defeat, but affirms human possibility. In "Prometheus," Shelley dwells in possibility, with all its windows and doors. In the "Triumph," as we shall see, the fairer house is deserted for the vision of human probability. This does not make the "Triumph" a palinode; it does evidence a human (not a creative) weariness in a very strong poetic nature. The hardening in the Milton of "Paradise Regained" and "Samson" is analogous; so in a different way is the despair of this world in the Spenser of the "Cantos of Mutabilitie." Of the English prophetic poets, only Blake endures in the vision of apocalypse in the *here* and *now* until the end, but Blake's myth is possibly the most formidable and organized ever created by a single man, and provided its maker with a faith which could not be defeated. Christianity is a better comforter than apocalyptic humanism; Spenser and Milton had a great deal more to fall back on than Shelley did. Blake's myth (in which he believed so totally that some among us, committed

6. Fogle, *Imagery*, p. 129.
7. E. B. Hungerford, *Shores of Darkness* (New York, Columbia Univ. Press, 1941), p. 182.

as totally to rival myths, defend ourselves uneasily by calling him "mad")
comprehended Christianity, and in his special vision of Christianity the
old Blake undoubtedly took considerable comfort. Blake's personal advantage over Shelley here is implicit in the contrast between his mythography, with its contrapuntal symbolism, and Shelley's stricter mythopoeia, with its single-stranded dialectic. No one can live on the bare
support of the I-Thou relationship; Judaism comes closest to it, but
grounds the Thou securely in the God of Abraham, Isaac, and Jacob.
Christianity personalizes the Thou to an even greater extent, with prag-
matic consequences that even a nonbeliever may envy. The moral hero-
ism of Shelley's agnostic faith in the mythopoeic mode, in the possibility
of sharing in reality through the I-Thou relationship only, without transcendental grounding, is at the least compelling. Whatever it may have
cost him as a man, it helped produce a body of poetry unique in its hon-
esty, refusing as it does to be anything but poetry, anything but mythmaking. Scholars who attempt to read it as philosophy, as discourse
animated primarily by speculative ideas, sin against it. Our own age
has learned to honor mythmakers, and claims to find in poetry a unique
form of knowledge. A Shelleyan irony is active in the refusal of such an
age to take Shelley very seriously. It may be that the fault lies not in
the critics but in the scholars, who continue to present the critics with
a philosophical Shelley, smothered by Platonism and other systems to
which the poetry, by being itself, actually opposes itself in its attempt to
visualize reality, to make a myth by its own power and in its own name,
not Plato's or Godwin's.

I have digressed, but in these chapters I shall not meet the morning star
in Shelley's poetry without digressing. Invariably, the appearance of the
morning star involves what is central in Shelley's mythmaking, and that
mythmaking, not previously studied, is the justification and the subject
claimed for this book.

Panthea has been delayed because her "wings were faint / With the
delight of a remembered dream." The remembered dream was one in
which the veil of corruption fell from the Titan's limbs, revealing the
equivalent to the New Testament's "risen body," but in its Blakean interpretation of the "Human Form Divine." With it came another dream,
momentarily forgotten by Panthea but suddenly recalled to her when
Asia reads a hint of it in her eyes. It is a kind of Behmenite dream, in
which one signature suddenly appears stamped on all natural things, the
word FOLLOW! Follow to the deep, the home of Demogorgon, is the
injunction. Before obeying, there are some points to be made about this
initial scene of Act II and some misapprehensions to correct.

Panthea's first dream has an element that critics consistently ignore
or misinterpret:

> the overpowering light
> Of that immortal shape was shadowed o'er
> By love; which, from his soft and flowing limbs,
> And passion-parted lips, and keen, faint eyes,
> Steamed forth like vaporous fire; an atmosphere
> Which wrapped me in its all-dissolving power,
> As the warm aether of the morning sun
> Wraps ere it drinks some cloud of wandering dew.
> I saw not, heard not, moved not, only felt
> His presence flow and mingle through my blood
> Till it became his life, and his grew mine,
> And I was thus absorbed . . .   [II.i.71–82]

And as this takes place in her dream, Panthea hears Prometheus mutter Asia's name. Ione wakes, having in her sleep been uneasily stirred by "something sweet, since it is sweet / Even to desire." When she kisses Panthea, the troubling element is stronger yet. Grabo thinks it to be mesmerism.[8]

Without agreeing with Bush's genial remark about a "seraglio," one still plainly perceives what in fact this element is. Panthea is surrogate for Asia until the dialectic shall accomplish a reversal (the point of the second dream). If you insisted on allegorizing this, then it might turn very sticky indeed. Read it literally and Panthea's dream is a schoolgirl's fantasy. Properly regarded, it makes an ironic but (toward Panthea and Ione) kindly point. Panthea is inadequate, Ione more so, on the level of Titanic sexuality. Apocalypse here, as in Blake, is incomplete without sexual fulfillment (Milton's vision of a higher degree of sexuality among the angels is parallel). One could claim Shelley, like Blake, as an ancestor for what is best in Lawrence, but critical followers of Lawrence might not be pleased at the genealogy.

Scene ii has received extensive scientific allegorizing at the hands of Grabo and Butter.[9] I need not again summarize my reasons for believing such allegorizings to be critically irrelevant.

The scene consists of a Sophoclean chorus of spirits, followed by a conversation between two fauns. The chorus is a lyrical exposition of the meaning of the downward journey of Asia and Panthea. Semichorus I defines the path of the journey in terms of Pottle's "narrowing image":

> The path through which that lovely twain
> Have passed, by cedar, pine, and yew,

8. Grabo, "Prometheus Unbound," p. 53.
9. Ibid., pp. 58–68. Butter, Shelley's Idols of the Cave, pp. 182–7.

> And each dark tree that ever grew,
> Is curtained out from Heaven's wide blue;
> Nor sun, nor moon, nor wind, nor rain,
>   Can pierce its interwoven bowers . . .   [II.ii.1–6]

The "narrowing image" is invoked as examples of what *can* pierce the "interwoven bowers" of this path are given. The path can be pierced by the transitory Thou, by momentary glimpses of relationship, by the narrowing images that convey the Beauty of the 1816 "Hymn":

> Nor aught, save where some cloud of dew,
> Drifted along the earth-creeping breeze,
> Between the trunks of the hoar trees,
>   Hangs each a pearl in the pale flowers
> Of the green laurel, blown anew;
> And bends, and then fades silently,
> One frail and fair anemone . . .   [7–13]

The picture is vivid, but the poetic excellence here has little to do with vividness. In the midst of phenomena, one image for an instant is confronted as reality, "and then fades silently." The dialectic of confrontation and reversal, of relationship and experience, of sharing and appropriation for one's self, the dialectic which is "Demogorgon's mighty law," is operative in such an image:

> Or when some star of many a one
> That climbs and wanders through steep night,
> Has found the cleft through which alone
> Beams fall from high those depths upon
> Ere it is borne away, away,
> By the swift Heavens that cannot stay,
> It scatters drops of golden light,
> Like lines of rain that ne'er unite . . .   [14–21]

Again the narrowing of the image and the programmatic shift from image to image convey the dialectic of Shelley's myth. If there is Necessity in that dialectic, then it is necessity with a small "n," the necessity of mythopoeic defeat, of "the swift Heavens that cannot stay."

In Semichorus II, the myth moves from confrontation of natural Thou's to the mutual confrontation of creatures, and the defeat of the myth, its tragic rhythm of alteration, augments in intensity of presentation as it approaches nearer to human relationship. The stanza is a foreboding of Swinburne's style, but at a level of controlled meaning that Swinburne did not often attain:

> There the voluptuous nightingales,
>   Are awake through all the broad noonday.

When one with bliss or sadness fails,
  And through the windless ivy-boughs,
  Sick with sweet love, droops dying away
On its mate's music-panting bosom;
Another from the swinging blossom.
  Watching to catch the languid close
  Of the last strain, then lifts on high
  The wings of the weak melody,
'Till some new strain of feeling bear
  The song, and all the woods are mute . . .   [24-35]

The individual relationship fails, "with bliss or sadness." The song of the nightingale, which is a narrowing image of such relationship, fails only to rise again. Line 29 is one of those Shelleyan commonplaces that now give most offence. The overcharged context provides some justification; these are "voluptuous nightingales." The adjective has been debased in our time, and can no longer be used as Shelley uses it here. The diction of this stanza is certainly erotic, but it is not vicious diction, conveying as it does intimations of a state of being which is not our own, though subject to our prime limitations.

The return of Semichorus I summarizes the dialectic of the downward journey:

There those enchanted eddies play
  Of echoes, music-tongued, which draw,
  By Demogorgon's mighty law,
  With melting rapture, or sweet awe,
All spirits on that secret way;
  As inland boats are driven to Ocean
Down streams made strong with mountain-thaw:
    And first there comes a gentle sound
    To those in talk or slumber bound,
  And wakes the destined soft emotion,—
Attracts, impels them; those who saw
    Say from the breathing earth behind
    There steams a plume-uplifting wind
Which drives them on their path, while they
    Believe their own swift wings and feet
The sweet desires within obey:
And so they float upon their way,
Until, still sweet, but loud and strong,
The storm of sound is driven along,
    Sucked up and hurrying: as they fleet
    Behind, its gathering billows meet
And to the fatal mountain bear
Like clouds amid the yielding air.   [41-63]

"Demogorgon's mighty law" I have already interpreted as being the dialectic of Shelley's myth of relationship. Read thus, the stanza is clarified in itself and in its relation to the remainder of the poem. We enter into the I-Thou relationship convinced that our wills are the agency behind the myth. But "those who saw," those who have learned the dialectic of reversal, the double-sided law of Demogorgon, know that an outward impulse is operative upon us as well. Moved by this fusion of grace and will we proceed on the stormy stream of relationship until we encounter "the fatal mountain" of Demogorgon, the point to which the relational event has run its full course. Like clouds borne to the mountain in their cycle of ocean → cloud → rain → mountain thaw → stream → ocean, even so our relationships are borne to the mountain (in which is situated Demogorgon's cave) in a mythic cycle of Thou → It → Thou.

The conclusion of scene ii, with its conversation of fauns, and scene iii, with its lyric of descent, need no analysis of the kind I am venturing here. Scene iv, set in the cave of Demogorgon, constitutes one of the central problems of the drama and needs close attention.

The history of "Demogorgon" (a spelling error transmuted into the most dreadful of gods) and my researches into that history I will consign to my notes.[1] The genesis of Shelley's Demogorgon is a fascinating problem, still not fully solved, but the *meaning* of Demogorgon in the poem has little to do with his genetic background.

The principal point to be noted about scene iv to begin with is its agnosticism. Faithful to the myth, the drama does not seek to know more of reality than the myth itself creates. The myth puts *its* faith precisely in what *can* be visualized, in what can then be confronted. Demogorgon cannot be visualized; you do not enter into relationship with a dialectic, but instead you are merely subject to it. Demogorgon is "a mighty darkness," "Ungazed upon and shapeless," a creature that has "neither limb, / Nor form, nor outline." He embodies the destiny of the relational event, its passing away into experience, *and* the contrary destiny—that of experience, its passing away into the relational event. The first process is that of Fall, the second of Redemption. To be this dual process, and nothing more, is to be considerably less than ultimate and to know

1. Theodontius, a Campanian philosopher who lived sometime between the 9th and 11th centuries, seems to be responsible for Demogorgon. Following Byzantine tradition, Theodontius assigned to Demogorgon (originally no more than an orthographical error) the fathership of the gods. Boccaccio popularized Demogorgon in his *Genealogy of the Gentile Gods,* which in turn was Peacock's principal source for his note on Demogorgon in *Rhododaphne,* Shelley's probable source. Hughes, ed., *Shelley,* p. 175, n. 1, gives the history of this derivation, and quotes Peacock's note. Two articles can be recommended as dealing with the genesis and career of Demogorgon: M. Castelain, "Démogorgon ou le barbarisme déifié," *Bull. Assoc. G. Bude, 36* (July 1932), 22–30; Cornelia C. Coulter, "The Genealogy of the Gods," *Vassar Mediaeval Studies* (1923), pp. 317–41. I have found, for myself, that a knowledge of Demogorgon's genesis does not aid much in one's reading of "Prometheus Unbound."

considerably less than everything. Demogorgon does not equivocate or evade—he quite simply *does not know* the answers to Asia's questions. They are the wrong questions for her to ask, for he knows only what *he* is. He tells Asia that he can reply to "All things thou dar'st demand," and the key word here is "dar'st." Courage is not in it; propriety is. And this is precisely what Asia comes to recognize before her dialogue with Demogorgon is done. Demogorgon can tell her only what she (and Prometheus) have already realized for themselves. All else *that can be known* she (and Prometheus) will have to discover through relationship, through a sharing in reality. Salvation is through the myth, and faith consequently must be restricted to the efficacy of the myth, the possibilities of poetry, of imaginative making. Not Christianity, not Platonism, not Godwinism is put forward in this scene, but rather a rejection of doctrine, an affirmation of an agnostic apocalypse, a humanism to be achieved through image-making powers but not through any specific images. "The deep truth is imageless," Demogorgon at length proclaims, and Asia is fully in agreement with him. Mutability dominates in the world of Itness, the state of experience—"Fate, Time, Occasion, Chance, and Change." "Eternal Love"—the confrontation of the I and the Thou—is alone not subject to experience. "And of such truths," as Asia remarks, "Each to itself must be the oracle"; received doctrine cannot perform this work. Yeats spoke of how "Prometheus Unbound" was to him in his youth "a holy book," and of how at first he hoped to reconstitute religion from the lyrical drama.[2] The old Yeats wrote of his disappointment with "Prometheus," of its failure to satisfy *in him* his expectations of its religion-making power. But his expectations were at fault and his impatience with Demogorgon unjustified. Demogorgon made the poem's plot incoherent, he complained; Demogorgon was there as a nightmare image to negate Shelley's images of desire.[3] The misunderstandings of one great poet by another who is very much in the same line of descent (here, from Spenser) can be a very valuable aid to our understanding of both poets. Yeats expected what Shelley *on mythmaking principle* refused to give. The point of scene iv, Act ii is that it refuses to put itself to us as Scripture—it precisely does not want to be "a holy book." The *Defence* knows all about the hardening of poetry into religion, and "Prometheus" knows what the *Defence* knows. Blake is what Yeats wanted, and in the final phase took. Blake offers *a* myth in place of religion—a contrapuntal myth which can fulfill all the functions of religion. Shelley is fiercely tentative—he gives us not a myth but only a fully conscious exemplification of the experiment of mythmaking. To Blake, the contraries make for progression; to Shelley the

2. W. B. Yeats, "The Philosophy of Shelley's Poetry," *Ideas of Good and Evil* (London, 1903), p. 91.
3. Yeats, "Prometheus Unbound," *Essays*, p. 57.

contraries are a program in themselves. Blake insists that he can liberate you from your condition; Shelley suggests that within your condition you cannot be liberated. Blake believes in *his* myth; Shelley only in myth itself. Yeats at length chose to emulate Blake, though he modified the tone of apocalyptic insistence back into the tone of the earlier Blake, that of cyclic irony. By doing so, he has gained a momentary reputation higher than that of either Blake or Shelley. Whether he will endure as they have endured and as they will endure is not a matter that even the most distinguished of our contemporary critics can well decide. His masters in vision—Spenser, Blake, Shelley—may at the last overshadow him, if only for having invariably *meant* as truth everything that they visualized in their poems.

Her questions dismissed, Asia holds to only one request for information: "When shall the destined Hour arrive?" The answer is of course *now*—"Behold!" With that answer, the concern of my thesis with scene iv is done.

The descent of Asia, ostensibly for information, actually in a quest for transfiguration, is followed by her reascent in more glorious form. She has descended because the rhythm of dialectic demanded it; the dark places required her as visitor before giving her up completely to the light. Not that she has ventured further into experience but only that she has found the point at which experience and relationship converge. And having found that truth, she is set free by it.

The opening of scene v, Act II, has provoked much argument over the time scheme of the drama, but Baker has a note which settled the difficulty to my satisfaction.[4] Asia's transfiguration is the mythic burden of this scene, and more nearly my own concern.

The suspended dawn ("The sun will not rise until noon," line 10) is suddenly illuminated by an outer manifestation of the inward change that has taken place in Asia, the change for which the descent was made. The lyrics that end the act attempt to communicate the nature of this transformation. Unfortunately, both lyrics have led an independent historical existence as anthology pieces, and the critical task in reading them begins with an attempt to restore them to context, so that a sense of strain is necessarily involved here in proper apprehension of two valuable poems.

Correct visualization is essential here, else both lyrics lack justification for their tone, for an intensity more narrowly developed and highly pitched than elsewhere even in Shelley. Asia is being modified back into her prelapsarian state; the songs must present her as incarnating an ultimate Thou. A mode of address not proper in lesser contexts is necessary here. The sublime is being affected, and the high style is therefore operative.

4. Baker, *Shelley's Major Poetry*, p. 108, n. 44.

The speeches of Panthea and Asia, preceding the "Life of Life" lyric and Asia's rejoinder, are probably vulnerable to Cleanth Brooks's strictures upon poetry that exhibits only primary impulses. The lyrics, as I shall show, are not liable to the charge, and are indeed built on ironic foundations that can withstand contemporary criticism.

The "Voice in the Air, singing," after Asia's transfiguration, is a Shakespearean device of the kind so persuasively analyzed in Knight's criticism. Samuel Barber's "Music for a Scene from Shelley" is the most successful attempt among several similar efforts to realize this "Voice."

Bush is entertaining, but perhaps not very instructive, on the lyrics that follow: "Then we come to the two lyrics, 'Life of Life' and 'My soul is an enchanted boat.' At this point all good Shelleyans face the east, and regard an attempt to discern the meaning as both prosaic and profane; those who desire more in poetry than rapturous reverie, who ask that feeling shall have direction as well as intensity, must not enter the temple with their thick-soled shoes." [5] Facing (I think) north-northwest as I write but walking barefoot into the temple, I pass to a close consideration of these two poems.

Fogle speaks of the "dazzling 'Life of Life' lyric, from which one may strip off layer after layer without arriving at any solid certainty." [6] To him, the poem embodies the "finite-infinite" conflict, which he finds at the heart of Shelley's imagery. I agree with his reading of the poem's imagery (indeed his study of Shelley's imagery seems to me to be definitive). I offer my reading here to supplement and in turn to be supplemented by his.

> Life of Life! thy lips enkindle
>   With their love the breath between them;
> And thy smiles before they dwindle
>   Make the cold air fire; then screen them
> In those looks, where whoso gazes
> Faints, entangled in their mazes.   [II.v.48–53]

This stanza has prompted Stephen Spender to demonstrate that he too can be a scrutinoid: "Unless one is carried away by the sheer intensity of this, one wonders how the last three lines work out. How can you be screened by looks which are also mazes in which whoever gazes becomes entangled and faints? An image which suggests a mental structure in the mind of the reader—and how could one draw such a picture?" [7]

The voices address Asia as "Life of Life"—a Word within a Word, a Thou within a Thou, ultimate reality directly confronted. But this "Life of Life," as is no surprise, Shelley presents as paradoxical in mani-

---

5. Bush, *Mythology and the Romantic Tradition,* pp. 147–8.
6. Fogle, *Imagery,* pp. 234–5.
7. Stephen Spender, *Shelley* (London, British Council, 1952), p. 32.

festation. She is always there to be apprehended; we are not always there to confront her. When confronted, her smiles "make the cold air fire," are life-giving, just as her lips are. But the smiles dwindle, just as the Beauty of the "Hymn" dwindled in each of the phenomena visited. The Thou becomes an It; "thy smiles" become "those looks," as the Thou becomes hidden. And the pursuit of It, questing for Thou, is hopeless; entangled in the mazes of the natural world, the pursuer will never achieve his quest. To be so entangled is to gaze on the It, expecting the Thou, and the result is conveyed by "faints." Instead of Asia's smiles, you see only her screening looks. The Thou will not remain fixed for you, whatever your devotion, for by your natural bondage to the realm of It you cannot always be there to be confronted yourself as a Thou. Spender's "mental structure" which he cannot draw is irrelevant· Shelley is not sending him to the sketching board.

> Child of Light! thy limbs are burning
> Through the vest which seems to hide them;
> As the radiant lines of morning
> Through the clouds ere they divide them;
> And this atmosphere divinest
> Shrouds thee whereso'er thou shinest.   [54–9]

The paradox becomes yet more extreme. This ultimate Thou has its reality, *for us,* to the extent that we can share in it without appropriating for ourselves. When we try to visualize the reality in itself, to appropriate it, we are defeated; precisely, we get a series of It's again. Fogle is apt: each Thou we attempt to grasp becomes only another veil of itness to be stripped off, an endless series of Thou's within Thou's, each becoming in turn an It as we pass out of relationship into analysis of our experience of the poem. Asia is Child of Light: all revealment then, revelation precisely; no concealment, no mystery. But the Light is so much Light *of* Light that its brightness puts our eyes out. Asia's limbs "are burning / through the vest" which only "seems to hide them." But the limbs are themselves the vest; the "burning through" is the vital phrase here, just as it is in the final lines of "Adonais":

> Whilst, burning through the inmost veil of Heaven,
> The soul of Adonais, like a star,
> Beacons from the abode where the Eternal are.

The star there is the morning star (as Baker's discussion well evidences).[8] Here in "Life of Life," the "burning through" is paralleled to the similar burning through the as yet undivided "clouds" of darkness by the light of morning. The clouds have not yet been divided; the vest hiding Asia has not yet been removed, for the vest is her limbs. "Seems

8. Baker, p. 248.

to hide" in line 55 is wonderfully ambiguous; her limbs only *seem* to be hidden, for they burn through the vest; yet the vest does hide them, because it seems to hide them. The final couplet confirms the paradox; the light which burns through the vest, or at least the burning-through itself, is "this atmosphere divinest." Or again, the light, or the burning through, cannot be distinguished from the vest, so the vest may be "this atmosphere divinest." And in a line which carries paradox to a climax, this most divine of atmospheres *shrouds* Asia wheresoever she *shines*. The stanza is calculated to defeat analysis; its imagery deliberately refuses to be unraveled. Asia's Thou is to be met, not explicated. The poetry itself here is determinedly anticritical, with superb aplomb. Faced by it, the New Critic, in love with his instrument of analysis, will throw away the poem, not the instrument.

> Fair are others; none beholds thee,
>   But thy voice sounds low and tender
> Like the fairest, for it folds thee
>   From the sight, that liquid splendour,
> And all feel, yet see thee never,
> As I feel now, lost for ever!   [60–5]

This third stanza weaves a variation on the lyric's central paradox. "None beholds thee" confirms the previous stanza. What is unbeheld needs to be visualized by invoking parallels, analogues of the seen. One begins with "fair are others"—the voice of Asia is "like the fairest." But her voice also "folds" her "from the sight"—the reference may well be back to the first stanza. Her lips enkindle the breath between them, and this fire of love helps conceal her. "That liquid splendour" has "sight," in the sense of "eye," as antecedent. The final couplet, like the final couplets of the first two stanzas, focuses on the paradox proper, the unseen radiance, and on the deprivation suffered by the I suddenly bereft of the Thou.

> Lamp of Earth! where'er thou movest
>   Its dim shapes are clad with brightness,
> And the souls of whom thou lovest
>   Walk upon the winds with lightness,
> Till they fail, as I am failing,
> Dizzy, lost, yet unbewailing!   [66–71]

The final stanza considers the effect of having met the ultimate Thou of Asia in relationship. She is the "Lamp of Earth," and Earth's otherwise "dim shades" can be brightly perceived wherever she moves. But when she has moved on, the shades dim again. I's, liberated by her confrontation, "walk upon the winds with lightness, / *Till* they fail." Fail they must, as the song's I now fails, in the dizzy and lost condition we have seen previously in the "Ode to the West Wind's" fourth stanza. The Thou seems to become an It, and the singer tumbles down again into the thorniness of experience. "Yet unbewailing!" he reminds us here as the lyric closes, for he fully knows the paradox inherent in the myth that sustains him. The Thou of Asia, by its nature, cannot become an It. But we, as I's, by our nature cannot sustain relationship with her. And this lyric confirms that truth, demonstrating by its structure that Asia's Thou "may properly only be addressed, not expressed." [9]

In reply to this lyric, Asia sings a greater poem to the Voice in the Air. Inwardly, she is going back to the earthly paradise, back to Beulah, the "married land," the seedbed of life, the Adonis Garden. She is being reborn that she may be fit bride for the reborn Prometheus. Singing directly out of the radiance of paradox, the "Life of Life" depicts a voyage beyond the comprehension of the senses, a journey from one state of existence to another. The technical achievement surpasses anything previous in Shelley:

> My soul is an enchanted boat,
> Which, like a sleeping swan, doth float
> Upon the silver waves of thy sweet singing;
> And thine doth like an angel sit
> Beside a helm conducting it.
> Whilst all the winds with melody are ringing.
> It seems to float ever, for ever,
> Upon that many-winding river,
> Between mountains, woods, abysses,
> A paradise of wildernesses!
> Till, like one in slumber bound,
> Borne to the ocean, I float down, around,
> Into a sea profound, of ever-spreading sound . . .   [72–84]

In "The Tower" Yeats, with deliberate casualness, remembered that "some moralist or mythological poet / Compares the solitary soul to a swan." [1] The solitary soul of Asia, the Thou speaking out of its Thouness, and not in relationship but with the impact of revelation, is compared by her to a sleeping swan, floating motionless on the silver waves of the "Life of Life" lyric. This is only *like,* momentary. *Like* the sleeping swan, she is poised for an instant in the lyric. But her soul *is* an enchanted boat, and is not just like one. This similitude is felt as identity, and is extended throughout the three stanzas of the poem. The enchanted boat moves without sail, without oars, "where never mortal pinnace glided." Her solitary soul moves, propelled by no force external to that soul. The soul of the Voice in the Air (Hughes wrongly, in my opinion,

9. Buber, *I and Thou,* p. 81.
1. "Nineteen Hundred and Nineteen," *Collected Poems,* p. 234.

identifies the Voice in the Air with the voice of Prometheus) [2] sits "like an angel" (messenger, guide) beside a helm, conducting the boat of Asia's soul with its song, and making the surrounding woods ring with melody. The boat-soul floats out of time—"ever, for-ever"—and out of any but visionary place, as the downriver journey continues to culminate in a somnambulistic descent into deep ocean.

With this descent, the laws of the natural state bind no longer. The Voice in the Air, poetry incarnate, lifts its pinions, just as the curious Hermaphrodite will do in "The Witch of Atlas," when the Witch insists that the boat of *her* desire go upstream, against the current. The winds of song's "most serene dominions" propel the boat-soul in defiance of nature:

> Meanwhile thy spirit lifts its pinions
> In music's most serene dominions;
> Catching the winds that fan that happy heaven.
> And we sail on, away, afar,
> Without a course, without a star,
> But, by the instinct of sweet music driven;
> Till through Elysian garden islets
> By thee, most beautiful of pilots,
> Where never mortal pinnace glided,
> The boat of my desire is guided:
> Realms where the air we breathe is love,
> Which in the winds and on the waves doth move,
> Harmonizing this earth with what we feel above. [85–97]

Her soul moves instinctively, in obedience to her harmonized will and desire; the boat responds to the lyric's prompting, and enters into a region of "Elysian garden islets," the poet's paradise envisioned at the conclusion of "Lines Written among the Euganean Hills" and "Epipsychidion." The nature of this region, with its paradoxical reality, greater and yet less than ours, is explored in the lyric's final stanza:

> We have passed Age's icy caves,
> And Manhood's dark and tossing waves,
> And Youth's smooth ocean, smiling to betray:
> Beyond the glassy gulfs we flee
> Of shadow-peopled Infancy,
> Through Death and Birth, to a diviner day;
> A paradise of vaulted bowers,
> Lit by downward-gazing flowers,
> And watery paths that wind between
> Wildernesses calm and green,

2. Hughes, ed., *Shelley*, p. 198.

> Peopled by shapes too bright to see,
> And rest, having beheld; somewhat like thee;
> Which walk upon the sea, and chant melodiously! [98–110]

Bush and Baker agree with E. M. W. Tillyard on the probable derivation of this ascent "to a diviner day" from the similar myth of reversed
cycle in Plato's *Statesman*.³ I do not find any essential similarity to
Plato's myth here; Asia is going back to a state of innocence ironically
perceived and paradoxically presented. Like Alice through the looking
glass, she is fleeing "beyond the glassy gulfs." The *tone* of the imagery is
all-important here. The voyage is *backward* through experience, the
object world of fallen nature. *Retreat* is the dominant pattern. Blake's
"Book of Thel" is the best analogue, as my discussion of "The Sensitive
Plant" attempts to evidence. This retreat to the lower paradise is fatal
for created beings, as Spenser's Bower of Blisse, Blake's myth, and
Shelley's last vision in "The Triumph of Life" make clear. Asia's order of
reality is sufficiently different from our own, the poem asks us to believe,
so that she can manage the journey backward to Beulah with impunity.
In Spenserian terms, she is re-entering the Gardens of Adonis momentarily and out of cycle to replenish what is vital in her in that seedbed of
life.

The icy caves of Age and the rough ocean of Manhood (the imagery
may be too public here) yield to the smooth ocean of Youth, deceptively
placid. As the ocean smooths to an extreme, it recedes to a surface that
can be characterized as "glassy gulfs." Here the imagery is more ro-
bustly organic and interwoven. The looking-glass world, peopled with
shadows, evokes Infancy and the attendant paradox: are we losing or
gaining in reality by this journey? But the voyage is too swift for doubts;
flight goes beyond Infancy and into the lower paradise of an unborn
world, fully parallel to the Gardens of Adonis and the land of Beulah.
And now paradox is crowded upon us: we go backward not through
Birth alone to "a diviner day" but "through Death *and* Birth." The
phrase, in context, is almost inexhaustible to meditation. "Birth" is our
birth into natural, everyday life, but what is "Death"? Death to the
lower paradise, but Death which is also Birth, a movement to a lower
reality which is yet richer in imaginative content and therefore more real
than the Beulah of creative repose. Death here is also Birth, but Birth
here is also Death. The equivalent nice balance of paradox is the Christian
vision of the Birth of Jesus, God being born into Death, man dying into
Birth, a vision which shades into the pattern of Pauline doctrine: dying
that you may be twice born, being born again that you may die into Birth,
not Death. I am paralleling a mode of paradox here, nothing else. Asia's

---

3. Bush, p. 148, n. 43. Baker, p. 108. E. M. W. Tillyard, letter in *TLS* (Sept. 29,
1932), p. 691.

song is not compatible with Christianity, offering as it does a counter-myth.

Through the looking glass, and we are in a world of talking flowers. Through the glassy gulfs, and we are in a *paradise* of vaulted *bowers,* illuminated by flowers that do not turn their faces to the sun, but "unnaturally" gaze downward in a richly suggestive figure. A world of winding watery paths, rivers of paradise, pulsing with life. A paradise, a park or garden, wildernesses tamed, "calm and green." And the inhabitants, dark with excessive light, "too bright to see," paradox epitomized; and "having beheld" what is "too bright to see," we rest. We are in the state of creative repose, inhabiting a Beulah in Bunyan's sense as well as Blake's or Isaiah's, a nature more real than nature because God has taken his delight in it, and it is "married land," Beulah; where Venus and Adonis perpetually are in union; an It redeemed into Thou. We are become *"somewhat* like thee," the lyrical Voices in the Air, which are more than natural, "which walk upon the sea." And having been included by Asia in her "we" and having sung her song, we can grant that like the Voice in the Air singing "Life of Life" we "chant Melodiously."

3

The opening scene of Act III, Jupiter's downfall, is powerfully imagined, but requires little commentary of the kind my thesis can provide. Jupiter speaks (line 18) of having "even now . . . begotten a strange wonder," a "fatal child" fathered upon Thetis. This child at "the destined hour" will rise from the throne of Demogorgon, having put on Demogorgon's might, and ascend to his father Jupiter. Next the fatal child will "redescend, and trample out the spark" of Promethean defiance. This is Jupiter's vision, set forth to Thetis:

> even then
> Two mighty spirits, mingling, made a third
> Mightier than either, which, unbodied now,
> Between us floats, felt, although unbeheld,
> Waiting the incarnation, which ascends,
> (Hear ye the thunder of the fiery wheels
> Griding the winds?) from Demogorgon's throne.
> Victory! victory! Feel'st thou not, O world,
> The earthquake of his chariot thundering up
> Olympus? . . .   [III.i.42–51]

This problem of "Father-Son Succession" is usefully dealt with by Baker, in Appendix 3 of his book.[4] I agree with Baker that Demogorgon is "a son of Jupiter only in the ironic sense that he is the agent who will

4. Baker, pp. 281–3.

dethrone him." But I do not agree with Baker's surmise that Jupiter expects Demogorgon to "ascend to Olympus, enter into and thus produce an incarnation of Jupiter's as yet 'unbodied' son." The "incarnation . . . ascends . . . from Demogorgon's throne," but that is not to say that Demogorgon is in any way involved in the incarnation, except possibly as intended victim. The fatal child is to replace Demogorgon, to put on his might, to leave his throne "vacant." Prometheus sees Demogorgon as being what indeed he is, dialectical, but Jupiter sees this dread power as being unidirectional. The fatal child, once incarnated, will do (his father hopes) what his father could not do, that is, usurp the power of Demogorgon, fix it more firmly still in its direction of Fall. But Jupiter mistakes his efficacy; the grim secret that Prometheus knows and will not reveal is that Jupiter *has engendered no child at all*. The dialectic has gone into reverse; the unbodied fatal child is "unbeheld" for a sound reason: he does not and will not exist. Not a menacing child but the infants of apocalypse have been born in this turn of the dialectic. The "wingèd infant" of Ione's vision of the moon chariot and the young Spirit of the Earth of Panthea's vision of "a sphere, which is as many thousand spheres," the dominant figures in Act IV, are counterpoises to the unborn child of Jupiter.

Demogorgon himself arrives in the Car of the Hour, and drags down Jupiter into the abyss. What follows, in scene ii, is perhaps the calmest moment in Shelley's poetry, a dialogue of deep peace between Ocean and Apollo.

The scene is set at the mouth of a great river in the island Atlantis, with Ocean reclining near the shore and Apollo standing beside him. Atlantis is chosen for implicit reasons close to Blake's symbolic purposes in utilizing that titanic lost island. Atlantis is fallen land, a human culture overborne by the Thunderer, now fallen himself. A restored Atlantis, a vision of the lower paradise, is a necessary concomitant to the fall of Jupiter.

Lewis and Bush have preceded me in recording an admiration for this scene of postlapsarian peace.[5] The language of Ocean and Apollo here is rounded and golden and manifestly Shakespearean in its authority. Pastoral tradition in English poetry, in its main Spenserian line, culminates in Ocean's vision of a pastured sea:

> Henceforth the fields of heaven-reflecting sea
> Which are my realm, will heave, unstained with blood,
> Beneath the uplifting winds, like plains of corn
> Swayed by the summer air; my streams will flow
> Round many-peopled continents, and round

5. Lewis, *Rehabilitations,* p. 33. I cannot find this reference anywhere in Bush, but I believe that some sentence of his first singled out this line.

> Fortunate isles; and from their glassy thrones
> Blue Proteus and his humid nymphs shall mark
> The shadow of fair ships, as mortals see
> The floating bark of the light-laden moon
> With that white star, its sightless pilot's crest,
> Borne down the rapid sunset's ebbing sea . . .   [III.ii.18–28]

The unpastured sea is Chaos; the pastured sea reflects heaven, and is a lower paradise. And there will be no more sea, in effect. The ships of a redeemed commerce among nations are analogically visualized in Shelley's favorite apocalyptic figure of the new moon with the old moon in its arms, guided by the evening star through its night journey. Apollo replies to this figure with its complement, which summons him to *his* journey of relationship:

> I hear
> The small, clear, silver lute of the young Spirit
> That sits i' the morning star.

In this final dawn the awakening sea cries out for its pastor's ministrations. The lines that carry this looking-up-to-be-fed by a hungry sea are quite simply the finest Shelley ever wrote:

> The loud deep calls me home even now to feed it
> With azure calm out of the emerald urns
> Which stand for ever full beside my throne.
> Behold the Nereids under the green sea,
> Their wavering limbs born on the wind-like stream,
> Their white arms lifted o'er their streaming hair
> With garlands pied and starry sea-flower crowns,
> Hastening to grace their mighty sister's joy.
>   [A *sound of waves is heard*.]
> It is the unpastured sea hungering for calm.
> Peace, monster; I come now. Farewell.   [41–50]

Line 49 is packed with more meaning than any eight words elsewhere in Shelley (or indeed, in all but a few poets) could sustain. A completed Spenserian vision is contained in that one line, which epitomizes Shelley's poetry in the broad. The imaginative force of the line lies ultimately without the sphere of analysis, but one can note how thoroughly the poem has earned the right to the line. The statement is final, definitive, hence its force; but justifying the statement is a wealth of the tentative, of the dangerous dialectic of Shelley's myth. The poem has explored the possibilities of what for its poet constitutes imaginative damnation: the universe of Itness, of subject-object experience. Having done so, the poem has done with that contrary of the dialectic and sings now of innocence. Sentimentality can be brought to the poem here by the wrong reader, but the poem has progressed beyond that state which belongs to a reader's realm of negations, not to the poem's world of contraries. The poem's impulse now is indeed primary; the secondary is irrelevant to it. The irony of modern criticism, a secondary impulse, cannot touch the poem now, for it is deflected by the primary irony of the poem's dialectic, file to its serpent. And next to the magnificence of line 49 is the rough affection of line 50, with its aura of deep peace as Ocean replies to his charge. The pauses in line 50 are remarkable, for they have cognitive content. The fatherliness that lies behind the affection of Ocean for his "monster" is held in the first pause, before "I come now." In that next pause, before the "Farewell" to Apollo, the profound satisfaction of the shepherd of the waves can be surmised. "Prometheus" may have been too ambitious a poem for a lyrical poet still in his middle twenties; certainly the third act in particular has dismaying features. But here, in at least one scene, Shelley voids all carping. One can reject the vision here on many grounds, if one desires to do so, but immaturity cannot well be among them.

In scene iii we are back in the Caucasus. Asia and Panthea have returned from their journey on the downward path of wisdom, and the mode of their return, in the triumphal car which bears the Spirit of the Hour, is signal enough to Hercules to unbind Prometheus. From this point on, Shelley is confronted by all the technical difficulties involved in depicting a lower paradise. *Lower* paradise, Beulah-land, it most certainly is, for in the cave in which the four-fold grouping of Prometheus, Asia, Panthea, and Ione will dwell, the theme for passionate discussion will be mutability:

> Where we will sit and talk of time and change,
> As the world ebbs and flows, ourselves unchanged.
> What can hide man from mutability?   [III.iii.23–5]

"Our selves unchanged," because we have retreated into the finality of our cave, out of the mutable earthly paradise. And within the Byzantine security of the cave, monuments of unaging intellect will be fashioned, in beauty of changeless metal. Within the cave

> We will entangle buds and flowers and beams
> Which twinkle on the fountain's brim, and make
> Strange combinations out of common things,
> Like human babes in their brief innocence . . .   [30–3]

Without the ballast of Itness, the other pole of the Promethean dialectic, the verse in Acts III and IV tends to be inferior to that of the earlier sections of the drama. In "The Witch of Atlas," as I shall show, an urbane, almost cynical tone tends to make firm the visionary texture.

Implicit in Acts III and IV is the possibility of apocalyptic reversal, as I have said, but it may be that a few explicit reminders of the *ouroboros* nature of the drama's myth might have improved the poetry here. In Blake, reality is reconstituted through strife, as the warring Zoas and their emanations come together again. In Shelley, all the strife is ended before the reconstitution begins. The rhetorical contrast is instructive. Shelley's Titans hold converse thus:

> And if ye sigh, then I will smile; and thou,
> Ione, shalt chant fragments of sea-music,
> Until I weep, when ye shall smile away
> The tears she brought, which yet were sweet to shed.

The "Four Living Creatures" of Blake's apocalypse converse together also, in their attempt at remaking reality. But the *tone* of discourse has little in common with Shelley's presentation, though in other matters similarities are instantly perceptible. One could wish that Prometheus and the triad of Oceanides were being depicted here:

> And they conversed together in Visionary forms dramatic which bright
> Redounded from their Tongues in thunderous majesty, in Visions
> In new Expanses, creating exemplars of Memory and of Intellect,
> Creating Space, Creating Time, according to the wonders Divine
> Of Human Imagination throughout all the Three Regions immense
> Of Childhood, Manhood & Old Age; & the all tremendous unfathomable
>   Non Ens
> Of Death was seen in regenerations terrific or complacent, varying
> According to the subject of discourse; & every Word & every Character
> Was Human according to the Expansion or Contraction, the Translu-
>   cence or
> Opakeness of Nervous fibres: such was the variation of Time & Space
> Which vary according as the Organs of Perception vary; & they walked
> To & fro in Eternity as One Man, reflecting each in each & clearly seen
> And seeing, according to fitness & order.
>
> > [Keynes, "Jerusalem," plate 98, p. 566]

Blake's diction is strong and nervous because his "Four Living Creatures" still have the capacity for disunion. The style's vigor is built on the potential tension between an anagogical thrust toward finality and the recalcitrant nature of the four human faculties which need to be combined in that thrust. The feminine, placid diction of scene iii, Act III of "Prometheus" results from the lack of felt potential toward conflict and separation in Shelley's "Living Creatures." The myth in Shelley that this thesis explores provides that potential in the abstract, but here in scene iii it unfortunately does not seem to be operative.

The strength of scene iii is not in this cave visualization, I think, but rather in the mythic device of the "curvèd shell" of Proteus and in the startled joy of a revivified Mother Earth. The shell is a Wordsworthian device, as Knight and Butter have noted, and I agree with Butter that Wordsworth made "the more precise and effective use" of it, at least in "The Prelude" if not in "The Excursion." [6] Neither Shelley's use of the shell nor his vision of an Earth redeemed into a mutual relationship of all her components can be said to illustrate new aspects of his mythopoeia. I pass therefore without further discussion to the final scene of Act III.

Earth in scene iii introduced a winged child, a Spirit of the Earth, whose function it was to guide Prometheus and Asia to yet another cave for their reuniting. This child is perhaps the least successful creation in the entire drama, in contrast to the remarkable child-visions of the last act. Lines 25–97 of scene iv are given over to a conversation between this child and Asia, an interplay of affection in which Beulah-land dissolves away into the bog of Namby-Pamby land. The necessary function of this conversation I cannot ascertain, and previous commentators are of little help here. The passage *is* decorative; it has *all* the characteristic faults of Shelley's poetry at that poetry's worst, and I would be dishonest if I attempted to defend it by barbing it around with the formidable irony of Shelley's myth of relationship. A poor consolation can be obtained by recalling the waste stretches in the last two books of "Paradise Lost." Lewis, very eminent advocate of the poem though he is, has confessed that he "must be content to say that Milton's talent temporarily failed him" in much of those last two books.[7] Partisan as I am, I can only say the same of Shelley here and at other moments in the two final acts of "Prometheus."

Milton, as Lewis points out, makes a great recovery at the end of his poem; so does Shelley at the end of Act III. The act, and the drama proper, conclude with a long (over one hundred lines) and eloquent speech by the Spirit of the Hour. The Spirit of the Earth, in his best passage, had described how:

> All things had put their evil nature off:
> I cannot tell my joy, when o'er a lake
> Upon a drooping bough with nightshade twined,
> I saw two azure halcyons clinging downward
> And thinning one bright bunch of amber berries,
> With quick long beaks, and in the deep there lay
> Those lovely forms imaged as in a sky.   [III.iv.77–83]

Nightshade berries devoured by the quick long beaks of azure halcyons, birds of abiding peace; the halcyons themselves have realized that night-

6. Knight, *The Starlit Dome*, p. 212. Butter, *Shelley's Idols of the Cave*, p. 198.
7. *A Preface to Paradise Lost*, p. 125.

shade no longer has noxious qualities, that all things have put their evil nature off. They forsake fish for apocalyptic berries. The Spirit of the Earth draws no morals; the Spirit of the Hour, emblem of the *now,* is left to summarize the meanings of the state of natural redemption, much as Demogorgon, at the close of Act iv, summarizes his own meaning, the dialectic which makes for the redemption of the state of nature.

The Spirit of the Hour, and the coursers which draw his moon-like car, henceforth will rest, "exempt from toil." The car, vehicular form of the now, the willing agent of apocalypse, will stand within the temple of Prometheus as reminder and against the day of reversal, we may surmise. A remarkable passage is the key to this concept:

> Yoked to it by an amphisbaenic snake
> The likeness of those wingèd steeds will mock
> The flight from which they find repose. [119–21]

This is another of those extraordinary prophetic ironies in which Shelley's mature poetry abides. The Amphisbaena (out of Lucan, according to Hughes) [8] is a mythic serpent~with a head at each end of its body. Like the Law of Demogorgon, it can move either way. Under the throne of the unknown God of this drama is coiled a "snake-like Doom" (ii.iii.97) perpetually ready to be unloosed through life's portal. Related to these serpents is the ouroboros, serpent swallowing its own tail, hermetic emblem of Blake's Orc cycle and of the cycle which struggles against eternity in Shelley's vision as well. Demogorgon, in his final speech, refers us again to the ouroboros, as we shall see. Here in Act iii the amphisbaenic snake yokes together the museum piece Car of the Hour and "the likeness of those wingèd steeds," the steeds themselves having "sought their birthplace in the sun" where they graze perpetually, "pasturing flowers of vegetable fire." This likeness of steeds, encased in its visionary museum, will *mock* "the flight from which they find repose." What we have here is Shelley's finest defiance of time, conveyed by a figure terrifying in its implications and fiercely triumphant in its immediacy. As in "The Witch of Atlas," we have also a clear anticipation of Yeats's "Byzantium," where visionary cocks can scorn aloud, in glory of changeless metal, every common bird, every time-bound and flesh-bound complexity of blood and mire, because they mock from within the artifice of Eternity. The flight of the Hours is over; the *likeness,* artifice of the winged steeds, standing in its Byzantine showcase, the temple of Prometheus, can therefore *mock* the now unnecessary flight. But it is not the steeds themselves that mock; only their artifice is involved. The steeds pasture in the redeemed sun, against a fatal Hour, the Hour of reversal, when relationship shall dissolve again. Therefore the likeness, the con-

8. Hughes, ed., *Shelley,* p. 204.

struct of Eternity, is yoked to the temporal car by the Amphisbaena, the two-way snake. The artifice can no more draw the Car than the Car the artifice. When the Hour of reversal comes again and the implicit burden of Shelley's myth is *when* and not *if,* then the Amphisbaena shall be unyoked, the artifice put aside, the steeds from the sun reattached, and car and Prometheus shall together be driven from the temple of Eternity.

The greater part of the speech of the Spirit of the Hour needs no analysis to mock its clear eloquence. The final passage will sustain commentary:

> The loathsome mask has fallen, the man remains
> Sceptreless, free, uncircumscribed, but man
> Equal, unclassed, tribeless, and nationless,
> Exempt from awe, worship, degree, the king
> Over himself; just, gentle, wise: but man
> Passionless?—no, yet free from guilt or pain,
> Which were, for his will made or suffered them,
> Nor yet exempt, though ruling them like slaves,
> From chance, and death, and mutability,
> The clogs of that which else might oversoar
> The loftiest star of unascended heaven,
> Pinnacled dim in the intense inane.   [193–204]

The "narrowing image" finds its ultimate home here, in the void of infinite space. The greatness of this passage is in its passionate undersong, which presents a contrary to every one of its overt affirmations, which replies to aspiration with the irreconcilability between transcendent desire and human limits. The triple burden, of chance and death and mutability, does not invalidate the aspiration toward an ultimate Thou, but it crushes the technique of relationship which alone can flesh that aspiration. One is tempted to substitute the word "ballast" for "clogs" in line 202; the "that which else" would no longer be poetry or any apprehensible reality, if unclogged, and the poet Shelley is aware of his ultimate paradox. The lyrical drama stops where it must, on the border of a region in which "the intense inane" might bear an unflattering double meaning. Poised at this limit of expression, the poem bends back on itself, forgets Prometheus and Asia, and bursts into a hymn of triumph.

4

Act IV is a sustained nuptial song in honor of the state of pastoral innocence, renewed relationship, into which all living substance has again emerged. More narrowly, it is a specific epithalamium for the reunion of Prometheus and Asia, who are carefully kept offstage throughout. As befits an epithalamium, much of the act is specifically sexual in nature. Prometheus and Asia are withdrawn into their cave; earth and moon enact a macrocosmic and hermetic analogy to the union of Titan and nymph.

Panthea and Ione, sleeping near the nuptial cave, awaken gradually during the act's first song. Their function is to be audience for a masque of interlocked song and rushing vision. They do not interpret, but they describe for us every vision that does not join in the song.

Roughly the first third of the act is an aesthetic disaster. The dead Hours pass first, hymning their own dirge, specters bearing Time to his tomb in eternity. Their strophes, like the choruses of liberated Spirits which follow, are mechanical little songs, exemplifying Shelley's near-fatal lyrical fluency. He cannot have taken much trouble in their composition, which is the only consolation a friendly reader can offer to other readers here. One stanza has interest as being perhaps the worst the poet ever produced:

> And our singing shall build
> In the void's loose field
> A world for the Spirit of Wisdom to wield;
> We will take our plan
> From the new world of man,
> And our work shall be called the Promethean.
>
> [IV.i.153–8]

This has about it a peculiar ignobility. One cannot extenuate it, Polonius-fashion, by assigning it to the sphere of the hortatory-prophetic. Fifteen years before, Blake had utilized the same impulse, with happier consequences:

> I will not cease from Mental Fight,
> Nor shall my Sword sleep in my hand
> Till we have built Jerusalem
> In England's green & pleasant Land.

This second apocalyptic laboring tune is steady and resolute, the hymn of a veteran prophet, sustained by the harshness of experience, visionary and otherwise. He will fight on until he wins, but every line counts the cost, knows the tyranny of time. A poem that sets itself among dark Satanic Mills begins to earn the right to sing of the New Jerusalem. Red Crosse sees the City in the distance, after he has survived the temptation of Despaire. Even if we overlooked the Poe-like jingle of Shelley's stanza, we would want it to glance back at earlier things in "Prometheus" before it threw itself so heartily into "the void's loose field." As it stands, it has the poetic quality of a cheerleader's chant.

Yet from this bathetic depth the drama rises suddenly to the poetic level of Ezekiel. Two visions suddenly burst forth from two openings in the forest surrounding the cave. Never fully analyzed or apprehended by critics of the poem, all too frequently ignored completely, these visions are the mythic culminations of "Prometheus Unbound." Everything else in Act IV can be briefly summarized; these visions require something more of an energy of response. The first and, as Blake would have said, less terrific of these visions is fittingly described by the gentlest and least of the Oceanides, Ione:

> I see a chariot like that thinnest boat,
> In which the Mother of the Months is borne
> By ebbing light into her western cave,
> When she upsprings from interlunar dreams;
> O'er which is curved an orblike canopy   210
> Of gentle darkness, and the hills and woods,
> Distinctly seen through that dusk aery veil,
> Regard like shapes in an enchanter's glass;
> Its wheels are solid clouds, azure and gold,
> Such as the genii of the thunderstorm   215
> Pile on the floor of the illumined sea
> When the sun rushes under it; they roll
> And move and grow as with an inward wind;
> Within it sits a wingèd infant, white
> Its countenance, like the whiteness of bright snow,   220
> Its plumes are as feathers of sunny frost,
> Its limbs gleam white, through the wind-flowing folds
> Of its white robe, woof of ethereal pearl.
> Its hair is white, the brightness of white light
> Scattered in strings; yet its two eyes are heavens   225
> Of liquid darkness, which the Deity
> Within seems pouring, as a storm is poured
> From jaggèd clouds, out of their arrowy lashes,
> Tempering the cold and radiant air around,
> With fire that is not brightness; in its hand   230
> It sways a quivering moonbeam, from whose point
> A guiding power directs the chariot's prow
> Over its wheeled clouds, which as they roll
> Over the grass, and flowers, and waves, wake sounds,
> Sweet as a singing rain of silver dew.   235

Grabo and Butter have worked out what they take to be the "scientific meaning" of this and the immediately subsequent vision.[9] Both visions, like that in "The Triumph of Life," stem ultimately from Ezekiel's vision of the Enthroned Man. Why not look for "science" behind

9. Grabo, *"Prometheus Unbound,"* pp. 139–43. Butter, pp. 153–6. Carl Grabo, *A Newton among Poets* (Chapel Hill, Univ. of North Carolina Press, 1930), pp. 151ff.

Ezekiel's vision as well as Shelley's then? The point is that neither Ezekiel's vision nor Shelley's is truth masked by a fair form. Fair form is as much of these truths as we can be given to work upon, for the form itself is the truth here. Not allegory but anagogy, vision, confronts us. The researches of Sir Humphry Davy will not aid in the difficult labor of understanding what it is that Ione *sees*.

Lines 206–9 are no problem; the natural comparison is to the new moon in the old moon's arms, a phenomenon that haunts Shelley's poetry. Everything subsequent in the vision is a positive development of Ezekiel's tradition of vision, just as the chariot in "The Triumph of Life" is a negative development in that same line.

That line of vision, running from Ezekiel through Revelation, Dante, Milton, to Blake and Shelley, I examine at some length in my chapter on "The Triumph of Life" (see pp. 231–6). Only the directly relevant details of that tradition will be cited now, as they seem useful in my discussion of the chariot of the moon infant and the sphere of the earth infant, here in Act IV.

The "wingèd infant" is borne by a chariot itself instinct with spirit, the wheels of which "roll / And move and grow as with an inward wind." Divinity is being conveyed, and no force exterior to divinity can therefore be the moving agent here (Ezekiel and Milton are precedents). The work of visualizing is deliberately impeded by paradoxes, as it is in Ezekiel. The wheels are "solid clouds"; the infant's plumes are as "sunny frost"; its eyes shine forth "with fire that is not brightness." And the infant is white beyond whiteness, a bewildering embodiment of the "colorless all-color." From 219–24 we get the words "white" or "whiteness" six times in six lines. Its face is white as snow, its plumes are frosty, its limbs are white, its robe is white, its hair is white. In all this whiteness, the impression is of white flame (as in "sunny frost"). The light from its eyes and its moonbeam wand is colorless; white fire again.

The "likeness of the glory of the Lord," Ezekiel's Enthroned Man, hovers behind this: "And I saw as the colour of amber, as the appearance of fire round about within it, from the appearance of his loins even upward, and from the appearance of his loins even downward, I saw as it were the appearance of fire, and it had brightness round about" (1:27). Derivative from this, and closer to Shelley's luminous infant, is Revelation's "one like unto the Son of Man": "His head and his hairs were white like wool, as white as snow; and his eyes were as a flame of fire" (1:14).

Who is Shelley's winged infant who rides in the moon chariot? Our only clue is that it approximates the Divine Man of Ezekiel and of Revelation. They are visions of a mature deity; here the Divine is embodied as an infant. Only Wilson Knight of all the critics of Shelley seems to me to be of use here, but my inability to apprehend him fully makes it difficult for me to profit by him as I should. He emphasizes the infant state, here and in the next vision, as being the vital element we need to grasp, and in this he is correct.[1] The myth of relationship in Shelley is human, agnostic even, in its emphasis. The apocalyptic infants here in Act IV have nothing to do with that myth but transcend it in a unique moment in Shelley's poetry. The winged infants are a kind of cherubim like the wingèd creatures who surround the Enthroned Man in Ezekiel's vision. They are divine emblems, and their infancy betokens the hope of finality present in the earthly paradise of the end of "Prometheus Unbound." Unlike the components of the drama's central myth of confrontation and reversal, there is no organic necessity to be pleaded for the winged infants. They burst into the lyrical jubilance of the final act as a gratuitous augury of permanence, which nothing in the myth itself can guarantee. Structurally, they serve an ingenious and subtle function, which I do not recall as ever having been mentioned in a commentary upon "Prometheus." The infant Spirit of the Moon leads in the Moon to her great wedding with a suddenly masculine Earth, led in by the formidable infant Spirit of the Earth. In effect, the infants give away the mythic planets in marriage.

"Prometheus Unbound" has already given us the Earth as universal mother and as a somewhat sticky child Spirit. In the passages between Earth and Moon to be examined after the second infant vision is dealt with, no consistent role or sex can be assigned the Earth. In the same way, little poetic consistency can be discovered between the Spirits of the Earth of Act III and of Act IV. The Earth Spirit of Act III is of unknown origin. Asia tells him:

> And never will we part, till thy chaste sister
> Who guides the frozen and inconstant moon
> Will look on thy more warm and equal light
> Till her heart thaw like flakes of April snow
> And love thee.
>   *Spirit of the Earth.* What; as Asia loves Prometheus?
>   *Asia.* Peace, wanton, thou art yet not old enough.
> Think ye by gazing on each other's eyes
> To multiply your lovely selves, and fill
> With spherèd fires the interlunar air?
>   *Spirit of the Earth.* Nay, mother, while my sister trims her lamp
> 'Tis hard I should go darkling.   [85–96]

In its own right, this little dialogue is abominably arch. Presumably, its function is to introduce the two visions I am now discussing. Fortunately for those visions, Shelley seems to have discarded his coy pur-

1. Knight, p. 222.

pose as he labored in the furnace of composition. The precocious brat of Act III shares only a title with the infant Spirit here, as Panthea describes him in his rushing onset:

> And from the other opening in the wood
> Rushes, with loud and whirlwind harmony,
> A sphere, which is as many thousand spheres,
> Solid as crystal, yet through all its mass
> Flow, as through empty space, music and light:
> Ten thousand orbs involving and involved,
> Purple and azure, white, and green, and golden,
> Sphere within sphere; and every space between
> Peopled with unimaginable shapes,
> Such as ghosts dream dwell in the lampless deep,
> Yet each inter-transpicuous, and they whirl
> Over each other with a thousand motions,
> Upon a thousand sightless axles spinning,
> And with the force of self-destroying swiftness,
> Intensely, slowly, solemnly roll on,
> Kindling with mingled sounds, and many tones,
> Intelligible words and music wild.
> With mighty whirl the multitudinous orb
> Grinds the bright brook into an azure mist
> Of elemental subtlety, like light;
> And the wild odour of the forest flowers,
> The music of the living grass and air,
> The emerald light of leaf-entangled beams
> Round its intense yet self-conflicting speed,
>   Seem kneaded into one aëreal mass
> Which drown the sense.   [IV.i.236–61]

Visualization is of central importance here, and is deliberately made difficult. The peculiar speed and complexity of this passage make it a kind of ancestor to Hart Crane's "The Bridge," and much in the "Cape Hatteras" and "Atlantis" sections of "The Bridge" strongly resembles elements in Shelley's lines here. The resemblance is, I think, significant. Both poets were primarily "primitive" mythmakers, their urge being toward the making of religion out of personal vision. Crane's poetry too is balanced on a dialectic between I-Thou confrontation and I-It experience. "Atlantis" is an enraptured attempt to address the bridge as a Thou, a mythic humanization of a mechanism. Admirers of either romantic poet will resent and reject the comparison, but Shelley born just a century later would have written a long poem very much like "The Bridge." The earlier poet is confronted by a flickering Thou in natural phenomena; the later meets the Thou in the phenomena of urbanized, machine-tooled existence. The terrors of the I-It experience are as eloquent in "The Tunnel" as in "The Triumph of Life."

The Thou of the sphere in the vision of the Earth chariot, quoted above, is too complicated to be confronted in relationship by a reader without an initial analytical preparation. But the impact of the vision precedes its full comprehension, much as it does in Ezekiel. This sphere, "which is *as* many thousand orbs involving and involved," is exactly analogous to the wheel of Ezekiel's vision of the cherubim: "the wheels and their work," but "behold one wheel," and "their appearance and their work was as it were a wheel in the middle of a wheel" (1:16). I take "orbs" in Shelley's "ten thousand orbs involving and involved" as being not just a synonym for "spheres" but as meaning, poetically, "eyes." "As for their rings, they were so high that they were dreadful; and their rings were full of eyes round about them four," as Ezekiel has it (1:18). I do not maintain that Shelley had Ezekiel in mind; Milton, influenced by Ezekiel and Revelation, would be influence enough here. Indeed, as Hughes notes,[2] Milton is most probably involved as another kind of influence beside that of the Divine Chariot:

> That day, as other solem dayes, they spent
> In song and dance about the sacred Hill,
> Mystical dance, which yonder starrie Spheare
> Of Planets and of fixt in all her Wheeles
> Resembles nearest, mazes intricate,
> Eccentric, intervolv'd, yet regular
> Then most, when most irregular they seem:
> And in thir motions harmonie Divine
> So smooths her charming tones, that Gods own ear
> Listens delighted.[3]

Details from this passage seem to join with those of Ezekiel's chariot in Shelley's vision. This is a vision paradoxical in the extreme. This sphere is one sphere yet many spheres, spheres within spheres. It is "solid as crystal" (Ezekiel uses the similitude of "the terrible crystal"—1:22), yet music and light flow through all its mass, as if through empty space. Milton's "mystical dance" and song is given its analogy in a heavenly sphere of fixed wheels, intricate in its mazes, eccentric, intervolved, yet most regular when seeming most irregular. We are baffled, but what to us is paradox delights God's ear. So is it with Shelley's sphere, as divine music, light, and song perform their regular irregularities in an epiphany of the deity otherwise unrevealed in "Prometheus" or in any of

2. Hughes, ed., *Shelley,* p. 205.
3. "Paradise Lost," Bk. 5, lines 618–25.

Shelley's mythopoeic poems. But there is more to Shelley's sphere here than that, involved as visualization has already become.

Shelley's sphere is an anagoge of the earth whirling itself on into apocalypse; intensely, solemnly, slowly, but with the force of self-destroying swiftness grinding toward finality. *Unimaginable* shapes people the sphere, while the phenomena of nature are transformed by it into "an azure mist of elemental subtlety," "one aëreal mass / Which drowns the sense." Not even the Blake of "Night the Ninth," "The Four Zoas," gives us a more energetically imaginative apocalypse than this. What suddenly lifts the passage from brilliance to greatness is in the astonishing and humanistic irony that follows:

> *Panthea.*   Within the orb itself,
> Pillowed upon its alabaster arms,
> Like to a child o'er wearied with sweet toil,
> On its own folded wings, and wavy hair,
> The Spirit of the Earth is laid asleep,
> And you can see its little lips are moving,
> Amid the changing light of their own smiles,
> Like one who talks of what he loves in dream.
> *Ione.* 'Tis only mocking the orb's harmony.   [261–9]

That last is a very great line indeed. Wilson Knight, in one of his fine perceptions, sees in it something analogous to the "purified consciousness" of Blake and the Jesus of the Gospels, in its "mocking" of "all such geometric eternities." [4] The Jesus reference is perhaps confusing; the Blake comparison seems to me to be brilliantly exact. Blake, reading Berkeley on Aristotle's geometrical theology, angrily snapped: "God is not a Mathematical Diagram." [5] In a gentle but highly persuasive irony, the sleeping infant Spirit mocks the harmony of his own orb, its less-than-human outline, its geometric eternity of intricate mazes. Coming where it does, the mocking produces a humor unique in kind, a value unlike any other value. Panthea directly after resumes her account of the relentlessly advancing vision, but we are now insulated against it; we know that we are to accept it as a vision of finality, but we know also that our human state mocks it as much as its final state mocks us. Reality is complex here, for the vision is as significantly less real than we are, as it is more real by its very nature. Few lines in poetry suggest as much as economically as Ione's line has done here.

The rest of Panthea's account can be summarized as having to do, first, with the increases in self-knowledge that a redeemed earth will reveal ("apocalypse" means a full revelation, an end to mystery) and,

4. Knight, p. 222.
5. Keynes, ed., *Blake*, p. 819.

second, with "cancelled cycles," the melancholy product of time, cancelled now because time *has* had a stop.

Lines 319–502 of Act IV consist of a lyrical duet, a *bel canto* display of Shelley's virtuosity, between a Moon and Earth prepared for the Great Marriage. In lines 338–49, the Earth sounds rather too much like the Earth Mother of Act I. Nevertheless, I read this as being a third mythic Earth, totally distinct from the Earth Mother and the Spirit of the Earth, though in this I disagree, in various ways, with Forman, James Thomson, and Rossetti, and with Hughes, who agrees with Rossetti. The sustained power of these two hundred lines of interlocked lyrics is largely dissipated, I believe, if the Earth is not maturely male and the Moon maturely female.

These lyrics need an extensive analysis, which I have not space for here. Briefly, they embody a sexual relationship in the highest degree, and their excellence can be demonstrated to follow from the remarkable tact with which they execute this vital subject. For my purposes here, it is enough to note that they demonstrate a solar universe redeemed out of experience into relationship.

What remains, after a fine dialogue between Panthea and Ione, illustrating a rejuvenation primarily in Panthea and secondarily in her sister, is the great pastoral scene, in which Demogorgon addresses a world of scattered Thou's, redeemed phenomena. Demogorgon addresses first Earth, which answers: "I am as a drop of dew that dies," that is, an It that is redeemed into Thou. Next Moon, which replies: "I am a leaf shaken by thee!"; It into Thou again, as in the "Ode to the West Wind." The outer spaces, the dead, the confused voice of elemental beings, and beasts and birds and foliage and lightning and wind and meteors and mists; all are addressed, and reply. "Thy voice to us is wind among still woods." Finally, man himself is addressed. All listen, as the drama concludes with a powerful didactic lyric, too familiar to be quoted here. Though overtly a hymn of triumph, it contains within itself the figure of the ouroboros, the serpent of time, with the implied hint that the dialectic can always be reversed. The actual burden of the lyric, being didactic, needs no paraphrase; no analysis is necessary of a meaning the poet spells out so plainly.

Buber, writing of the bare outlines of a dialectic that Shelley has fleshed so well, dwells at last upon defeat, paradoxical reversal:

> The times in which the living Word appears are those in which the solidarity of connexion between *I* and the world is renewed; the times in which the effective Word reigns are those in which the agreement between *I* and the world is maintained; the times in which the Word becomes current are those in which alienation between *I* and the world, less of reality, growth of fate, is completed

—till there comes the great shudder, the holding of the breath in the dark, and the preparing silence.[6]

Shelley's times are the last mentioned; "Prometheus Unbound," for all its blemishes, is the kind of augury Buber suggests as appropriate for such times: a great shudder, a holding of the breath in the dark, a preparing silence.

6. Buber, *I and Thou,* p. 119.

6

"The Sensitive Plant"

"THE Sensitive Plant" (composed at Pisa, March 1820, and published in the "Prometheus Unbound" volume in that year) is best understood as a prelude to a greater visionary poem by Shelley, "The Witch of Atlas" (composed at San Giuliano, near Pisa, August 14–16, 1820, and first published in the *Posthumous Poems, 1824*). Because "The Sensitive Plant" is so directly a mythopoeic poem, it has been misread frequently and has received less than adequate evaluation. The reading I shall present here takes as context only the remarks I have made in my first chapter on the nature of mythmaking in poetry, and the means one might employ in understanding and evaluating it. As archetypal analogues to this poem, Spenser's "Muiopotmos: or the Fate of the Butterflie" and Blake's "The Book of Thel" have seemed to me appropriate and useful.

Sourly enough, the special plea might be made that the Victorian cult, botanical and social, of the Sensitive Plant, has done Shelley's poem real harm. "Sensitive Plant" is hardly a term of approbation when given human applications, and Shelley scholars have not helped much toward discouraging that notoriously popular "reading" of the poem in which Plant equals Shelley.

Admittedly, the "tone" of "The Sensitive Plant" is a critical problem, but the problem is one that an adequate reading of the poem can resolve, and the resolvement, as I hope to show, will be in the poem's favor. The tone of "The Sensitive Plant" is itself an anagoge of that poem's meaning, just as the very similar tones of "Muiopotmos" and "Thel" are important aspects of the meanings of those poems. I am aware that "tone" is an ambiguous term as I now employ it, but no better one exists to hand. Any reader of the three poems I am describing will know what I mean when I say that their tones are "fragile," purely affective as that term must be in this context. They are "light" poems about something which is very serious, the state of being most generally referred to as the earthly or lower paradise, categorized by Blake as Beulah or the state of innocence; by Spenser as the Garden of Adonis; not categorized but still depicted by Shelley in several places, most notably in Act III of "Prometheus," in "The Witch of Atlas," and here in the garden of "The Sensitive Plant."

148

Spenser is the ancestor here, as so often, of both Blake and Shelley, and is therefore to be considered first, though I shall not hesitate to categorize aspects of "Muiopotmos" in terms of Blake and Shelley. I am not endeavoring to read the meanings of one poet into another but rather to clarify three poems by considering them together, before investigating one of them in particular.

"Muiopotmos," one of the finest things by Spenser outside of the "The Faerie Queene," has suffered at the hands of many scholarly historical allegorizers. The Clarion-Aragnoll incident has been read as alluding to conflicts between Spenser and Lady Carey, Raleigh and Essex, Spenser and Burghley, Sidney and Oxford, Burghley and Essex, and, last and best, Elizabeth and the Armada.[1] Ernest de Sélincourt has protested eloquently against these interpretations of what he reads as delightful mock-heroic: "It is surely a mistake to read into this delicious *jeu d'esprit* a moral or satirical intention." [2] Agreed, but while "Muiopotmos" is what de Sélincourt describes it to be, it *is* something else also, and that something else, together with much in "The Faerie Queene," marks the historical beginning in English poetry of what develops into the romantic mythmaking of Collins, Blake, Shelley, and Keats. Here I am concerned with a very specific kind of influencing, though it is influencing through example rather than the influence of verse line upon verse line. The history here is the record of the communication not of ideas but rather of a visionary attitude and a mythmaking technique which results from, and poetically justifies, that attitude. However neutral and descriptive I make this account, it will still present itself as polemic, for polemic is implicit (even in Spenser) in the visionary attitude itself here. And perhaps, in these days, when so much of Spenser and Shelley is categorized, disparagingly, as a "Poetry of the Will," in which the "Will" performs the work more properly the province of the "Imagination," polemic from a visionary stance which is made explicit may do some good. The real case of a Spenserian against the mode of Donne is not so often presented as it might be in our generation, and an attempt at it in these chapters, whatever its shortcomings, is not likely to be redundant. When we have reached the stage at which Brooks can find Milton of the Minor Poems more metaphysical than Spenserian, and this for the sake of critically redeeming those poems, then it is surely time for a judicious counterattack.[3] Spenser and Shelley will bury their own undertakers, as they have done before, but if the time of that entombment can be hastened, a few of us at least will be glad. Drayton, a

1. C. G. Osgood and H. G. Lotspeich, *The Minor Poems, the Works of Edmund Spenser* (2 vols. Baltimore, The Johns Hopkins Univ. Press, 1947), 2, 599.
2. Ernest de Sélincourt, Introduction to the Oxford Standard Authors' *Spenser,* p. xxiv.
3. Cleanth Brooks and John E. Hardy, eds., *Poems of Mr. John Milton* (New York, Harcourt, Brace, 1951), pp. 242ff.

great Spenserian poet fallen in his old age upon evil days of neglect, the days of Jonson and Donne, wrote the appropriate motto for our contemporary situation in his own vision of Beulah, the poet's earthly paradise, in "The Muses Elizium":

> This beastly brood by no meanes may abide
> The name of their brave ancestors to heare,
> By whom their sordid slavery is descry'd,
> So unlike them as though not theirs they were,
> Nor yet they sense, nor understanding have,
> Of those brave Muses that their country song,
> But with false lips ignobly doe deprave
> The right and honour that to them belong;
> This cruell kinde thus viper-like devoure
> That fruitfull soyle which them too fully fed;
> The earth doth curse the age, and every houre
> Againe, that it these viprous monsters bred.
> I see the plagues that shortly are to come
> Upon this people cleerely them forsooke:
> And thus am light into Elizium,
> To whose straite search I wholly me betooke.[4]   [109–24]

With "Muiopotmos" as historical allegory or mock-heroic this discussion need not deal; with "Muiopotmos" as a romantic poem, an augury of innocence or intimation of the earthly paradise, a presentiment of Blake's Beulah-land and Shelley's "breathing Garden" (the phrase is Blake's), another level of meaning, one which is very much *in* the poem, is opened up.

Blake's vision embraces the worm of "The Book of Thel"; so Spenser's embraces Clarion, the young butterfly, and we are to remember the lovely myth of Cupid and Psyche as we follow Clarion's adventures:

> Report is that dame *Venus* on a day,
> In spring when flowres doo clothe the fruitful ground,
> Walking abroad with all her Nymphes to play,
> Bad her faire damzels flocking her arownd,
> To gather flowres, her forhead to array:
> Emongst the rest a gentle Nymph was found,
> Hight *Astery,* excelling all the crewe
> In curteous usage, and unstained hewe.
>
> Who being nimbler joynted than the rest,
> And more industrious, gathered more store

4. John Buxton, ed., *Poems of Michael Drayton* (2 vols. London, Routledge, 1953), *1,* 284.

Of the fields honour, than the others best;
Which they in secret harts envying sore,
Tolde *Venus,* when her as the worthiest
She prais'd, that *Cupide* (as they heard before)
Did lend her secret aide, in gathering
Into her lap the children of the spring.

Whereof the Goddesse gathering jealous feare,
Not yet unmindful, how not long agoe
Her sonne to *Psyche* secrete love did beare,
And long it close conceal'd, till mickle woe
Thereof arose, and manie a rufull teare;
Reason with sudden rage did overgoe,
And giving hastie credit to th' accuser,
Was led away of them that did abuse her.

Eftsoones that Damzel by her heavenly might,
She turn'd into a winged Butterflie,
In the wide aire to make her wandring flight;
And all those flowres, with which so plenteouslie
Her lap she filled had, that bred her spight,
She placed in her wings, for memorie
Of her pretended crime, though crime none were:
Since which that flie them in her wings doth beare.   [113–44]

The function of these stanzas in the poem is to remind us that the
Greek word psukhē means both soul, spirit, mind on the one side, day-
flying moth or butterfly on the other. Our psyches, which are Eros objects, beloved of Cupid, are as butterfly-winged. In "the fate of the
butterflie," Clarion, we are to read an augury of our own experience.

That experience begins in the state of innocence, in the "gay gardins"
to which the "fresh" Clarion's desire carries him:

To the gay gardins his unstaid desire
Him wholly caried, to refresh his sprights:
There lavish Nature in her best attire,
Powres forth sweete odors, and alluring sights;
And Arte with her contending, doth aspire
T' excell the naturall, with made delights:
And all that faire or pleasant may be found,
In riotous excesse doth there abound.

There he arriving, round about doth flie,
From bed to bed, from one to other border,
And takes survey with curious busie eye,

Of everie flowre and herbe there set in order;
Now this, now that he tasteth tenderly,
Yet none of them he rudely doth disorder,
Ne with his feete their silken leaves deface;
But pastures on the pleasures of each place.

And evermore with most varietie,
And change of sweetnesse (for all change is sweete)
He casts his glutton sense to satisfie,
Now sucking of the sap of herbe most meete,
Or of the deaw, which yet on them does lie,
Now in the same bathing his tender feete:
And then he pearcheth on some braunch thereby,
To weather him, and his moyst wings to dry.

And then againe he turneth to his play,
To spoyle the pleasures of that Paradise:
The wholsome Saulge, and Lavender still gray,
Ranke smelling Rue, and Cummin good for eyes,
The Roses raigning in the pride of May,
Sharpe Isope, good for greene wounds remedies,
Faire Marigoldes, and Bees alluring Thime,
Sweet Marjoram, and Daysies decking prime.

Coole Violets, and Orpine growing still,
Embathed Balme, and chearfull Galingale,
Fresh Costmarie, and breathfull Camomill,
Dull Poppie, and drink-quickening Setuale,
Veyne-healing Verven, and hed-purging Dill,
Sound Savorie, and Bazil hartie-hale,
Fat Colworts, and comforting Perseline,
Colde Lettuce, and refreshing Rosmarine.

And whatso else of vertue good or ill
Grewe in this Gardin, fetcht from farre away,
Of everie one he takes, and tastes at will,
And on their pleasures greedily doth pray.
Then when he hath both plaid, and fed his fill,
In the warme Sunne he doth himselfe embay,
And there him rests in riotous suffisaunce
Of all his gladfulnes, and kingly joyaunce.   [161–208]

This garden, together with its analogue in "The Faerie Queene," the
Garden of Adonis (Book 3, Canto VI), is the prototype of Drayton's
"poets paradice," Elizium, "the muses only bower of blisse" in the in-

troductory quatrains of "The Muses Elizium"; of Milton's Eden garden in Book 4 of "Paradise Lost"; of Blake's Beulah-land throughout the engraved works; finally of Shelley's garden in "The Sensitive Plant" (where Milton's garden, as Baker notes, is an influence also [5]) and of much else in Shelley and Keats.

This "gay Gardin" in "Muiopotmos" depicts, or rather embodies, a state of innocence, a first imaginative world through which visionary poets and their readers must pass. This world of first imaginative wonder, the child's world visualized with an intensity so great that the objects of perception are become confronting Thou's, is not a world where any of us can long abide. There is a constant movement of living substance through Spenser's Garden of Adonis; if the movement ceased the garden would become only another Bower of Bliss. The major visionary poets see this first state of innocence as being a natural structure that the world of experience will shatter, inevitably, for the natural world, especially in its best aspects, is mutable. One unreality destroys another. An aspect of Blake's central meaning in his early work sums the matter : there are two contrary states of the soul, innocence and experience, which satirize one another. "Muiopotmos," lines 1–216, is a Song of Innocence; "Muiopotmos," lines 217–440, is the contrary Song of Experience. "The Sensitive Plant," Parts 1 and 2, is another Song of Innocence, to which Part 3 opposes a Song of Experience, with the brief conclusion as emblem. "Paradise Lost," on a huge scale, is a Song of Experience following an unwritten Song of Innocence, of imaginative triumph, as Tillyard has conjectured, with the brief prelapsarian vision of Book 4 hearkening back to a state of innocence.[6] "The Witch of Atlas," the major text to be examined in the next chapter, is an extended Song of Innocence to which "The Triumph of Life" may be regarded as the contrary expression.

Examined in this light, "Muiopotmos" is revealed as something more than mock-heroic and radically different from allegory, at least from "allegory" in its modern critical and derogatory sense. The garden of "Muiopotmos" is very lovely but unreal or, better, unreal (deliberately) but very lovely. The fate of young Clarion is the fate of Blake's fly, whose "summer play / My thoughtless hand / Has brush'd away." Shining in all his splendor, Clarion is unreal, for his splendor is unearned and has no chance of survival in the deceptively lovely but still fallen natural world. The poem, for all its butterfly lightness, is a complaint of Mutability, a "sundry small poem of the World's Vanitie," the failure of the natural world to attain to a timeless vision, when no more change shall be.

In the poem's garden, which gathers together a manifold of natural delights from differing regions of the earth, Clarion's presence and dom-

5. Baker, *Shelley's Major Poetry*, p. 197.
6. E. M. W. Tillyard, *Milton* (London, Chatto and Windus, 1934), p. 112.

inance convey overtones of archetypal Adam in Eden, for his is "kingly joyaunce":

> What more felicitie can fall to creature
> Than to enjoy delight with libertie,
> And to be Lord of all the workes of Nature,
> To raine in th' aire from earth to highest skie,
> To feed on flowres, and weeds of glorious feature,
> To take what ever thing doth please the eie?   [209–14]

Keats perceptively selected the first two of these lines to serve as the epigraph to his first volume, the Poems of 1817, most of which deal with the visionary poet's first state of innocence, with nature in its kindliest but still unredeemed aspects, in short with what Blake called Beulah. Lines 209–14 of "Muiopotmos" climax that poem's Song of Innocence. Following is the song in which the gay gardins are transmuted into the cobweb of Aragnoll.

The Ovidian story of the genesis of Aragnoll's hatred for Clarion (lines 257–356) is beautifully told, but does not belong to the aspect of the poem's meaning that I am examining but rather to its mock-heroic, light-hearted side. There is no humor or grace in Aragnoll the spider, the "wicked wight" who prepares for Clarion a literal Agony in the Garden. A butterfly is emblematic of a human psyche; a spider tends to assimilate to that Satan whom Blake considered god of the natural world, tempter into a deceitful garden. After an organically necessary lament of Mutability (lines 217–40), Spenser sings the Tempter in the Garden:

> It fortuned (as heavens had behight)
> That in this gardin, where yong *Clarion*
> Was wont to solace him, a wicked wight
> The foe of faire things, th' author of confusion,
> The shame of Nature, the bondslave of spight,
> Had lately built his hatefull mansion,
> And lurking closely, in awayte now lay,
> How he might anie in his trap betray.   [241–8]

The complexity of tone here, with its nice balance between mock-heroic and romantic disillusion, is carried over into the final stanzas depicting a mock fall as Clarion is trapped in Aragnoll's web, but is then resolved in the poem's final lines into something grim, abrupt, quite horrific:

> There the fond Flie entangled, struggled long,
> Himself to free thereout; but all in vaine.
> For striving more, the more in laces strong

> Himselfe he tide, and wrapt his winges twaine
> In lymie snares the subtill loupes among;
> That in the ende he breathelesse did remaine,
> And all his yougthly forces idly spent,
> Him to the mercie of th' avenger lent.
>
> Which when the grisly tyrant did espie,
> Like a grimme Lyon rushing with fierce might
> Out of his den, he seized greedelie
> On the resistles pray, and with fell spight,
> Under the left wing stroke his weapon slie
> Into his heart, that his deepe groning spright
> In bloodie streames foorth fled into the aire,
> His bodie left the spectacle of care. [425–40]

There is no moral in this, as Clarion has fallen not through fault but only as every creature must, out of a state of innocence into the world of experience. But there is lament here, lament for Clarion's (and the world's) vanity, a vanity engendered by lack of recognition that visionary innocence is mutable.

Before paralleling "Muiopotmos" with "The Sensitive Plant," I turn to Blake's "The Book of Thel" as another poetic reflector for Shelley's poem. "Thel" is overtly a Song of Innocence–Song of Experience contrary, and therefore will require a less extensive summary than I allowed for "Muiopotmos."

Frye's summary of "The Book of Thel" is concise and to me seems definitive. I quote it here because it is better and more useful than anything I could say about "Thel":

> All life is born in Beulah, and the energy of that life impels the infant Orc to push his way out of it into our world of Generation. When plants grow out of the place of seed, we see the growth as an ascent, but imaginatively it is a descent to a lower world. But as, according to Blake, nothing achieves reality without going through physical existence, the descent must be made. The failure to make it is the theme of *The Book of Thel*. Thel is an imaginative seed: she could be any form of embryonic life, from a human baby to an artist's inspiration, and her tragedy could be anything from a miscarriage to a lost vision. To insist on an exclusive interpretation would vulgarize the poem into the wrong kind of allegory. Being an embryo in the world of the unborn, Thel longs to be of "use," that is, to develop her potential life into an actual one and hence come into our world of Generation. . . . But, hearing the groans of a fallen world tormented in its prison, she becomes ter-

rified and escapes back to the unborn world . . . Thel's abode is the garden "of him that walketh in the garden in the evening time," the Eden of Genesis, by "the river of Adona" . . .[7]

Frye also comments on the "fragility" of "The Book of Thel" as part of its meaning. Thel's world of innocence, Beulah, is mutable, dissolving, arbitrary, "a looking-glass world of talking flowers." Beulah, like Spenser's Garden of Adonis (demonstrated by Frye to be Blake's prototype here), is a state in which substance prevails but form is constantly mutable; the upper paradise, of artist, visionary or of the orthodox religious, is one in which form shall be eternal and substance plastic. The tone of Beulah poems—"Muiopotmos," "The Book of Thel," "The Sensitive Plant," "The Witch of Atlas"—ought to and does reflect the mutable nature of the state. Thel's lament for Beulah is characteristic (and very Shelleyan in the varied profusion of figures by which Thel describes herself):

"O life of this our spring! why fades the lotus of the water,
"Why fade these children of the spring, born but to smile & fall?
"Ah! Thel is like a wat'ry bow, and like a parting cloud;
"Like a reflection in a glass; like shadows in the water;
"Like dreams of infants, like a smile upon an infant's face;
"Like the dove's voice; like transient day; like music in the air.
"Ah! gentle may I lay me down, and gentle rest my head,
"And gentle sleep the sleep of death, and gentle hear the voice
"Of him that walketh in the garden in the evening time."
                                                    [Keynes, p. 162]

Following this lament are dialogues between, successively, a "lilly" and Thel, a cloud and Thel, and (after Thel addresses an infant worm, which can only weep in reply) a clod of clay and Thel. The burden of the dialogue is that everything that lives is holy, that precisely everything can be entered into an I-Thou relationship with by Thel, once she has passed out of Beulah into the ordinary world of Generations. She voluntarily (for it must be voluntary, hence her name, Thel, will or wish) passes into Generation or Experience, but she flees back "unhinder'd" into Beulah when she sees Experience and hears its song in the final lines of the poem. She cannot accept it that Clarion must be destroyed by Aragnoll, that the Sensitive Plant must die in winter and not be reborn in the spring of the year. But Beulah will turn into Ubro for her, the Garden of Adonis into a Bower of Bliss, for the state is not one in which she can abide, the Genesis garden of Eden is only a place she *must* fall from. Like Clarion or the Plant, she will be destroyed in any case, but without their recompense of having passed through Generation, our life here.

7. Frye, *Fearful Symmetry*, pp. 232-3.

"The Sensitive Plant" in its garden description may echo both "Mui-opotmos" and Milton's Eden Garden; they are certainly its precedents, but the verbal echo is fairly inconclusive ("Muiopotmos" is definitely echoed in the stanza to Mary introducing "The Witch of Atlas," as we shall see). But influence is less important here for understanding of Shelley's poem than conceptual parallels are, which is why I have discussed "Muiopotmos" and "Thel" at some length. The Sensitive Plant is kin to Clarion and Thel; they are all dwellers in Beulah whose lives are shattered by the breaking-in of the world of Generation, visions of Innocence which fade under the impact of Experience. Blake in "Auguries of Innocence" pointed the moral of such visions:

> The Catterpiller on the Leaf
> Repeats to thee thy Mother's grief.

In much the same way we are involved in the fate of Spenser's Butter-flie and of Shelley's Sensitive Plant. With this as background, I begin my reading of "The Sensitive Plant," which opens as Song of Innocence, vision of Beulah, a state Blake categorized as "three-fold," that is, as being primarily "sexual," a "married" (that is what "Beulah" means in Hebrew) state of lover, beloved, and offspring, in which all "phenomena" are necessarily humanized Thou's, the natural world mythopoeically perceived.

> A Sensitive Plant in a garden grew,
> And the young winds fed it with silver dew,
> And it opened its fan-like leaves to the light,
> And closed them beneath the kisses of Night.
>
> And the Spring arose on the garden fair,
> Like the Spirit of Love felt everywhere;
> And each flower and herb on Earth's dark breast
> Rose from the dreams of its wintry rest.
>
> But none ever trembled and panted with bliss
> In the garden, the field, or the wilderness,
> Like a doe in the noontide with love's sweet want,
> As the companionless Sensitive Plant.   [1–12]

The diction, which has been questioned, performs a precise work: the plant's opening of its leaves to the light and closing them with darkness is a natural fact; a "sensitive plant" is more responsive to such, and other stimuli, than any other garden growth. In this lower paradise, this garden of Shelley's poem, the Spirit of Love is felt everywhere, as it is in Blake's "sexual" threefold world of Beulah. The Spirit of Love is felt in the light to which the Plant is sensitive, and in the winds which bring it dew. The Sensitive Plant *trembles* more than the other flowers and herbs; the word accurately conveys natural fact. It *pants* because as Smart says in a memorable verse in the "Jubilate Agno": "flowers can breathe and Pope's carnations knew him." And it trembles with bliss and pants with bliss because it inhabits a lower paradise, in which it is known and loved and knows and loves, as a Thou in relation to other Thou's.

After a descriptive catalogue (lines 13–58) of all the inhabitants of the garden, "this undefilèd Paradise," the *relationship* between them is stressed:

> For each one was interpenetrated
> With the light and the odour its neighbour shed,
> Like young lovers whom youth and love make dear
> Wrapped and filled by their mutual atmosphere.
>
> But the Sensitive Plant which could give small fruit
> Of the love which it felt from the leaf to the root,
> Received more than all, it loved more than ever,
> Where none wanted but it, could belong to the giver . . .
>
> [66–73]

Lines 72–3, obscure in their syntax, have been aptly paraphrased by Swinburne: "[The Sensitive Plant] felt more love than the flowers which gave it gifts of light and odour could feel—all the more thankful and loving for the very barrenness and impotence of requital which made these gifts a charity instead of an exchange." [8]

This mutual interpenetration between the flowers is the mark of their state of Innocence—they are sustained in their world because they stand in relation to one another; they have no objects and are no objects to others; they encounter no soul or dryad of the other flowers, but the flowers themselves. The exception is the Sensitive Plant, which receives but cannot give, which is addressed by light or odor but which cannot reply. Because it does not stand in relation, it becomes an *object* of love, and in that reduction from relationship to experience is presaged its destruction. I am aware that Shelley may not consciously have intended such a meaning, but I cannot see that Shelley's intention is of any primary importance in this. Wilson Knight's remark on the "myth-making faculty at work" in Shelley's poetry is relevant here, for we are confronted by "that queer business of using one's imaginative experience to create something surprising to oneself." [9] The mythmaking Shelley, what Blake termed in himself "the real man, the imagination," gave us the two stanzas I have just paraphrased; the "philosophical" Shelley, a spectral

8. Quoted by Hughes, ed., *Shelley*, pp. 210–11.
9. Knight, *The Starlit Dome*, p. 226.

being who delights modern Shelley scholars, gives us the next stanza, with its jarring reminiscence of Plato:

> For the Sensitive Plant has no bright flower;
> Radiance and odour are not its dower;
> It loves, even like Love, its deep heart is full,
> It desires what it has not, the Beautiful!   [74–7]

This Song of Innocence of Part 1 of "The Sensitive Plant" is climaxed in the vision of the Lady of the Garden in Part 2:

> There was a Power in this sweet place,
> An Eve in this Eden; a ruling Grace
> Which to the flowers, did they waken or dream,
> Was as God is to the starry scheme.

Baker has explored the parallel between this Lady and Milton's Eve in a thorough and useful manner.[1] Each tends a lower paradise, but one difference between them is absolute. Eve has a quite consubstantial Adam near to hand; Shelley's Lady has a more remote paramour:

> She had no companion of mortal race,
> But her tremulous breath and her flushing face
> Told, whilst the morn kissed the sleep from her eyes,
> That her dreams were less slumber than Paradise:
>
> As if some bright Spirit for her sweet sake
> Had deserted Heaven while the stars were awake,
> As if yet around her he lingering were,
> Though the veil of daylight concealed him from her.   [13–20]

Grabo, trying to puzzle out the poem as the kind of allegory it assuredly is not, asks: "Is not the Lady of the garden but another of Shelley's idealizations of Intellectual Beauty who appears in so many guises from Queen Mab to the Witch of the *Witch of Atlas?*"[2] There seems to be little point in attempting to reduce all of Shelley's poems into the one poem, aside from the lack of any necessity for categorizing the Lady in the garden of "The Sensitive Plant." The vocabulary of mythopoeia is sufficient to explain the Lady's function in the poem; speculations on her status need not go beyond what is stated in the first stanza of Part 2 of the poem. She is "a ruling Grace" in the garden; she is to the flowers "as God is to the starry scheme."

Her function in the poem is akin then to the function of God's grace in our world. In the more neutral vocabulary of mythmaking, God becomes the eternal Thou (and one can name this transcendent Thou what

1. Baker, pp. 197–9.
2. Grabo, *The Magic Plant,* p. 284.

one pleases) through to whom a particular Thou may be a glimpse. The plants of the garden in Shelley's poem are confronted by one another in mutual relationship; they serve as particular Thou's for one another, and each of them is therefore for the others a glimpse through to the more general Thou embodied in the Lady. Her work, in effect, is to be a Thou which can never for them become an It, and ultimately her work must fail, for Mutability rules her as well as the garden. Though she bears away from the garden and into "the rough woods far aloof" "all killing insects and gnawing worms," all things which will not enter into mutual relationship, nevertheless she herself "ere the first leaf looked brown" is borne away by the mutable cycle. The meaning of her death, in the aspect which I choose to emphasize here because it is, strictly speaking, *the* mythopoeic aspect of the poem, is a conceptual rather than a moral kind of meaning. She dies because the poem's "undefilèd Paradise" is a lower and not an upper paradise, a place of repose and seedbed of life rather than a place of wakeful creativity, of life twice born. Blake would not have lamented her death but Spenser most certainly would, and Part 3 of "The Sensitive Plant," with its dark vision of the passing of Innocence into Experience, is a very fearful lament. Only "The Triumph of Life," among Shelley's poems, presents a pageant of decay to match this one.

A. T. Strong, a very sympathetic critic of Shelley, nevertheless could condemn Part 3 of "The Sensitive Plant," because in it "Shelley evidently scorns beauty of subject, and strives to portray the sinister for its own sake." [3] Nobody is likely to criticize Shelley in that way just now. The fashionable criticism of "The Sensitive Plant" now would be that the poem is a veritable monument to what Eliot first termed "dissociation of sensibility." Pottle has given us an admirably concise summary of this aspect of the New Critical case against Shelley: "He exhibits dissociation of sensibility: though he is even too much aware of the disgusting, the ugly, the painful, and the horrible, he puts all the beauty into one poem and all the ugliness into another, or he sorts them out in different portions of the same poem." [4]

That last is exactly what Shelley does in "The Sensitive Plant": all that he can visualize as beauty is in Part 1: as ugliness, in Part 3. But that in itself is part of the meaning and the poetic strength of "The Sensitive Plant." Shelley, like Spenser and Blake, is writing about different states of being, each existing independently of the other. These states are *contraries,* though in our lives they are mingled. If you reject (as many now do) this kind of writing, then you are rejecting a kind of *poetry* or, at the very least, what our ancestors considered to be poetry.

3. A. T. Strong, *Three Studies in Shelley* (London, Oxford Univ. Press, 1921), p. 142.
4. Pottle, "The Case of Shelley," *PMLA, 67* (1952), 601.

Ultimately the whole question is an affective one, and the visionary poet must address his reader as Bunyan does, asking:

> Dost thou love picking meat? Or would'st thou see
> A man in the clouds, and have him speak to thee?

The decay and death pictured in Part 3 of "The Sensitive Plant" are not of the mutable, natural world alone but also of Shelley's (or any man's) confrontation of that world as a Thou. The relational event (which is here the poem) has run its course, and the Thou has become an It. The confrontation of life by life is replaced by the experience of a dead (not an inanimate) world. It is not, I think, an accident that personification, which is so minor an element in the first two parts of the poem, is dominant in Part 3. Things exist to be personified in Part 3; from the universe of Shelley we are back suddenly to that of prosopopoeia, and stanzas occur reminiscent of Collins:

> For Winter came: the wind was his whip:
> One choppy finger was on his lip:
> He had torn the cataracts from the hills
> And they clanked at his girdle like manacles;
>
> His breath was a chain which without a sound
> The earth, and the air, and the water bound;
> He came, fiercely driven, in his chariot-throne
> By the tenfold blasts of the Arctic zone.   [86–93]

This is very distinguished verse, but the point about it (and this is a *critical* point) is that it is a very different kind of creation from that which I am attempting to study in these chapters. Parts 1 and 2, whether you judge them to be good or bad, are in the mythopoeic mode (as I have defined it); Part 3 is not, and this shift from one mode to another is one way of getting at the meaning of "The Sensitive Plant" (I acknowledge of course that there are others, but they are not my subject here, and seem to me to distort the poem's meaning in their various ways). In the world of experience, objects of experience can survive; the Sensitive Plant cannot, for mutual relationship with all that surrounds it is necessary to its existence:

> When Winter had gone and Spring came back
> The Sensitive Plant was a leafless wreck;
> But the mandrakes, and toadstools, and docks, and darnels,
> Rose like the dead from their ruined charnels.   [110–13]

Nothing is said here of the plants of the garden which rose again alive, and nothing need be said of them, for natural fact is not vital to the poem at this point. The poet knows, as well as we know, that natural cycle perpetuates much that is beautiful, but the concern of the poem is with a particular Sensitive Plant, just as "Muiopotmos" directly dealt with the fate of Clarion, an individual butterfly. One garden at least is dead, and with it its Lady and the Sensitive Plant. One vision, at least, of the lower paradise is ended; one poem attempting to perpetuate the revelation of a Thou has compelled itself to commemorate the passing of Thou to It. Another Song of Innocence has transmuted itself to a Song of Experience. What remains is the epilogue of the poem's *conclusion,* in which the uncertain anapaests are replaced by a measured iambic movement in six quatrains replete with conversational grace. Nothing is urged upon us here, but with quiet conviction and gentlemanly tact (as Donald Davie notes) [5] a visionary suggestion is offered us:

> Whether the Sensitive Plant, or that
> Which within its boughs like a Spirit sat,
> Ere its outward form had known decay,
> Now felt this change, I cannot say.
>
> Whether that Lady's gentle mind,
> No longer with the form combined
> Which scattered love, as stars do light,
> Found sadness, where it left delight,
>
> I dare not guess; but in this life
> Of error, ignorance, and strife,
> Where nothing is, but all things seem,
> And we the shadows of the dream,
>
> It is a modest creed, and yet
> Pleasant if one considers it,
> To own that death itself must be,
> Like all the rest, a mockery.
>
> That garden sweet, that lady fair,
> And all sweet shapes and odours there,
> In truth have never passed away:
> 'Tis we, 'tis ours, are changed; not they.
>
> For love, and beauty, and delight,
> There is no death nor change: their might
> Exceeds our organs, which endure
> No light, being themselves obscure.   [114–37]

5. Donald Davie, *Purity of Diction in English Verse* (New York, Oxford Univ. Press, 1953), pp. 154–5.

Compare to this the great stanza in which Spenser's Dame Nature replies to the claim of dominion over all things made by Mutabilitie:

> I well consider all that ye haue sayd,
> And find that all things steadfastnes doe hate
> And changed be: yet being rightly wayd
> They are not changed from their first estate;
> But by their change their being doe dilate:
> And turning to themselues at length againe,
> Doe worke their owne perfection so by fate:
> Then ouer them Change doth not rule and raigne;
> But they raigne ouer change, and doe their states maintaine.[6]

Compare also two memorable sentences of Blake's "The Marriage of Heaven and Hell":

> If the doors of perception were cleansed every thing would appear to man as it is, infinite.
> For man has closed himself up, till he sees all things thro' narrow chinks of his cavern. [Keynes, p. 187]

There is no "mysticism" in any of these passages—Shelley's, Spenser's, or Blake's,—and those who find mysticism in them are only shirking the labor of understanding. Aldous Huxley has recently taken to mescalin to induce "vision," and has had the temerity to entitle his record of this experimentation *The Doors of Perception.* Buber, in his sober consideration of a tree at the beginning of *I and Thou,* cleanses the doors of his perception as Blake meant them to be cleansed. Everything appears to man as it is, "infinite," when man enters into relation with any "thing," when I says Thou. The tree is encountered as a "single whole," and is "now no longer It." And this comes about "if I have both will and grace," but not by the aid of a Dark Night of privation or of mescalin.

Even so, this is the burden of the conclusion of "The Sensitive Plant," augmented by the belief stated in the stanza I have quoted from Spenser. Our organs are obscure, narrow chinks in our self-enclosed caverns. The light which puts out our eyes is darkness to us, as Thoreau had it. Garden, and Lady, and the Sensitive Plant, being rightly weighed, dilate their being by change but do not lose it. Spenser would even have it that they "doe their states maintaine," and Shelley expresses the same hope as "a modest creed." Blake, committed to contraries, without which he could visualize "no progression," would not have agreed. Spenser, as a Christian, is imaginatively consistent here; so are Shelley and Blake as more independent visionaries, with Blake having the advantage of tougher-mindedness. Faith is parallel to vision momentarily, while received myth

6. *Faerie Queene, 2,* Bk. 7, Canto VII, stanza LVIII.

for once does not clash with mythopoeia. All three poets face and meet the technical difficulty of visualizing the substance of the things they hope for and of presenting the evidence of things that we at least cannot see. I do not think that it is their supposed Platonism (or Neoplatonism) that is responsible for bringing Shelley and Spenser together here in closer agreement than Blake is with either. Blake's vision is codified, is mythographic; Blake is fully conscious of what he is doing. Beulah is a lower paradise fully categorized; an earthly paradise whose name and nature is fully known. The visionary gardens of Spenser and of Shelley (paradise, the Greek *paradeisos,* means a garden or park) are more ambiguous and less deliberate places. Blake's advantage is that in consequence he is more aware of the limitations of a *lower* paradise than Spenser or Shelley, i.e. he apprehends impermanence more readily and with less protest than they do. Whether the advantage is always a *poetic* advantage is for an individual reader to judge.

A few months after the composition of "The Sensitive Plant," Shelley returned in vision to Spenser's "gay gardins." "The Witch of Atlas" (August 14–16, 1820; first published in the *Posthumous Poems,* 1824) was the result. No more Spenserian poem has been written in the language than this "visionary rhyme," as Shelley termed it, and to me it seems also the best and most characteristic of all Shelley's works. I turn now to its consideration.

7

"The Witch of Atlas"

T. S. ELIOT, in one of his rare and authoritative footnotes, has assured us that we may dismiss "The Witch of Atlas" as a "trifle." [1] Nevertheless, it is Shelley's best long poem, the most individual and original of his visions, and the supreme example of myth-making poetry in English. In it the Spenserian tradition culminates, more gloriously even than it does in Blake. And from it, as much as from Blake, the finest poems of Yeats derive their ancestry, as Knight has noticed. "The Witch" is the central document in my argument, more so than "Prometheus" or "The Triumph of Life," for "The Witch" is *purely* a product of mythopoeia (with a mythographic element, suggestive of Blake, in its extraordinarily extensive counterpointing of mythic material from other poets against its own unconditioned imaginings). In this three-day loose-to-his-soul Shelley *created* as absolutely as any poet has ever done. Douglas Bush would have it that in "The Witch" Shelley is guilty of self-indulgence, of "playing by himself in public." [2] Fortunately, Shelley has anticipated his critics here, and has barbed his poem with an ironic grace, an urbane self-awareness, which can resist any criticism. Part of the glory of "The Witch," as I shall show, is that it is splendidly and overtly anticritical. It sets deliberate traps for analytic critics and learned exegetes, and arms itself, at each stage of its progress, with what must be termed visionary cynicism, a peculiar and effective attitude shared in only by Blake and the late Yeats among English poets. I am making the highest claims for "The Witch" because it can sustain them and because even its most sympathetic critics have undervalued it, allegorized it to death, condescended to it, or, worst of all, have submerged it in a mass of esoteric Neoplatonic and chemico-physical doctrine.

Tate has very persuasively condemned romantic poetry as being "allegory, a discourse in things, but on the understanding that they are translatable at every point into ideas." [3] "The Witch of Atlas" is any-

1. T. S. Eliot, *The Use of Poetry and the Use of Criticism: Studies in the Relation of Criticism to Poetry in England* (Cambridge, Mass., Harvard Univ. Press, 1933), p. 84, n. 1.
2. Bush, *Mythology and the Romantic Tradition*, p. 139.
3. Tate, *Reactionary Essays*, pp. 90–1.

thing but that kind of allegory, yet every one of its more serious critics
has made it into just that in his reading. E. E. Kellett labelled the Witch
as "creative imagination," and systematically translated the poem "at
every point into ideas" on that basis.[4] Hughes translated on the basis of
the Witch being the *anima mundi*.[5] Bush, wary of translating, calls the
Witch Asia "on a holiday." [6] Knight, in a brilliant series of observations
to which I am very much in debt, calls her "a dream-projection and,
partly, an incarnation of poetry itself." [7] Baker, warier even than Bush,
offers a catalogue of equivalences for the Witch:

> But she is also a female counterpart of the prankish Hermes of the
> Homeric Hymn; she is Vergil's Massylian priestess; she is Una,
> and she is Alma; she is the joyous nymph of "L'Allegro" bidding
> loathed melancholy an impolite adieu, and bringing quips and cranks
> (and even wanton jollity) into the vacated place; she is a female
> Archimage without evil intent, and she is Eve before the Fall. In
> short, the witch is a composite portrait of all the womanly grace,
> wisdom, beauty, and sympathy that Shelley could conceive of . . .[8]

This is still translation, still reduction. What the Witch *is* is herself,
a mythopoeic projection, a Thou confronted, and she can and ought to
be studied as such. What follows here is an attempt at such a study, a
study in anagogy, Dante's "fourth sense," "and this is when a scripture
is spiritually expounded which even in the literal sense, by the very
things it signifies, signifies again some portion of the supernal things of
eternal glory." [9] The literal form of Shelley's poem, "by the very things it
signifies, signifies again" rather than instead of, as Tate would have it.
What it is that is signified again by it, ought in some measure to be
demonstrated by my reading.

Something of the tone of the *ottava rima* "The Witch of Atlas" may
be derived from Shelley's own *ottava rima* "Hymn to Mercury," freely
rendered from the Homeric Hymn a little over a month before the making of "The Witch" (this conjecture is original with Bush, to whom I
am indebted).[1] Incidentally, "The Witch" *and* the Shelleyan "Hymn to
Mercury" seem to me to owe something to the tone and versification of
the opening Canto of "Don Juan." At the least, Byron stands in relation
to "The Witch" much as Coleridge does to "Mont Blanc"; they provide
for Shelley the modern instance of *form* that he adopts for his poem.

4. E. E. Kellett, *Suggestions* (Cambridge Univ. Press, 1923), p. 114.
5. A. M. D. Hughes, "Shelley's 'Witch of Atlas,'" *MLR, 7* (1912), 508–16.
6. Bush, pp. 139–40.
7. Knight, *The Starlit Dome*, p. 226.
8. Baker, *Shelley's Major Poetry*, pp. 213–14.
9. *The Convivio of Dante Alighieri*, trans. P. H. Wicksteed (not on title page),
Temple Classics ed. (London, Dent, 1912), p. 64.
1. Bush, p. 140.

Ultimately, "The Witch of Atlas" owes more to the Renaissance mythological narrative, the epyllyon of Spenser and Drayton, both of them
masters of digression. But there is a sharp turn to the digressiveness of
"The Witch" which is more Byronic than Spenserian. Wonder and
invention are there in profusion, as is what I have termed the irony of
vision, of Blake and Yeats, but a deliberate cynicism is present as well,
and the cynicism is the urbane variety practiced by one group of "the
liberal schism," the wits of Holland House, Byron's sometime milieu.

Six stanzas dedicate "The Witch of Atlas," stanzas headed "To Mary
(On Her Objecting to the Following Poem, upon the Score of Its Con-
taining No Human Interest)." Contrast these stanzas with the Dedication of "Laon and Cythna" some three years before, where fourteen
stanzas headed "To Mary" form an ecstatic confession, not so much, you
can grasp, of what had happened to the relationship between the Shelleys
(which is, I am glad to say, not my subject anyway) but of what had
happened to Shelley's art and his attitude toward it. From idealistic
dream-making of the fulfillment of desire, he had passed to fully conscious mythopoeia with its knowledge that desire is unfulfillable. From
an attempt to mix vision and history, he had moved to vision alone. Most
and best of all, he had learned to barb his vision, to polemicize from a
specifically visionary stance, to undercut his critics. Here is the tenth
stanza of the Dedication of "Laon":

> Is it, that now my inexperienced fingers
>   But strike the prelude of a loftier strain?
> Or, must the lyre on which my spirit lingers
>   Soon pause in silence, ne'er to sound again,
>   Though it might shake the Anarch Custom's reign,
> And charm the minds of men to Truth's own sway
>   Holier than was Amphion's? I would fain
> Reply in hope—but I am worn away,
> And Death and Love are yet contending for their prey.
>
> [82–90]

That swooning away at the close does not help much, even when we
realize that the poet of these lines believed himself at the point of dying
when he wrote them. That Shelleyan swoon has been confused by modern
readers with the prophetic descent from being caught up in the spirit
which figures in the "Hymn to Intellectual Beauty," the "Ode to the
West Wind," the "Ode to Liberty," and the "Epipsychidion," and no
amount of rational, learned argument seems likely at this time to dis-
suade most readers from thus worse compounding. But here, at least, no
confusion exists in the common reader's reaction. The assumptions of this
and of the other stanzas of the Dedication to "Laon" are in fact presump-
tions; the poem overtly legislates, and is available for translation of the

"one-for-one" variety. Here are the stanzas dedicating "The Witch of Atlas" and answering the objection that the poem contains "no human interest"

I

How, my dear Mary,—are you critic-bitten
    (For vipers kill, though dead) by some review,
That you condemn these verses I have written,
    Because they tell no story, false or true?
What, though no mice are caught by a young kitten
    May it not leap and play as grown cats do,
Till its claws come? Prithee, for this one time,
Content thee with a visionary rhyme.

II

What hand would crush the silken-wingèd fly,
    The youngest of inconstant April's minions,
Because it cannot climb the purest sky,
    Where the swan sings, amid the sun's dominions?
Not thine. Thou knowest 'tis its doom to die,
    When Day shall hide within her twilight pinions
The lucent eyes, and the eternal smile,
Serene as thine, which lent it life awhile.

III

To thy fair feet a wingèd Vision came,
    Whose date should have been longer than a day,
And o'er thy head did beat its wings for fame,
    And in thy sight its fading plumes display;
The watery bow burned in the evening flame.
    But the shower fell, the swift Sun went his way—
And that is dead.—O, let me not believe
That anything of mine is fit to live!   [1–24]

The next three stanzas, which develop this opening by a comparison with Wordsworth, can best be considered when the opening is first precisely apprehended. These first stanzas read most bitingly in juxtaposition to Mrs. Shelley's "Note on 'The Witch of Atlas,' " in which she rather nervously defends herself from their graceful reproach:

This poem is peculiarly characteristic of his tastes—wildly fanciful, full of brilliant imagery, and discarding human interest and passion, to revel in the fantastic ideas that his imagination suggested. The surpassing excellence of *The Cenci* had made me greatly desire that Shelley should increase his popularity by adopting subjects that would more suit the popular taste than a poem conceived in the abstract and dreamy spirit of the *Witch of Atlas.* It was not only that I wished him to acquire popularity as redounding to his fame; but I believed that he would obtain a greater mastery over his own powers, and greater happiness in his mind, if public applause crowned his endeavours. The few stanzas that precede the poem were addressed to me on my representing these ideas to him. Even now I believe that I was in the right. . . .

Shelley shrunk instinctively from portraying human passion, with its mixture of good and evil, of disappointment and disquiet. Such opened again the wounds of his own heart; and he loved to shelter himself rather in the airiest flights of fancy, forgetting love and hate, and regret and lost hope, in such imaginations as borrowed their hues from sunrise or sunset, from the yellow moonshine or paly twilight, from the aspect of the far ocean or the shadows of the woods,—which celebrated the singing of the winds among the pines, the flow of a murmuring stream, and the thousand harmonious sounds which Nature creates in her solitudes. These are the materials which form the *Witch of Atlas:* it is a brilliant congregation of ideas such as his senses gathered, and his fancy coloured, during his rambles in the sunny land he so much loved.[2]

This Marian view of "The Witch of Atlas" and of Shelley's poetry in general can be all too easily assimilated to the popular *and* New Critical misconceptions of that poetry. Mrs. Shelley was no more fit a reader for "The Witch" than either William Godwin or Mary Wollstonecraft would have been. The central point Mrs. Shelley makes is the one that Shelley's dedicatory stanzas so deftly parry—does "The Witch of Atlas" manifest "human interest and passion"? Mrs. Shelley says "no," seeing "The Witch" as a deliberate escape from human realities, and proceeds to rhapsodize sloppily, as Shelley's poetry *never* does, about "yellow moonshine."

The stanzas of dedication have nothing shrill in them, no demands, only an ironic courtliness. The tone is the tone of the Conclusion to "The Sensitive Plant," the tone of Spenser, and the appeal, appropriately enough, is to the "Muiopotmos," as a prime example of the fragility and value of "visionary rhyme" as well as a prototype for a "holy song" about the state of being of the lower paradise. These opening stanzas plainly set the poem in Blake's Beulah, a state of the imagination rather than our state of nature.

The first stanza invests all its meaning in its social grace, with an underlying menace in the figure of the kitten as symbolic of the Beulah-

2. Hutchinson, ed., *Works of Shelley,* pp. 429-30.

world (I assume that by now I have earned the right to import this Blakean term into the discussion of Shelley's poetry). "The Witch" tells "no story, false or true," not because it lacks a narrative element but rather because its events are not our events. "The Witch" celebrates the world of relationship, the state of innocence; our world is that of experience, our state is mutable and generative. "The Witch" is not a mouser, as good poems depicting or constituting experience are. But, like a young kitten, "The Witch" leaps and plays as poems of experience, grown cats, do; when the kitten's claws have grown, it will leap out of Beulah into the world of experience, and will know how to employ those claws. So, meanwhile, even to the most nonvisionary of critics, with their insistence on the mimetic obligation a poem is under, the necessity of its doing justice to our world of existent things, It's of experience, everyday values—even to these the poem modestly makes the request:

> Prithee, for this one time,
> Content thee with a visionary rhyme.

In the next stanza, the Beulah symbol switches to a butterfly, and the butterfly, we may be reasonably certain, is Spenser's Clarion:

> Of all the race of siluer-winged Flies
> Which doo possesse the Empire of the aire,
> Betwixt the centred earth, and azure skies,
> Was none more fauourable, nor more faire,
> Whilst heauen did fauour his felicities,
> Then Clarion . . .   [17–22]

> For he so swift and nimble was of flight,
> That from this lower tract he dar'd to stie
> Vp to the clowdes, and thence with pineons light,
> To mount aloft vnto the Christall skie . . .   [41–4]

Compare that, in phrasing and tone, to Shelley:

> What hand would crush the silken-wingèd fly,
> The youngest of inconstant April's minions,
> Because it cannot climb the purest sky,
> Where the swan sings, amid the sun's dominions?

Least important here in this vital resemblance are what *may* be the actual echoings of Spenser by Shelley: "silken-wingèd fly" from "silver-winged flies"; "climb the purest sky" from "mount aloft vnto the Christall skie"; possibly "the sun's dominions," in this context, from "the Empire of the aire." [3] More important for the significance of the

3. Carlos Baker, "Literary Sources of Shelley's 'Witch of Atlas,'" *PMLA*, 56 (1941), 472-9, is my source for these analogues between Spenser and Shelley.

poem is the conceptual use that Spenser is being put to here. Whose hand, Mary is rhetorically questioned (and potential critics with her), would crush the infant butterfly because it is not a death-defying swan? Underlying is the question: who cares to reject a poem like "Muiopotmos" (or "The Witch") once he has realized just what kind of a poem it is? The singing swan, climbing into the purest sky amid the sun's dominions, is an image of death, of imaginative finality, an emblem of a poetry greater in kind than visions of a lower paradise.

The sun metaphor for Mary is urbanely cruel. The butterfly's doom is to die as day dies—the lucent eyes and eternal smile of day, which proceed from the sun, become hidden at twilight as great wings of darkness are folded over them. The butterfly, the psyche, loses the life the eyes and smile gave to it. Day's countenance is "serene as thine," Mary's, until the wings blanket it. The implication is that Mary, like the sun or day, determines whether the vision—fly, psyche, poem—is to survive or not. In the next, the third stanza, Mary's rejection of the poem, here hinted at, is made central, and the image for her action is the swift, merciless, mutable sun in his passage. A "wingèd Vision," perhaps "The Witch of Atlas," beats its wings for fame, seeks to live longer than the butterfly's day of the second stanza. The rainbow of hope momentarily burns in the evening flame, but is then dissolved. With Mary's rejection, the sun goes his swift way, the vision's day passes, and it is dead. The plaintive protest is self-deprecatory; an ironic bow of a creator to his wife, undercut by all that comes before and after it. "O, let me not believe / That anything of mine is fit to live!" If you will not care for it, is the graceful undertone.

So far the dedicatory stanzas have sought to categorize the poem as Spenserian vision, the vision of "Muiopotmos" and the Garden of Adonis (which is echoed, as we shall see, in the opening stanzas of the poem proper, in the account of the Witch's birth). The "human interest" in the poem is not experiential, but is to be mythopoeic, relational, an augury of innocence. The remaining stanzas of dedication are just a smack at Wordsworth, but a relevant smack in their place.

Shelley's "Peter Bell the Third" (composed at Florence, October 1819, thus preceding "The Witch of Atlas" by some ten months) is one of his poems of merit which have no part in these chapters. Its subject is Wordsworth as shuffler, and it parodies aspects of "Peter Bell" which are not relevant to these final three dedicatory stanzas to "The Witch":

IV

Wordsworth informs us he was nineteen years
    Considering and retouching Peter Bell;
Watering his laurels with the killing tears
    Of slow, dull care, so that their roots to Hell

Might pierce, and their wide branches blot the spheres
Of Heaven, with dewy leaves and flowers; this well
May be, for Heaven and Earth conspire to foil
The over-busy gardener's blundering toil.

V

My Witch indeed is not so sweet a creature
As Ruth or Lucy, whom his graceful praise
Clothes for our grandsons—but she matches Peter,
Though he took nineteen years, and she three days
In dressing. Light the vest of flowing metre
She wears; he, proud as dandy with his stays,
Has hung upon his wiry limbs a dress
Like King Lear's 'looped and windowed raggedness.'

VI

If you strip Peter, you will see a fellow
Scorched by Hell's hyperequatorial climate
Into a kind of a sulphureous yellow:
A lean mark, hardly fit to fling a rhyme at;
In shape a Scaramouch, in hue Othello.
If you unveil my Witch, no priest nor primate
Can shrive you of that sin,—if sin there be
In love, when it becomes idolatry.   [25–48]

Grabo thought these last three lines to be a "challenge" to the reader
to "unravel" the "playful web of mystification" in the poem, thus mistaking Shelley's tone entirely.[4] Newman White was closer to the lines
when he reproved Grabo and identified Shelley's urbane warning as being directed against committing the sin of Actaeon.[5] The point against
Wordsworth *here* has never, I think, been adequately considered. The
stanzas have the tone of gentlemanly jest—the nineteen years–three days
contrast, the tribute to Ruth and the Lucy poems, the figure of the over-
busy gardener, finally the disturbing but sardonic appearance of the
devil in Peter. Strip Peter and you behold vision fallen back into what
Blake calls Ulro, the state of being of the isolated It, the real hell. Unveil Shelley's Witch and run the risk of being blinded or transformed, for
you will behold vision naked, the state of Beulah. The *Defence*, as almost always, is what is needed for glossing: "Few poets of the highest
class have chosen to exhibit the beauty of their conceptions in its naked
truth and splendour; and it is doubtful whether the alloy of costume,

---

4. Carl Grabo, *The Meaning of "The Witch of Atlas"* (Chapel Hill, Univ. of North
Carolina Press, 1935), p. 24.
5. White, *Shelley, 2*, 218.

habit, &c., be not necessary to temper this planetary music for mortal ears." [6]

The underlying point about Wordsworth's "Peter Bell" is that it *was* once vision. Traces of vision are still prominent in the poem's prologue, though pushed over the precarious border into Namby-Pamby land, realm of the childish rather than the childlike:

> "I know the secrets of a land
> Where human foot did never stray;
> Fair is that land as evening skies,
> And cool, though in the depths it lies
> Of burning Africa.
>
> "Or we'll into the realm of Faery,
> Among the lovely shades of things;
> The shadowy forms of mountains bare,
> And streams, and bowers, and ladies fair,
> The shades of palaces and kings!
>
> "Or, if you thirst with hardy zeal
> Less quiet regions to explore,
> Prompt voyage shall to you reveal
> How earth and heaven are taught to feel
> The might of magic lore!"   [96–110]

These are the last words the "little Boat, / Shaped like the crescent-moon" is able to say to Wordsworth. In this little boat, the poet has sailed "among the stars" and through all the earth's waters. But now, Wordsworth puts the boat from him:

> "My little vagrant Form of light,
> My gay and beautiful Canoe,
> Well have you played your friendly part;
> As kindly take what from my heart
> Experience forces—then adieu!"   [111–15]

Experience bids farewell to innocence; Wordsworth casts out vision. So Shelley must have read it, and with justification. As for the little boat:

> Off flew the Boat—away she flees,
> Spurning her freight with indignation!   [171–2]

And this is the last we see of Wordsworth, as the prologue ends, and the deliberately now-visionary poem of "Peter Bell" begins:

6. Shawcross, ed., *Shelley's Criticism,* p. 130.

I spake with faltering voice, like one
Not wholly rescued from the pale
Of a wild dream, or worse illusion;
But straight, to cover my confusion,
Began the promised Tale.

[186–90]

He had abandoned vision, and vision was not slow to abandon him. Not unrelated to this abandoned boat of "Peter Bell" is the visionary boat of the Witch of Atlas, in which she too adventures among the stars, on all the seas, and into the realm of Faery. In thus adding to a host of sources found for the Witch's boat, I am not rejecting the work of previous source hunters. "Nothing but" is the reverse to the principle on which "The Witch of Atlas" works. I claim for my source, or parallel, that it has the value of critical significance; it helps us understand both "The Witch" and, if not "Peter Bell," then certainly at least Shelley's reaction to "Peter Bell." Wordsworth puts away his little boat: Shelley's Witch claims it, and her voyages therein are the substance of Shelley's poem. That, I believe, is one reason why "Peter Bell" is relevantly involved in the dedicatory stanzas to "The Witch of Atlas." The visionary boat, rejected and reclaimed, is a prime vehicle for contrast. And, with that contrast made and with full warning given that we are moving into vision, into a state of being not that of "Peter Bell," we are ready to begin reading Shelley's poem.

I

Before those cruel Twins, whom at one birth
Incestuous Change bore to her father Time,
Error and Truth, had hunted from the Earth
All those bright natures which adorned its prime,
And left us nothing to believe in, worth
The pains of putting into learnèd rhyme,
A lady-witch there lived on Atlas' mountain
Within a cavern, by a secret fountain.

[49–56]

In "Mont Blanc" (line 44) Shelley had written of "the still cave of the witch Poesy." Poetry is a witch because, like magic, it competes with religion and philosophy as a discipline apprehending reality. The Witch of Atlas is called a witch for much the same reason; we are not to apprehend her through religion or philosophy (Grabo notwithstanding) but through poetry (which is not to say that she allegorically represents poetry). She is a Titaness (a friendlier relative of Spenser's Mutabilitie), a granddaughter to Atlas ("Her mother was one of the Atlantides," line 57) and a great-grandniece to Prometheus. She shares therefore in Shelley's activation of the Titanic myth which I discussed in my fourth chapter.

She lived on her grandfather's mountain before the Fall, before the end of the Saturnian golden age, when Time ruled in time's despite:

> There was the Heaven and Earth at first,
> And Light and Love; then Saturn, from whose throne
> Time fell, an envious shadow; such the state
> Of the earth's primal spirits beneath his sway,
> As the calm joy of flowers and living leaves.

Thus Asia, speaking of the age of Kronos (ii.iv.32–6). Shelley in the first stanza of "The Witch" adumbrates the myth of the Fall of Kronos; "Incestuous Change," the Titanese Mutabilitie, bears to her father Time those cruel twins, Error and Truth. This adumbration of myth is primarily urbane, not "serious," and it fulfills the function of defending visionary poetry. In effect it is *the* instance in Shelley's poetry of a protest against a certain kind of antipoetic attitude stemming from natural science, a protest found also in Blake, Wordsworth, and Keats (and in their eighteenth-century predecessor, Smart). We have heard so much, since Whitehead, of Shelley the passionate chemist, that we are likely to overlook the plain meaning of the first stanza of "The Witch of Atlas." Error and Truth, cruel twins, Blake's "cloven fiction," have hunted all the "bright natures" of vision from the earth; nothing is left to be believed in, to be "worth / The pains of putting into learnèd rhyme," which last is what "The Witch of Atlas" is. They are verses that "tell no story, false or true" (line 4, dedication) and therefore have nothing to do with the reign of the cruel twins. But what is philosophy but the kingdom of the twins, and science also?

The cavern in which the Witch dwells, with its enclosed "secret fountain," has not lacked for allegorical interpreters. Grabo again is the most comprehensive and learned of the commentators:

> The cavern then is a symbol of souls living in this world after their descent from the divine world into mortality and before their descent to the realm of Pluto. Water is the symbol of material things, of the world of generation . . . [the] cavern . . . symbolizes a soul shut apart to itself in the individuality and isolation which is characteristic of human life. . . .
>
> Of the Witch, living in her cave by "a secret fountain," we can say for the moment no more than that she is associated with some stream of divine energy: whether the creative energy of nature, the divine energy of intellect, or that which is but another name for the energy of intellect, the fountain of beauty . . .[7]

7. Grabo, *The Meaning of "The Witch,"* pp. 26–7.

Yeats, the pioneer student of Shelley's "symbolism," was happily indefinite when he considered Shelley's use of the cavern: "It may mean any enclosed life, as when it is the dwelling-place of Asia and Prometheus, or when it is 'the still cave of poetry,' and it may have all meanings at once, or it may have as little meaning as some ancient religious symbol enwoven from the habit of centuries with the patterns of a carpet or a tapestry." Most generally, Yeats saw Shelley's caverns as symbolizing "the mind looking inward upon itself," and his fountains as sources whence water, "his great symbol of existence," flowed forth as the substance of life.[8]

The most recent comprehensive student of Shelley's symbols, Peter Butter, gives us a rather more (perhaps rather too) thorough an account of cavern and fountain:

(1) A cave may be emblematic of life on earth, shut in from eternity. Any enclosed place, like a bower or heavily-shaded place among trees, may be used in the same way. (2) A cave may be the human mind, or an individual mind, or a secret place within the mind. Especially this image is used for the mind turning in upon itself . . .

Fountains or wells may be used figuratively for the source of anything; more specifically for a source of inspiration within the mind, or . . . for the source of life itself.[9]

After all this, I suggest that it is sufficient and even advisable to read the "cavern" and "secret fountain" of line 56 as not being as specifically symbolic as even the most generalized equations offered us by Grabo, Yeats, and Butter. The Witch, before vision was hunted from the earth, led a deliberately segregated existence "within a cavern," cut off from mankind. In her cavern a secret fountain was prominent; its purpose we learn in stanzas XXVIII–XXX. We sleep to rebuild our tissues. The Witch never sleeps, but all night she lies in trance within her fountain. In winter she resorts to a nearby well, where she can lie snug in "crimson fire." The suggestiveness of this is vast, yet the invitation to particularize it as extended to the individual reader requires individual precision, if the poem is not to be falsified. The central point to be observed is that the principle is not that of the Behmenite picnic, in which the author supplies the words, and the reader the meanings, but even more is it not the "nothing but." The fountain and well can mean as many precise things as does the biblical phrase "water of life," employed so repeatedly and so differently. I read the burning fountain of the Witch as embodying also (not as nothing but) what Blake calls the "Eden fire," the flame of human desire and creativity, burning atop the

8. Yeats, *Ideas of Good and Evil*, pp. 98, 100, 96.
9. Butter, *Shelley's Idols of the Cave*, pp. 60, 66.

water of life, or life-giving water. But here, I am convinced, the poem invites more than a solitary reader; rather does it demand a great number of "and also's."

What follows in the poem, as several scholars have noted,[1] is a deliberate linking with Spenser's Beulah vision, the Garden of Adonis:

II

> Her mother was one of the Atlantides:
> The all-beholding Sun had ne'er beholden
> In his wide voyage o'er continents and seas
> So fair a creature, as she lay enfolden
> In the warm shadow of her loveliness;—
> He kissed her with his beams, and made all golden
> The chamber of gray rock in which she lay—
> She, in that dream of joy, dissolved away.   [57–64]

The relevant parallel in Spenser (the opening "Her" here is Belphœbe) is:

> Her mother was the faire *Chrysogonee,*
> The daughter of *Amphisa,* who by race
> A Faerie was, yborne of high degree,
> She bore *Belphœbe,* she bore in like cace
> Faire *Amoretta* in the second place:
> These two were twinnes, and twixt them two did share
> The heritage of all celestiall grace.
> That all the rest it seem'd they robbed bare
> Of bountie, and of beautie, and all vertues rare.
>
> It were a goodly storie, to declare,
> By what straunge accident faire *Chrysogone*
> Conceiu'd these infants, and how them she bare,
> In this wild forrest wandring all alone,
> After she had nine moneths fulfild and gone:
> For not as other wemens commune brood,
> They were enwombed in the sacred throne
> Of her chaste bodie, nor with commune food,
> As other wemens babes, they sucked vitall blood.
>
> But wondrously they were begot, and bred
> Through influence of th'heauens fruitfull ray,
> As it in antique bookes is mentioned.
> It was vpon a Sommers shynie day,

---

1. Among others, Baker, "Literary Sources of 'Witch,'" and F. L. Jones, "Shelley and Spenser," *Studies in Philology, 39* (1942), 662–70.

> When *Titan* faire his beames did display,
> In a fresh fountaine, farre from all mens vew,
> She bath'd her brest, the boyling heat t'allay;
> She bath'd with roses red, and violets blew,
> And all the sweetest flowres, that in the forrest grew.
>
> Till faint through irkesome wearinesse, adowne
> Vpon the grassie ground her selfe she layd
> To sleepe, the whiles a gentle slombring swowne
> Vpon her fell all naked bare displayd;
> The sunne-beames bright vpon her body playd,
> Being through former bathing mollifide,
> And pierst into her wombe, where they embayd
> With so sweet sence and secret power vnspide,
> That in her pregnant flesh they shortly fructifide.   [IV–VII]

Source study is so often a fruitless kind of exercise that one is surprised and disheartened to see neglected an instance where it might be made a major aid to critical understanding. Bush and Baker, among other scholars, have noted the influencing I have just cited, but like other scholars they have been contented in simply recording their recognition of Shelley's debt. But in Shelley's debt to Spenser (here and throughout the poem) what counts is the use to which Shelley has put Spenser, a use dependent on Shelley's understanding of Spenser, which itself can be valuable to us. The use made of Spenser by Shelley and Blake (and less substantially, though as extensively, by Keats) is an important part of the critical history of *The Faerie Queene,* and in these days constitutes an aid to reading *The Faerie Queene* which Spenser scholars are not wise to neglect, however curiously backward a technique it may seem to approach a prototype, the Garden of Adonis, by means of its imaginative derivatives, Blake's Beulah or Shelley's various earthly paradises.

Spenser's Garden of Adonis, as C. S. Lewis has most influentially interpreted it,[2] is the conceptual center of *The Faerie Queene;* it is Spenser's most successful original myth (for all the ascribing it to sources in the *Variorum* edition of Spenser) and certainly his most influential visualization (Drayton, Milton, Blake, Shelley, and Keats are a considerable progeny for a poetic concept to have influenced). Its import in *The Faerie Queene* is inexhaustible; what I have to say about it here is altogether incomplete, but is offered as the main outline of the reading given it by the poet of "The Witch of Atlas," on the evidence that *the poem itself,* "The Witch," provides.

The Garden of Adonis is a bower of lawful *passive* pleasure, of a

2. C. S. Lewis, *The Allegory of Love* (London, 1938), pp. 324ff.

sanctified sexual relationship, of "chastity" in its Spenserian, which is to say its best, sense. I use "passive" as Shelley (and Blake) would have used the word, for the garden is (quite deliberately, one is sure) a place of *passive* imaginative activity, in which only natural creation goes on. The creativity of the garden is eternal (until Christian apocalypse, "when no more Change shall be") but its creations are not; they are mutable. In the Garden of Adonis, as in Blake's Beulah or the state of existence embodied in "The Witch of Atlas," forms constantly pass away, but substance always endures to be converted into new forms again. The Garden of Adonis is equivalent to the Eden garden of Genesis or to Milton's Garden of Eden (which, as Milton scholarship has long told us, partially derives from it), the paradise from which (Christianity teaches us) our forefathers fell. It is not equivalent to the paradise to which we may return (as Spenser's Christianity taught him) or to the kind of upper paradise visualized in Blake's Eden, where the forms of the artist's creation are eternal (and this, no more than in Shelley, is not Platonic, strictly *or* loosely). In the heaven of Christianity substance has not prevailed, but ordained form has; in Spenser's Garden of Adonis the sad reverse is envisioned, celebrated, and yet lamented:

> there is the first seminarie
> Of all things, that are borne to liue and die,
> According to their kindes.

> All things from thence doe their first being fetch,
> And borrow matter, whereof they are made,
> Which when as forme and feature it does ketch,
> Becomes a bodie, and doth then inuade
> The state of life, out of the griesly shade,
> That substance is eterne, and bideth so.
> Ne when the life decayes, and forme does fade,
> Doth it consume, and into nothing go,
> But chaunged is, and often altred to and fro.

> The substance is not chaunged, nor altered,
> But th'only forme and outward fashion;
> For euery substance is conditioned
> To change her hew, and sundry formes to don,
> Meet for her temper and complexion:
> For formes are variable and decay,
> By course of kind, and by occasion;
> And that faire flowre of beautie fades away,
> As doth the lilly fresh before the sunny ray.

> Great enimy to it, and to all the rest,
>   That in the *Gardin* of *Adonis* springs,
>   Is wicked *Time,* who with his scyth addrest,
>   Does mow the flowring herbes and goodly things . . .
>
> But were it not, that *Time* their troubler is,
>   All that in this delightfull Gardin growes,
>   Should happie be, and haue immortall blis:
>   For here all plentie, and all pleasure flowes,
>   And sweet loue gentle fits emongst them throwes,
>   Without fell rancor, or fond gealosie;
>   Franckly each paramour his leman knowes,
>   Each bird his mate, ne any does enuie
> Their goodly meriment, and gay felicitie.   [xxx–xli]

These magnificent stanzas, which I have marred by excerpting from their necessary context, are what "The Witch of Atlas" wants us to keep in mind as we read it. *That* is why the Witch, in stanza ii, is born, as Belphœbe and Amoret are born, by an *aura seminalis*. The allusion tells us that the Witch has been born into the Garden of Adonis; that the garden *is* the pastoral scene of the poem. The allusion sets the visionary scene, and it sets the tone: one of mingled celebration and lamentation, the last being for the mutability of the lower, earthy paradise, specifically dealt with in stanzas xxii–xxv of the poem, as we shall see. As in "The Sensitive Plant" we are in Blake's "married land," Beulah, the world of innocence, of mythopoeic relationship.

As befits the state of innocence, Shelley narrates his Witch's engendering with a childlike (not childish) mischief; the tone of wonderment mocks the professional source hunter, tells us where we are and what we are doing, tones down the insubstantiality of the vision, and, best of all, mocks at itself and any more tedious pretensions it may have:

III

> 'Tis said, she first was changed into a vapour,
>   And then into a cloud, such clouds as flit,
> Like splendour-wingèd moths about a taper,
>   Round the red west when the sun dies in it:
> And then into a meteor, such as caper
>   On hill-tops when the moon is in a fit:
> Then, into one of those mysterious stars
> Which hide themselves between the Earth and Mars.

IV

> Ten times the Mother of the Months had bent
>   Her bow beside the folding-star, and bidden

With that bright sign the billows to indent
The sea-deserted sand—like children chidden,
At her command they ever came and went—
Since in that cave a dewy splendour hidden
Took shape and motion : with the living form
Of this embodied Power, the cave grew warm.   [65–80]

Expectation is that a mother will carry her child within her womb, but this is a visionary poem to an extreme, and that commonplace expectation is not fulfilled by it. The birth of the Witch, according to the poem's text, seems to be more marvelous even than the analogous births of Belphœbe and Amoret.

The Sun (line 62) kisses the nymph with his beams, impregnates her, and makes the cavern her womb. His force is too great for her; in a "dream of joy," not joy itself, she is "dissolved away," while "the chamber of gray rock," the cavern itself, is "made all golden." The poem's touch on the Witch's mother is very light; her transformations are all in the realm of " 'Tis said" (line 65), but whatever may have become of her, she is not in the cave when the Witch is born *full-grown*.[3] After the set time of gestation "a dewy splendour *hidden* / Took shape and motion" *"in that cave."* And "with the living form / Of this embodied Power, *the cave grew warm."* No mother is in sight when suddenly this vision is to be seen within the cave, not an infant but

V

A lovely lady garmented in light
From her own beauty—deep her eyes, as are
Two openings of unfathomable night
Seen through a Temple's cloven roof—her hair
Dark—the dim brain whirls dizzy with delight.
Picturing her form; her soft smiles shone afar,
And her low voice was heard like love, and drew
All living things towards this wonder new.   [81–8]

She is more visionary still than Belphœbe and Amoret; she shares with them the Sun as father, but her mother is at least something of a question. If we wished to practice a severely reductive reading we could make that "chamber of gray rock" the poet's brain, womb impregnated by Apollo in the guise of the Sun so as to produce the Witch. But we do better to avoid even that: a secret cave sustains the Sun's force, which "one of the Atlantides" cannot sustain, and brings forth the Witch, altogether mature. As a child of the Sun, the Witch will manifest an energy more than human; she will transcend Beulah and her form, unlike anything else in the Garden of Adonis state, will be eternal.

3. *Shelley*, 2, 216–17. White seems to confuse mother and daughter here.

Stanza v, quoted above, resembles the "Life of Life!" lyric in "Prometheus," ii.v, in that it combines ecstatic apprehensions of a visionary lady with a maddening (to some) refusal to provide images of the lady which can be visualized. The lady is clothed only in the light of her own beauty, but the light is strong enough to put out Shelley's eyes. *Her* eyes are wonderfully "deep," and their deepness is splendidly conveyed by the image of two openings of night seen through a temple's cloven roof, but the night itself is imageless, "unfathomable." Her hair is "dark"—that is as concrete a detail as we get. But is it helpful or provocative of anything but impatience to be told that "the dim brain whirls dizzy with delight, / Picturing her form"? Shelley has forgotten that it is not his primary business to give us his own affective reaction to what is after all his own creation. Whether deliberately or not, in effect he has evaded a technical problem here, one which he went some way toward solving in "Life of Life!" If there were much more of this affective evasion in his poetry than in fact there is, it would be very difficult to defend properly against the modern critical onslaught.

In any case, her beauty and her receptiveness draw to her all the inhabitants of her pastoral domain (stanzas vi–xi), inhabitants drawn largely from Spenser's Faery Land (she has a touch of Una in her at this point, as scholars have noted).[4] As in Act iii of "Prometheus" we witness a culmination of English pastoral tradition, a procession of heraldic and emblematic beasts, of old Silenus and Dryope and Faunus and universal Pan, of the pasturers of the sea itself:

x

> And every nymph of stream and spreading tree,
>   And every shepherdess of Ocean's flocks,
> Who drives her white waves over the green sea,
>   And Ocean with the brine on his gray locks,
> And quaint Priapus with his company,
>   All came, much wondering how the enwombèd rocks
> Could have brought forth so beautiful a birth;—
> Her love subdued their wonder and their mirth.   [121–8]

(Lines 126–7, incidentally, with their reference to "the enwombèd rocks" having brought forth so beautiful a birth, I take as being confirmatory of my reading of the manner of the Witch's birth.)

Herdspeople and pastoral kings complete the procession with the addition of a few visionary grotesques, worthy of Beddoes:

> Pigmies, and Polyphemes, by many a name,
>   Centaurs, and Satyrs, and such shapes as haunt
> Wet clefts.—and lumps neither alive nor dead,
>   Dog-headed, bosom-eyed, and bird-footed.   [133–6]

4. Baker, "Literary Sources of 'Witch,'" seems to have priority here.

Grabo's Witch, being Minerva, Venus, Proserpine, Diana, Isis, and a good deal besides,[5] attracts all of these worshipers presumably because there is nothing which she cannot do for them, having as she does the combined powers of the whole mélange of goddesses she somehow comprehends. Shelley's Witch draws the procession because she embodies a supreme offer of relationship, because she offers the possibility of confronting everything in her pastoral world as an ultimate Thou. And most simply, because she is beautiful:

XII

For she was beautiful—her beauty made
    The bright world dim, and everything beside
Seemed like the fleeting image of a shade:
    No thought of living spirit could abide,
Which to her looks had ever been betrayed,
    On any object in the world so wide,
On any hope within the circling skies,
But on her form, and in her inmost eyes.

XIII

Which when the lady knew, she took her spindle
    And twined three threads of fleecy mist, and three
Long lines of light, such as the dawn may kindle
    The clouds and waves and mountains with; and she
As many star-beams, ere their lamps could dwindle
    In the belated moon, wound skilfully;
And with these threads a subtle veil she wove—
A shadow for the splendour of her love.   [137–52]

If she were not to veil herself, then the life of her pastoral world would cease. Without It man cannot live; activity without objects of experience (line 142) is impossible. Philosophical or theological interpretation, here as elsewhere in the poem, is redundant.

The thirteenth stanza has been praised, aptly, by Knight, for the brilliance of its phrasing, for its attempt to "compress the intangible into concrete forms."[6] I partly agree with Fogle that "Shelley is in some respects the antithesis of Blake: his is the generalizing imagination, Blake's the particularizing,"[7] but I am not prepared to believe with Fogle that this antithesis is in any way to Shelley's advantage. Blake moves from the perception of an ultimately human Thou to its embodiment in minute particular Thou's; Shelley far too often forgets that you confront an ultimate Thou only through a particular Thou, else you have

---

5. Grabo, The Meaning of "The Witch," pp. 38–9.
6. Knight, p. 224.
7. Fogle, "Image and Imagelessness," Keats-Shelley Journal, 1 (Jan. 1952), 27.

forsaken poetry for some other discipline. The generalizing imagination seems to me, as it did to Blake, something of a contradiction in terms. Shelley was cursed with the generalizing passion to the extent that Shelley the man wanted to be a philosopher, early and late (and a very bad one he would have made, if "philosopher" is to have any precise meaning as a word), but Shelley the poet had strength enough to resist the man's inherent abstractness. Indeed, he had strength enough to dare to utilize his own weakness, and to do as much toward redeeming "the generalizing imagination" for poetry as can perhaps be done. Pottle's summary, usefully quoted in part by Fogle,[8] seems likely to be the definitive concise account of Shelley's visualization:

> He seldom uses a firmly held, developed image, but pours out a flood of images which one must grasp momentarily in one aspect and then release. He is fond of figures within figures. He imposes his will on the object of experience: he does not explore "reality," he flies away from it. He seldom takes a gross, palpable, near-at-hand object from the world of ordinary perception and holds it for contemplation: his gaze goes up to the sky, he starts with objects that are just on the verge of becoming invisible or inaudible or intangible and he strains away even from these.[9]

A remarkable thing about this very accurate and acute summary is that it is meant as part of a syllabus of errors that the fathers of the New Critical faith might draw up against Shelley, but is also in fact, if not in intention (and it may be that also, for all I know), a catalogue of Shelleyan poetic virtues, of the characteristic excellences of Shelley's poetry, some of them excellences scored against the grain, if you would have it so. The summary I have quoted above seems to me in fact to be the practical demonstration in Shelley of the consequences of the mythopoeic technique which is the subject of this thesis. The image Shelley seeks is one which can embody the confrontation of life by life, the living which is a meeting of Thou's, relationship as dialogue, in which experience and its necessary objects disappear. But each particular Thou, as he imagistically lights upon it, becomes for him an It also. The relational event quickly runs its course; the image cannot hold the Thou. Hence the "flood of images," as well as the "figures within figures," for this quest toward confrontation seeks a relationship at the cost of commonplace observation. "Reality" for it is not the reality of observer and object observed, and a figure within a figure is therefore not less "real" for it than a figure within a world of things. And most certainly in this mythopoeia it will seem as if the poet "imposes his will on the object of experience," for that *is* the mode of operation of mythopoeia, to strive to

8. Ibid., p. 35.
9. Pottle, "The Case of Shelley," *PMLA,* 67 (1952), 601.

do away with It's, with objects of experience, with experiencing and being experienced itself. Pottle rightly puts the "reality" from which Shelley flies in quotes; for the question here is "whose reality?" and the answer is forever disputable. Finally, the generalizing passion comes into play; the particular Thou's with their attendant mutability are rejected, and Shelley's visualization strains upward, toward the evanescence of Thou, seeking desperately for the Thou that cannot by its very nature become for us an It, and seeking (of necessity) vainly.

Fogle, following Pottle as I do here, achieves an insight partially invalidated for me by its unnecessary involvement with Platonics, the specter which hangs so heavily over Shelley criticism that one can despair of ever lifting it, even in part. Writing of Shelley's "narrowing image" and citing the famous image of the fading away of the morning star into the dawn ("To a Skylark," lines 21–5) in illustration of this phenomenon "in which the truth, receding, dwindles to a point," Fogle goes for sanction to Platonism, though it is "a Platonism which comes to terms with literature":

> Shelley is expressing not a surrender, not a passive emotion, but the result of intellectual effort pushed to its furthest reaches, with all the difficulties and dangers which are involved in it. He presents a full cycle of the confrontation, of the struggle, and of the victorious defeat of the human spirit at full stretch. What seems superficially to be formlessness and the shattering of order is really the synthesis of form and formlessness, of expansion and determination, of image and imagelessness. As such, it is the wholly consistent result of absorbing into art a system of thought which has not been, to put it mildly, without influence in the world, and is not lightly to be banished by even the most confident criticism.[1]

That "system of thought," as Fogle had made clear, is Platonism. But the phenomenon in Shelley's poetry which Fogle is describing is one with the mythopoeic theme and technique that is studied here. I do not prefer my practical account here to Fogle's; we are getting at the same thing from different directions. What I do deprecate is that Fogle draws sanction and critical vocabulary for this matter from outside Shelley's poetry; I do not. I urge mythopoeia and its principles (so evident in Shelley's poetry when one realizes that personification is what one brings to it, not what one finds there) as the proper technique for reading here precisely because sanction and vocabulary for it can be drawn from the poetry. Platonism, or anything akin to it, is another kind of discipline entirely, as Plato well realized when he shut the mythmakers out of his Just City.

I have digressed from stanza XIII and its remarkable instance of Shel-

1. Fogle, "Image and Imagelessness," pp. 35, 27, 25–6.

ley's frequently operative "particularizing imagination" in which vision
is concretized. Out of her compassion for created things, the Witch
weaves a ninefold "subtle veil" whose function it is to be "A shadow for
the splendour of her love." I take this ninefoldness to have imaginative
force rather than to be accidental. Witches, in all traditions of magic, are
associated with ninefoldness. Both the Muse and the Night-Mare embody a ninefold vision. In Blake the number is used very strictly, always
in conjunction with evil. Magic in "The Witch of Atlas" (and everywhere in Shelley) is altogether white, and a ninefold veil, a supremely
evil symbol of natural mystery in Blake (Vala, the name of the "agèd
mother" who sings the nine fallen "Nights" of "The Four Zoas," is
derived from the Norse Eddic *Völuspa* and from the word "veil"), is
here an emblem of mercy. The nine strands of the Witch's veil are twined
from "three threads of fleecy mist," "three long lines of light," dawnlight, and three beams of the evening star ("ere their lamps could dwindle / In the belated moon"). To Grabo mist, light, and starbeams are
"symbols of the divine fire." [2] I demur again at the arbitrariness of this
kind of reading. Confrontation of an ultimate Thou in the Witch separates the components of creation off from experience, ends life as we
know it. To spare created things, the Witch veils herself in particular,
transient Thou's, flickering on and off in mist, dawnlight, and star-
beams. The best analogue is, suitably enough, in the "Hymn to Intellectual Beauty," where Shelley first clearly presented the name and nature
of his mythopoeia, his search for a Thou which would not become an It.
In the "Hymn" the shadow of the Thou floated among us "as summer
winds," "like moonbeams," "like hues and harmonies of evening," "like
clouds in starlight," "like mist o'er mountains driven." These are the
stuff, the transient Thou's, the mythopoeic components, out of which the
veil of the lady is woven in stanza XIII. "Symbols of the divine fire" belong to theism, not to the agnostic confrontations of a Thou which constitute Shelley's mythopoeia. Grabo, as before, imports myth from without the poem.

　　Stanzas XIV–XX are devoted to describing the magical contents of the
Witch's cave. They are the properties peculiar to the lower paradise.
First, visions of relationship, such as were depicted in the "Hymn to
Intellectual Beauty" and the dedicatory stanzas to "The Revolt of Is-
lam":

XIV

The deep recesses of her odorous dwelling
　　Were stored with magic treasures—sounds of air,
Which had the power all spirits of compelling,
　　Folded in cells of crystal silence there;

2. Grabo, *The Meaning of "The Witch,"* p. 43.

> Such as we hear in youth, and think the feeling
>   Will never die—yet ere we are aware,
> The feeling and the sound are fled and gone,
> And the regret they leave remains alone.

Next, lines that might come out of the Beulah-land of Blake, refining the Garden of Adonis:

> And there lay Visions swift, and sweet, and quaint,
>   Each in its thin sheath, like a chrysalis,
> Some eager to burst forth, some weak and faint
>   With the soft burthen of intensest bliss . . .   [153–64]

The tone here resembles that of "The Book of Thel"; if you comprehend the nature of the technical difficulties involved in presenting an unborn state, then the tone is acceptable, is indeed necessary and altogether appropriate for the work it must perform.

The wondrous odours, beneficent liquors, manuscripts, and other apocalyptic objects which form the Witch's stock need no paraphrase, no explication. With stanza XXI the poem begins a new movement; genesis and description of the Witch give way to her activities, but only after the poem's climax (XXII–XXV), a Spenserian lamentation over and acceptance of the mutability that reigns even in the Garden of Adonis, as the emphasis shifts from lower *paradise* to *lower* paradise, and nature again cries out against the order of grace.

At first the Witch lived alone, but when her beauty and promise of relationship had attracted all the denizens of her world, an illusion of togetherness, an appearance of shared reality was created. In stanzas reminiscent of and exactly parallel to Spenser's "Two Cantos of Mutabilitie" (this suggestion of influence is my own), the Witch herself, gently but firmly, dissolves this illusion:

XXII

> The Ocean-nymphs and Hamadryades,
>   Oreads and Naiads, with long weedy locks,
> Offered to do her bidding through the seas,
>   Under the earth, and in the hollow rocks,
> And far beneath the matted roots of trees,
>   And in the gnarlèd heart of stubborn oaks,
> So they might live for ever in the light
> Of her sweet presence—each a satellite.

XXIII

> 'This may not be,' the wizard maid replied;
>   'The fountains where the Naiades bedew

Their shining hair, at length are drained and dried;
   The solid oaks forget their strength, and strew
Their latest leaf upon the mountains wide;
   The boundless ocean like a drop of dew
Will be consumed—the stubborn centre must
Be scattered, like a cloud of summer dust.

XXIV

'And ye with them will perish, one by one;—
   If I must sigh to think that this shall be,
If I must weep when the surviving Sun
   Shall smile on your decay—oh, ask not me
To love you till your little race is run;
   I cannot die as ye must—over me
Your leaves shall glance—the streams in which ye dwell
Shall be my paths henceforth, and so—farewell!'—

XXV

She spoke and wept:—the dark and azure well
   Sparkled beneath the shower of her bright tears,
And every little circlet where they fell
   Flung to the cavern-roof inconstant spheres
And intertangled lines of light:—a knell
   Of sobbing voices came upon her ears
From those departing Forms, o'er the serene
Of the white streams and of the forest green.   [217–48]

These stanzas are the thematic center of *The Witch of Atlas,* and taken together constitute one of what seem to me to be the heights of Shelley's poetic achievement, comparable to Act III, scene ii of *Prometheus,* the "Ode to the West Wind," the closing stanzas of "Adonais," and Rousseau's speeches of self-revelation in "The Triumph of Life." Because they determine what is most vital in the establishment of the complexity and unity of the poem's theme and structure, as well as for their high intrinsic value, I shall deal with these stanzas at some length. The remainder of the poem, if these stanzas are read aright and fully valued, can then be more summarily explicated.

Why, of all the pastoral subjects of the Witch, are the "ocean-nymphs and Hamadryades, / Oreads and Naiads, with long weedy locks" selected out to present the petition not to be parted from her? The question has not been asked by the scholars who have written of the poem, but critically it is a legitimate question and the answer to it (if I have found the proper one) may well be illuminating.

These petitioners are all nymphs: ocean nymphs, hamadryads (oak nymphs), oreads (mountain nymphs), and naiads (water nymphs, belonging to fountains). Shelley was a good enough classicist to have known a great deal about nymphs and what they betoken. In any case, their associations form a legitimate part of their meaning in "The Witch of Atlas."

Hermes was the son of Zeus by the mountain nymph Maia, a birth we have seen paralleled in that of the Witch of Atlas. Hermaphroditus was a son of Hermes (as was Pan) and came to his peculiar grief through arousing the passion of a nymph. Shelley's Witch, in her prankishness-to-come in the poem, clearly resembles the Hermes of Shelley's version of the Homeric hymn and is to be accompanied by her version of Hermaphroditus. Add these to the appealing nymphs, and you perceive how the poem moves in the pastoral world of the *numphai*.

Who were the nymphs, by the canons of Greek myth? "The word *numphe* meant a female being through whom a man became the *numphius*, i.e. the happy bridegroom who had fulfilled the purpose of his manhood." [3] The term might be applied to goddess or earthly maiden, but if some being was referred to simply as a "nymph," then something more specific was meant. Nymphs proper were not eternal beings; dryads died with their oaks, naiads ceased with their fountains. Nymphs lived a long time, much longer than humans, but nevertheless at last they died. But of all natural mortal things, they survived longest. Kerényi quotes an ancient formula for computing a nymph's span of life: "Nine human spans lives the chattering rook; a stag as long as four rooks; a raven as long as three stags; a palm as long as nine ravens; and as long as ten palms live the beautiful-haired nymphs, the daughters of Zeus." [4]

Nymphs are appropriate dwellers in the Garden of Adonis, for they represent an unfulfilled state, a paradise lower, a sea still unpastured, Blake's feminine threefold Beulah state not yet become the upper creative paradise, the fourfold Eden. Nymphs await the bridegroom; the passage from numphe to numphius, the passive female to the male then actively fulfilled by her, is the movement toward apocalypse, exemplified in the action of "Prometheus Unbound." But the play-poem "The Witch of Atlas" never passes from Beulah to Eden, as "Prometheus" does; it abides with Spenser in the Garden of Adonis, while with Spenser it utters the lamentation for the Garden of the "Cantos of Mutabilitie."

The nymphs then are the most characteristic and most long-lived inhabitants of the Witch's pastoral paradise; they are therefore closer in relationship to the Witch than any of her other subjects, and their appeal to her is consequently the strongest that can be made. But the paradox of Shelley's mythopoeia is fully operative in that appeal; the appeal is ungrantable. The conflicting claims of love and mutability are re-

3. Kerényi, *The Gods of the Greeks*, p. 177.
4. Ibid.

solved for mutability; from the conflict the poetry of these stanzas comes into being.

The nymphs in stanza XXII in effect offer to hallow their several worlds to the Witch, to worship and obey her in all their local habitations, in return to live "for ever" as satellites to her sun. Her reply first summarizes the mutability of the nymphs, with the severely sad "This may not be." The fountains at length are drained and dried, and the naiads with them. The solid oaks forget their strength, strew their last leaves, and die, and the dryads die with them. At length, temporal mutability will have run its course, and as the time when no more change shall be draws near, the boundless ocean will be consumed and the ocean nymphs with it. At last the stubborn center itself must be scattered, the earth itself be dispelled like a cloud of summer dust, and the oreads who had offered their homage "under the earth, and in the hollow rocks" to the Witch, must be scattered with it. The two stanzas, XXII and XXIII, are rigorously integrated with one another.

Stanza XXIII echoes the boast of Spenser's Titaness Mutabilitie as she asserts her sway:

> Yet mauger *Ioue,* and all his gods beside,
> I doe possesse the worlds most regiment;
> As, if ye please it into parts diuide,
> And euery parts inholders to convent,
> Shall to your eyes appeare incontinent.
> And first, the Earth (great mother of vs all)
> That only seems vnmov'd and permanent,
> And vnto *Mutability* not thrall;
> Yet is she chang'd in part, and eeke in generall.   [XVII]

And her summary embraces all that from the earth springs, the earth's tenants, and all that is of ocean, river, lake, pool, and all that is of air and fire as well (Book 7, Canto VII, stanzas XVIII–XXV). Nature's reply to Mutabilitie is implied in the Witch's vision of ocean and earth coming to their end.

The pathos of stanzas XXIV–XXV of "The Witch of Atlas" is handled with a tact, a humane control which ought to absolve Shelley permanently from accusations of proneness to sentimentality or emotional abandonment. The Witch's gentle firmness gives way to her own grief in lines that catch the modulations of her struggle with herself. She will not sigh or weep at the inevitable, she begins by saying, as she would have to do if she loved the nymphs until their "little race is run." She schools herself to a stoicism bordering on a necessary cruelty, without being able to accept that schooling. The device of dashes, generally misused by Shelley, is for once employed masterfully by him. The Witch, in her struggle, leaps from thought to thought, painfully attempting to maintain her bearing. "I cannot die as ye must"—the self-justification is untinged by insincerity. Finally comes the attempt to face the cruelty of what is inexorable:

> 'over me
> Your leaves shall glance—the streams in which ye dwell
> Shall be my paths henceforth, and so—farewell!'   [238-40]

With that last, her control gives way—"She spoke and wept." The scene fades out in Keats-like fashion; our eyes move to her fountain, that dark and azure well which will never stop flowing, and we watch it sparkle beneath the shower of her tears and fling reflections upon the cavern roof. The tears are mutable also; the circles of light they cast are "inconstant spheres"; the nymphs and their fountains find epitaphs in "intertangled lines of light" playing on the walls of the Witch's cavern, reflecting the distress of her consciousness. As the "departing Forms" (the word is wonderfully apt) fade out, their sobbing voices complement her tears as a "knell." They move out of Innocence into the death-to-come of Experience; they will be objects of experience, and experience objects themselves; relationship for them is over as they part from the Witch. Substance prevails in but forms depart from the Garden of Adonis. This exit from Beulah is analogous to the departure of Adam and Eve from their garden; something of the tenderness of the closing lines of "Paradise Lost" is carried over in this vision of the nymphs departing:

> o'er the serene
> Of the white streams and of the forests green.

Stanzas XXVI–XXX provide a transition to the playful Witch, whose more characteristic activities dominate the remainder of the poem. All day the Witch sits aloof, forgetting her grief by "spelling out scrolls of dread antiquity" or by weaving poetry "upon her growing woof." We need to avoid pressing too hard upon this point, but she weaves poetry even as she establishes relationships; if she incarnates anything then she incarnates the mythopoeic faculty, so varied a mode that it is as well to read her as incarnating only herself, as meaning something because she is something.

What she weaves is a fire that dims natural fire, a flame like the flames of Blake's Eden or Yeats's Byzantium:

XXVII

> While on her hearth lay blazing many a piece
> Of sandal wood, rare gums, and cinnamon;
> Men scarcely know how beautiful fire is—
> Each flame of it is as a precious stone

> Dissolved in ever-moving light, and this
> Belongs to each and all who gaze upon.
> The Witch beheld it not, for in her hand
> She held a woof that dimmed the burning brand.   [258–64]

Shelley's fire is Byzantine; unreal with the hardness of the "flame" that burns in precious stones, unreal also in that like the flickering fire in the stone it is perpetually "dissolved in ever-moving light." Its final unreality is that it "belongs to each and all who gaze upon" it. But all this "unreality" of the Witch's hearth-fire has another edge: less real than the fire we know, but more real as well. Less real because it cannot burn us (like Yeats's "agony of flame that cannot singe a sleeve" and Blake's "How is it we have walked through fire and yet are not consumed"); more real because it cannot be quenched. The operative paradox in much of "The Witch of Atlas" that is to follow is the paradox enshrined also in Keats's "Nightingale" and "Urn" odes and Yeats's "Byzantium" poems. Here in stanza xxvii of "The Witch" the paradox begins to emerge; the burning spindle of the Witch dims even her own hearth-fire:

> The Witch beheld it not, for in her hand
> She held a woof that dimmed the burning brand.

The Witch's color is green, emerald green (I am not suggesting that we are to visualize the lady as having green skin). Grabo is sensible, if too explicit, in seeing this green as being "symbolic of the earthly aspect of Venus." [5]

The Witch clearly is green as April is green; her green endures "as April's green endures"; the symbolic use of color here is parallel to the color schemes of Blake and Jung. The presiding genius of a Garden of Adonis or Beulah land will take the color of natural, growing life.

Lying in trance at night in her cavern's fountain (or in winter in her outdoor burning fountain) the Witch assumes the posture of disciplined contemplation, suggesting eastern affinities: "Open eyes, closed feet, and folded palm." As befits the patroness of Beulah, the Witch is essentially passive; her best fulfillment is in repose, especially when winter comes upon her world (stanza xxx). The remainder of the poem (xxxi–conclusion) will see her in action, but at best that action will be serious play.

From stanza xxxi on the poem demands different treatment from what I have hitherto given it. The poet's imagination goes off on urbane holiday, taking the excursion boat discarded by Wordsworth at the opening of "Peter Bell." What count most from now on in the poem are its reverberations, those visionary overtones which, as in the later

5. Grabo, p. 52.

Yeats (Knight notes this),[6] are deliberately undercut by a frequent employment of irony in comparison and cynicism in phrasing. The properties henceforward are even more purely visionary: the magic boat and the Hermaphrodite. What anchors these properties is an irony which bites deep by virtue of its civilization and complexity, as well as its critical direction, for if it holds up the poem's events for an urbane contemplation, still more does that contemplation damage the realities of our daily lives. The states, as in Blake, are contraries; most obviously Experience satirizes Innocence, but more profoundly Innocence satirizes the contrary state.

The account of the poem's genesis is itself a thrust at readers looking for "nothing but" interpretations. "Some say" (line 289) that the boat was wrought by Vulcan for Venus to be the chariot for her morning star, but, delightfully, "it was found too feeble to be fraught / With all the ardours in that sphere which are," in which we can observe a good-natured toning down at work. "Others say" (line 297) that Cupid-as-gardener was responsible for it, which to the poet seems no more and no less likely. Whether Apollo bought it in chariot form from the disgruntled Venus, changed it into a boat, and gave it to his daughter the Witch; or whether Cupid stole a seed (Hermes-like), sowed it in the morning star, and so grew a gourd which, scooped out, made this boat; these individual versions of genesis are not important. What is important is what both accounts have in common; the boat has its beginning in the sphere of the morning star. As Yeats first realized, Shelley's most consistent, indeed dominant and ruling symbol is the morning star. I have examined already its function in the visions of Act IV of "Prometheus"; its final, triumphant use by Shelley is in the "Adonais," a poem largely outside of the sphere of this special study, as I explained in my first chapter. Yeats rightly characterized Shelley's morning star as being the "star of infinite desire," probably being influenced in this by Blake's conception of human desire as being necessarily infinite. Under the aspect of mythopoeia, its principles and the necessary defeat of those principles, I have analyzed that desire in Shelley into what seem to me to be its components. The desire to confront a Thou in all things, to stand in relation to everything that is created as a reality meeting a reality, seems to me to underlie Shelley's myth of human desire. What it gives that myth is direction and a dialectic; what it takes away from that myth is the possibility of a realization of the myth within the limitations of either poetry or human life. The morning star, surviving the night longer than the other stars but fading nevertheless with the dawn into the light of everyday, into the sunlight, is a perfectly appropriate symbol for the mythmaking Thou, the desire of the poet. As such it is used again and again in Shelley's poetry, reaching a negative culmination, as we shall

6. Knight, p. 230.

see, in "The Triumph of Life," a poem concerned with that fading away
of vision into the light of the day, the cold glare of life which too soon
deforms. Here in "The Witch of Atlas" the everyday triumph of It is
relegated to an uneasy background. The boat which carries us through
the latter half of the poem is quarried from the morning star symbol;
like the pinnace which takes Asia back to primordial depths, it is "the
boat of my desire." As such, it is ultimately a frail vehicle: the morning
star at length fades; the boat of my desire will be borne back by the
stream. But, like Asia's boat, the boat of desire, the vehicle of the Thou,
can swim for a while against the stream; the mutable morning star is
ever reborn (D. H. Lawrence, whether or not influenced by Shelley in
this I do not know, uses the morning star in *The Plumed Serpent* as a
symbol of the recurrent strength of male desire). We are made to be
conscious of the frailty of the Witch's boat by its morning-star associations, but as I hope I have indicated, we are also made conscious of a
good deal more.

Stanza xxxiv is vital for comprehending the boat's nature, before we
examine its singular crew member, the Hermaphrodite:

> This boat she moored upon her fount, and lit
>   A living spirit within all its frame,
> Breathing the soul of swiftness into it.
>   Couched on the fountain like a panther tame,
>   One of the twain at Evan's feet that sit—
>   Or as on Vesta's sceptre a swift flame—
> Or on blind Homer's heart a wingèd thought,—
>   In joyous expectation lay the boat.   [313–20]

Grabo reads the "living spirit," "soul of swiftness" and "swift flame"
of the above all as electricity.[7] Whatever the Witch's creative fire may
be read as (Blake's "fires of Intellect" will do as well as any reading),
it is that fire, drawn from the cavern's fountain, which is to animate the
boat. The emphasis on swiftness is an Ariel characteristic for which
Shelley is famous, and is difficult to comprehend cognitively. The popular conception of Shelley is of the spirit praying for swiftness, founded
on the "tameless, and swift, and proud" of the great "Ode" and the self-
portrait in "Adonais" of the spirit pantherlike, beautiful, and swift. This
popular notion, the reaction of the common reader (whose taste for
Shelley, however bad its reasons, does not seem to have abated for all
the adverseness of the New Criticism), is not a misconception. What lies
behind Shelley here is the biblical notion of the swiftness of spirit,
whether in its Jewish version of the nabi suddenly being carried up into
the spirit and hurried along by it, or in its Christian aspect of the contrast
between the swiftly answering spirit and the more sluggishly respond-

7. Grabo, pp. 55–6.

ing flesh. The movement of images in Shelley is in itself a metaphorical analogue to this movement of spirit, as I have said several times in these chapters. However well we comprehend Shelley's mythmaking, the *speed* at which it moves resists analysis. Relational events run their course for all of us; the Thou's we confront can all too quickly become objects of our experience. If Shelley is mythopoeically abnormal, it is only in the swiftness with which his myths are made and unmade. This kind of swiftness is perhaps not the business of what tries to be scholarly criticism, but can scarcely be reduced by the more prevalent modes of psychology. What needs to be remembered in any case is that the spirit so perpetually stretched thin by this outrageous swiftness is of an extraordinary toughness. Until "The Triumph of Life" we shall not see its resilience impaired.

In line 317 the "Evan" at whose feet two panthers sit is Bacchus (Locock derives the name from "Evoe," the Bacchanalian cry).[8] The boat is "couched on the fountain like a panther tame"; the emphasis on tamed swiftness is appropriate for a visionary boat of desire whose employment is suggestive of the use of vision for the making of poetry. The hearth of Vesta, as Grabo sensibly remarks, is a "symbol of creative energy," [9] and even more, as I am compelled to add, of creative energy domesticated, tamed. The symbolizing force of the boat is made most explicit in the comparison of its couching at the fountain to a similar couching of "on blind Homer's heart a wingèd thought." The boat is coiled in creative desire, a pent Ariel knowing it is soon to be released: "In joyous expectation lay the boat."

What it awaits is the completion of its crew, a completion which provides the last major interpretative problem of the poem, and one which has recently become a creative obsession in Knight's distinguished Shakespeare criticism. Because Knight's concern with this problem has been and is likely to be influential, and is in some ways at least helpful in reading "The Witch of Atlas," I shall consider it at some length, together with other scholarly readings of the meaning of the Hermaphrodite, which need to be considered first.

Douglas Bush feels that the meaning of Shelley's Hermaphrodite "remains dubious," and is content to probe that meaning with a question: "Is it simply that the Witch, in her immortal loneliness, must create for herself a companion of ideal perfection?" Perhaps more helpfully, he also points out the rather puzzling parallel between Shelley's Hermaphrodite and Spenser's False Florimell. Finally, Bush also notes that Ovid's Hermaphroditus "was a scion of Atlas." [1]

Baker follows Bush closely in all of these suggestions, and does not

8. Locock, ed., *Poems of Shelley, 2,* 656.
9. Grabo, p. 55.
1. Bush, *Mythology and the Romantic Tradition,* p. 142 and n. 33.

attempt to *explain* the Spenser parallel. Is Shelley's Hermaphrodite falsely beautiful, spuriously chaste, as False Florimell is? Baker, like Bush, sees the Witch's motive in creating the Hermaphrodite to be one of assuaging loneliness.[2] Grabo's view needs to be quoted here for the sake of fairness and completeness: "The Hermaphrodite, then, in Shelley's symbolism, is a natural personification of the two complementary forces of the world, of attraction and repulsion, of love and hate, for there are two fluid principles in electricity, the positive and the negative, the resinous and vitreous, the masculine and the feminine, as they are variously designated." [3]

Wilson Knight's remarks seem to me to be more immediately useful here, whatever their final value:

> The Witch creates out of "fire and snow" mingled with "love" a new being resembling Goethe's Homunculus, the mixture recalling the sunny-ice of Coleridge's dome, symbol of the purified, yet inclusive, poetic consciousness. This seraph-form is *sexless,* its bosom swelling "lightly" with "full youth," yet incorporates *the best of both sexes,* strength and gentleness, and is excessively beautiful with an artistic "purity." It is thus super-sexual rather than a-sexual, as is the creative consciousness, and, perhaps, the evolutionary or transcendental goal of mankind.[4]

Before attempting to utilize or evaluate this as interpretation, a glance needs to be taken at Knight's final phrase and its consequences in his later work. The phrase is a germ of Knight's "Phoenix" concept, recently expounded in his study, *The Mutual Flame,* and applied there by him both to the "Epipsychidion" and "The Witch of Atlas." [5] I shall return to Knight's Phoenix in my chapter on "Epipsychidion," where it is a more fully relevant concept, but desire at least to introduce a consideration of it here. Knight, even where misleading, is valuable as a warning; his work, especially at this point, illustrates the danger of criticism of visionary poetry passing over into independent vision. The motive is altogether generous; the desire is for understanding, but the actuality suddenly becomes the creation of an individual and inferior poetry. Rapt in the consequences of poetry, Knight develops the poem's anagoge for himself. Valuable as this may be (to himself and to others), it ceases to be criticism. Knight's Phoenix has replaced Shelley's Hermaphrodite; the ostensible object of criticism has been abandoned.

The Hermaphrodite, according to Knight, is in "The Witch" a representative of something unambiguously positive, of a purified creative consciousness, of a sexuality more vital than human sexuality, incor-

2. Baker, *Shelley's Major Poetry,* p. 211.
3. Grabo, p. 60.
4. Knight, pp. 228–9.
5. G. Wilson Knight, *The Mutual Flame,* London, Macmillan, 1954.

porating as it does *"the best of both sexes."* Finally, the Hermaphrodite, as Knight tells us in *The Mutual Flame,* is a type of the Phoenix, a creation which "properly surpasses all normal and easily conceived perfection," an apocalyptic completeness toward which Knight's favorite poets are held to drive, scorning merely natural sexuality in the process. My concern here is only to demonstrate that Knight has misread Shelley's poem by neglecting to read its phrases closely enough. The Witch's Hermaphrodite is a more paradoxical creature than Knight realizes, in addition to being presented as rather less of a good thing than he supposes. Literary psychologists have worked Shelley up into a sexual tangle by similar misreadings of the Hermaphrodite, and my corrections here are directed as much against them as against Knight. The failure of Bush and Baker to account for the function of the False Florimell analogue can be redressed as well, if my reading is correct. And, if it be correct, it will serve also to reduce whatever plausibility Grabo's notion of the Hermaphrodite as an electrical fixture may otherwise possess.

We need to bear in mind the kind of personal isolation in which the poem has by now set Shelley's lady. By her very nature, she has been forced to reject ultimate relationship with any living being. She reigns over a Beulah-world, replete with sexuality, but she herself is to be perpetually a maid, "a sexless bee" as line 589 of the poem will have it. She cannot die and she cannot be fulfilled, until presumably the order of nature is altogether abolished. She chooses not to voyage alone nevertheless, but the necessity of her status and function compels her to create a mockery of herself for companion, a False Florimell to her True Florimell. What she creates is spuriously ideal, less than human, a *thing,* an It which is incapable of entering into relationship with her. That is not of course the entire story about the Hermaphrodite, for that Byzantine creation is in many abstract, lifeless ways ideal, but ideal almost exactly as Yeats's similar vision is ideal. The Byzantine dome, lit by starlight or moonlight, disdains "all mere complexities," but the "mere" is packed with conflict between opposing orders of reality. These complexities are what we have in the lives we lead by sunlight, and they are very nearly all that we have got, the fury and the mire that run in our human veins. Shelley, all his critical reputation to the contrary, opposes the two orders of reality, human and Byzantine, as ambivalently, self-mockingly, and rather more passionately than Yeats does. And the passion, as much as in Yeats, is the passion of self-conflict, though the urbanity and indirection of "The Witch of Atlas" may trap the unwary reader, as Yeats is less likely to do. Shelley's poem makes curiously overt, descriptive statements about the Hermaphrodite, which it then proceeds to counter by its description of the Hermaphrodite in action, or rather in lack of action. The Hermaphrodite is neither altogether positive nor altogether negative as a creation ; it is very simply the best the Witch can do for herself in her necessary isolation, and as such it constitutes both

an apotheosis and a criticism of the Witch's state of being, of the lower
paradise of the poem and the visionary state of Beulah, the possibility of
Innocence and relationship in general. This Song of Innocence by Shelley has a self-awareness of limitations not found in similar poems by
Spenser and Blake (at least, short of his major epics, Blake fights shy
of the ambivalence of presentation in which desire, though dominant,
already senses its contrary; he uses a contrary expression to balance his
vision of Beulah). And that self-awareness, for which contemporary
criticism gives Shelley so little credit, preferring its straw man Shelley
enslaved by his own "primary impulses," is a major part of the pro-
tective fur which surrounds "The Witch of Atlas," as it amuses itself
in kittenish Innocence while it waits for its claws to develop fully.

I turn to the relevant stanzas, in which the Hermaphrodite is brought
into its dubious being:

XXXV

Then by strange art she kneaded fire and snow
        Together, tempering the repugnant mass
With liquid love—all things together grow
        Through which the harmony of love can pass;
And a fair Shape out of her hands did flow—
        A living Image, which did far surpass
In beauty that bright shape of vital stone
Which drew the heart out of Pygmalion.

XXXVI

A sexless thing it was, and in its growth
        It seemed to have developed no defect
Of either sex, yet all the grace of both,—
        In gentleness and strength its limbs were decked;
The bosom swelled lightly with its full youth,
        The countenance was such as might select
Some artist that his skill should never die,
Imaging forth such perfect purity.

XXXVII

From its smooth shoulders hung two rapid wings,
        Fit to have borne it to the seventh sphere,
Tipped with the speed of liquid lightenings,
        Dyed in the ardours of the atmosphere:
She led her creature to the boiling springs
        Where the light boat was moored, and said: 'Sit here!'
And pointed to the prow, and took her seat
Beside the rudder, with opposing feet.   [321–44]

A Spenserian witch, to save her son's reason (and her own life) made a "repugnant mass" of purest snow into the False Florimell (Book 3, Canto VIII, stanzas v–ix), but tempered the stuff of creation not "with liquid love" but "with fine Mercury, / And virgin wex." Most important, Spenser's witch makes a Florimell *which is also an Hermaphrodite,* as Bush and Baker overlook. "In the stead / Of life, she put a Spright to rule the carkasse dead," and the spright is a male:

> A wicked Spright yfraught with fawning guile,
> And faire resemblance aboue all the rest,
> Which with the Prince of Darknesse fell somewhile,
> From heauens blisse and euerlasting rest;
> Him needed not instruct, which way were best
> Himselfe to fashion likest *Florimell,*
> Ne how to speake, ne how to vse his gest,
> For he in counterfeisance did excell,
> And all the wyles of wemens wits knew passing well. [VIII]

The spright is a female impersonator of archaic vintage, almost a type of Milton's Belial, patron of sodomy and outwardly the fairest, inwardly the grossest spirit who fell with Satan. In Spenser's next stanza, adroit use of gender changes establishes the hermaphroditical nature of this spright: the witch at the beginning of the stanza *"Him* shaped thus, she deckt in garments gay," but then "she forth *her* brought / Unto her sonne." The fitting embodiment of spurious chastity, of snowy, seeming beauty, has the hint of the cities of the plain in it. Remembering this, let us again consider Shelley's false Witch of Atlas, as it were, made by the true Witch (as we are all agreed) for company's sake.

The Hermaphrodite is "a living Image" (line 326), whose beauty surpasses Pygmalion's creation. The equivalents to "a living Image" are Yeats's visions in "Byzantium" of an "image . . . / Shade more than man, more image than a shade," an image of "the superhuman," "death-in-life and life-in-death," and of a golden cock, which can scorn in the glory of its changeless metal, its artifice of eternity, the common bird, a complexity of mire and blood. Specific resemblances of later stanzas to Yeats's "Byzantium" poems will be traced below; the conceptual resemblance is of use here.

This "living Image" is a "sexless thing"; its "growth" from fire and snow under the Witch's hands not having been generative, it outwardly displays "no defect / Of either sex, yet all the grace of both"; it is an image of "perfect purity," its countenance displays the never-to-die skill of its maker. *But* when all that has been said for the Hermaphrodite, its "positive" case is at an end, for as the poem goes on to make clear, the Hermaphrodite is only an object for the Witch to experience, a useful toy at best, otherwise only a distraction; as much a toy, as much a deceitful image of real flesh as the False Florimell is.

What Knight thinks to be "the evolutionary or transcendental goal of mankind" is in the poem's view only a robot. It has got to be led to the boat by the Witch, ordered to sit in the prow (the Witch takes the rudder), and promptly falls into a deep sleep, from which it is roused only at its creator's command, and then only for *use,* to enable the boat to go against nature, to ascend labyrinthine rivers against the stream, or to winnow the Elysian air far above the earth. In function at least, it is surely not a very glorious goal toward which to evolve or transcend.

This awakened Hermaphrodite Knight regards as "representing poetry fully *conscious*" [6] (in Knight's reading Witch, boat, and Hermaphrodite somehow all represent poetry). If one alters this to the statement that Shelley's Hermaphrodite spreads its wings most fully in Yeats's "Byzantium" poems, then I suspect one can come closer to a proper reading of that awakening. The Hermaphrodite is an artifice only, and the Witch plainly realizes this. But, in her state, the Hermaphrodite is the best *permanent* being she can create or assist in creating; the Nymphs are capable of relationship, but cursed by the natural consequences of that capability; what can love, what can address a Thou must also die. In Shelley's myth, a poem is a relational event which has run its course by being set down; once on the page a poem is an It. Shelley's poems generally begin in relationship, are defeated, and end as artifice. Not so "The Witch of Atlas"; like the "Byzantium" poems it begins as artifice. "The Witch" is a poem about mythmaking more than it is a mythmaking, as "Mont Blanc" and the "Ode to the West Wind" are. The Hermaphrodite is its supreme artifice. If poetry is what Wallace Stevens calls it, a supreme fiction, then in some sense the Hermaphrodite is poetry; but "The Witch of Atlas," though urbane, is not that sophisticated. The Hermaphrodite is the best means available for the boat of the Witch's mythopoeic desire to move against the course of nature; to oppose natural reality with a reality at once supra- and preternatural. The commentators on "The Witch of Atlas" have neglected that preternatural aspect of the Hermaphrodite, but it is in the poem as much as the supranatural is; the beautiful mouth of the Hermaphrodite is more beautiful than the mouths of the nymphs, but it is a mouth that has no moisture and no breath and only breathless mouths can summon it.

What remains in the poem is the record of the Witch's voyagings and pranks. She goes first to an antarctic subsidiary lower paradise, there to receive the reports on "all that had happened new / Between the earth and moon" since "her ministering spirits" had last brought her intelligence. The gathering of spirits and the "imperial tent" they build for the Witch to hold her assembly are based, as Knight and Baker note, on

6. Knight, *The Starlit Dome,* p. 229.

Milton's account of the creation of Pandemonium.[7] Baker's contrast between the two assemblies seems to me to be mistaken—"a concourse of the daemons of love in place of the *omnium gatherum* of hateful demons in Milton's nether world." That is an orthodox theistic contrast foreign to the antinomian spirit of "The Witch of Atlas." The Witch herself, as she moves about the earth in the final stanzas of the poem, is hardly an upholder of orthodox morality, religion, or politics; Blake-like, she is an apotheosis of desire, and encourages its human manifestations as being the prime value. I take the allusion to Pandemonium to be a sympathetic one; certainly the contrast between "daemons of love" and "hateful demons" is not one embedded in the poem's text. This is another Titanic assembly, like Pandemonium, the allusion in effect says; spirits of desire, of the antinomian impulse, are met together.

These remarkable stanzas (xxxviii–end), as Knight observes,[8] compensate for their sheer visionary quality by suddenly thrusting a late Yeatsian visionary cynicism into the midst of the texture of the ideal. Other forebodings of the late Yeats can be found here as well; as the Witch's boat masters the waves, the unpastured sea protests:

> Beneath, the billows having vainly striven
> Indignant and impetuous, roared to feel
> The swift and steady motion of the keel. [414–16]

Yeats's uncontrollable sea, tormented by the gong, torn by Arion's dolphin, is frequently foreshadowed in "The Witch." (Knight points to the seraphic boys who in stanza LVIII are seen "bridling tame water-snakes, / Or charioteering ghastly alligators," as being analogous to Yeats's "Astraddle on the dolphin's mire and blood, / Spirit after spirit!," a parallel reinforced, as it seems to me, by the conceptual closeness of "Byzantium" and "The Witch of Atlas").[9]

To the resemblances Knight detects I desire to add the following, to clinch the case for influence and to understand better "The Witch" and "Byzantium" by one another's light: Yeats's "drowsy Emperor" of "Sailing to Byzantium," whose presence is so strong in "Byzantium," owes something to the emperor of Shelley's poem; under the Witch's influence

LXXIV

> The king would dress an ape up in his crown
> And robes, and seat him on his glorious seat,
> And on the right hand of the sunlike throne
> Would place a gaudy mock-bird to repeat

7. Ibid., p. 230; Baker, p. 212.
8. Knight, pp. 230, 233.
9. Ibid., p. 231.

The chatterings of the monkey.—Every one
  Of the prone courtiers crawled to kiss the feet
Of their great Emperor, when the morning came,
  And kissed—alas, how many kiss the same!

LXXV

The soldiers dreamed that they were blacksmiths, and
  Walked out of quarters in somnambulism;
Round the red anvils you might see them stand
  Like Cyclopses in Vulcan's sooty abysm,
Beating their swords to ploughshares;—in a band
  The gaolers sent those of the liberal schism
Free through the streets of Memphis, much, I wis,
To the annoyance of king Amasis.   [633–48]

"The Witch of Atlas," even more than "Prometheus" (and like "Prometheus" an enthusiasm of the young Yeats), seems to have become a
permanent part of the mature Yeats's poetic mind. The two stanzas
above, their units fragmented and then brought together into another
imaginative harmony, seem to me to be among the materials from which
"Byzantium" was created. Spenser's "Prosopopoia: or Mother Hub-
berds Tale," lines 1059–63 and 1082–5, would seem to have influenced
Shelley's grotesque ape-dressed-as-king, whose parts are kissed by the
prone courtiers; but that "gaudy mock-bird" who repeats the ape's chatterings is Shelley's own, and is an ancestor to the metallic bird in "Sailing to Byzantium" whose function it is "to keep a drowsy Emperor
awake," and who appears in the third stanza of "Byzantium." "Byzantium" opens with a vision of night, when "the Emperor's drunken soldiery are abed" and "night-walkers' song" can be heard. Here in Shelley
the emperor's soldiers, under the Witch's nocturnal influence, "walked
out of quarters in somnambulism." Dreaming that they are blacksmiths,
they beat their swords into ploughshares, standing around the red anvils. In "Byzantium" a similar vision is mingled with still stranger
events, but is present nevertheless.
  At midnight on the emperor's pavement the red anvils of smiths are
to be seen, but they are the anvils of dream, with flames that no faggot
feeds nor steel has lit. Here blood-begotten spirits die away into a dance
in which all complexities of fury leave; here, on another level, the soldiers beat their swords into ploughshares. In Yeats's last stanza the
golden smithies of the emperor appear, to break the flood of the unpastured sea, to control what is uncontrollable. Like Shelley's emperor's
soldiery turned smiths, they are agents of an apocalypse; with the Shelleyan influence may be mingled remembrances of Blake's Los, the imaginative shaper, the cosmic blacksmith who hammers out the upper para-

dise of Eden as a thoroughly human artifice, a construct of eternity. The fires of Blake's Eden and of Shelley's Witch-state thus burn on in "Byzantium" together.

This ambiguous final state of "The Witch of Atlas" is our life as caught in the serio-comic vision of the Witch herself, even as our life was termed a "mockery" by the conclusion to "The Sensitive Plant." Thus, our moon seems "like a sick matron wan" (line 455) ; the "liquid surface" of our life is troubled by the disturbances we force upon ourselves, but the Witch's state of being has its foundation in deeper waters:

> But she in the calm depths her way could take,
> Where in bright bowers immortal forms abide
> Beneath the weltering of the restless tide.   [550–2]

I have avoided chronological discussion of the latter half of "The Witch of Atlas" because that part of the poem does not progress, in narrative or theme, from stanza to stanza as the first half of the poem does. The Witch, as a kind of muse of mythopoeia, is predicated as a force eternally operative; her story cannot be concluded until the stubborn center itself is scattered. Meanwhile, for those she most favors she can do this (and again, one can hear the late Yeats in the concluding lines of the stanza) :

LXX

> For on the night when they were buried, she
>   Restored the embalmers' ruining, and shook
> The light out of the funeral lamps, to be
>   A mimic day within that deathy nook;
> And she unwound the woven imagery
>   Of second childhood's swaddling bands, and took
> The coffin, its last cradle, from its niche,
> And threw it with contempt into a ditch.   [601–8]

Grabo, with that dogged consistency that compels at length a puzzled personal respect, finds Neoplatonism dominant in this stanza.[1] By now, my divergence from Grabo has reached a point which makes dispute impossible, and Grabo's comments on this stanza seem to me to be his doctrine's *reductio*. What counts in this stanza, what overwhelmingly counts is the gesture the words make, not the supposed pseudophilosophical background. To accept Grabo is to reduce very good poetry to bad poetry, and that surely in a critic is the primal sin. Stanza LXX is not a statement of belief in an esoteric variety of immortality; it is a gesture of confidence in the reality of relationship and the unreality of experience; death belongs to experience, life and poetry to relationship.

1. Grabo, pp. 99–100.

The coffin is the "last cradle" of second childhood; a believing Christian
could make that gesture also, but it would have a different meaning
than it does here as made by an agnostic mythmaker.

There are stanzas in "The Witch of Atlas" that I have not examined
here, but my special approach has perhaps contributed what insight
into the poem that it is (or I am) capable of contributing. The poem
ends with an urbane ease that shames even its sympathetic critic and
with a promise that Shelley was not to live to fulfill. "Epipsychidion,"
examined next, is a rhapsody in praise of human relationship which
breaks off, of necessity, in the ecstasy of the perception of a Thou, a
Vita Nuova which leads only to the "Inferno" of "The Triumph of
Life," in which the myth of relationship is devastated (a weaker term
will not do). The last seventeen stanzas of the "Adonais" are a personal
triumph, but evade the whole problem of Shelley's characteristic myth.
Though he thought and declares otherwise, Shelley in the last stanza
of "The Witch of Atlas" is saying his farewell to the muse of mythopoeia, the innocence of Beulah. To lapse (I hope) altogether into the
subjective, I find myself reading into this last stanza a unique sadness,
extraneous to it perhaps but unavoidable with the advantage of retrospect:

LXXVIII

These were the pranks she played among the cities
    Of mortal men, and what she did to Sprites
And Gods, entangling them in her sweet ditties
    To do her will, and show their subtle sleights,
I will declare another time; for it is
    A tale more fit for the weird winter nights
Than for these garish summer days, when we
Scarcely believe much more than we can see.   [665–72]

8

"Epipsychidion"

THE orthodox scholarly account of "Epipsychidion" which seems to me most complete, with regard to biographical data and the poem's sources, is to be found in the late Newman I. White's *Shelley*.[1] As always in these chapters, my criticism of the poem is deliberately incomplete, focuses only on what I have chosen to call its mythopoeic aspect, and needs to be supplemented by some such account as White's. Biographical fact is necessary for a complete approach to the "Epipsychidion" in particular, among Shelley's poems. I emphasize my deliberate incompleteness because here it is carried to an extreme: I shall have no occasion even to *mention* Emilia Viviani's life in my account of the poem. As for the poem's supposed sources, I shall refer to them only when they seem to me to have critical value, to be involved in the poem's meaning. The Platonic "sources" of the poem do not seem to me to be critically relevant; my reading of the poem, entire, is what I offer in evidence of that irrelevance. Indeed here, as so often, the Platonizings of Shelley scholars have done real critical harm; so sympathetic a reader of Shelley as C. S. Lewis has turned away from "Epipsychidion" under the impression that in the poem Shelley is attempting to stand upon a certain rung of the Platonic ladder, that rung being one that Lewis does not believe to exist.[2] It is time to kick away the ladder which not Shelley's poem but its Platonizing interpreters have set up.

Dante, as Knight and Baker have most clearly recognized, is the chief influence on and the really useful critical parallel to the "Epipsychidion."[3] But even Dante is more useful here as contrast rather than as parallel to Shelley. The human love celebrated in "Epipsychidion" has no Christian warrant; the poem attacks marriage because it must in order to be true to itself. The mythopoeic technique of Shelley's vision is counter to orthodox morality as it is counter to orthodox religion; the real analogue to "Epipsychidion" is in Blake's "The Marriage of Heaven and Hell" with its apotheosis of human desire. Shelley scholars (Knight is again an honorable exception, for all his eccentrici-

1. White, *Shelley, 2,* 253–69.
2. Lewis, *Rehabilitations,* p. 27.
3. Knight, *The Starlit Dome,* p. 238; Baker, *Shelley's Major Poetry,* pp. 220–4.

ties) have a way of mollifying "Epipsychidion's" meanings to make the poem more acceptable, in doctrine, to themselves and others. But the duty of a scholarly expositor is to the text of the poem, and misreading a text is never justifiable.

Grabo has the Emilia of the poem down as "the Uranian Venus or the Witch of the *Witch of Atlas* or Asia of *Prometheus*—all personifications of the spirit of love and beauty in nature." [4] Baker offers us a "mystical idea," drawn from Shelley's prose fragment "On Love" and, as we might expect of a professedly "mystical idea," it is not an unconfused one, mixing Plato and more popular notions:

> The Idea which bears the name of Emilia in *Epipsychidion* may be defined as that part of the inmost soul which participates in the world-soul. Shelley had attempted an exposition of this mystical idea in the prose fragment, "On Love." Here Shelley defines the epipsyche (the "soul within our soul" which gave him the title of his poem) as a miniature of the inmost self. It is, however, a self as purified of "all that we condemn or despise" that it is in fact the "ideal prototype of everything excellent and lovely that we are capable of conceiving as belonging to the nature of man." It is in itself as sexless as an angel, for on the spiritual plane where Shelley is standing, sexual distinctions are of no consequence. He indicates its completely ideal character by comparing it to a special kind of selective mirror which "reflects only the forms of purity and brightness." This is the Idea behind the figure of Emilia in *Epipsychidion.*[5]

Grabo wants to read one poem into another and Neoplatonism into the mélange. Baker wants to read the prose Shelley into the poetry, a process that Shelley himself warned against, and one which is more than usually fatal in regard to *Epipsychidion*. "On Love," like all of Shelley's philosophical fragments, is thirdhand stuff and without literary or philosophical value. Of all Shelley's prose only the *Defence* lives, and that is because it is more a visionary poem about poetry than it is a reasoned argument. I affirm the "unscholarly" heresy that a student of Shelley's *poetry* is best off not having read any of the prose but the *Defence*. The letters sometimes help; more usually they do not, and two years of steady reading in them have not sufficed for me to find too much of permanent literary or human value therein. They will not sustain comparison with the letters of Shelley's disciple Beddoes, let alone Wordsworth or Keats. The poet Shelley was infinitely wiser and better than the philosopher Shelley or the man Shelley, from the beginning to the end of his career. Shelley himself wrote in a letter to the

4. Grabo, *The Magic Plant*, p. 338.
5. Baker, p. 219.

Gisbornes that "The poet and the man are two different natures; though they exist together, they may be unconscious of each other, and incapable of deciding on each other's powers and efforts by any reflex act." [6]

"Epipsychidion" is the poem by Shelley in which the confrontation of a Thou in one human being by the I in another and the relational event which ensues from such a confrontation are most clearly set forth as poetic subject and theme. That kind of confrontation is quite overtly what "Epipsychidion" is *about,* and Platonics, mysticism, depth psychology simply are not in it. "Emily" could be read as Platonic Idea, Christian or Jewish Sophia or Shekhina (as Spenser's Sapience in "An Hymne of Heavenly Beautie" is sometimes read), Jungian anima, Blakean emanation, Dantean Beatrice, and finally, Shelleyan epipsyche (if we accompany Baker to the enlisting of the prose Shelley). But all these readings, even the last, substitute other counters for the words of the poem "Epipsychidion." (I myself would earlier have been inclined to read Emily as an instance of what Blake usually calls an emanation, which Northrop Frye accurately summarizes as meaning in Blake "the total form of all the things a man loves and creates." [7] I still find this a better guide to what Emily *is* and means *in* the poem than I find the epipsyche of Shelley's "On Love" to be, but it now seems to me an unnecessary reduction also and one which takes away more from the concrete value of Shelley's poem that it gives in return.) I shall demonstrate that the critical vocabulary of mythopoeia itself is perfectly adequate for the imaginative comprehension of "Epipsychidion": it is as "Thou" that the poem addresses Emily, and in this particular "Thou" we have what Emily is, and also a critical tool, a way of comprehension and evaluation, for discovering the kinds of meaning that Emily and the poem embody. Shelley's "soul within our soul" and Blake's hypostasis of all that a man loves *and creates* are formulations which approach categorizing the mythopoeic creation of relationship when a man utters and confronts a Thou, but they are by comparison to a poem or any other fully human act rather clumsy entities because they *do* abstract, because they *are* formulations. Criticism of a poem must also to an extent abstract, formulate, but it is good to keep that kind of necessary clumsiness to a minimum. The poem says "Thou"; we can at least attempt the critical experiment of saying "Thou" after it. As for "Thou," we know of it not because we have read Buber (though he can help us to talk about it), but because we have read poems and stood in relationship to other people. And with this as preamble, I turn now to a reading of "Epipsychidion."

Knight remarks of the poem that "what would normally be climax-

6. Ingpen, ed., *Letters of Shelley, 2,* 883; letter of July 19, 1821.
7. Frye, *Fearful Symmetry,* p. 73.

impressions in poetry are here a level style." [8] The poem is a kind of extended or narrative lyric, and the style of emotive climax is dominant in the more than six hundred lines. The figures are profuse, as always in Shelley, but their variety is more than usually justified. They present particular Thou's, individual confrontations, and through them the poem tries to present confrontation, the fact of relationship, as an entity. But, Baker and his Platonics and Knight with his own curious ideas aside here, confrontation in the poem is between the I of a man and the Thou of a woman. Very simply (but because of Baker and Knight, this needs to be said), "Epipsychidion" is a poem about heterosexual love. Blake ends "Jerusalem" with a frankly visualized plate in which Albion and Jerusalem reunite in apocalyptic intercourse. "Epipsychidion" is not quite that healthy a poem, but Lawrence-like it aspires toward just that image of integration. A good part of its complexity stems from the multiform inner obstacles, in a human being, that impede the attainment of just such a vision.

"Epipsychidion" carries as motto a sentence from an essay on love by Emilia Viviani: "The soul in love lances itself out of the created, and creates in the infinite a world for itself, and for itself alone, how different from this obscure and fearful den!" [9] This (it is Medwin's translation) is sentimental and incoherent, and is a bad augury of some sentimentalities and incoherencies in the poem to come. It would be dishonest to gloss over them; "Epipsychidion" has many flaws. But these faults, though they cannot be condoned, do not vitiate what is critically valuable about the poem. Shelley did not succeed completely in cutting the poem's genetic hawsers; the poem is to a certain extent a private and not a public performance. To that extent it is mostly very bad; Shelley's overt parallel of his poem to Dante's *Vita Nuova* is hardly justified. Dante wrote in terms of a convention, and did it consistently and honestly. Shelley, in this poem, wanted to have it both ways: to employ a convention but at the same time to disown it. The result is sometimes coterie verse. As Knight protests, "Emily—the name is scarcely suitable." [1] Beatrice, as a name, has public, in this case Christian, meaning; Emily, as a name, has not.

There are other irritants in the private apparatus of the poem, devices which lack critical justification. The Advertisement gave Shelley great trouble; three drafts exist, in addition to the version published as preface to the poem. Shelley might well have spared himself the trouble; the Advertisement, even in its final version, does not help us to comprehend anything of value in the poem. The fiction of a young poet, not Shelley,

8. Knight, p. 234.
9. White, 2, 257.
1. Knight, p. 234.

who died at Florence while "preparing for a voyage to one of the wildest of the Sporades," presumably there to dwell with "Emily," was undoubtedly intended to save Shelley (and Mrs. Shelley) some social embarrassment. But as an appendage to the poem, it embarrasses even the sympathetic reader.

The sun-moon-comet figures in the poem, biographically associated by scholars with Emilia, Mary, and Claire Clairmont, respectively, are by contrast fully integrated into the poem and read best with their biographical referents forgotten. Only in line 601, in a kind of epilogue, does the coterie aspect of the poem reappear in troublesome form. Marina, Vanna, and Primus, pet names of Shelley for Mary, Jane Williams (Giovanna), and Edward Williams ("Primus" as Dantesque best or first friend), are out of place at the poem's conclusion, contributing by the invocation of their *particular* names nothing to its significance.

The meaning of the poem's title is disputable, but I agree with Locock that "the word is formed on the analogy of 'epicycle,' and would mean literally 'A little additional soul,' or, as Shelley himself puts it (line 238), 'this soul out of my soul.' " [2] More clearly even than in "Prometheus," Shelley puts the relationship of love between humans into mythopoeic terms, defines the reality of that relationship as an activity in which both lovers share without attempting to appropriate for themselves.

The opening stanza, translated from Dante, is a successful "fit audience though few" device, a rhetorical trick if you would have it so, but here an effective one. The reader is invited into a charmed circle, or else warned to stay out. There is a first hint of paradox: the "reasoning" of the poem will provide "hard matter" for the aspiring reader to work upon; it is available for misinterpretation.[3]

The first twenty lines of the poem proper are suspended between private and public declaration; they suggest frustrated intensity, as though the poem had already been in progress for some length. More baffling, they are all invocation, but so are the next fifty lines, and indeed, to a lesser degree, so is the remainder of the poem. What we have here is a rhapsody, and very nearly a static one, devoted to direct address and to little else. This curious structure is itself thematic; what is involved is an ultimate effort to grasp a Thou firmly and never to let the confrontation subside. The direct challenge is to the limits of poetry, and the limits necessarily triumph. The resultant failure has an excitement and value matched by few poems, for few poems can teach us so much about what poetry can and cannot do.

At line 16 is a reference to our life as "this low and worldly shade," which the poem will develop later. The Thou of Emily has moved in these

2. Locock, ed., *Poems of Shelley, 2,* 453.
3. Hutchinson, ed., *Works of Shelley,* p. 454.

opening lines from "Sweet Spirit!" to "Poor captive bird!" to "High, spirit-wingèd Heart!" At line 21 this progression of heightenings suddenly ascends to divinity, to the ultimate Thou, in a veritable fireworks display of alternate images, rejected as swiftly as they are pronounced:

> Seraph of Heaven! too gentle to be human,
> Veiling beneath that radiant form of Woman
> All that is insupportable in thee
> Of light, and love, and immortality!
> Sweet Benediction in the eternal Curse!
> Veiled Glory of this lampless Universe!
> Thou Moon beyond the clouds! Thou living Form
> Among the Dead! Thou Star above the Storm!
> Thou Wonder, and thou Beauty, and thou Terror!
> Thou Harmony of Nature's art! Thou Mirror
> In whom, as in the splendour of the Sun,
> All shapes look glorious which thou gazest on!   [21–32]

No image here cancels another, but again no image here supports another. The poem affirms images but no image; it declines to take the antipoetic, antihuman way of union which denies images. But by modern critical belief, a poem affirms an image or several images; a poem does not affirm a principle, an infinity of images. "Epipsychidion" exists to record the struggle of image-making; as is so frequent in Shelley, it is a poem about poetry, and consciously so. Directly following this display of images is the consciousness of that display:

> Ay, even the dim words which obscure thee now
> Flash, lightning-like, with unaccustomed glow;
> I pray thee that thou blot from this sad song
> All of its much mortality and wrong,
> With those clear drops, which start like sacred dew
> From the twin lights thy sweet soul darkens through,
> Weeping, till sorrow becomes ecstasy:
> Then smile on it, so that it may not die.   [33–40]

What helps this is its urbane graciousness; what would be extravagance is modified by social irony, by the poem's awareness that it is adopting a way of speaking, heightening a convention of love-making. The poem, for all its Italian roots, is not an exotic; with "The Witch of Atlas" it can claim Elizabethan ancestry. Its ardor, however intense, is gentlemanly; its exaltation of a particular Thou has parallels in Spenser, Sidney, and a host of their contemporaries and followers; like them, it assumes something of the social climate of a court, and a court in which chivalrous love is not without honor.

Having established its tone, "Epipsychidion" proceeds on its way of elucidation. Emily is "Youth's vision thus made perfect"—a Thou which will not perpetually depart as the Beauty celebrated in the 1816 "Hymn" perpetually departs. With this declaration comes the subsidiary declaration of love, and with it a sudden descent into the world of organized experience: a poem about mythopoeic confrontation becomes also a poem about and a polemic against the social custom of marriage. The descent is inevitable; if you give absolute primacy to mythmaking and reject all myth that is received, then legal and sacramental marriage will follow legal and sacramental religion into the realm of what is discarded.

The theme of marriage and its iniquities has been sounded in the poem's opening couplet, is picked up again here (lines 46–51), and will receive full development in the famous passage (lines 147–59) about "the longest journey" which I shall examine below. Counterpointed against that theme here is the poem's most urgent element, the desire for a union with the Thou that will go beyond human limitations. "Would we two had been twins of the same mother!" bursts forth (line 45), and we begin to understand better the curious theme of incest in Shelley, beginning in "Laon and Cythna," dimly figured in "Prometheus," and culminating here in "Epipsychidion." If the Thou is always becoming an It, why not by-pass the way of relationship? Why should not the I discover a Thou which is already one with it? The answer is one which the Greeks and the Jews, so apart in sexual and social morality otherwise, gave with one voice. Communion of an I with an I is selfhood-communion, destructive of all relationship, destructive of the city and the nation, abominated by the gods and by God. Shelley's myth is an impulse toward life; counter to it is Shelley's antimyth, driving toward death because of despair in the myth. In "Epipsychidion" the myth and its contrary have intensified to their extremes, and appear side by side. The poem violently alternates between the quest for relationship and the quest for destruction, a sweet, mystical annihilation. The two quests are antithetical: the first is rational and poetic; the second is less than rational and attempts to destroy the poem.

In line 52 one of the momentary triumphs of the second way is recorded: "I am not thine: I am a part of *thee*." Paradoxical as it may seem, that line is no part of the poem's ideal but of that ideal's contrary, and in the dialectic of the poem it will emerge again and again until at last, at the poem's conclusion, it triumphs. With that surrender, this *Vita Nuova* will have prepared us for the "Inferno" of "The Triumph of Life."

Recovering momentarily from the deliberate imaginative collapse of line 52, the poem soars off again into an affirmation of images, in a passage beginning and ending with an expressed awareness of poetic limits:

Sweet Lamp! my moth-like Muse has burned its wings
Or, like a dying swan who soars and sings,
Young Love should teach Time, in his own gray style,
All that thou art. Art thou not void of guile,
A lovely soul formed to be blessed and bless?
A well of sealed and secret happiness,
Whose waters like blithe light and music are,
Vanquishing dissonance and gloom? A Star
Which moves not in the moving heavens, alone?
A Smile amid dark frowns? a gentle tone
Amid rude voices? a belovèd light?
A Solitude, a Refuge, a Delight?
A Lute, which those whom Love has taught to play
Make music on, to soothe the roughest day
And lull fond Grief asleep? a buried treasure?
A cradle of young thoughts of wingless pleasure?
A violet-shrouded grave of Woe?—I measure
The world of fancies, seeking one like thee,
And find—alas! mine own infirmity.   [53–71]

The "infirmity" is of the muse itself, with its singed wings, able at
best to render the Thou by a swan song of self-immolation. The attempt
to express "all that thou art" proceeds again by a multiplicity of image-
makings, precariously linked by a formula akin to that of the "narrowing image." The Thou of Emilia is likened to a series of Thou's surrounded or encased by experiential It's. A sealed and secret well, its
waters separated off from the surrounding gloom; a fixed star in the
moving heavens; a smile amid frowns; a gentle tone amid rude voices;
a light amid darkness; all of these Thou's are solitudes, refuges, delights,
sheltering the I from the universe of things.

The remaining images are conditioned by the same dominant figure
of the refuge. The lute soothes the roughness which surrounds it; the
treasure is buried in earth; innocence is cradled; the violets shroud off
Woe in its grave, but paradoxically they shroud off Woe from Woe.
What is buried in the Thou's presence nevertheless lurks outside as well
as inside its tomb. This last figure in effect breaks the pattern of the
imagery, and the poet again asserts the impotence of his making of
analogies. He *measures* the world of fancies against his awareness of
confrontation of the Thou, and he finds his "own infirmity" in the process
of search. The Thou has no bounds, is unconditioned, and cannot therefore be placed in a context of space and time. But images are necessarily
bounded and conditioned, and belong to the universe of It. Unable to
focus the Thou of Emilia in his poem by direct confrontation, the poet
turns to chronicling the history of this particular Thou, the *history* even
of a Thou being set in the context of space and time.

The transition from confrontation to history is gradual and inconstant until the passage beginning with line 190. What begins as history at line 71 passes rapidly into a rhapsody of images again, descends yet once more into the realization of the limits of expression, and climaxes in three passages of high rhetoric, sermons on love. Summary of this transition will bring us to the movement beginning at line 190; summary cannot be slighted for the "structure" of this poetic rhapsody is embedded in its circular dialectic, and transition from movement to movement provides us with an opportunity to work in closer to that dialectic.

> She met me, Stranger, upon life's rough way,
> And lured me towards sweet Death; as Night by Day,
> Winter by Spring, or Sorrow by swift Hope,
> Led into light, life, peace. An antelope,
> In the suspended impulse of its lightness,
> Were less aethereally light: the brightness
> Of her divinest presence trembles through
> Her limbs, as underneath a cloud of dew
> Embodied in the windless heaven of June
> Amid the splendour-wingèd stars, the Moon
> Burns, inextinguishably beautiful . . .   [72–82]

We are back to the "Life of Life" lyric celebrating Asia's transfiguration in this account of the meeting with Emilia. The language of rapturous paradox is employed to convey a reality which transcends the world of our experience, the world in which we appropriate for ourselves. The shared reality of relationship, in which what is loved cannot be imaged for fear that self-appropriation may commence, is represented here by the irony of a figure of the loved one which cannot be apprehended, strictly speaking. As in the "Life of Life" lyric, the reader is confronted by a divine brightness *trembling through* limbs, but the limbs themselves are the only evidence for such brightness, and tremble through the brightness. The Thou cannot become an It, if we are given no object to experience, but the poem demands a figure, a verbal object. Only paradox can provide a figure which is no figure, in which the outer covering and the essence contained are interchangeable, and therefore scarcely to be grasped before they have passed over into each other once again.

The brightness of her presence is indeed so great that it cannot be contained:

> The glory of her being, issuing thence
> Stains the dead, blank, cold air with a warm shade
> Of unentangled intermixture, made
> By Love, of light and motion: one intense
> Diffusion, one serene Omnipresence,

Whose flowing outlines mingle in their flowing,
Around her cheeks and utmost fingers glowing
With the unintermitted blood, which there
Quivers, (as in a fleece of snow-like air
The crimson pulse of living morning quiver,)
Continuously prolonged, and ending never,
Till they are lost, and in that Beauty furled
Which penetrates and clasps and fills the world . . .

[91–103]

This is one of those passages in Shelley's poetry which are inexhaustible to analysis and which it is superfluous to praise. The passage I have
quoted just previous to this prepares us for the difficulties of these lines.
The "unentangled intermixture, made / By Love" repeats a Spenserian
line-and-a-half of "The Witch of Atlas"—"all things together grow /
Through which the harmony of love can pass." [4] The "light and motion"
which intermix so well here to vivify "the dead, blank, cold air" stem
from the just antecedent figures of Asia-like brightness and antelope
swiftness and lightness (antelope, panther, snake, swan, in about that
order seem to be the favored natural creatures in Shelley's poetry).
The Thou of Emilia is here successfully realized and apotheosized as being light and motion only, each refined to an intensity singular even for
Shelley. "Glory" (line 91) is the key word in this rhapsody akin to a
Catholic poet's celebration of the Virgin. Hopkins, writing on "The
Blessed Virgin Compared to the Air We Breathe," approximates Shelley in some Crashaw-like lines:

> I say that we are wound
> With mercy round and round
> As if with air.[5]

Even so, here in Shelley, the Thou of Emilia has intensely diffused to
become a serene Omnipresence, the very air that the I breathes. And the
form of Emilia, already precariously balanced between limbs trembling
through brightness and a brightness trembling through limbs, is further
transfigured by this process of intense diffusion until it becomes one
with that spiritual Beauty first maturely visualized by Shelley in the
1816 "Hymn to Intellectual Beauty," a report of the heart which balanced out the grim sister-hymn of 1816, "Mont Blanc," with its report
of the head on the impossibility of natural religion and the remoteness

---

4. "The Witch of Atlas," stanza xxxv, lines 323–4.
5. "No one would have complained of the unreality of his [Shelley's] poetry or of
its want of substance if his subject-matter, like Crashaw's, had been the Christian
religion instead of that religion which he was always trying to discover and express
for himself." Pottle, "The Case of Shelley," *PMLA, 67* (1952), 594. Pottle, by his
own account, is paraphrasing Clutton-Brock.

of divinity, the inaccessibility of the Thou. Here in "Epipsychidion," at
this point, the accessible Thou of the spiritual, the "intellectual" Beauty,
is suddenly raised to its climax of availability, and the glory of Shelleyan
grace is celebrated as never before or after in the poetry considered in
these chapters. The outlines of the Thou of Emilia, themselves already
flowing, mingle yet again in this sudden overflowing, and the "unintermitted blood" which flows in Emilia burns through this vision of the
Thou, reminding us of its human basis. Only in that Beauty whose
function it is, like the unconditioned grace of other religions, to pene-
trate and clasp and fill the world with itself are the flowing outlines of
this particular Thou lost.

Having achieved this climax of confrontation, the poem's I seeks
again to embody the confrontation in figures, but this time with a fuller
consciousness of the necessary self-defeat of such an enterprise. In lines
115–21, Emilia is termed successively an image, a shadow, a reflection,
a metaphor, and ultimately a vision. What follows, with programmatic
inevitability, is a self-conscious descent into the awareness of inadequacy
to sustain relationship, or even to describe it (lines 123–9). Another
burst of affirmation of relationship (lines 130–46) and we are ready to
move decisively from confrontation into history. But the confrontation
first forces from the I three sermons on true love, attempts to justify,
rhetorically, the action of the will in giving primacy to relationship over
everything that might conflict with it. The first of these three passages
of high rhetoric is the most effective and the most famous, being a classic
attack on the social institution of marriage. Something of the fluent
power of the style of "The Triumph of Life" is forecast in these lines:

> Thy wisdom speaks in me, and bids me dare
> Beacon the rocks on which high hearts are wrecked.
> I never was attached to that great sect,
> Whose doctrine is, that each one should select
> Out of the crowd a mistress or a friend,
> And all the rest, though fair and wise, commend
> To cold oblivion, though it is in the code
> Of modern morals, and the beaten road
> Which those poor slaves with weary footsteps tread,
> Who travel to their home among the dead.
> By the broad highway of the world, and so
> With one chained friend, perhaps a jealous foe,
> The dreariest and the longest journey go.   [147–54]

"Thy wisdom" is the lesson the "Epipsychidion" by necessity embodies, and is possessed in the highest degree by the Emilia of the poem.
The lesson concerns the consequences of giving the myth of relationship
primacy over all received notions of morality. The myth demands pri-

macy; it makes an absolute demand upon its believers. Consequently, if you resist the myth (and all of us must, to some degree or other, for without It we cannot live, as Buber observes) you cannot be expected to accept this passage on its own terms. What remains is the rhetoric, powerful enough to compel attention if not to convince. What additionally remains, in the context of the poem, is the application of these lines to the poem's ostensible theme, the apparition of the Thou in Emilia and the attempt of the poet's *I* to express the reality of that apparition. Applied to Emilia, these lines lead to the conclusion that her individual Thou is one among many, all of which, when confronted, can provide glimpses into the ultimate Thou. What the poem celebrates then is not the relationship with Emilia but relationship (in its special mythmaking sense) itself.

The two following sermons (lines 160–73 and 174–89) are less effective, though Ellsworth Barnard persuasively argues for their high value. Indeed, Barnard claims that in them "the question of sex is simply forgotten, and the conception of love becomes indistinguishable from that of the New Testament." [6] I am not competent to discuss the conception (or conceptions) of love to be found in the New Testament, but I cannot believe that Shelley's teaching here has much in common with that of Christianity. I cannot understand these lines if they are not to be read as being predicated against the foundations of Christian marriage:

> Narrow
> The heart that loves, the brain that contemplates,
> The life that wears, the spirit that creates
> One object, and one form, and builds thereby
> A sepulchre for its eternity.   [169–73]

To marry and adhere to one only is to build a sepulcher for your eternity: how Barnard explains this as the lore of the New Testament I do not know. As I have said, this defense of "free love" is quite simply a practical consequence of Shelley's unrelenting adherence to the myth of confrontation presented in his poetry. The Thou is a vanishing image: the Spirit of Beauty flits from one epipsyche to another. The third sermon varies the same theme: "If you divide pleasure and love and thought, / Each part exceeds the whole." Relationship is unlimited: Thou has no bounds.

Lines 190–344 are a unit, the history of the I of the protagonist and his quest for the Thou. Lines 190–216 establish the initial confrontation of the I and the Thou in the poet's youth, the presentation here being directly analogous to that given in the "Hymn to Intellectual Beauty."

---

6. Ellsworth Barnard, ed., *Shelley: Selected Poems, Essays, and Letters* (New York, Odyssey Press, 1944), p. 370.

Thou departs, almost as quickly as it came, and lines 217–55 deal with the poet's attempt to re-encounter this ultimate vision. The image is again that of the dizzy moth seeking the narrowing morning and evening star, and finding instead "a radiant death." The Thou passes "into the dreary cone of our life's shade" : the evening star is obscured by the shadow our earth throws into the heavens. Though a voice tells the I that the phantom he seeks is beside him (as, of course, it is, ready to be confronted everywhere) the I lacks understanding, and is precipitated upon its quest:

> And in that silence, and in my despair,
> I questioned every tongueless wind that flew
> Over my tower of mourning, if it knew
> Whither 'twas fled, this soul out of my soul;
> And murmured names and spells which have control
> Over the sightless tyrants of our fate;
> But neither prayer nor verse could dissipate
> The night which closed on her; nor uncreate
> That world within this Chaos, mine and me,
> Of which she was the veiled Divinity . . .   [235–44]

The I of the 1816 "Hymn" "called on poisonous names with which our youth is fed," but "was not heard." Here the same "names and spells," "prayer," and "verse" fail to dissipate the night into which the Thou has vanished. Received doctrines cannot help in this quest. Lines 242–4 are especially difficult: Baker's gloss seems to me to be helpful here: "Shelley is making a distinction between the chaos (the *not-me* or that which lies outside the epicenter of the soul) and the *me* (the central firm microcosm within the chaos, 'the world of thoughts that worshipped her'). The idea recurs in lines 345–346. . . ." [7]

The quest, as is traditional, proceeds through misadventures. The first substitute for the Thou (lines 256–66) is a kind of Duessa. Those that follow (lines 267–71) manifest the dialectic of reversal, Thou to It, all too quickly. When the poet's I at length turns in on itself in desperation, suddenly a remote Vision of the Thou is given:

> One stood on my path who seemed
> As like the glorious shape which I had dreamed
> As is the Moon, whose changes ever run
> Into themselves, to the eternal Sun . . .   [277–280]

"Like," but not the same; like as moon to sun, in that she borrowed the radiance of the Thou, without incarnating it. Not to be condemned, for being what she had to be, but inadequate in any case and incapable

7. Baker, p. 229, n. 28.

of the relationship necessary for the I's survival as a man. From this
Death-in-Life, encased in a sea of ice, the protagonist is liberated by a
full advent of the fiery Thou, in a sudden effluence of vision:

> Soft as an Incarnation of the Sun,
> When light is changed to love, this glorious One
> Floated into the cavern where I lay,
> And called my Spirit . . .   [335–8]

Lines 345–83, which follow upon this advent, constitute a prayer to
the ultimate Thou and its particular anticipatory Thou's (the moonlike
lady, already celebrated, and a cometlike confrontation, related to the
morning and evening star symbolism by which Shelley pictures poetry
itself as vanishing relationship) to abandon the I never again. Why all
three, is the inevitable query aroused in us. The dialectic of the myth has
been understood too well, is the proper response. The I asks for "alternate
sway" because he knows that contraries (not negations) are necessary
in this kind of relationship. Even the Thou of Emilia will alternately
fade and then come into the light again. During the night the I desires
the moon, and at morning and evening, the creative transitions, he needs
"the star of Death / And Birth," the comet, star of "Even and Morn."
On the practical level, you can be accurate in describing this as a program
for polygamy, whatever the orthodox admirers of Shelley have written
to the contrary. The Thou fades, momentarily but perpetually: the I falls
into the cold common hell of Itness if unprovided for, if left without other
confrontations of the Thou.

But the poem does not pause to argue the practical; it seeks (and at-
tains) a more individual defeat. The myth will destroy itself, in its paradoxical double commitment to an awareness of human limitations and
to the transcendent value of an infinite desire. The culmination of "Epipsychidion" manifests this awareness of defeat; defeat itself fleshes the
myth's last appearance in "The Triumph of Life."

The pastoral vision of Beulah-land, the earthly paradise of the Witch
of Atlas, dominates the closing passages of "Epipsychidion." The beauty
of these passages (lines 388–572) is intricate and deserving of analysis,
but stands apart from my thesis. The vision of attempted union (and
its failure) is very much my concern:

> We shall become the same, we shall be one
> Spirit within two frames, oh! wherefore two?
> One passion in twin-hearts, which grows and grew,
> Till like two meteors of expanding flame,
> Those spheres instinct with it become the same,
> Touch, mingle, are transfigured; ever still
> Burning, yet ever inconsumable:

> In one another's substance finding food,
> Like flames too pure and light and unimbued
> To nourish their bright lives with baser prey,
> Which point to Heaven and cannot pass away:
> One hope within two wills, one will beneath
> Two overshadowing minds, one life, one death,
> One Heaven, one Hell, one immortality,
> And one annihilation. Woe is me!
> The wingèd words on which my soul would pierce
> Into the height of Love's rare Universe.
> Are chains of lead around its flight of fire—
> I pant, I sink, I tremble, I expire!   [573–91]

But love (the sensible love of the emotions) does not unify; it unites in act, but it does not unite in essence. The countermyth has taken control and concludes the poem. Not by accident this account of union passes to "one annihilation." With that recognition the poem collapses, and its seer collapses back into a less rare universe. He has denied the poem's myth, and the poem cannot be continued without it. Unwilling to face the dialectic of reversal which "Prometheus" accepted, the repassage of every Thou back to an It again, "Epipsychidion" concludes by leaping the gap between I and Thou. With this leap relationship ends, poetry ceases, and life triumphs over the poet. The astonishing merit of "Epipsychidion" is not diminished by this conclusion: the poem remains as a unique attempt to extend and realize the limits of relationship and expression.

9

"The Triumph of Life"

T HE fragment of an "Inferno," "The Triumph of Life," the work which occupied Shelley at the time of his death, has seemed to some of his critics a kind of palinode, to others a reaffirmation in its relation to Shelley's previous major poems.[1] My own reading of earlier poems by Shelley in these chapters ought to have made clear that the central myths in Shelley's mature poems, from the 1816 Hymns through to "Epipsychidion," are never compatible with the beliefs that the natural man is not in serious need of redemption or that natural religion is possible. The affinities of the author of the prose tract *A Refutation of Deism* are with the author of the prose tract *There Is No Natural Religion*. Blake went through Christianity to reach his apocalyptic humanism; Shelley passed through the Enlightenment to attain eventually an apocalyptic humanism very akin to Blake's. Though they begin so differently, each ultimately presents a religion parallel to but in competition with Christianity, and completely counter to any naturalistic doctrine. The youthful disciple of Swedenborg lived to mock mysticism in his mature works; the young Godwinian survived long enough to feel that, in the human condition, good and the means of good are irreconcilable. The popular misconception of the mature Blake and the mature Shelley probably will always prevail, but it is disappointing to find so many scholars, supposedly close readers of Blake or Shelley, who still believe that Blake was a mystic and a Christian and Shelley an ill- (or well-) compounded mash of Godwinian and Platonist. "The Triumph of Life," to me, does not seem to be in any way a palinode to Shelley's earlier major poems, as it must seem to those who have misread the earlier works. Neither can I consider it as precisely a reaffirmation of previous poems, as it does more than reaffirm. It has finality about it; for all its unfinished state it is the most finished, the most

1. As ought to be plain from my account of Shelley's myth, "The Triumph of Life" cannot be palinode *or* reaffirmation. The world of the "Triumph" is a world deliberately emptied of myth, a world of *things*. In this world the myth is neither retracted (palinode) nor reversed (reaffirmation). The myth is simply absent, and the poem deals with the consequences of precisely that absence. The "myth" of the "Triumph" is thus seen to be an antimyth; the "Triumph" is a myth-*unmaking* poem, and is properly Shelley's last work.

ruthlessly and objectively realized of all Shelley's visions. The full implications latent in all of Shelley's mythmakings are finally visualized in this account of the triumph of life over almost all human integrity and aspiration. The cry of St. Paul, to be delivered from the body of this death, natural human life, might serve as motto to this poem if Paul himself, and all those who would give his answer to that rhetorical question, were not seen as being chained to the triumphal chariot of life with the other "spoilers spoiled," in the lines which embody the last and most impressive of Shelley's many rejections of doctrinal and institutional Christianity:

> And Gregory and John, and men divine,
>
> Who rose like shadows between man and God;
> Till that eclipse, still hanging over heaven,
> Was worshipped by the world o'er which they strode,
>
> For the true sun it quenched . . .   [288-92]

I maintain then that "The Triumph of Life" has been misread by the few commentators who have written on it at any length. If I seriously dissent here from these critics—chiefly A. C. Bradley, F. Melian Stawell, and Carlos Baker—at the same time I acknowledge my indebtedness to all of them for their valuable work on the poem's sources and on many of its difficult passages. The text of "The Triumph of Life" is still quite uncertain, and may always remain so, in spite of the labors of many devoted editors, beginning with Mrs. Shelley, who first published the poem in the *Posthumous Poems* (1824, pp. 73–95). Rossetti, Richard Garnett, Locock, Mathilde Blind, and Bradley all contributed emendations to the text, not all of which are acceptable from my standpoint as a critic of the poem's meaning. The task of interpretation is complicated also by the editorial problem of having to decide whether certain lines are in the text of the poem or not. Garnett's recovery of line 281 and the first two words of line 282 appears in all modern standard editions of Shelley's poems, but the same scholar's recovery of what would be half of line 544, lines 545–7, and the first word of line 548 of the fragment, does not appear in some modern standard editions, including the 1904 Oxford edition, edited by Thomas Hutchinson, which is the text I have preferred for quotations throughout these pages. I am in no way qualified to contribute anything toward the settlement of the "Triumph's" text, beyond judging in several places which of alternate readings is more consistent with my interpretation of the poem. I shall adhere throughout my commentary to Hutchinson's text, and when I am compelled to deviate from it I shall try to indicate why and by what authority I do so.

Edward Dowden was the first scholar to point out the influence of Petrarch's "Trionfi," a series of six *terza rima* poems, on Shelley's "Triumph," instancing the first of the "Trionfi," "The Triumph of Love," as the likeliest source for Shelley's poem.[2] Bradley detailed Petrarch's influence, but rightly considered it as being much less important than the pervasive influence of Dante on the poem.[3] Miss Stawell made an attempt to demonstrate Goethe and Calderon as influences, not very successfully to my mind, but also apprehended the important relationship between Shelley's "Triumph" and Wordsworth's "Immortality" ode, following Todhunter and anticipating Knight and Baker in this recognition.[4] Baker has completed the source study by showing the possible influences of Byron's "The Prophecy of Dante" and Shakespeare's *Tempest* on Shelley. Baker also has the credit of being the first (to the best of my knowledge) to have traced at length a Spenserian influence in the poem.[5] Petrarch, Dante, Goethe, Calderon, Wordsworth, Byron, Shakespeare, and Spenser form a very imposing list of influences for a fragment of 548 lines to have to sustain; indeed, one could wonder in advance how much of Shelley there can be in a fragmentary poem so burdened with the influences of the most distinguished names in European poetry. The worry is needless. Worthy of critical notice in the reading of "The Triumph of Life" are the influences of Dante and Spenser: the first, stylistic and to some extent conceptual; the second, primarily the influence of visionary example. The analogue of Wordsworth's ode counts for something also. Petrarch, Goethe, Calderon, Shakespeare, and Byron all may have had some bearing on the genesis of the poem, but a study of their influencing of the poem's composition will not help us to comprehend its meaning. Finally, for all the influencing, supposed or genuine, "The Triumph of Life," in style and conception, is as startlingly original as any of the mature poems of Shelley. If it resembles any other poem, that poem is the "Epipsychidion," which stands in relationship to it as the *Vita Nuova* does to the *Commedia*.

Critical estimates of "The Triumph of Life" vary greatly. Oliver Elton, one of the most discerning and sympathetic of Shelleyan critics, failed to understand the "Triumph" to the extent that he considered the entrance of Rousseau into the poem to be an intrusion. Elton nevertheless did the "Triumph" the justice of thinking it to be the "hardest" of Shelley's poems to comprehend and judge, though his summary verdict

2. Edward Dowden, *The Life of Percy Bysshe Shelley* (London, Kegan Paul, 1926), p. 554.
3. A. C. Bradley, "Notes on Shelley's 'Triumph of Life,'" *MLR*, 9 (Oct. 1914), 441ff.
4. F. Melian Stawell, "Shelley's 'Triumph of Life,'" *Essays and Studies by Members of the English Association* (Oxford, 1914), 5, 104ff; Wordsworth suggestion, p. 124. Todhunter, *A Study of Shelley*, p. 289. Knight, *The Starlit Dome*, p. 253. Baker, *Shelley's Major Poetry*, p. 258.
5. Baker, pp. 258, 266, 260, respectively.

went against it: "Greatness no one can fail to see in *The Triumph of Life;* but that it could have been a good poem, unless it had been put back into the crucible, is difficult to suppose." [6] In our own time the "Triumph" has been found to be incoherent by Leavis,[7] but has been praised by Eliot as being better Dantesque verse than Eliot himself can write.[8] Hazlitt, writing in 1824, though as violent an anti-Shelleyan as Leavis (and on much the same grounds, insofar as I apprehend Leavis), felt compelled to a reluctant tribute to balance out his very Leavisite condemnation: "Anything more filmy, enigmatical, discontinuous, unsubstantial than this, we have not seen; nor yet more full of morbid genius and vivifying soul."

In the same review Hazlitt commented on and complained of the poem's bitterly paradoxical title: "The poem entitled the *Triumph of Life,* is in fact a new and terrific *Dance of Death;* but it is thus Mr. Shelley transposes the appellations of the commonest things, and subsists only in the violence of contrast." [9] Unfinished as the poem is, I find the attempts of some of its critics to envision its potential climax as joyous and optimistic and its title as indicative of such a conclusion to be very mistaken. Miss Stawell decided that either the poem would have ended with the conqueror Life conquered, or else that Shelley would have composed a second "Triumph" to accomplish his idealistically proper aim.[1] Her evidence for such an assumption, besides her firm belief that no long poem by Shelley would resolve itself in despair as to the human condition, was the analogue provided by Petrarch's "Trionfi," where the triumph of Love (over man) was followed in turn by the triumphs of Chastity over Love, Death over even a chaste Mortality, Fame over Death, Time over Fame, and finally Divinity over Time. Hazlitt, whatever his difficulties with the poem itself, was a better reader of its title than Miss Stawell. The analogy, if there is one, itself is to be read as ironic, for the title of the poem needs to be read as the triumph of life over human integrity, and the "life" of the title is Death-in-Life.

The opening of the poem, with its precision, speed, and directness, did not result from a first inspiration. The canceled opening, as first published by Mathilde Blind [2] (who had it from Garnett), is remarkably weak and very unlike the tone of any part of the poem as we have it:

> Out of the eastern shadow of the Earth,
> Amid the clouds upon its margin gray
> Scattered by Night to swathe in its bright birth

6. Elton, *Survey,* *2,* 210–11.
7. Leavis, *Revaluation,* p. 231.
8. T. S. Eliot, "Talk on Dante," *The Adelphi, 27* (1st Quarter, 1951), 110–12.
9. P. P. Howe, ed., *The Complete Works of William Hazlitt* (London, Dent, 1933), *16,* 274.
1. Stawell, "Shelley's 'Triumph,'" p. 130.
2. *Westminster Review,* July 1870. See Hutchinson, ed., *Works of Shelley,* p. 569.

> In gold and fleecy snow the infant Day,
> The glorious Sun arose: beneath his light,
> The earth and all. . . .

With that, contrast

> Swift as a spirit hastening to his task
> Of glory and of good, the Sun sprang forth
> Rejoicing in his splendour, and the mask

> Of darkness fell from the awakened Earth . . .

Not only has vigor replaced the too pretty imagery but each word in the final version has its function and adds to the meaning; in the first opening the "infant Day" is there for decoration only. Indeed, in that version all of the first four lines are made unnecessary by "The glorious Sun arose" in line 5, for that is all that they are trying to state. Shelley came to realize just this quite quickly, and threw out his initial lines. As he rewrote them, the sun, an emblem of major importance in the poem, appears almost immediately, to execute its "task of glory and of good," to remove the "mask of darkness" from the "awakened Earth." Better to wait until the sun reappears in the "Triumph," I think, before any estimate of what it signifies is made, than to adopt Bradley's manner of instantly drawing upon Plato and Dante and Shelley's earlier poetry to identify the emblem.[3] The sun is a varied and ambiguous symbol in the "Triumph" rather than the simple counter for all that is good and of God, as the critics have taken it to be. Until we have examined all the functions of the sun and its surrogates in this poem, we ought not to allow ourselves to fix its meaning *in the poem*. Here, in the scene setting (lines 1–40) of the poem's double vision, the sun's function is as definite as it is limited, and (within those limits) it does denote a supreme authority and a necessary good.

What follows this first appearance of the sun can best be described as a series of natural acts of worship of the sun by all the simply natural components of the earth. The mountain snows are "smokeless altars"; the ocean contributes its "orison"; the birds pray by tempering "their matin lay" (like small monks); the flowers (like acolytes) swing their censers, while the sun kindles their "orient [i.e. "morning"] incense," so that they can send "their odorous sighs up to the smiling air." So that

> in succession due, did continent,

> Isle, ocean, and all things that in them wear
> The form and character of mortal mould,
> Rise as the Sun their father rose, to bear

3. Bradley, "Notes on 'Triumph,'" p. 444.

> Their portion of the toil, which he of old
> Took as his own, and then imposed on them . . . [15–20]

Bradley noted the resemblance between this and that passage in "The Boat on the Serchio" (1821) which encouraged Browning and Barnard, among others, in the belief that Shelley would have been among the Christians had he lived:

> All rose to do the task He set to each,
>   Who shaped us to His ends and not our own;
> The million rose to learn, and one to teach
>   What none yet ever knew or can be known.
>   And many rose
> Whose woe was such that fear became desire;—
> Melchior and Lionel were not among those;
> They from the throng of men had stepped aside,
> And made their home under the green hill-side. [30–8]

Bradley quoted only the first four lines above when he commented on them; I have continued the quotation for a few lines because even that much more of the text will evidence the dangers that Bradley incurred by isolating that orthodox quatrain. "All" in that first line, reads Bradley, means all things; "one" in the third line is the "He" of the first, the deity-representing sun. All *things* possibly but, as the ensuing lines demonstrate, not all men are included in that first line's "all," including the poem's heroes (one of them a Shelley surrogate, at that). Switching back to the "Triumph," the pattern is repeated, as Bradley suggested, but the pattern is not precisely the one that Bradley found. The sun as benevolent tyrant ("imposed," line 20) has to do with "all *things*" that are mortal, but not with man, and therefore not with the protagonist of this poem. As all things rise, in answer to the summons of the sun, the poet does the reverse; he makes day into his night, night into his day (see my reading of "To Night" in Chapter 1). The natural world cannot suffer from the prime Shelleyan sin of remorse; it can sleep and wake with the sun. Man is other than simply natural and breaks the natural pattern. Hence, the "But" which begins the first entry of man into the "Triumph":

> But I, whom thoughts which must remain untold
>
> Had kept as wakeful as the stars that gem
> The cone of night, now they were laid asleep
> Stretched my faint limbs beneath the hoary stem
>
> Which an old chestnut flung athwart the steep
> Of a green Apennine: before me fled
> The night; behind me rose the day; the deep
>
> Was at my feet, and Heaven above my head . . . [22–8]

The Shelleyan identification with and idealization of stars as opposed to sun and moon (especially, as seen in "Adonais," of the morning and evening star) is again expressed. The recurrent image of "the cone of night" (which I have examined already in its appearance in "Prometheus" and "Epipsychidion"), the conical shadow which our earth casts into the sky, is here seen as partially redeemed by the stars that gem it, just as poets wakefully illuminate "the dreary cone of our life's shade." With the natural night past, the sun obscures the stars, and the poet sleeps. In the vision of Rousseau, which takes place within the poet-protagonist's vision, the ultimately obscuring sun will figure again.

Miss Stawell effectively summarized the natural setting which follows this first hint of the ambiguity of the sun as symbol in the poem (an ambiguity that neither she nor Bradley nor Baker ever recognized, with certain unfortunate results in interpretation later in the poem, as I shall evidence). The poet (as set forth in lines 22–8) rests at sunrise on a mountain slope, on a spur of the Apennines near the coast (at Lerici). His view is westward to the sea, his back to the east. The chariot of the vision comes up behind him, over the spur, from the east, up from the valley of birth described in Rousseau's vision. On the farther side, the eastern side, of this valley, rises the mountain of lines 312 and 452. As Miss Stawell remarked, the vision of the poet and the vision within a vision of Rousseau form one coherent picture in terms of natural setting.[4]

The coming of the vision is presented in traditional terms, rather reminiscent of Langland's prologue but having affinities with Chaucer and Spenser also.[5] The most curious aspect of Shelley's presentment is that it is deliberately archetypal; the emphasis is on a renewal of visionary circumstances:

> When a strange trance over my fancy grew
> Which was not slumber, for the shade it spread
>
> Was so transparent, that the scene came through
> As clear as when a veil of light is drawn
> O'er evening hills they glimmer; and I knew
>
> That I had felt the freshness of that dawn
> Bathe in the same cold dew my brow and hair,
> And sate as thus upon that slope of lawn
>
> Under the self-same bough, and heard as there
> The birds, the fountains and the ocean hold
> Sweet talk in music through the enamoured air,
> And then a vision on my brain was rolled.   [29–40]

4. Stawell, "Shelley's 'Triumph,'" p. 112 and n. 1.
5. Todhunter, *Study of Shelley*, pp. 284–5.

(In line 33 I take it that we are to read "hills" as the antecedent of "they," and ought to interpose a comma between them.)

Through "a veil of light," analogous to the last clear light of sunset, the vision is *renewed*. The point to be grasped is that this seer is a poet, not unaccustomed to visions, for this is essential to an understanding of the poem. Fundamentally, "The Triumph of Life" is as concerned with "optics" as Brooks found Wordsworth's great ode to be.[6] The strength of contending lights and the visions they inform, and the obliteration of one kind of light by another; these are the real themes and the major figures of "The Triumph of Life." The seer here is a poet because the "Triumph," like so many of Shelley's works, is a poem about poets and poetry, their relation to one another and to the life and light of everyday, as well as to another life and light contrasting to that of everyday.

In lines 41–175 we have the first movement of the poem, a vision of natural life and the natural man. As the poet lies in his trance (one in which his reason still functions, the meaning of "wondrous thought," line 41, and "waking dream," line 42), he sees "a public way" akin to that "broad highway of the world" in the "Epipsychidion " which is trodden by the convention-bound slaves making "the dreariest and longest journey" of legalized marriage. This straight and narrow way, by which Death-in-Life marches on to Death, is the vision of *our* life. Aimlessness, inconsequence of movement, meaninglessness of dying, all are conveyed:

> Methought I sate beside a public way
>
> Thick strewn with summer dust, and a great stream
> Of people there was hurrying to and fro,
> Numerous as gnats upon the evening gleam,
>
> All hastening onward, yet none seemed to know
> Whither he went, or whence he came, or why
> He made one of the multitude, and so
>
> Was borne amid the crowd, as through the sky
> One of the million leaves of summer's bier . . .   [43–51]

Shelley's genius for varied, rapid, and nonextended images is extraordinarily apt in its application here. The way (an ironic word, with something of Blake's fierceness of prophetic irony, when we remember that "way" is the correct translation for so many religious terms: the Hebrew Torah, the Chinese Tao; the "public way" here contrasts deliberately with the religious "way of man," way to salvation, path to

6. Cleanth Brooks, "Wordsworth and the Paradox of the Imagination," *The Well-Wrought Urn* (New York, 1947), pp. 114–38.

righteousness, etc.) is "thick strewn with summer dust, and a great stream of people . . . hurrying." The people, by suggestion, are only as dust, or as gnats, or as dead leaves. What is emphasized is the great numbers, the meaningless multiplication of ciphers, the lack of individuality in the way. The dust, the gnats, the leaves, the people are all alike, in that one speck of dust is much like another; one gnat, one leaf, one person, each like all the others. Emphasized as much are haste and blindness-in-haste, in lines forming an epigraph for the unexamined human life:

> All hastening onward, yet none seemed to know
> Whither he went, or whence he came, or why
> He made one of the multitude . . .

Finally, the lines suggest powerlessness, related to the lack of individuality. Dust collects dust, gnats attract gnats, the leaves are impelled helplessly through the sky, the rush of the crowd of people bears the single person along. The tone is the opening tone of Koheleth, Solomon as preacher, the vanity of human activities, wishes, futurities, existence itself.

> Old age and youth, manhood and infancy,
>
> Mixed in one mighty torrent did appear,
> Some flying from the thing they feared, and some
> Seeking the object of another's fear . . .   [52–5]

This senseless flooding is no product of the stages of youth and age, but encompasses each chronological grouping of our lives. Some flee death; others pursue it. Worse is that all objectives in this trek are unreasonable; what is sought by some is feared by others, and with reason. The rhetorical turn of lines 54–5 is peculiarly effective in emphasizing the inability to escape from our fears as well as the confusion among us about the objects of desire.

> And others, as with steps towards the tomb,
> Pored on the trodden worms that crawled beneath,
> And others mournfully within the gloom
>
> Of their own shadow walked, and called it death;
> And some fled from it as it were a ghost,
> Half fainting in the affliction of vain breath . . .   [56–61]

Those fleeing from or toward death are complemented by, first, those who march toward it helplessly, fascinated with horror at the vision of physical corruption that the worms present to them. Next, there are those who are stricken *in this life* with despair at viewing the shadow of their own mortality, and thus live their deaths in advance. Finally are those who deny death as having no reality, but who deny out of fear and know that their vocal denial is vain expense of breath. But all of these are small minorities; the mass of men do not reflect on death at all. *Their* dance of death is completely automatic and compulsive; it is the dance of *busyness,* of empty activity, serious folly:

> But more, with motions which each other crossed,
> Pursued or shunned the shadows the clouds threw,
> Or birds within the noonday aether lost,
>
> Upon that path where flowers never grew,—
> And, weary with vain toil and faint for thirst,
> Heard not the fountains, whose melodious dew
>
> Out of their mossy cells forever burst;
> Nor felt the breeze which from the forest told
> Of grassy paths and wood-lawn interspersed
>
> With overarching elms and caverns cold,
> And violet banks where sweet dreams brood, but they
> Pursued their serious folly as of old.   [62–73]

This dance is wildly irregular; men's motions *cross* one another—crossing as interference, dispute, vindictiveness is here restored to something of its root physical meaning—men get in one another's way as they pursue or shun *shadows,* shadows created by inconstant clouds, themselves blacking the sun, or by *lost* birds, blinded "within the noonday aether." The sterile, flowerless path is clearly the way of competition. There is nothing esoteric (or, on the other side, banal) about the "fountains" which these "faint for thirst" competitors are too engrossed to hear. The waters of life are not to be invoked lightly by any poet; the poem earns their entrance or it does not, and then we resent their intrusion. What is best in our natural life surrounds the sterile "public way" here, and the presentation of it eludes commentary. The final word of the poet, before the cold glare of the chariot of Life breaks into his poem, is one of compassionate condemnation, as he shakes his head in a kind of wonderment:

> but they
> Pursued their serious folly as of old.

"Their serious folly" is "the principle of Self," of which, as Shelley said, money is a visible incarnation. Throughout these poems upon which I have tried to comment, this principle is opposed to Poetry as the Mammon against the God of this world, an opposition analogous to Blake's cosmic war of Imagination against Selfhood, also expressed in this world as a warfare of Poetry and Mammon, the competitive instinct.

What follows in "The Triumph of Life," from this point and this recognition, is the entrance of the first of the two major visionary projections of the poem, the triumphal car of the conqueror, Life (the second is the "Shape all light"). Upon the detailed interpretation of these projections, any critical reading of the "Triumph" must be judged, for without a comprehensive understanding of the anagoge of these representations, I do not think that the poem itself can be understood. Since I reject all prior interpretations of both these visions, I shall present a full accounting of those interpretations, each in its place.

The poet-protagonist resumes:

> And as I gazed, methought that in the way
> The throng grew wilder, as the woods of June
> When the south wind shakes the extinguished day,
>
> And a cold glare, intenser than the noon,
> But icy cold, obscured with blinding light
> The sun, as he the stars. Like the young moon . . .   [74–9]

As the chariot approaches, the passing throng (which is now that portion of the crowd directly in front of the chariot, the fierce young who dance to destruction under its juggernaut wheels) is seen to grow wilder, and the simile of the south wind shaking woods at twilight is evoked. The woods are shaken most fiercely just before the day is extinguished; the frenzy of the young dancers becomes greatest just before the advancing chariot overrolls them. Just after are two and one-half lines which are a key passage of the whole poem and which stand out in their frightening eloquence even from their context:

> And a cold glare, intenser than the noon,
> But icy cold, obscured with blinding light
> The sun, as he the stars.

Shelley's hatred of cold became part of his poetic equipment, as I have already evidenced in discussing "Mont Blanc," "Prometheus," "The Sensitive Plant," and "Epipsychidion," and as Fogle has well demonstrated.[7] Here, in these lines, it achieves its most successful *use* in Shelley's poetry. The repetition, "but icy cold," drives in the effect of this incredibly intense, blinding cold glare given off by the chariot of Life. Light absolutely without heat, which obscures the warm but less bright light of the sun, just as the sun's light obscures the light of the stars. In these few lines the optical theme of the "Triumph" is summarized, with that last phrase "as he the stars" prophesying the Shape's (the sun-

7. Fogle, *Imagery*, pp. 74–6.

surrogate's) obscuring of the light of poetry. (In Rousseau's vision later in the poem, Rousseau, the archetype of the poet, and the morning and evening star are being identified, just as Keats, again the archetype of the poet, and the morning and evening star are identified in "Adonais.") *The light of nature destroys the inner light of the poet, only to be obliterated in turn by the real light of everyday life,* not the warm sun but the more than moonlike cold car of Life:

> Like the young moon—
>
> When on the sunlit limits of the night
> Her white shell trembles amid crimson air,
> And whilst the sleeping tempest gathers might—
>
> Doth, as the herald of its coming, bear
> The ghost of its dead mother, whose dim form
> Bends in dark aether from her infant's chair,—
>
> So came a chariot on the silent storm
> Of its own rushing splendour . . .   [79–87]

The sinister phenomenon of the new moon with the old moon in its arms, prophetic of storm, introduces the "silent storm" of the "rushing splendour" of the advancing chariot, the Shape resting in the chariot as the old moon rests in the new. Recall Ione's vision:

> I see a chariot like that thinnest boat,
> In which the Mother of the Months is borne
> By ebbing light into her western cave,
> When she upsprings from interlunar dreams . . .

The visualization here is the same, but this chariot, its occupant Shape, and its charioteer are distinct from any previous Shelleyan chariot and figures:

> So came a chariot on the silent storm
> Of its own rushing splendour, and a Shape
> So sate within, as one whom years deform,
>
> Beneath a dusky hood and double cape,
> Crouching within the shadow of a tomb . . .   [86–90]

Why a chariot? Shelley scholars seem to accept its presence as being part of the inevitable machinery of a triumphal pageant, but that is only to thrust the question a stage further back. Knight is an honorable but unclear exception, and even he will not take us very far: "The symbol

is important in Dante, Milton, Shelley, and Keats, suggesting a tran-
scendence-in-motion to be both compared and contrasted with domes.
We may, provisionally, call it 'dynamic eternity.' " [8] I must confess to
not understanding Knight here, even when I attempt to set his remark
in the total context of his very imaginative criticism. For want of help
then, I will digress on "chariots" before returning to the chariot of Life
in the "Triumph," taking the Bible and Blake as aids in this essay at
symbolology.

I am indebted to Frye's commentary on Blake here:

> The body which is the form of the soul's energy is called by Blake
> the "Vehicular Form." The most natural symbol for this vehicular
> form in its complete divine state would be either a chariot or a
> throne, depending on whether the god is conceived as moving or
> sitting still. The chariot is found in the allegorical pictures of the
> Renaissance depicting the triumphs of gods or virtues: in the *Bha-
> gavadgita* Krishna, the divine imagination of Arjuna, is Arjuna's
> charioteer, and the same figure occurs in the *Phaedrus*. Now a
> chariot is drawn by animals, who thereby become symbols of the
> god: thus in the triumphs just mentioned Venus is always drawn
> by doves, Juno by peacocks, Bacchus by leopards, and so on. In
> Ezekiel God is visualized in a chariot surrounded by four "living
> creatures" full of eyes resembling an eagle, an ox, a lion and a man.
> In the Book of Revelation Ezekiel's chariot has become a throne,
> and here the same expression "living creatures" is used . . . The
> reason why the animals who draw the chariot become symbols of
> the driver is that otherwise the suggestion is that the driver is de-
> pendent on an external power for his energy.[9]

What is most worth exploring here, for my purposes, is the chariot
of Ezekiel's vision, which is the direct influence on the divine chariots
of Milton and Blake and possibly an influence (in itself or through
Milton) on the chariot of Life in Shelley's triumph (but my argument
here, as will be seen, is quite independent of the notion of influencing,
and relies instead upon Ezekiel, Milton, and Blake as providing archetypal analogues to Shelley's chariot). Here is Ezekiel's vision (in part):

> 4. And I looked, and, behold, a whirlwind came out of the north,
> and a fire infolding itself, and a brightness was about it, and out
> of the midst thereof as the colour of amber, out of the midst of the
> fire.
>
> 5. Also out of the midst thereof came the likeness of four living
> creatures. And this was their appearance; they had the likeness of
> a man.

8. Knight, p. 251.
9. Frye, *Fearful Symmetry*, pp. 272-3.

6. And everyone had four faces, and everyone had four wings. . . .

10. As for the likeness of their faces, they four had the face of a man, and the face of a lion, on the right side : and they four had the face of an ox on the left side ; they four also had the face of an eagle. . . .

12. And they went every one straight forward : whither the spirit was to go, they went ; and they turned not when they went.

13. As for the likeness of the living creatures, their appearance was like burning coals of fire, and like the appearance of lamps : it went up and down among the living creatures ; and the fire was bright, and out of the fire went forth lightning. . . .

15. Now as I beheld the living creatures, behold one wheel upon the earth by the living creatures, with his four faces.

16. The appearance of the wheels and their work was like unto the colour of a beryl : and they four had one likeness : and their appearance and their work was as it were a wheel in the middle of a wheel.

17. When they went, they went upon their four sides : and they turned not when they went. . . .

19. And when the living creatures went, the wheels went by them : and when the living creatures were lifted up from the earth, the wheels were lifted up. . . .

24. And when they went, I heard the noise of their wings, like the noise of great waters, as the voice of the Almighty, the voice of speech, as the noise of an host : when they stood, they let down their wings.

The chapter terminates in the vision of "the likeness of a throne" appearing over the cherubim and their chariot, with a flaming "likeness as the appearance of a man" upon the throne. The vision of the chariot is my concern, and the verses most relevant to that vision and to Shelley's chariot vision are the verses I have given above.

Even these verses are too complex for any interpretation here, granting that I were competent enough to interpret them, which I am not. This vision of "the wheels and their work"—the *Ma'aseh Merkabah,* "Work of the Chariot"—inspired a long tradition of visionary commentary, beginning with the Essenes, passing to the *Merkabah* mystics of Jewish medieval Spain, and climaxing in the Hasidic movement. The tradition of Christian commentary is not so extensive but is of great importance, since the Enthroned Man on the firmament above the chariot has always been read as direct prophecy of the Son of God. Only what is central in all this commentary on the chariot can be of use here.

Frye is incorrect in saying that God is visualized in this chariot :

by Jewish or Christian interpretation either an emanation of God, or Christ, is involved. Frye is right in pointing out that the chariot is not being drawn by any power but that of the Enthroned Man: there are in fact no animals in this chariot's shafts; the wonder-winged cherubim, each with four faces, are the *wheels* of the chariot; the power that moves the chariot is not in the cherubim but in the Enthroned Man. The whirl-wind and fire that accompany the chariot come from the north, which traditional commentary explains by pointing out that the north is the quarter from which the sun never shines, so that Ezekiel can know that this fire and brightness transcend the fire and brightness of the sun, just as God transcends the sun, and thus realize instantly that the "fire in-folding itself, and a brightness about it" is directly from God, not from nature.

Ezekiel's visionary chariot comes in the midst of a whirlwind, Shel-ley's on the "storm of its own rushing splendour." Ezekiel's cherubim each have four faces and four wings; we are not allowed to see any beasts drawing the chariot. Shelley's charioteer has four faces; we are not allowed to see the "wonder-wingèd team," for the narrator is dazzled:

> The shapes which drew it in thick lightenings
> Were lost:—I heard alone on the air's soft stream
> The music of their ever-moving wings.

Ezekiel emphasizes this dazzling brightness again and over again, and emphasizes as well, again and again, the single-mindedness of the cherubim: "And they went every one straight forward . . ." "And they turned not when they went. . . ." These are also dominant characteristics of the chariot of Life in Shelley.

Here is Milton's chariot, directly influenced by Ezekiel:

>   forth rushed with whirl-wind sound
> The Chariot of Paternal Deitie,
> Flashing thick flames, Wheele within Wheele undrawn,
> It self instinct with Spirit, but convoyd
> By four Cherubic shapes, four Faces each
> Had wondrous, as with Starrs thir bodies all
> And Wings were set with Eyes, with Eyes the Wheele
> Of Beril, and careering Fires between;
> Over thir heads a chrystal Firmament,
> Whereon a Saphir Throne, inlaid with pure
> Amber, and colours of the showrie Arch.
> Hee in Celestial Panoplie all armd
> Of radiant *Urim,* work divinely wrought,
> Ascended, at his right hand Victorie

> Sate Eagle-wing'd, beside him hung his Bow
> And Quiver with three-bolted Thunder stor'd,
> And from about him fierce Effusion rowld
> Of smoak and bickering flame, and sparkles dire . . .   [749–66]

Those "thick flames" of 751 are very like Shelley's "thick lightenings" of line 96. Once again, as Frye points out, it is made clear that the "four Cherubic shapes" are not drawing the chariot; they "convoy" it in very much the modern naval meaning of "convoy"; they surround the chariot. For the chariot is "It self instinct with Spirit"; it does not need to be drawn by beasts. These two visions of the chariot—Ezekiel's and Milton's—are to be kept in mind as I turn back to Shelley. Before that return, for the sake of the instructive analogue, I pause to consider Blake and his assumption of this tradition.

Ezekiel's vision of the cherubim was taken by Blake as a starting point for the mythography of "The Four Zoas" (four "living creatures," Zôa, in Revelation's version of Ezekiel's vision). The Four Zoas are the four cherubim, the four faculties of Unfallen Man or divine Enthroned Man, Albion; Blake named them: first, Luvah (Orc in time, as opposed to the Unfallen Luvah, the faculty of Love, the loins of a man's body, the stars of the fallen universe, the "state" of generation, the season of spring, etc.); second, Urizen (Satan in time, faculty of wisdom, the head of a man, the sun in nature, the "state" of Eden, the season summer, etc.); third, Tharmas (covering Cherub in time, faculty of power, heart of a man, moon in nature, the "state" of Beulah, autumn, etc.); fourth, Urthona (Los in time, faculty imagination, the body of man viewed as a whole, and since Blake believed that "that call'd Body is a portion of Soul discern'd by the five Senses, the chief inlets of Soul in this age," therefore the soul of man, mountains in nature, the "state" of winter, etc.). I have given just enough abstract summary of the Zoas here as to make Blake's myth at this point reasonably clear.

Blake is not far from either orthodox Jewish or orthodox Christian interpretation of Ezekiel's cherubim when he categorizes them as Love, Wisdom, Power and Imagination, the difference residing in his assigning of these faculties to archetypal Man, while Jewish interpretation sees the cherubim as personifying attributes of God (and His emanation in the Enthroned Man) and Christian as attributes of Christ, as in the Miltonic chariot in the passage above.

Gray visualized Milton as riding in a divine chariot in "The Progress of Poesy" (and, as Frye points out, Gray refers to Ezekiel's chariot in his own note on the appearance of Milton in that ode).[1] Blake, with all this in mind, was able to culminate this tradition of the divine chariot in the opening lyric of his "Milton":

1. Ibid., p. 274.

Bring me my Bow of burning gold:
Bring me my arrows of desire:
Bring me my Spear: O clouds unfold!
Bring me my Chariot of fire.

This is Blake's own invocation to his "Muse," a daughter of Inspiration as opposed to the classical "daughters of Memory," whom he hated. What that invocation is can be understood only when you have followed out the tradition of Ezekiel's chariot of fire and know Blake's modification of the tradition. Unfallen, divine, that is, altogether human Man rides in the chariot, convoyed by his four attributes of Power, Love, Wisdom, and Imagination, and drawn by no force external to himself. This is Blake's development of the chariot, following upon Ezekiel and Milton; but *in deliberate contrast* to Ezekiel and Milton, and in a kind of complement to Blake, is the chariot of Shelley's last vision, the chariot of Life in the poem to the consideration of which I now return:

So came a chariot on the silent storm
Of its own rushing splendour, and a Shape
So sate within, as one whom years deform,

Beneath a dusky hood and double cape,
Crouching within the shadow of a tomb;
And o'er what seemed the head a cloud-like crape

Was bent, a dun and faint aethereal gloom
Tempering the light.   [86–93]

Knight calls this Shape "Moneta-like," [2] but he is profoundly mistaken, as I shall show. Baker calls her "Worldly Life," and attempts to equate her with Spenser's Lucifera, which is certainly an influence here, as Locock hinted.[3] Baker proceeds by the equation: Shelley's Shape equals Lucifera, Lucifera equals Worldly Pride; Shelley's Shape equals Worldly Pride or Worldly Life. Baker has in mind a distinction between the lower Venus (affiliated to Shelley's Shape) and the higher (of which he finds "Iris," in this poem, to be a representative). But this distinction—between lower and higher Venus, Worldly and other-than-Worldly Life—is Baker's. It is not, as I shall show, to be found in Shelley's poem. Baker's error is that he desires to import into the "Triumph" Shelley's supposed distinctions, or at least the distinctions which he, Baker, has read in Shelley's earlier major poems. This desire to find a pattern, especially one which will link up all of Shelley's "epipsyche" figures (the

2. Knight, p. 251.
3. Baker, p. 260. Locock makes this suggestion in his relevant note in *Poems of Shelley,* 2.

visionary maiden of "Alastor," Cythna, Asia, the Witch of Atlas, the Lady of the Garden in "The Sensitive Plant," Emilia, Urania, and now "Iris"), is not a critical desire. You must begin by reading closely "The Triumph of Life," without preconceptions. If there are elements in the "Triumph" which cannot be assimilated into the "pattern" of Shelley's earlier poetry, into the fabric of his vision, then surely it is better to alter the pattern, restitch your notion of the fabric, than it is to alter the poem, to rewrite it by misreading.

John Todhunter read the Shape as being "a type of the phenomenal— what Blake calls the 'vegetable,' as opposed to eternal, life." [4] This, especially the Blake comparison, is coming closer to the poem, but the opposition Todhunter found is not, I think, there in the poem. Miss Stawell thought the Shape of Life to be equivalent to what the New Testament means by "the World," and (with eloquence) amplified this reading of the Shape to include : "the evil side of human society in the earthly order, those elements, terrible and alluring, in the rush of circumstance and in the passions of men that combine to fetter, deform, and crush personality. So that 'Life' conquers when a man fails in right action, and still more when his character becomes the plaything of circumstance." [5]

That is noble, though platitudinous, but has nothing to do with "The Triumph of Life" and its Shape of Life. The poem calls the shape "Life," without qualification, and Rousseau in the poem does the same, nor is any "higher" Life opposed to this Life in the poem's text. In the lines now under consideration (87–93) we learn only this : that the Shape of Life in the chariot is deformed, dusky, shrouded, *indefinite*. The Enthroned Man or the Christ nakedly blazed with light, and had the hardness and definite form of something agatelike. The Shape of Life is hidden "beneath a dusky hood and double cape," crouches "within the shadow of a tomb," and over what "seems" *her* (see line 240) head "a cloud-like crape was bent." The Enthroned Man had clearly human lineaments, but Life, pertaining only to the natural in man, is not quite human. The crape (suggestive of mourning) tempers the light with "a dun and faint aethereal gloom," for the light itself here is only that of the chariot. Life, categorically, we can identify with natural life, with all of the life that a merely natural man lives. Much to confirm this reading will be brought forth as we go further into the poem. The other components of the vision are the concern now : the charioteer, the "wonder-wingèd team," and the chariot itself.

> Upon the chariot-beam
> A Janus-visaged Shadow did assume

4. Todhunter, p. 285.
5. Stawell, "Shelley's 'Triumph,'" pp. 113–14.

> The guidance of that wonder-wingèd team;
> The shapes which drew it in thick lightenings
> Were lost:—I heard alone on the air's soft stream
>
> The music of their ever-moving wings.   [93–8]

The team is concealed from us, but Baker has ventured on an identification: the "steeds," he says, "are 'wonder-wingèd' hours." This "may
be conjectured," he writes, from lines 97–8 above.[6] But the "steeds" are
Baker's surmise; they are not mentioned in the poem. Baker's "conjecture" is also very much his own; "The music of their ever-moving wings"
does not necessarily suggest hours to me. The cherubim of Ezekiel's
vision have ever-moving wings, but are not therefore hours. I suspect
that the meaning of Shelley's team, as of his charioteer, is rather to be
sought with Ezekiel's or Milton's vision in mind. That the shapes of
the team "in thick lightenings/were lost" I take as a hint that this
chariot, like a chariot of divinity, needs no force external to it in order
to go forward. Shelley has divided up the attributes of the cherubim between that obscured team and the charioteer. The team (and it would
be of four) has the ever-moving cherubic wings; the charioteer has the
four faces, each with its set of eyes. Just as the cherubim "convoy,"
guide the chariot in Ezekiel and Milton, so a four-faced demonic cherub
serves as charioteer here, while the "team" provides an analogue for the
cherubim as wheels. As confirmation of this studied guesswork and as
interpretation of a difficult and much-debated passage, I shall proceed to
consider the state of the charioteer:

> All the four faces of that Charioteer
> Had their eyes banded; little profit brings
>
> Speed in the van and blindness in the rear,
> Nor then avail the beams that quench the sun,—
> Or that with banded eyes could pierce the sphere
>
> Of all that is, has been or will be done;
> So ill was the car guided—but it passed
> With solemn speed majestically on.   [99–106]

In Ezekiel's vision of cherubim-as-chariot-wheels we may remember
this passage:

> 18. As for their wings, they were so high that they were dread-
> ful; and their rings were full of eyes round about them four.

6. Baker, p. 259, n. 4.

This vision of a multiplicity of seeing eyes is taken up by Milton:

> four Cherubic shapes, four Faces each
> Had wondrous, as with Starrs thir bodies all
> And Wings were set with Eyes, with Eyes the Wheels
> Of Beril, and careering Fires between . . .

The same influence is at work in the "Purgatorio's" Triumphal Chariot of the Church, which Bradley considered a possible influence upon Shelley's chariot: [7]

> even as star follows star in the heavens, four creatures came after them, each one crowned with green leaves.
>
> Everyone was plumed with six wings, the plumes full of eyes; and the eyes of Argus, were they living, would be such.
>
> To describe their form, reader, I spill no more rhymes; for other charges bind me so, that herein I cannot be lavish.
>
> But read Ezekiel, who depicts them as he saw them coming from the cold region, with whirlwind, with cloud, and with fire;
>
> And as thou shalt find them in his pages, such were they here, save that as to the pinions John is with me, and differs from him.
>
> The space within the four of them contained a car triumphal, upon two wheels, which came drawn at the neck of a grifon.

Dante avowedly follows Revelation 4 here, rather than Ezekiel, as to the number of wings:

> 6. And before the throne there was a sea of glass like unto crystal: and in the midst of the throne, and round about the throne, were four beasts full of eyes before and behind.
>
> 7. And the first beast was like a lion, and the second beast like a calf, and the third beast had a face as man, and the fourth beast was like a flying eagle.
>
> 8. And the four beasts had each of them six wings about him; and they were full of eyes within: and they rest not day and night, saying, Holy, holy, holy, Lord God Almighty, which was, and is, and is to come.

Dante, like Ezekiel and Revelation and also Milton, emphasizes the innumerable eyes of the cherubim. Dante does not attempt to describe the cherubim, any more than Shelley describes the obscured shapes of his "wonder-wingèd team." Dante piously gives Ezekiel as descriptive

7. Bradley, "Notes on 'Triumph,'" p. 443.

reference, claiming that he has other charges upon himself. Somewhere in the background here is the long Jewish and Judeo-Christian tradition of not attempting to describe the *Ma'aseh Merkabah,* Work of the Chariot, any more graphically than the deliberately obscure Ezekiel described it, for fear of prying into the divine mystery.

The tradition of the multiplicity of cherubic eyes, from Ezekiel and Revelation through Dante and Milton, culminates where one might expect it to culminate, in Blake. I must refer the reader here to Blake's painting in "illustration" of Dante's Triumphal Chariot of the Church, in the passage from the "Purgatorio" quoted above.[8] Blake's illustration, as again one might expect, is closer to Ezekiel than it is to Dante's text. The cherubim surround the chariot, and their four wings each are alive with dozens of eyes. More intensely visionary is the chariot itself, for it consists of a platform mounted upon a single whirlpool of a wheel, and in that whirlpool are to be seen the faces of cherubim and many detached eyes, all in rapid motion. Blake is pressing his vision of the "Vehicular Form" to its limit; he is making clear his belief that the body is the form of the soul's energy, that body and soul are one, in this picture of the cherubim drawing themselves along. For my immediate purpose, which is the contrast between this tradition of cherubic eyes and Shelley's reversal of that tradition, I draw attention to Blake's deliberate overall effect in his painting, the effect of the dominance of the plethora of eyes over everything else in the scene. Dante, according to his commentators, means the eyes to indicate the knowledge of things past and future. I do not think that so restrictive a meaning need be attached to the eyes anywhere in this tradition of Ezekiel-through-Blake. What is important, I think, is that there are a plethora of eyes and they are open; *they can see.* Blake might have said of these cherubic eyes what Keats said about "intelligences" which were "atoms of perceptions— they know and they see and they are pure, in short they are God." [9] These cherubic eyes, in Blake's belief, would be those eyes with which we see God, and these would be the very same eyes with which He was able to see us, since, by Blake's belief, we see God when we perceive *as* He, and He *as* we. Shelley would have ultimately agreed with Blake on this, according to my argument as to the necessary consequences of Shelley's mythmaking commitment, with the all-important difference that Shelley's emphasis would be on the banding in our life here of those eyes with which we could see or be seen by divinity. This at last brings me back to Shelley's vision of the charioteer, and the problems of interpretation which that vision has provided for Shelley scholars.

    8. The best reproduction I know of is to be found in Albert S. Roe's *Blake's Illustrations to the Divine Comedy,* Princeton, 1953.
    9. M. B. Forman, ed., *The Letters of John Keats* (London, Oxford Univ. Press, 1948), p. 336.

The charioteer, "a Janus-visaged Shadow," has four faces, like the cherubim, except that every one of those faces "had their eyes banded." The team of cherubim (as I believe them to be, rather than Baker's horse-like "hours") travel with great speed, but the guiding cherub cannot guide ("Speed in the van and blindness in the rear") for he cannot see. All the light given off by the chariot ("the beams that quench the sun") is to no avail, because of this blindness. The next two lines are difficult:

> Or that with banded eyes could pierce the sphere

> Of all that is, has been or will be done;   [103–4]

Rossetti is followed by Hutchinson and Woodberry in putting a stop at the end of line 102 (a dash by Hutchinson, a colon by Woodberry) and thus reading these lines so that "*that* with banded eyes" is taken to be the charioteer with eyes bandaged, who would be able to "pierce the sphere" if his eyes were unbound. This seems correct to me, and is consistent with the interpretation that I offer. The cherub could see all that there is to be seen—present, past, or future—were his eyes not bound. The cherubim convoying the divine chariot, with their manifold of unbanded eyes, can see just that. The meaning here, I take it, is in the contrast. The divine chariot's progress is meaningful because of the see-ing eyes; this chariot's progress is meaningless:

> So ill was the car guided—but it passed
> With solemn speed majestically on.   [105–6]

That "with solemn speed" I read as a gravely and bitterly ironic mock-ing, in contradistinction here to Knight, who says that the point is that "though a figure of death and blind destruction" the Shape of Life, like the chariot, "yet possesses dignity." [1]

I shall sum up what I have said about the Shape of Life, the chariot, and the charioteer, before proceeding to examine the interpretations which I hope either to modify or to demonstrate to be unacceptable. The dis-torted Shape of Life is, quite literally, Life, our daily life, the natural life of man. The chariot, its unseen team, and its charioteer all derive from the fourfold tradition of Ezekiel's vision of cherubim, developed by the New Testament, Dante, Milton, and (unknown to Shelley) Blake, but they derive from Ezekiel or Dante or Milton only in standing de-liberately in contrast to that vision of cherubim. Where chariot and cherubim are "instinct with Spirit" in the Christian tradition, here in Shelley chariot and cherubim (team and charioteer) are instinct with the reverse of Spirit, are possessed by Death-in-Life. The warm light of the Christian chariot is matched by the cold glow, the "icy glare" of the chariot of Life. The manifold blazing eyes of the Christian cherubim

---

1. Knight, p. 251.

are balanced by the "banded eyes" of Shelley's four-faced charioteer. Shelley's whole vision subsists in this terrifying irony of contrasts, with its wealth of awful meanings, most of which you miss if you fail to see the contrasts as being such. No critic of "The Triumph of Life" seems ever to have pointed to this deliberate contrast (why "four Faces" otherwise, or the other details of vision which are so close, though reversed), let alone develop it, though any critic who recognized the Dante analogue (Bradley) or the Spenser (Baker) would have been able to do so by tracing the Dantesque or Spenserian triumphal chariots back to their ultimate source in Ezekiel. Before going on in my reading of the poem, I am impelled, because of my divergence from all previous readings, to examine those earlier interpretations of the charioteer, in particular, and of the chariot of Life and its occupants in general.

Todhunter identified the charioteer as the "Human Intelligence," thus allegorizing it in the broad.[2] Bradley, followed by Locock and Stawell, equated the charioteer with Destiny or Necessity, on the basis of the allusion in "Hellas," line 711, to "the world's eyeless charioteer, Destiny." [3] Hughes, followed by William Cherubini, took the charioteer to be "the unspiritualized intelligence, the 'calculating faculty,' which is said in *A Defence of Poetry* to thwart or stifle the imagination; a sorry coachman of the passions of men, blinded to the saving truths, but with the eyes to see through that disability to the four corners of Nature for the truths that do not profit or deliver." [4] Barnard read the charioteer as "the human soul, blinded by evil desires and by the careless or cowardly acceptance of base superstition, corrupt institutions, and degrading customs and conventions (in short all that is personified by the figure of Life) and hence unable to see any meaning in the past or present, to say nothing of foreseeing or influencing the future or passing beyond time into Eternity." [5] Most recently Baker has decided that the charioteer "is the type of the poet who has been hoodwinked by the worldly life, and does not therefore own the skill—which for Shelley was the true use of great poetry—to guide aright the chariot of worldly life." [6]

We are back again at the "every man his own allegorist" situation, which Newman White deplored in regard to "Prometheus" and which I have concurred in deploring in regard to the whole of Shelley's mature mythmaking poetry. No necessity can be demonstrated in any of this allegorizing, and each critic can very persuasively demolish the allegorizer who has come before him in this procession of latter-day victims chained to the chariot of Life. All allegorizers have been bothered

2. Todhunter, p. 285.
3. Bradley, "Notes on 'Triumph,' " p. 447.
4. Hughes, *The Theology of Shelley*, p. 13. Also William Cherubini, "Shelley's 'Own Symposium': The Triumph of Life," *SP, 39* (1942), 559–70.
5. Barnard, ed., *Shelley, Selected Poems, Essays, and Letters*, p. 492.
6. Baker, pp. 260–1.

by the four faces of the charioteer; no one has been able adequately to
account for them. I have quoted Hughes on the four faces; the other
critics and editors follow Bradley in believing the four faces to look
toward past, present, future, and eternity, one face for each. Baker fits
his interpretation of the charioteer to this: "The ideal poet can see in
all these directions; the imperfect poet is blinded to them." [7]

Aside from what I regard as questionable forcing in all of this allegorizing, how does the poem benefit by this one-for-one mode of finding
equivalents? Surely it is one thing to interpret a poem, but another thing
entirely to translate a poem into terms and figures not its own. All of
the scholars I have cited (and I regard them all as distinguished Shelleyans, to whom I am indebted) in effect give notice of their failure to
read "The Triumph of Life" as a poem by trying to make it into a very
different *kind* of poem from what in fact it is. It belongs to what Blake
termed Vision, not Allegory, and, as Blake said, the two kinds must be
kept distinct, as I tried to indicate in my initial chapter. The precise form
in which Shelley visualizes in the "Triumph" is itself an anagoge of his
meaning. If you take your eyes away, at any point in the poem, from
Shelley's own figures, then you will fall inevitably into misreading of the
meaning, for the meaning is the total form that Shelley's series of visions
(and everything in this poem *is* visualized for you) assumes when you
can be certain you have seen all of them as clearly as Shelley has presented
them. As soon as you have identified the abstraction you believe the
chariot of Life and its occupants to be, then just that soon you have
stopped reading Shelley's poem. Shelley's chariot, Shape of Life, and
charioteer are themselves, not something else. They are forms seen in a
poet's vision, and what they mean is not something in addition to what
they are.

What they are I have tried to indicate by bringing them into contrast
with figures in analogous visions, contrasts which I think the poem deliberately invites. Further indication depends upon reading the rest of
the poem, to which I now return. The chariot has passed on:

> The crowd gave way, and I arose aghast,
> Or seemed to rise, so mighty was the trance,
> And saw, like clouds upon the thunder-blast,
>
> The million with fierce song and maniac dance
> Raging around—such seemed the jubilee
> As when to greet some conqueror's advance
>
> Imperial Rome poured forth her living sea
> From senate-house, and forum, and theatre,
> When   upon the free

7. Ibid., p. 260, n. 7.

> Had bound a yoke, which soon they stooped to bear.
> Nor wanted here the just similitude
> Of a triumphal pageant, for where'er
>
> The chariot rolled, a captive multitude
> Was driven . . .   [107–20]

The gap in line 115 presumably should be filled by whatever figures one might regard as having been most responsible for the extinction of the Roman republic. The comparison is fully adequate for the poem's purpose; the "million" conquered by Life are like the citizens of imperial Rome who "stooped to bear" the yoke of empire, and who poured forth to greet the recipients of imperial triumphs without realizing that they themselves had been triumphed over by the empire. Raging "with fierce song and maniac dance" they had celebrated their own victimization, as those conquered by Life do so in the poem. Another contrapuntal strand of a triumphal chariot has been woven into the poem. The triumphal procession of Life is a mockery, a diabolic *parody* of the triumphal procession of Ezekiel's Enthroned Man, Dante's Church, Revelation's and Milton's Christ, Blake's Divine Man (this last unknown to Shelley). But it is an exact parallel to the triumphal procession of a Roman general, and also to the procession of juggernaut, as will be seen in lines 161–2.

The poem proceeds to an analysis of the captive multitude, with the word "all" pealing throughout:

> all those who had grown old in power
> Or misery,—all who had their age subdued
>
> By action or by suffering, and whose hour
> Was drained to its last sand in weal or woe,
> So that the trunk survived both fruit and flower;—
>
> All those whose fame or infamy must grow
> Till the great winter lay the form and name
> Of this green earth with them for ever low;—
> All but the sacred few. . . .   [120–8]

If you count up these "alls" you count up to not less than everybody as having been vanquished by Life, except for "the sacred few" who are considered next in the poem. Readers who take a less darksome view of history or their own lives have tended to soften the explicit statement made by these lines. "Good or bad," these captives have failed to possess their souls, and have been overcome by Life. Such aging is certainly not approved or desired by the poem, and the point about it is that it is *not* distinct from the "enfeebled exhaustion" of the other aged victims of

Life. *All* similarly have been conquered by Life; there is the emphasis. The lines could not well be clearer as to this. The "captive multitude" includes *all,* whether grown old "in power *or* misery," whether having "subdued" age (living intensely in spite of it) "by action *or* by suffering," whether dying "in weal or woe," whether their "fame *or* infamy must grow" until an end is brought by an apocalyptic winter. To have endured is counted as nothing here; I cannot understand how Miss Stawell saw praise for the captives, rather than pity, in the pathetic line:

> So that the trunk survived both fruit and flower . . .

A final "all" sums up, as we are told of the handful of the unconquered:

> All but the sacred few who could not tame
> Their spirits to the conqueror's—but as soon
> As they had touched the world with living flame,
>
> Fled back like eagles to their native noon,
> Or those who put aside the diadem
> Of earthly thrones or gems till the last . . .
>
> Were there of Athens or Jerusalem,
> Were neither mid the mighty captives seen,
> Nor mid the ribald crowd that followed them,
>
> Nor those who went before fierce and obscene. [128–37]

Because I deviate twice from Hutchinson's text here, I am compelled to pause to justify those deviations. Hutchinson, in line 129, read "conquerors," following Mrs. Shelley. Bradley emended to the singular "conqueror," as did Rossetti before him and Locock and Miss Stawell after him. Barnard and Baker both have adopted the same reading more recently.[8] Now, I agree that the conqueror, Life, is meant, but I suggest, though lamentably on no authority, that "conqueror's" is a better emendation. Better, I think, because of the sense obtained and because it would be a less drastic emendation. Shelley, I am told, was notoriously careless in punctuation, and it is surely less drastic to insert an apostrophe than it is to drop the final letter of "conquerors." As for the sense, I read "All but the sacred few who could not tame / Their spirits to the conqueror's [spirit]," which I consider better balanced and more meaningful, as it clarifies the nature of the struggle between what is vital about "the sacred few" in opposition to Life, their "spirits" against her "spirit."

My other deviation from Hutchinson is in the unfinished line 133, where I have added "till the last" to Hutchinson's "Of earthly thrones

---

8. A. C. Bradley, "Notes on Passages in Shelley," *MLR, I* (1905–06), 31–2, gives the best reasons for adopting this emendation.

or gems." My authority here is Locock and, through him, Garnett. Locock states that Garnett, after consulting the Bodleian manuscript of
"The Triumph of Life," communicated this phrase to him.[9] While it still
leaves the line imperfect, of course, the phrase does fill out the sense, and
is consistent, as I will show, with the reading I would give this passage in
any case. Until some new edition of Shelley is given to us and clears this
matter up, I feel justified in regarding "till the last" as part of the text
of the poem.

Baker agrees with many previous readers in assuming that Socrates
and Jesus are among "the sacred few," which is safe conjecture and
which is justified, since the text of the poem forces us into conjecture
here. But Baker's reading is one I am compelled to modify: "The 'sacred
few' were those who established contact with the 'living flame' of heavenly
light and did not lose it by taming their spirits to the cold glare of the
worldly life. Evidently Christ and Socrates are foremost among the
sacred few." [1] This glosses over, it seems to me, what is most important
about the sacred few and what is very clearly expressed in the lines in
question (128–34). The spirits of these few were too fierce to be tamed
even by whatever elements of Selfhood these few had ("could not tame").
Not the "worldly life," but life itself, our life, attempted to triumph over
these few, and was defeated only because they *chose to die* to our life, to
all of our life. They did not choose to suffer and endure, to be sanctified
by suffering. Those who did so choose are among the group of captives
described in lines 120–4, and are at one with the "sacred few" of Baker,
on the basis of the paraphrase by Baker that I have quoted above. A
Christian saint could fit Baker's reading, but not Shelley's poem, as to
membership in "the sacred few." Saints frequently have "their age subdued . . . by suffering," and saints clearly are involved in Rousseau's
identification of "those chained to the car" in lines 208–15. Who else are
"they who wore . . . wreaths of light" (line 210) than the saints?

The "sacred few," those whose might *could* repress "the mystery
within" (what this means in the poem I shall attempt to clarify below,
after dealing with Rousseau's appearance), preserved their sacredness
by voluntary martyrdom—no milder interpretation of lines 128–37 can
do justice to the text. Shelley's figure is that of a fiery eagle which flies
down from its high place of soaring, briefly touches the world below,
and then immediately returns to its home. The light of "the world"
(Life) is an icy glare, a deadly cold flame. The light of the "sacred few"
is a "living flame." When the two flames meet, the spirits of the few rebel
rather than lose their warmth in order to acquire the cold flame of Life,
the conqueror's spirit. They flee back instead to "their native noon," to
the full warmth of the source of their living flame. Literally, they choose

to die. The statement is as grim and unequivocal as it is in "Adonais," and as frequently misread as "Adonais" is. The "pure spirit" remains pure only because it flows soon enough "back to the burning fountain whence it came." If it stayed, then inevitably it could not be secure "from the contagion of the world's slow stain." The Selfhood, "the mystery within" which Shelley, like Blake, recognized as the imagination's great enemy, would have triumphed, a Quisling within, in aid of Life's triumph over the individual's spirit, no matter who the individual. If Socrates and Jesus are "those who put aside the diadem / Of earthly thrones or gems till the last . . . / . . . of Athens or Jerusalem," then they are so because of their martyrdoms, their refusals to compromise their visions. (What can be made of "were there" at the beginning of line 134? The words are meaningless in context, as the very point of the passage is that the "sacred few" *were not there* amid the captives bound to the chariot. I am inclined to accept Rossetti's emendation of "were there" to "whether," as well as his emendation of "or" to "for" at the beginning of line 132.[2] There is no either-or here: the sacred few are those who flee back to their native noon, *and* who put aside the diadem. The text would then read—with a full stop at the end of line 131—

> All but the sacred few who could not tame
> Their spirits to the conqueror's—but as soon
> As they had touched the world with living flame,
>
> Fled back like eagles to their native noon.
> For those who put aside the diadem
> Of earthly thrones or gems till the last . . .
>
> Whether of Athens or Jerusalem,
> Were neither mid the mighty captives seen,
> Nor mid the ribald crowd that followed them,
>
> Nor those who went before fierce and obscene.

There would seem to be no textual authority for these emendations by Rossetti, but without them I do not see how this passage can be construed.)

A grouping of Jesus and Socrates is more than questionable. Against Shelley's "And Socrates, the Jesus Christ of Greece," in the fragments connected with "Epipsychidion," one can properly set Blake's bitter comment on Byron's linking of Socrates and Jesus: "If Morality was Christianity, Socrates was The Savior."[3] What justifies Shelley's probable grouping here is just this: that Socrates and Jesus are the most commonly

2. Locock, *2*, 480.
3. Keynes, ed., *Blake*, p. 825.

accepted examples of individual integrities which refused to be triumphed over by Life. They, and the few like them, martyrs of Athens or Jerusalem (and "Athens" and "Jerusalem" can be taken here as embodiments of faiths, philosophic and religious), are therefore not among "the mighty captives seen," though the bulk of their supposed followers *are* there to be seen. Nor are they to be seen in "the ribald crowd" of the old, following the chariot, nor amid the younger victims of life "who went before fierce and obscene":

> The wild dance maddens in the van, and those
> Who lead it—fleet as shadows on the green,
>
> Outspeed the chariot, and without repose
> Mix with each other in tempestuous measure
> To savage music, wilder as it grows,,
>
> They, tortured by their agonizing pleasure,
> Convulsed and on the rapid whirlwinds spun
> Of that fierce Spirit, whose unholy leisure
>
> Was soothed by mischief since the world begun,
> Throw back their heads and loose their streaming hair;
> And in their dance round her who dims the sun,
>
> Maidens and youths fling their wild arms in air
> As their feet twinkle; they recede, and now
> Bending within each other's atmosphere,
>
> Kindle invisibly—and as they glow,
> Like moths by light attracted and repelled,
> Oft to their bright destruction come and go,
>
> Till like two clouds into one vale impelled,
> That shake the mountains when their lightnings mingle
> And die in rain—the fiery band which held
>
> Their natures, snaps—while the shock still may tingle;
> One falls and then another in the path
> Senseless. . . .   [138–60]

Todhunter, with Locock following him, identified "that fierce Spirit" of line 145 as the lower Venus, Venus Pandemos.[4] I distrust this suggestion (which probably has its ultimate origin in Mrs. Shelley's note on

4. Locock, *2*, 481.

the fragmentary "Prince Athanase")[5] because it lends itself to a distinction between Venus Pandemos and Venus Urania which is not true to the theme and tone, to the text, of "The Triumph of Life." With some such distinction in mind, critics have been able to make "Iris," the rainbow embodiment, into a representative of the higher Venus, and thus seriously misread the poem. There is no necessity for "that fierce Spirit" to be anything but the Spirit of the conqueror, Life. The Shelley of "Athanase" may have distinguished between the two Venuses as being present in this life; the Shelley of the "Triumph" believes that the two, in this life, are in fact one.

The dancers of these lines "outspeed the chariot," whirl themselves to exhaustion at a pace more relentless than the swift advance of Life itself. This passage, one of the most powerful and integrated of the poem's visions, needs only the commentary of retrospect, needs to be measured against the passion and belief of all those previous visions of the possibility of human love, from "Alastor" through "Epipsychidion" and the poems to Jane Williams, with which Shelley had occupied himself. In my chapter on "Epipsychidion" I attempted to demonstrate that a close reading of Shelley's myth of sexual love, psyche and epipsyche relationship, always reveals an underlying pattern in which the myth is defeated, the defeat being the myth's culmination. The recognition always exists, *in the poems themselves,* that the Thou of the beloved, the Thou in relation to which the lover attempts to take up his stand, must become at the last yet another It, an object that the lover experiences. "Epipsychidion," as I have said, is not a Platonic exercise, not a hymn to free love, not another idealization of the Shelleyan epipsyche (I doubt that any such idealizations exist, at least in any poem that I have examined in these chapters). "Epipsychidion" is a denial, a protest against the myth which it embodies so admirably, a myth which has it that in this life love and the means of love are irreconcilable ultimately (again, I do not state this as *Shelley's* belief but as the belief of his *poems*). In the same way poetry and the means of poetry, good and the means of good are here irreconcilable in "our mortal day," in which power and will rule in opposition and where necessarily "the good want power . . . the powerful goodness want," "the wise want love, and those who love want wisdom"; the world of "The Triumph of Life" as much as of Act I of "Prometheus," the world of our life, in which "all best things are thus confused to ill." The celebration and lament of "Epipsychidion" resolve into the poem's climax, in which Shelley in effect finds the release of St. Ignatius, the escape of "My Eros is crucified." In the cold inferno of "The Triumph of Life" there is no escape, and the poem as we have it does not attempt one.

5. Hutchinson, ed., *Works of Shelley*, p. 165.

Like the Carnal Sinners of Dante's "Inferno," where

> The hellish storm, which never rests, leads the spirits
> with its sweep; whirling, and smiting it vexes
> them . . .

so, here, *all* human lovers are visualized as "convulsed and on the rapid whirlwinds spun." The *experience* of love itself, supplanting the *relationship* of lovers, is seen as destructive, as a falling away into the realm of It must seem. The figures of destruction are those recurrent in Shelley: lovers,

> Like moths by light attracted and repelled,
> Oft to their bright destruction come and go . . .

and again, "like two clouds into one vale impelled," they dissipate their substance in the storm of their contact. And the chariot rolls over them:

> nor is the desolation single,

> Yet ere I can say *where*—the chariot hath
> Passed over them—nor other trace I find
> But as of foam after the ocean's wrath

> Is spent upon the desert shore . . .   [160–4]

Bradley's paraphrase of this effective if grisly passage seems to me to be the correct one.[6] Those falling fall congested together; the desolation is always double at the least. The *where* of line 161 is the where of the several points at which the lovers are crushed by Life's chariot. The juggernaut passes over them too suddenly for the points of contact to be established by the observer, and the lovers are reduced to being the backwash of the chariot. While

>   behind,
> Old men and women foully disarrayed,
> Shake their gray hairs in the insulting wind,

> And follow in the dance, with limbs decayed,
> Seeking to reach the light which leaves them still
> Farther behind and deeper in the shade.

> But not the less with impotence of will
> They wheel, though ghastly shadows interpose
> Round them and round each other, and fulfil

6. Bradley, "Notes on 'Triumph,'" p. 448.

> Their work, and in the dust from whence they rose
> Sink, and corruption veils them as they lie,
> And past in these performs what   in those.   [164–75]

What is central here is not an opposition of light and shade, but rather the grim paradox that the cold light of the car is at one with shade, that the shadows cast in it are necessarily ghastly. The old men and women, not dignified but "foully disarrayed," continue the obscene dance performed by the young. Their efforts are directed toward drawing abreast of Life's chariot again; their lust is toward being juggernauted. All their striving toward the cold glare of the chariot is impotent; they are left "still farther behind and deeper in the shade." The shade I take to be the backward shadow of the chariot, though this is surmise. The will of the aged dancers is strong but impotent, an infernal condition productive of the most extreme suffering. When the chariot of Life is far enough ahead of them, then they are no longer in its shade, but instead in the cold glare they project their own shadows, which come to cover them, so thickly that finally shadows "interpose . . . round each other." When all is shadow then death has triumphed, not over Life but over Death-in-Life. The dancers return to "the dust from when they rose"—they have gone from death to death. Against the "sacred few" who are twice born are set these millions who are twice died. The image of the mask, first employed in the poem's opening when the mask of darkness fell away from the countenance of awakened earth, and to be used again at the close of the poem as we have it, when "mask after mask" passes from the faces of the conquered, exposing corruption, is involved here in its complement, the veil, an ambiguous, multiform symbol throughout Shelley's poems. "Corruption veils them as they lie," but what is there left of them which is not already corruption? The point, as I take it here and at the poem's conclusion, is that the victims of Life are masked or veiled only as an onion is skinned. When all the masks are peeled away by the aging process, then nothing at all remains. As the young were reduced to the foam of the chariot's backwash, so indeed the old come to the same fate. Corruption falls away, and not this incorruptible remains but rather just nothing, foam, backwash of Life's chariot. So the passage properly ends:

> And past in these performs what   in those.

"These" are the old, "those" the young dancers. "Past," the aging process, "performs" in the old exactly what the omitted word (something like "present" surely) "performs" in the young. To age behind the chariot, or to be immediately juggernauted by it, is to come to the same thing: from the corruption of Death-in-Life you pass to the corruption-veiled nothingness of Death. No Christian poet has ever visualized the depravity of the natural man in his "given" condition more convincingly than Shelley, the opponent of Christianity, has done here.

With sure artistic instinct, at just this point, the poem mounts to its first climax with the entrance of Rousseau, *the* poet, above all others, of the natural man; the unique archetype of the celebrant of the body of this death, which is the human body of this life as the poem views it. Many commentators have noticed the equation: that Rousseau is to Shelley in "The Triumph of Life" as Virgil is to Dante in the *Commedia*. No commentator has asked, why Rousseau? The question needs to be asked, though in a sense it does answer itself. Who else but Rousseau could serve as the Virgil to guide Shelley through the inferno of "The Triumph of Life"? The poem is Rousseau's palinode, not Shelley's, just as the recent "Brother to Dragons" of Robert Penn Warren embodies Jefferson's palinode, not the poet's, though in each case consciousness of error exists also in the poet-protagonist. Implicit in the myths of Shelley's major poems is a realization that the limitations of this existence mark the human condition as fallen. Nowhere in Rousseau, to the best of my knowledge, is the equivalent realization to be found. No biographical support in the life of Rousseau can be found for his realization in Shelley's "Triumph" that life conquers us to our loss. The late Irving Babbitt classified both Rousseau and Shelley as "emotional naturalists," but does not seem ever to have bothered reading "The Triumph of Life," no single mention of it being made in *Rousseau and Romanticism,* a book which constantly examines Rousseau, Shelley, and Rousseau's influence upon Shelley. However, this is perhaps to be expected in a book which dismisses Shelley as an "eleutheromaniac" and Blake as "only a romantic aesthete." [7]

In his *Proposals for an Association, etc.* (1812), Shelley wrote of Rousseau, a decade before the composition of "The Triumph of Life": "Rousseau gave licence by his writings, to passions that only incapacitate and contract the human heart:—so far hath he prepared the necks of his fellow-beings for that yoke of galling and dishonourable servitude, which at this moment, it bears." [8] Nevertheless, writing in 1816 to Peacock, Shelley speaks of "the divine beauty of Rousseau's imagination, as it exhibits itself in 'Julie.' " [9] In *A Defence of Poetry* (1821) Rousseau is listed among those poets who "have celebrated the dominion of love, planting as it were trophies in the human mind of that sublimest victory over sensuality and force." Later in the *Defence,* Rousseau is distinguished from the other agents of the Enlightenment—Locke,

7. Irving Babbitt, *Rousseau and Romanticism* (Boston, Houghton Mifflin, 1919), p. 152 for Blake, p. 189 for Shelley.
8. David Lee Clark, ed., *Shelley's Prose* (Albuquerque, Univ. of New Mexico Press, 1954), p. 67.
9. Ingpen, ed., *Letters of Shelley, 2,* 489.

Hume, Gibbon, and Voltaire—as having been "essentially a poet," while the others "were mere reasoners." [1] Of Rousseau's poetic greatness Shelley had certainly too exalted an opinion; he speaks once of "French literature, which the great name of Rousseau alone redeems." [2] Of Rousseau as thinker, Shelley's most astonishing estimate is to be found in the *Essay on Christianity* (1815): "Rousseau . . . is, perhaps, the philosopher among the moderns who, in the structure of his feelings and understanding, resembles most nearly the mysterious sage of Judea. It is impossible to read those passionate words in which Jesus Christ upbraids the pusillanimity and sensuality of mankind, without being strongly reminded of the more connected and systematic enthusiasm of Rousseau." [3] This is an aberration, as the poet of "The Triumph of Life" was to recognize. The statements on Rousseau that I have quoted previously are more to the point of the "Triumph." Rousseau was a great poet, and his dominant theme was human love. His imagination had the intensity of divine beauty, but this intensity carried in itself the danger of self-enslavement and enslavement of its converts. Thus that prophecy of the "Triumph" a decade before: a "yoke of galling and dishonourable servitude" results from those Rousseauistic "passions that only incapacitate and contract the human heart."

It is as the poet-celebrant of natural religion and natural passion that Rousseau now makes his appearance in the poem, chastened but generous still; confessing his errors of vision so that others may not follow him into slavery. Virgil, by Dante's beliefs born into a state of nature at a time antecedent to the institution of an order of grace, guides Dante because fundamentally he is taken to represent the best that a poet may attain to in a state of nature only. But he represents that best because, among other virtues human and poetic, he harbored throughout his poetry a longing after grace, a lament for possessing nothing more than mutable nature, and, finally, a prophecy of redemption (so, at least, Dante read the fourth "Eclogue"). Shelley, as opposed to Dante, is not a Christian poet. But precisely because he is not, he is the fit poet for the chastened Rousseau to guide. As Dante comes under an order of grace in contrast to Virgil, so the poet of "Prometheus" knows of a kind of grace (not Christian) which Rousseau has neglected. The worst violence that can be done to "The Triumph of Life" would be to read into it an acknowledgment of original sin by either Shelley or Rousseau. Not Christianity but an apocalyptic humanism is herein opposed to the naturalistic humanism of Rousseau. Blake's opposition to Rousseau is exactly one with this. "Prometheus Unbound," like Blake's "Milton," is a work in contradistinction to Christianity in its institutional, "received"

1. Shawcross, ed., *Shelley's Criticism*, pp. 144–5; 150.
2. Clark, p. 236.
3. Ibid., p. 209.

form. "The Triumph of Life," like "Jerusalem," is in contradistinction to a merely naturalistic humanism, but in the name of another humanism. Knight misleads when he writes that Shelley in the "Triumph" "is denouncing the limitations of a purely humanistic existence" and that Rousseau is "chosen to typify the naturalistic or humanistic philosopher," for Knight does not comprehend what is being countered against Rousseau's vision by Shelley.[4] Knight nevertheless is a better guide here than Baker, who gives no evidence of realizing that Rousseau is in the poem as the chastened prophet of the inherent goodness of the state of nature.[5] Blake, throughout his mature work, recognizes deism as his chief contemporary enemy rather than the orthodox Christianity which he desires to transfigure. Shelley, in the "Triumph," has come to the same realization, recognizing, as Blake did, that natural religion is the enemy within himself, in his Selfhood proper. "Mont Blanc," the first of Shelley's poems that I have examined at length in these chapters, could have had as its motto the Blakean "There Is No Natural Religion," for that is in fact its theme. "The Triumph of Life," which comes here at the end, might carry the same motto. Frye has pointed out that if we take the titles of Blake's two early tracts—*There Is No Natural Religion* and *All Religions Are One*—we shall find that they "contain the whole of his thought if they are understood simultaneously. Any sectarian bigot could assent to the former alone, and any Deist to the latter alone." [6] One way of defining the difference between Blake and Shelley would be to point out that while Shelley's poetry assents to both of Blake's statements, only the first receives emphasis in it. The *All Religions Are One* side of Blake is responsible for mythography, the contrapuntal symbolism of which Shelley does not attempt. The denial of natural religion, with its acknowledgment of a God and a Nature which are frankly It's, is responsible for the mythopoeia, the attempt to confront a Thou, which Shelley and Blake do have in common.

I return now to the "Triumph" at line 176. Dante, after his encounter with Matilda ("Purgatorio," Canto XXVIII, a meeting which has its sinister parallel and possible "diabolic parody" in Rousseau's meeting with the Shape, as I shall show), is approached by the divine pageant of the triumphal chariot of the Church, just as Rousseau will be approached by the diabolic pageant of the triumphal chariot of Life, after he has been dealt with by the Shape. As the pageant approaches, Dante cries out "Che cosa è questa?" "What thing is this?" which as Bradley noted is paralleled by Shelley's "And what is this?" concerning the pageant of Life.[7] The Dantesque parallel I mention again here only because I do

4. Knight, p. 252.
5. Baker, pp. 262ff.
6. Frye, *Fearful Symmetry*, pp. 345–6.
7. Bradley, "Notes on 'Triumph,' " p. 443.

not think the Rousseau-Shape meeting can achieve its full meaning without it, and some evidence that Shelley consciously held in mind Cantos XXVIII and XXIX of the "Purgatorio" at this point in his own poem is welcome to me. (There is also Shelley's translation into *terza rima* of lines 1–51 of Canto XXVIII, done not long before the "Triumph's" composition, to be put in evidence here.)

Rousseau's condition is grimly just; he has been assimilated to nature all too completely, and the Dantesque horror of his state, in which his desires have been mockingly fulfilled, is powerfully conveyed:

> Struck to the heart by this sad pageantry,
> Half to myself I said—'And what is this?
> Whose shape is that within the car? And why—'
>
> I would have added—'is all here amiss?—'
> But a voice answered—'Life!'—I turned, and knew
> (O Heaven, have mercy on such wretchedness!)
>
> That what I thought was an old root which grew
> To strange distortion out of the hill side,
> Was indeed one of those deluded crew,
>
> And that the grass, which methought hung so wide
> And white, was but his thin discoloured hair,
> And that the holes he vainly sought to hide,
>
> Were or had been eyes . . . [176–88]

Rousseau has attained completely to the state of nature; grotesquely, he has become a part of what Blake calls the Vegetative universe, the state of Generation, the world in which only a vegetable is comfortably at home. Rousseau's metamorphosis is opposite to the metamorphoses which are accomplished by mythopoeia. A man has become an old root; rather than a natural object having been humanized, a human being has been naturalized. The pathetic human pride left in Rousseau is exposed in his attempt to hide the remnants of his eyes. The detail is vital to the poem's optics; Rousseau can no longer *see*. Either his eyes have been blinded by the glare of Life's chariot, or else they have been "banded," like the eyes of the charioteer. In place of eyes he has "holes." He does not see Shelley; he hears Shelley's words and replies to them, or else he intuits Shelley's thoughts ("of my thought aware," line 190), but not as Virgil can read Dante's thoughts, by gazing on his face, which was Bradley's comparison. What counts again here is contrast, between the keen-eyed Virgil, looking for grace, and the blinded Rousseau, well past that hope. The deeper contrast is one that I have already discussed, between the chariot pageant, alive with innumerable eyes, and its parody, in which no eyes live. Out of this last condition, Rousseau gives warning:

> 'If thou canst, forbear
> To join the dance, which I had well forborne!'
> Said the grim Feature (of my thought aware).
>
> 'I will unfold that which to this deep scorn
> Led me and my companions, and relate
> The progress of the pageant since the morn;
>
> 'If thirst of knowledge shall not then abate,
> Follow it thou even to the night, but I
> Am weary.'—Then like one who with the weight
>
> Of his own words is staggered, wearily
> He paused; and ere he could resume, I cried:
> 'First, who art thou?'   [188–99]

"The Grim Feature" (in the Latin sense of *factura*, "creature," as Forman noted) [8] is an uncomfortable remembrance, possibly, of "Paradise Lost," Book 10, line 279, where Death, son begotten by Satan upon Sin, sniffs the smell of mortal change on earth, and prepares to go forth to claim his carrion feast:

> So sented the grim Feature, and upturn'd
> His Nostril wide into the murkie Air,
> Sagacious of his Quarrey from so farr.

Here in the "Triumph," the terming of Rousseau as "the grim Feature," by calling up this passage, serves to emphasize the state that Rousseau is in, though Rousseau has the generosity of spirit to warn Shelley against joining in the dance that leads only to the condition of a carrion feast for Death.

The progress of the pageant of the triumphal car of Life has begun with morn, the world's morn and the morn of Rousseau himself, as his account will show. Rousseau's speech, here and throughout until he begins the story of his own conquest by Life, has the eloquence of bitter irony, a romantic irony which has gone into reverse, so to speak. Rousseau has fallen by the wayside with the other aged victims described in lines 165–75. Shelley is still young; if he joins in the dance, he can continue in it until his own nightfall. The phrasing of Rousseau's speech is masterful in its economy, and is very heavily indebted to Dante in style, though not in particular turns of speech. Rousseau "will unfold that which to this

8. Locock, *2*, 481.

deep scorn" led himself and the other dancers, "this deep scorn" being both the state Rousseau is now in, one worthy of deep scorn as well as the attitude which Rousseau, Farinata-like, has toward his own state: "come avesse lo inferno in gran dispitto," as if Rousseau also entertained great scorn of hell.[9] Rousseau's "If thirst of knowledge shall not then abate, / Follow it thou even to the night" to Shelley has a savage edge. "Thirst of knowledge" will not serve to save anyone from joining in the dance, as Rousseau goes on to clarify in what to me are the finest lines of the poem:

> 'Before thy memory,
>
> 'I feared, loved, hated, suffered, did and died,
> And if the spark with which Heaven lit my spirit
> Had been with purer nutriment supplied,
>
> 'Corruption would not now thus much inherit
> Of what was once Rousseau,—nor this disguise
> Stain that which ought to have disdained to wear it . . .'
>
> [199–205]

Rousseau began at least with a spark lit in his spirit; a flame which had light *and* heat. It was his own business to supply the proper nutriment for the spark; he failed, and he subsists now in the hell of his awareness of this failure, and the responsibility for it. Corruption, which veils the aged victims of the chariot as they lie outstretched by the wayside (line 174), now veils not Rousseau but "what was once Rousseau." A disguise now stains not that which can disdain to wear it, for what *is* now in place of Rousseau is no different from the vegetative disguise, but rather "that which ought to have disdained to wear it," the original Rousseau, endowed not only with Selfhood, "the mystery within," but with that saving spark of imaginative vision which, as we shall see, was stamped out by the Shape all light, by the light of the everyday world. And yet, Rousseau's case is still relatively individual; he is as corrupt as any of Life's victims, but the way of his corruption, though as deadly, was nobler than that of the captives chained to the chariot, and because of this he has the lesser doom of falling in weariness with the aged millions rather than that of being chained to the chariot with the other famous and infamous leaders of men and men's thoughts. As in the imperial Roman triumphs, where the barbarian leaders were led in chains near the conqueror's chariot or actually bound to it, thus suffering greater dishonor than the mass of captives, their followers; so here, with "the wise, the great, the unforgotten," as Rousseau bitterly puts it, after indulging in a final and more pathetic outburst of pride:

9. "Inferno," X, 36.

'If I have been extinguished, yet there rise
A thousand beacons from the spark I bore'—
'And who are those chained to the car?'—'The wise,

'The great, the unforgotten,—they who wore
Mitres and helms and crowns, or wreaths of light,
Signs of thought's empire over thought—their lore

'Taught them not this, to know themselves; their might
Could not repress the mystery within,
And for the morn of truth they feigned, deep night

'Caught them ere evening.'   [206–15]

Line 210 comprehends ecclesiastical leaders, warriors, rulers, and, finally, canonized saints or mystics; their headgear being "signs of thought's empire over thought," a clear recognition of tyranny as being not merely that of external restraint but more significantly that of the dominance of the spirits of men by other spirits. Self-knowledge, the awareness of the Mammon within which can only be slain by the Poetry within, does not come through any system of belief accepted in itself to these wise, these great, these unforgotten. Their truth is a feigned truth, and with it they begin to participate in the pageant of the triumphal car; before the pageant closes for them it has been exposed as only feigned, for it cannot keep them from being triumphed over by the conqueror Life. Blake also attacked "mystery," the "mystery within" of the Selfhood, and the Mystery without, enshrined by orthodox Christianity, as being the great enemy of the Imagination. Yet Christianity, in one of its traditions at least, is as opposed to the concept of Self as Blake and Shelley were. At random, one could cite Boethius: "In other living creatures ignorance of Self is nature; in man it is vice"; the *Theologica Germanica*: "Only the Self burns in hell" and "Your own Self is your own Cain that murders your own Abel"; William Law: "What could begin to deny Self, if there were not something in man different from Self?"; and many others. Shelley in line 210 is overstating his own poetic case, and his formulation there is not altogether defensible. His "sacred few" are perhaps more numerous than he realized, however closely we apply his own terms to their definition.

Among the captives is the Titan Napoleon, whose death had inspired from Shelley those astonishing stanzas (beginning "What! alive and so bold, O Earth?") published with "Hellas" in 1821. Here the appearance of the conqueror conquered is responsible for one of the central statements, moral and metaphysical, in Shelley's poetry:

I felt my cheek
Alter, to see the shadow pass away,
Whose grasp had left the giant world so weak

That every pigmy kicked it as it lay;
And much I grieved to think how power and will
In opposition rule our mortal day,

And why God made irreconcilable
Good and the means of good . . . [224–31]

With these lines what the "Triumph" has to say about life, our life, is complete. What remains in the work of the poem is the necessary account of how the imaginative spark of Rousseau, the poet, has come to be extinguished. While Shelley broods in despair on the contraries of mortal existence, Rousseau continues to name the mighty captives, separating himself from their condition. The "spoilers spoiled," Voltaire and the "benevolent despots" guided by his enlightened principles, come in review as the defeated:

'For in the battle Life and they did wage,
She remained conqueror. I was overcome
By my own heart alone, which neither age,

'Nor tears, nor infamy, nor now the tomb
Could temper to its object.' [239–43]

The key and difficult phrase, if we are to understand this important passage, is "temper to its object." Bradley has an ingenious discussion of this phrase proposing four possible meanings for it, none of which seems to me to be correct, though I have profited by studying his alternatives.[1] "Its" in line 243 I take to refer to Rousseau's heart; "object" is more difficult, but I take it to be not simply the object of Rousseau's love or loves, as Bradley proposes in his second alternative reading, but rather as the objects of all of Rousseau's desires, as elusive as those desires were infinite. None of Life's weapons, "neither age, nor tears, nor infamy, nor now the tomb" succeeded in tempering Rousseau's heart to that heart's object, that is, to bring the object to attainable level, to limit the desire by reducing the heart's infinite capacity to desire. Had his heart been tempered to its object, so changed that it would have been content with the gratifications offered by Life, then Life would have conquered him. As it is, he was overcome nevertheless, not directly defeated by life, but self-defeated, overcome by his own heart alone, all of

1. Bradley, pp. 451–2.

whose impulses he took to be naturally good. The consequences of that belief and the circumstances of that self-defeat, the placing of himself in a position where Life inevitably would triumph over him, will be seen in his account of himself beginning with line 300.

Against Rousseau's explanation of "the spoilers spoiled," the conquerors conquered, rises the cry of Shelley, ensuing from his brooding upon the irreconcilable contraries:

> 'Let them pass,'
> I cried, 'the world and its mysterious doom
>
> 'Is not so much more glorious than it was,
> That I desire to worship those who drew
> New figures on its false and fragile glass
>
> 'As the old faded.'   [243–8]

The point of this is that the protagonist still has not understood the full meaning of the pageant, or else that the impact of that meaning has not yet fully come upon him. Rousseau is quick enough to correct:

> 'Figures ever new
> Rise on the bubble, paint them as you may;
> We have but thrown, as those before us threw,
>
> 'Our shadows on it as it passed away.'   [248–51]

To reinforce the somber universality of this point Rousseau continues his recital of the great captives who are bound to the chariot. Plato, unlike Socrates, is there:

> 'The star that ruled his doom was far too fair,
>
> 'And life, where long that flower of Heaven grew not,
> Conquered that heart by love, which gold, or pain,
> Or age, or sloth, or slavery could subdue not.'

Bradley (followed recently by Butter) was the first to unravel the curious pun (very uncharacteristic of Shelley) involved here.[2] Plato, by tradition, in his old age fell in love with a boy named Aster. 'Αστήρ is Attic for "star" as well as the name of a flower which withers quickly, just as Plato's Aster died quite young according to the story. Plato was conquered by life through love; Socrates resisted the blandishments of such as Alcibiades. Alexander and Aristotle are next among the captives, Aristotle provoking a Baconian interlude which blemishes the poem, as it is an intrusion.

2. Ibid., p. 449.

More important, for the poem's meanings, are "the great bards of elder time," who are also among the captives:

'See the great bards of elder time, who quelled

'The passions which they sung, as by their strain
May well be known: their living melody
Tempers its own contagion to the vein

'Of those who are infected with it—I
Have suffered what I wrote, or viler pain!
And so my words have seeds of misery—

'Even as the deeds of others, not as theirs.'   [274–81]

The contrast between Rousseau and the classical poets, as drawn by Rousseau himself, is of a nature that might delight those modern critics of Rousseau, like Babbitt, who excel in demonstrating Rousseau's lack of the classical virtues of behavior and expression. The elder bards sang only after subduing themselves, with the result that their still "living melody" conveys passions only at that lower intensity where the mass of men experience passions. But Rousseau both expressed what he suffered and suffered what he expressed (he seems to assume that the elder bards, having quelled their passions for expressive purposes, no longer suffered them). As a result, whereas the elder bards could not make their readers sympathetically miserable, it was Rousseau's curious achievement (according to himself) that he could. "Theirs" in line 281 I take to refer to the words, not the deeds, of the bards (as any sustained reader of Shelley knows, one of his great faults is his heroic disregard of antecedents). Rousseau's words have seeds of misery ready for their readers, just as the deeds of some men are seeds of misery. The classical achievement (or failing, if you are with the still-unchastened Rousseau in regard anyway) is that their words contrived to be more impersonal. As for what conquered these bards or how, we already know the answers. They quelled their passions, but not the mystery within. They created, but did not recreate their own selves.

The last of the captives are Shelley's final rejection of institutional Christianity:

And then he pointed to a company,

'Midst whom I quickly recognized the heirs
Of Caesar's crime, from him to Constantine;
The anarch chiefs, whose force and murderous snares

Had founded many a sceptre-bearing line,
And spread the plague of gold and blood abroad . . .   [282–7]

"Caesar's crime" was the final overthrow of the republic. "Anarch chiefs" is hardly fair, from an historian's viewpoint, but then the "Triumph" is not history, despite Elton's objections as to the inadequacy of Shelley's view of history in it. Most significant is that Shelley ends his procession of emperors with Constantine. Constantine tied together the empire and the Church, the Church thus participating in spreading "the plague of gold and blood":

> And Gregory and John, and men divine,
>
> Who rose like shadows between man and God;
> Till that eclipse, still hanging over heaven,
> Was worshipped by the world o'er which they strode,
>
> For the true sun it quenched . . .   [288–92]

Gregory the Great is appropriate, as the true founder of the independent political power of the papacy. Which of many Johns is involved, there is no way of telling, and Shelley could surely have been more specific. The "true sun" of line 292 is not the sun of every day, but a sun beyond that sun, as Rousseau's ensuing account of his conquest by Life will make clear.

Rousseau, after a further boast that he at least, unlike the ecclesiastics, has created, not destroyed, though his creation "be but a world of agony," is entreated by Shelley to end the recital of captives and commence his own story. (As incidental points, "replied" in line 293 is clearly a mistake, as Rousseau at that moment has nothing to which to reply; and the naming of Rousseau as "the leader" in that line is another Dantesque tag, Virgil being frequently referred to as "lo duca.") Rousseau's vision has been so flagrantly and so frequently misread, in details and in total meaning, by all of the "Triumph's" commentators that I am compelled to examine it line-by-line again in order to justify my own reading.

> 'Now listen:—In the April prime,
> When all the forest-tips began to burn
>
> 'With kindling green, touched by the azure clime
> Of the young season, I was laid asleep
> Under a mountain, which from unknown time
>
> 'Had yawned into a cavern, high and deep;
> And from it came a gentle rivulet,
> Whose water, like clear air, in its calm sweep
>
> 'Bent the soft grass, and kept for ever wet
> The stems of the sweet flowers, and filled the grove
> With sounds, which whoso hears must needs forget

'All pleasure and all pain, all hate and love,
Which they had known before that hour of rest;
A sleeping mother then would dream not of

'The only child who died upon her breast
At eventide—a king would mourn no more
The crown of which his brows were dispossessed

'When the sun lingered o'er his ocean floor
To gild his rival's new prosperity.
Thou wouldst forget thus vainly to deplore

'Ills, which if ills can find no cure from thee,
The thought of which no other sleep will quell,
Nor other music blot from memory,

'So sweet and deep is the oblivious spell;
And whether life had been before that sleep
The Heaven which I imagine, or a Hell

'Like this harsh world in which I wake to weep,
I know not.'

Before attempting to comment on this passage, I am compelled to explain the text that I have quoted. "They" in line 320 may be a mistake in number; "whoso" in line 318 clearly requires "he" in line 320. In line 322 I have followed Locock's text and not Hutchinson's. Hutchinson has "Her only child who died upon the breast," following Mrs. Shelley's text, but Locock explains that his reading, which is more natural in any case, was communicated to him by Garnett after an examination of the manuscript.[3]

Bradley, Stawell, and Baker all interpreted the passage quoted above (lines 308–35) as "a symbolic representation of Rousseau's birth,"[4] which I believe to be the beginning of their misreading of Rousseau's account. Rather is it, as I must show, a symbolic representation of that process of rebirth described by Wordsworth in the "Intimations" ode, in which a poet passes from his initial vision into a time when vision ceases in its original sense, and another kind of vision may or may not succeed it; or again, described by Blake as a passage out of the land of Beulah into the world of Generation, out of Innocence into Experience, or into something worse than Generation, into the hell of Ulro, equivalent to Life in Shelley's "Triumph." In short, lines 308–35 are not, I think, about the process of birth but about the process of "growing up," of passing from boyhood to manhood, or from dependence upon nature

3. Locock, 2, 482.
4. Bradley, p. 454; Stawell, p. 124; Baker, p. 265.

to a recognition that it is dangerous to depend upon nature for too much. In a sense, Shelley at this point anyway is closer to Wordsworth's ode than even Miss Stawell and Baker realized.

Bradley's account of the physical detail of the scene, followed and developed by Baker, seems to me to be largely correct.[5] I differ on the necessity of interpreting it as symbolic of physical birth. Bradley points out that the "cavern" of line 313 is "orient" (line 344) in that it is an opening in the mountain which rises on the eastern side of the valley where Rousseau stands. The cavern is thus open to the west; the rising sun can flow through it because it is not a cavern in the usual sense but the roofed opening of a deep gorge or ravine which rends the mountain from top to bottom. Bradley gives several other instances in Shelley's poetry in which a cavern is not a hollow in something hard but is rather a deep woody recess. Baker says that "the symbolism of the deep cavern *through* the mountain is that of the passageway to this life" and cites "birth's orient portal" in "Hellas" (line 202). He cites also Wordsworth's ode (line 59), "Our birth is but a sleep and a forgetting," as being parallel to Rousseau's waking into "this harsh world" (an unconscious memory of Hamlet's charge to Horatio? as an allusion it would serve no purpose here) and not remembering how things were in his antenatal state.[6] If you hold very closely to the text, it is not possible to maintain this very pretty reading as being necessary, and you will also face the disadvantage of not leaving Rousseau very much time in which to be overcome by his own heart alone, in which enough of Rousseau can develop so that Life will have something more than an infant in swaddling bands over which to triumph. One can show as much necessity (or as little) in a reading of the ravine here as a passageway between childhood and the beginnings of manhood. "In the April prime"—that is, not at the birth of the vegetative year, but *in its first prime*—"when all the forest-tips began to burn / with kindling green"—not when they were first born, when the season was *new*, but when it was *young*—"touched by the azure clime / of the young season," the young Rousseau passed into a vision, "was laid asleep," a passing which implies a previously wakeful state, which there is no necessity again to denominate "prenatal." (Incidentally, Locock emends "forest-tips" to "forest-tops" on the basis of "The Witch of Atlas," xxxix.2, a reading in which I do not follow him because I am not sure that the figure is not damaged by it, and one which would not affect my interpretation here but which could damage Baker's.)[7] The instrument of Rousseau's first lapse in memory is not his birth, but is in the sound of the "gentle rivulet" in the cavern, a rivulet allied, as I shall show, to the Nature Shape and her

5. Bradley, p. 454; Baker, pp. 265–6.
6. Baker, p. 262, nn. 16, 17.
7. Locock, 2, 282.

nepenthe; for this rivulet, as Baker surmised, is one with the river which flows out of the cavern.[8] As Bradley observed, the geography of the scene once out of the cavern is very similar to that of "Purgatorio," Cantos XXVIII and XXIX, a point which I shall have to develop.[9]

The geography of the "Triumph" is consistent and continuous. The mountain is north-south (as Baker suggested),[1] and is cut through by the cavern east-west. On the east of the mountain Rousseau spent his infancy and very early youth. When he is laid asleep in the cavern he is there because he has progressed from the eastern side of the mountain through the cavern passageway to a kind of centerpoint in the cavern where a well or fountain is found. The fountain issues first in a west-flowing gentle rivulet, the sound of which lulls him asleep. The rivulet as it flows westward broadens into a stream or river. The rivulet, like the sun, is a natural phenomenon and, like the sun, it plays a prominent part in Rousseau's self-defeat, his seduction by Nature to a point where he is another victim of the conqueror Life.

The effect of the rivulet's sound is that Rousseau's childhood vanishes into oblivion. The poem's complexity of tone here is extraordinarily rich: the rivulet is "gentle," as nature in its better aspects can appear gentle, and if its sound washes away remembrances of pleasure and love, it obliterates memories of pain and hate also. The sleep it induces is "sweet and deep." Nevertheless, when Rousseau wakes out of that sleep it is to "weep" in this harsh world, described simply as "a Hell," while the forgotten existence may have been the heaven he imagines. And then, to continue his vision,

> 'I arose, and for a space
> The scene of woods and waters seemed to keep,
>
> 'Though it was now broad day, a gentle trace
> Of light diviner than the common sun
> Sheds on the common earth, and all the place
>
> 'Was filled with magic sounds woven into one
> Oblivious melody, confusing sense
> Amid the gliding waves and shadows dun . . .'   [335–42]

For a while, unobliterated by the light of the common sun, all that Rousseau sees still has a trace of that diviner light he had known before his sleep. Traces of that earlier existence appear in sounds as well, but confusedly, as for a final time, before the light of nature, embodied in the sun, has its way with him. In the great vision of the Shape representing Nature, the "Triumph" comes to its climax:

8. Baker, p. 266.
9. Bradley, p. 442.
1. Baker, p. 265.

'And, as I looked, the bright omnipresence
Of morning through the orient cavern flowed,
And the sun's image radiantly intense

'Burned on the waters of the well that glowed
Like gold, and threaded all the forest's maze
With winding paths of emerald fire; there stood

'Amid the sun, as he amid the blaze
Of his own glory, on the vibrating
Floor of the fountain, paved with flashing rays,

'A Shape all light, which with one hand did fling
Dew on the earth, as if she were the dawn,
And the invisible rain did ever sing

'A silver music on the mossy lawn;
And still before me on the dusky grass,
Iris her many-coloured scarf had drawn:

'In her right hand she bore a crystal glass,
Mantling with bright Nepenthe; the fierce splendour
Fell from her as she moved under the mass

'Of the deep cavern, and with palms so tender,
Their tread broke not the mirror of its billow,
Glided along the river . . .
                        .   .   .   .   .
'And still her feet, no less than the sweet tune
To which they moved, seemed as they moved to blot
The thoughts of him who gazed on them; and soon

'All that was, seemed as if it had been not;
And all the gazer's mind was strewn beneath
Her feet like embers; and she, thought by thought,

'Trampled its sparks into the dust of death;
As day upon the threshold of the east
Treads out the lamps of night, until the breath

'Of darkness re-illumine even the least
Of heaven's living eyes—like day she came,
Making the night a dream . . .'   [345-90]

Bradley began what has become the prevalent and persuasive misreading of these and the following passages in the poem. The Shape of Nature he took to be a daughter of the sun, *therefore* a manifestation of the Ideal, exactly like the Witch of Atlas.[2] She is "a Shape all Light" (line 352); so is the Witch "garmented in light" (line 81). She bears "a crystal glass, mantling with bright Nepenthe" (lines 358–9); the Witch gives "strange panacea in a crystal bowl," which entrances those who take it. Bradley succumbed here to the fatal temptation of forgetting to read the poem he was supposedly discussing. Resemblances between the Witch of Atlas and the Shape are simply not in it; Bradley was being taken in exactly as Rousseau was, which is a terrible irony. The Shape is a diabolic parody of the Witch of Atlas or Dante's Matilda; that is part of the meaning of the "Triumph." When Bradley came to lines 385–8, the terrible vision in which the Shape tramples the *sparks* of Rousseau's mind, thought by thought, "into the dust of death," he blandly observed that the reader might hastily conclude thereby that the Shape was to be taken for "a malevolent being." This "mistake," he went on to say, might be confirmed by the fact that Rousseau's draught from the Shape's crystal glass is followed by the sudden appearance of the chariot of Life. In both these cases he interpreted as follows: what was involved was "the effect of a revelation of the ideal in obliterating the modes of thought and feeling habitual before that revelation."[3] But is *that* what is happening here? Is this to be considered as "the effect of a revelation of the ideal"?

'And all the gazer's mind was strewn beneath
Her feet like embers; and she, thought by thought,

'Trampled its sparks into the dust of death . . .'

Those sparks are the same as "the spark with which Heaven lit my Spirit" which Rousseau previously mentioned, as he lamented his fall. And *how* does Bradley's interpretation account for the sudden appearance of the car of Life directly Rousseau has drunk the nepenthe? Is the cold chariot somehow part of the "revelation of the ideal"?

Miss Stawell followed Bradley in believing the Shape to be the "Spirit of supreme good," but then she also wrote a happy ending for the "Triumph" which saw the conqueror conquered. Of the nepenthe and its effect she eloquently wrote: "The dream of a sublime rapture awakes his craving for anything rapturous, however base: that is the paradox and tragedy in his desire. The Nepenthe in the cup appears to be such a dream, inspired and perilous, the dream of an all-satisfying experience in which love—'the Nepenthe love'—may be, for Rousseau as for Shelley, the

2. Bradley, p. 455.
3. Ibid., p. 454.

deepest element, but which, as Rousseau's cry for knowledge shows, is wider than love in the ordinary sense." [4] Here the critic has given way to the most fatal of temptations; she is at work writing her own poem, and palms it off on Shelley. There is quite literally no warrant in the text of the "Triumph" for anything in the paragraph just quoted.

Most recently, Baker has followed the interpretation of Bradley and Miss Stawell, broadly speaking, and in the process has gone further in writing his own poem. Not content with confusing the Shape and Iris, the rainbow, Baker sees her as the final Shelleyan goddess, the last vision of the epipsyche: "One last time, though objectively now in Rousseau's life-story, Shelley reincarnated in woman's shape his conception of the source of true poetic power—this time as Iris, many-colored goddess of the rainbow, prismatic reflector of the rays of the supernal sun." For his account of the Shape as beneficent spirit, Baker deserves to be quoted in full, since I must insist that he is mistaken at every point in his reading here:

> It has sometimes been quite wrongly supposed that the Iris-figure is intended to be a creature with evil connotations. Thus she is said to blot out "the thoughts of him" who watches her swift movement, and one by one to trample them out, like sparks or embers, into "the dust of death." But from what follows it is plain that these are dark and evil thoughts, not thoughts in general, for her action is com- pared to that of day "upon the threshold of the east" treading out the lamps of night. Similarly, when Rousseau asks for some ex- planation of the mysteries of his origin and his present condition, the goddess offers him her cup of Nepenthe, the bright cordial of her own Elysium, with the invitation: "Quench thy thirst [for knowledge]." But even as he touches "with faint lips" the cup which she raises, his brain becomes as sand and a new vision (that of Worldly Life and the "cold bright car") bursts on his sight. The usual explanation is that as a result of drinking from Iris' cup, Rousseau's spiritual senses were overcome by the cold new vision. Actually, however, he is not said to drink, but only to touch his lips to the cup. Had he drunk the bright Nepenthe, he could have quenched his youthful thirst for knowledge of the mysteries. But at the crucial moment his courage failed, his brain became "as sand," his thirst remained unquenched, and the bright cold vision of worldly life burst in. [5]

The first misreading to be charged against Baker here is his statement that the thoughts of Rousseau which the Shape tramples out "are dark and evil thoughts, not thoughts in general." The text of the poem quite

4. Stawell, "Shelley's 'Triumph,'" p. 126.
5. Baker, pp. 264–5, 267.

definitely reads "And *all the gazer's mind* was strewn beneath / Her feet like embers; and she, thought by thought, / Trampled its sparks into the dust of death." "Its sparks" clearly refers to "all the gazer's mind" and "all the gazer's mind" clearly does mean "thoughts in general" and *not* just "dark and evil thoughts," about which the text says nothing. As for Baker's demonstration here, it collapses when it reveals itself as part of his general misreading of the role that the light of everyday plays in the poem. "As day upon the threshold of the east / Treads out the lamps of night" *is* exactly analogous to what the Shape is doing, but what *is* it? Day is treading out the stars, "the lamps of night," equivalent to the poets who are the lamps of this world, and who are extinguished by the light of everyday, the common sun (not supernal, as Baker has it). And how does this passage, which to Baker proves that the Shape tramples only upon "dark and evil thoughts" just as day tramples on the lamps of night, go on? Day treads out the stars "until the breath / Of darkness re-illumine even the least / Of *heaven's living eyes.*" "Heaven's living eyes" would be incompatible in itself as a supposed parallel to "dark and evil thoughts"; how much more so in this poem, with its contrast between "banded eyes" and holes that had once been eyes on the one hand, and the living eyes of Ezekiel's or Dante's chariot vision on the other.

I will pass over Baker's description of the Shape's cup of nepenthe as "the bright cordial of her own Elysium," a phrase which I find impenetrable. What cannot be passed over is Baker's unique discovery that Rousseau does not drink from the cup of nepenthe; Rousseau's "great failure of nerve" is the somewhat Hemingwayish characterization Baker makes of this. The answer to Baker's originality here is to quote the relevant lines:

> 'Arise and quench thy thirst, was her reply.
> And as a shut lily stricken by the wand
> Of dewy morning's vital alchemy,
>
> 'I rose; and, bending at her sweet command,
> Touched with faint lips the cup she raised,
> And suddenly my brain became as sand . . .' [400–5]

I take it that "touched with faint lips the cup," by itself and even more definitely in this context, means that Rousseau in fact does drink from the cup. What else can it mean? Ambiguity does not serve any purpose here. If Shelley meant to indicate that Rousseau did not drink, he would surely have made so important a point a bit clearer. As it is, he employs an idiom, to touch a cup with one's lips, which means that one drinks.

Even Hughes, a very great Shelley scholar, was unfortunately in the

Bradley tradition of reading the "Triumph" when he wrote: "The Shape
or Spirit who meets Rousseau in the dawn of his manhood and gives him
the overmastering potion is, as in *Alastor* and *Epipsychidion,* ideal
beauty or the vision of it, fatal to the weak will, and only not so to the
saints and sages who have no part in the ghastly pageant." [6] Exceptions
to what I regard as this tradition of misreading are Todhunter, Locock,
and, most of all, Yeats. Todhunter identified the Shape as a "temptress"
who betrays Rousseau into the power of Life,[7] while Locock regarded the
Shape as malevolent because she stamps Rousseau's thoughts into the
dust of death.[8] Unfortunately, neither Todhunter nor Locock could reconcile this aspect of their interpretations with their assumption that the
sun, and all connected with it, is an emblem of good and of God in the
poem. Yeats had nothing to say of the Shape, but nevertheless he was the
first critic of Shelley to realize that Shelley's emblem of good, whenever
morning star is opposed to sun, is the star, and it was Yeats who wrote
that in "The Triumph of Life" the sun's "power is the being and source
of all tyrannies." [9] Butter has recently said that Yeats's statement "is
certainly nonsense as applied to *The Triumph of Life,*" [1] but my pages
on the poem ought by now to have made it clear that it is Butter, and not
Yeats, who is talking nonsense here. Butter quotes line 77–9 of the
"Triumph" to refute Yeats, but the lines bear Yeats out:

> And a cold glare, intenser than the noon,
> But icy cold, obscured with blinding light
> The sun, as he the stars.

Butter claims that Yeats must be confusing the light from the car and
the light from the sun. Yeats nowhere does so, and the point of these
prophetic lines in the poem, as I have already indicated, is that the glare
of the chariot does obscure the light of the sun, but that the light of the
sun in turn obscures the purer light of the stars.

I return to the first appearance of the Shape now, having surveyed
something of the history of its interpretation. In the passage beginning
at line 343, the rays of the sun come in through the east-west cavern,
from its eastern side. The "sun's image" burns on the waters of the
fountain and amid that image a rainbow appears, as the Shape drawing
her many-colored scarf. Here in the "Triumph" the sun, the light of
common day, manifests itself at this point in its most seductive representative, the rainbow. The light of nature's part in the pageant is to
seduce the poet by displaying its best aspect. Once he has given in to
this supposed beauty and good of nature, forgetting (because of his "rebirth") his early imaginative powers which transcended nature and which

6. Hughes, *The Theology of Shelley,* p. 13.
7. Todhunter, *A Study of Shelley,* p. 289.
8. Locock, *2,* 283.
9. Yeats, *Ideas of Good and Evil,* p. 138.
1. Butter, *Shelley's Idols of the Cave,* pp. 145–6.

alone could have given his eyes vision that the icy glare of life would not obscure, then life substitutes its glare for the illusory light of the natural sun.

As for the nepenthe that the Shape bears, it is in fact to be regarded as just that, strangely enough; nepenthe, a drug inducing forgetfulness of an earlier, divine existence *in this world.* Miss Stawell, in the paragraph I have quoted from her above, gratuitously brought in a phrase from "Prometheus Unbound," "the nepenthe, love," to allegorize unnecessarily. Recently, Cherubini has debated with himself as to whether the nepenthe is love or beauty, and has also opted for love on the basis of the phrase in "Prometheus." [2]

The scenery in which the Shape moves is a kind of parody or parallel to the scenery in "Purgatorio" xxviii–xxix in which Dante meets Matilda in her earthly paradise (Bradley, as I have said, first noted the parallel). Dante sees Matilda across the water of Lethe river, a draught of which washes away all memory of sin. Rousseau sees the Shape upon the waters of a Lethe-like (see line 463) river here, but a draught of this water washes away all memory, in this case of the divine youth of Rousseau, the spark with which heaven lit his spirit.

Matilda is the genius of her Eden, like the Witch of Atlas and, more exactly, the Lady of the garden in "The Sensitive Plant." The Shape is parody of this, just as Blake's Vala, his nature goddess, is. The Shape, like Vala, is a type of Rahab, the New Testament Great Whore embodied in the natural world which is a snare for the visionary. That this is the first time such a figure has appeared in Shelley's poetry, after a long succession of Asias, is what is responsible for so many critics greeting the Shape as a final embodiment of an Asia-figure. Rousseau learns better, like Keats's knight-at-arms, awakening on his cold hill's side.

To Dante, led by Matilda, there comes "a sudden brightness," *un lustro subito,* as the pageant of the triumphal chariot of the Church approaches. When Rousseau, as bidden by the Shape, has drunk the nepenthe,

> 'so on my sight
> Burst a new vision, never seen before,
>
> 'And the fair shape waned in the coming light,
> As veil by veil the silent splendor drops
> From Lucifer, amid the chrysolite
>
> 'Of sunrise, ere it tinge the mountain-tops . . .' [410–15]

Just as the sun dims Lucifer, the morning star, so now that Rousseau has given in to his own heart alone, through his love of and belief in nature (and himself as child of nature), the glare of Life's chariot dims the

2. Cherubini, "Shelley's 'Own Symposium,'" p. 562.

rainbow, emblem of the sun. Lines 77–9 are being recapitulated. The sun
and the rainbow cannot honor their commitments, and Rousseau's birth-
right has been tempted from him. The rainbow fades, and soon its
memory replaces the extinguished memory of the earlier and purer light,
which has no part in this nostalgia of the rainbow as:

> 'a day-appearing dream,
> The ghost of a forgotten form of sleep;
> A light of heaven, whose half-extinguished beam
>
> 'Through the sick day in which we wake to weep
> Glimmers, for ever sought, for ever lost . . .'   [427–31]

"Wake to weep" in line 430 echoes line 334, as if to demonstrate that
Rousseau's fall is now complete, from divinity through nature down to
life. The "new vision, never seen before," of life, is now his vision:

> 'But the new Vision, and the cold bright car,
> With solemn speed and stunning music, crossed . . .'   [434–5]

And with the chariot is its ghostly procession of victims, of whom
Rousseau is now one himself:

> 'But all like bubbles on an eddying flood
> Fell into the same track at last, and were
>
> 'Borne onward.—I among the multitude
> Was swept—me, sweetest flowers delayed not long;
> Me, not the shadow nor the solitude;
>
> 'Me, not that falling stream's Lethean song;
> Me, not the phantom of that early Form
> Which moved upon its motion—but among
>
> 'The thickest billows of that living storm
> I plunged, and bared my bosom to the clime
> Of that cold light, whose airs too soon deform.'   [458–68]

The statement of the failure of the natural world to save its prophet
could not be clearer. Flowers, the shadow and solitude of covert places,
the song of the Lethean stream, the indistinct remains of the rainbow,
these avail Rousseau nothing. The "living storm" of the chariot's rushing splendor, the cold glare of this life, is what engulfs him, not the natural
world to which he thought he had surrendered his heart. In the airs of
the clime of this life, his spirit is quickly deformed. Before the chariot
had even begun to climb out of the cavern of fountain and streams, over
its western slope, a last and most terrible vision was presented to Rous-

seau, a vision worthy of Dante, who receives an overt and fitting tribute in lines 471–80. Beyond the shadow of our night, the dreary cone of this life's shade, the "cone of night" of line 23 of the "Triumph," is the third sphere, the sphere of Venus, just barely touched by the farthest point of earth shadow. Sweet notes move that sphere, "whose light is melody to lovers," but the world is forever deaf to those notes, though they are sung, and sung best, by Dante. In our world rather, is to be visualized the fearful "wonder worthy of his rhyme," a vision fit for the "Inferno": the grove grows dense with shadows, gray with phantoms, and the air is peopled with dim forms. Madness sweeps over the dancers, and the end is come upon them:

'I became aware

'Of whence those forms proceeded which thus stained
The track in which we moved. After brief space,
From every form the beauty slowly waned;

'From every firmest limb and fairest face
The strength and freshness fell like dust, and left
The action and the shape without the grace

'Of life. The marble brow of youth was cleft
With care; and in those eyes where once hope shone,
Desire, like a lioness bereft

'Of her last cub, glared ere it died; each one
Of that great crowd sent forth incessantly
These shadows, numerous as the dead leaves blown

'In autumn evening from a poplar tree.
Each like himself and like each other were
At first; but some distorted seemed to be

'Obscure clouds, moulded by the casual air;
And of this stuff the car's creative ray
Wrought all the busy phantoms that were there,

'As the sun shapes the clouds; thus on the way
Mask after mask fell from the countenance
And form of all; and long before the day

'Was old, the joy which waked like heaven's glance
The sleepers in the oblivious valley, died;
And some grew weary of the ghastly dance,

'And fell, as I have fallen, by the wayside;—
Those soonest from whose forms most shadows passed,
And least of strength and beauty did abide.'

' "Then, what is life?" I cried.' . . .   [516–44]

The process of deforming is one in which hope degenerates into a hope-less lust of desire, in which the human is reduced to the animal level. All the valuable qualities—beauty, strength, freshness, innocence of youth—emanate from the dancers as shadows, the figure of the fall of dead leaves from an autumn poplar being exact and functional as parallel here. Each of the shadows (line 530) resembles the original from which it fell and also the other shadows which fell from that same form "at first," but the shadows, abstractions of the concrete human qualities, next become distorted also, first by the "casual air," which moulds them into cloudlike forms, and next by the cold glare from the car, bitterly and brilliantly termed "the car's creative ray."

The concrete qualities of life's victims become distorted, in them-selves and in their abstractions. The closing lines take us back to the cavern of Rousseau's sleep, and make it clear that everyone, in some measure, has had Rousseau's experience. As mask after mask falls, only corruption is revealed beneath.[3] Long before their lives are over, the sleepers who were waked by joy, "like heaven's glance," in "the oblivi-ous valley," the cavern where Lethe runs, experience the death of that joy. Some, like Rousseau, weary of the ghastly dance, fall by the way-side, their strength and beauty passed off in shadows. With these lines, Rousseau's account is complete. The despairing cry of Shelley—"Then, what is life?"—makes an effective end to the poem, no matter how much more Shelley may have intended to write. The lines recovered by Garnett are frankly not promising:

                    The cripple cast
His eye upon the car, which now had rolled
Onward, as if that look must be the last,

And answered, 'Happy those for whom the gold
Of . . .'

Whatever the tenor of Rousseau's reply might have been, the reply itself is superfluous. The myth adumbrated by "The Triumph of Life" is complete; it is the whole poem that answers Shelley's question. My

3. Baker, p. 268, misreads this figure. He says that at this point "The masks are gradu-ally assumed, and grow on." But Shelley writes: "Mask after mask *fell* from the coun-tenance / And form of all"; lines 536–7, italics mine.

reading ought to have made clear what that answer is. The final aspect of Shelley's mythopoeia is that the myth, and the myth's maker, are fully conscious of the myth's necessary defeat. There are no Thou's of relationship in "The Triumph of Life"; the poem commemorates the triumph of the "It" of experience.

Index

Works cited, except Shelley's own, will be found under the author's name.